CRITICAL PRAISE FOR MASQUERADE

D0711856

MASQUERADE

LOWELL CAUFFIEL

PINNACLE BOOKS
KENSINGTON PUBLISHING CORP.

http://www.pinnaclebooks.com

PINNACLE BOOKS are published by

Kensington Publishing Corp.
850 Third Avenue
New York, NY 10022

First Zebra Printing: December, 1989

First Pinnacle Printing: November, 1997
10 9 8 7 6 5

Printed in the United States of America

For my Father and Mother

Are we really happy here with this lonely game we're playing?
Looking for words to say.
Searching but not finding understanding anywhere,
We're lost in a masquerade.

> "This Masquerade" by LEON RUSSELL

Nothing is at last sacred but the integrity of your own mind.
Abide in the simple and noble regions of thine own life.
Trust thyself. To believe in your own thoughts, to believe that what
is true for you in your own private heart is true for all men; that is
Genius.

> Preface to *Principles of Counseling and Psychotherapy*
> by W. Alan Canty

It's almost irresistible. She's so deliciously low—so horribly dirty!

> Professor Higgins to Pickering in *My Fair Lady*

Author's Note

Masquerade is not a so-called "fictionalization" of the W. Alan Canty murder case. It is a work based on police records, trial testimony, three hundred hours of interviews with thirty-five key characters, and other proven methods of journalistic legwork conducted over a period of two years. The extensive dialogue is reconstructed from the best memory of those involved and, wherever possible, was carefully cross-checked with documents, testimony, and other reliable sources in the story.

The patients of W. Alan Canty portrayed in this book have requested anonymity for fear of embarrassment and repercussions for having undergone psychotherapy. Some are recovering alcoholics. Their fictitious names will appear in italic type in the first reference.

Prologue

We were jammed into the jury box, waiting for the first witness, when the main door of the courtroom swung open and the widow made her way toward the bench. More than a dozen reporters and artists filled the enclosure for the preliminary exam, simply because there was no other place to sit.

She wore a smart blue suit and medium heels, with her shiny hair pulled up in a french twist. Her eyes were swollen, her attractive face fatigued, but she marched up the aisle between the rows of spectators as though all of hell wasn't going to stop her.

Her name was Jan Canty, a Ph.D., psychologist, and marriage counselor, and wife of W. Alan Canty, Ph.D., psychologist, and murder victim. As she headed to the front of the courtroom, it occurred to a number of us that this had been a week quite unlike any other, even for a town numbed by six hundred homicides a year.

The headlines had progressed from PSYCHOLOGIST DISAPPEARS AFTER LEAVING OFFICE to POLICE THINK THEY'VE GOT CANTY'S BODY to BODY PARTS FOUND ON I-75 to TORSO FOUND MAY BE PSYCHOLOGIST'S. There were reports as well of more body parts found buried in an "animal boneyard" 250 miles to the north, near the tourist town of Petoskey, Michigan.

The suspects facing preliminary examination on murder and mutilation charges were a young street whore named Dawn Marie Spens and her pimp, John Carl Fry, an ex-con known on the streets as Lucky.

Spens, once an honor student from the suburb of Harper Woods, sat sleepy-eyed at the defense table. She wore ragged jeans, a tattered baby blue blouse, and a pair

9

of cheap black high heels with mesh toes. Fry relaxed at her side, his body weight shifted to one elbow. His white head was shaved, his mustache chiseled. His thick arms and barrel chest were like those of a professional wrestler.

Police still hadn't found all of Alan Canty, but the reporters in the jury box were just beginning to put the story together. There was talk in Homicide that the psychologist was the prostitute's regular customer, though the proposition seemed unlikely under the courtroom's bright lights.

"Jesus, she's nothing," one reporter whispered, eyeing Spens. "Maybe she's a terror in bed."

There was speculation that Canty had spent $140,000 on the girl over eighteen months, and there were reports that he'd fashioned a second identity for himself as well. In the tough sections of the city's smoggy south side he had taken on another name and was known as a general practitioner.

It seemed an unlikely role for the fifty-one-year-old psychologist. His mother was a former president of the Detroit school board and a longtime leader of the PTA. His late father was a nationally known criminologist and a former executive director of the psychiatric clinic serving the city's largest court.

Some of us in the jury box already had portrayed the victim as an author, a teacher, and an expert on autism. He was a prominent professional with a flourishing practice in the Fisher Building, one of the city's most impressive office addresses.

When the first witness sat down, her back was erect. Jan Canty was only six feet from us on the stand. Yes, she knew the victim. Yes, they were married nearly eleven years. Yes, the last she heard from him, he was on his way home from the office, planning to stop at a grocery store for coffee.

No, she hadn't given anyone permission to dissect her husband's body.

There was nothing more about their life together, only answers that shored up the prosecutor's charge of mutilation. We all wondered what she knew, but she left as quickly as she came.

Then a homicide cop began bringing forth witnesses through a door behind the bench. Soon it was clear why

10

Jan Canty had waited outside, instead of with the others in the witness room. The proceeding took on a cinematic quality, the homicide cop a casting director as the standing-room-only audience murmured with each new character.

Visually, they all were striking. An unshaven southsider lumbered forward to testify in yellowed jeans and a faded black T-shirt. Another wore a gold earring, his arm tattooed with dragons and assorted slogans. A neighbor of the suspects raised his hand to be sworn, displaying a scorpion tattooed across his middle finger. One young blonde looked innocent enough with her turned-up nose and tiny frame. Then everyone saw the blue tattoo scrawled across her right triceps. Another waddled to the stand looking as though she was going to deliver any day. She was an odd sight—so pregnant, but so close to such murder and mayhem.

They all seemed incapable of sharing anything in the life of the first witness of the day.

When the exam was over, I left the Frank Murphy Hall of Justice and decided to drive from downtown to take a look at the victim's home in Grosse Pointe Park. Already I suspected that even a lengthy magazine story wasn't going to cover the distance between the two sets of images I saw in the court.

The drive out Jefferson Avenue along the Detroit River was stratified like a sociological core sample of class variations.

Once lined with ma-and-pa stores and thriving industrial plants, Jefferson was a broken chain of boarded building fronts and party stores fortified by bulletproof glass. A stretch of stylish high rises still stood, but only a few blocks away were some of the most economically depressed neighborhoods in the United States.

They weren't much different than the streets that had produced the group of witnesses in court. Nobody in sight resembled the billboard over one burned-out building: a man in a designer tuxedo, savoring a snifter of Martell cognac.

Then, at Alter Road, Jefferson Avenue became the gateway to the Pointes—Grosse Pointe, Grosse Pointe Park,

Grosse Pointe Farms, Grosse Pointe Woods, and Grosse Point Shores. Since the nineteenth century, these suburbs have been the home of the Motor City's industrial aristocracy.

Old rail and auto money developed the most affluent sections — people with such names as Ford, Fisher, and Dodge. Some exceeded extravagance. Anna Dodge, wife of auto pioneer Horace Dodge, imported European craftsmen to build Rose Terrace, her monument to eighteenth-century French architecture. It was razed a few years back, but most of the other stone-walled estates remained along the shores of Lake St. Clair.

For years the Grosse Pointers took the term "exclusive" literally. Until a 1960 lawsuit, the suburbs were known for their "point system," a checklist used by realtors to weed out prospective buyers. They awarded "points" on the basis of ethnic background, complexion, religious affiliation, and other such values.

That day I drove out Jefferson, the contrast was most dramatic at the foot of Alter Road, the boundary between Detroit and Grosse Pointe Park.

To the east, a manicured municipal park complete with swimming pool and tennis courts. Men in cashmere sweaters and women in the latest jogging apparel strolled by the mansions on Windmill Pointe Drive.

To the west, there was a trailer town and a littered Detroit city park. Teenagers in jeans and T-shirts milled about a parking lot. Obscenities and heavy metal rock boomed from rusted autos as the youths passed joints and sucked on cans of beer.

Even the trees appeared to mind the border. A cathedral ceiling of towering elms shaded Berkshire Road, where Alan and Jan Canty owned a six-bedroom, six-bath, Tudor-style home with a five-car garage sporting doors of stained and varnished wood. Just across Alter, Dutch elm disease had ravaged most of Detroit's tall timber, leaving the streets virtually barren.

It was as though the Pointes were impervious to disease. But there was no real magic at work. Grosse Pointers could afford a costly, experimental treatment from Europe to save their elms. In time I would discover that W. Alan

Canty, a concerned professional and valued resident, purchased the deluxe therapy. Money and a little planning. It's the way many problems are solved in the Pointes.

Part One
1983

Chapter 1

*Very few individuals, regardless of their "intellect,"
can view their own emotional behavior objectively.*
— W. Alan Canty, 1973,
Principles of Counseling and Psychotherapy

The black Buick broke from the congestion at the Fisher
Building and wheeled into the surging traffic on Third Avenue. Executives in wool suits and power ties of steel gray and
scarlet hustled from the world headquarters of General Motors, stirring the New Center's streets for the lunch hour. But
after a few blocks, only the granite tower of the Fisher dominated the Buick's rear-view mirror as the car headed south.

The man in the black Buick knew the drive well. If two
and a half miles of Third Avenue between the New Center
and downtown portrayed the character of the Motor City,
Detroit could boast as many faces as Eve.

The Buick glided by the pampered landscaping and
scrubbed windows of Burroughs Corporation, then cut the
western edge of Wayne State University. It passed the campus's nineteenth-century homes, the University's contemporary architecture by Minoru Yamasaki, the 118 cobalt
security lights. The blue beacons marked phones to campus
police and burned small halos into the gray day.

When the Buick crossed Forest Avenue, the only university building left ahead was Wayne State's mortuary school.
At Martin Luther King Jr. Boulevard, a church sign reminded the driver that "Christ Died for Our Sins." It sometimes lured a convert or two but also inspired a metaphor
locals evoked to describe the people in the surrounding
blocks:

"Those motherfuckers would steal Jesus off the cross,
then go back for the nails."

17

The Cass Corridor, as the area just north of downtown is called, was marking its fourth decade as Detroit's Hell's Kitchen. The area inspired studies on urban decay and provided stark scenery for the film *Beverly Hills Cop*. But its main contribution to the Motor City remained dope, despair, and sex.

Unlike flashing porn strips that lure johns in other towns, the Cass Corridor had only broken glass to supply its limited accents of glitter. Street whores strolled blocks lined with weedy lots and gutted brick tenements. More stylish girls worked the saloons, perched along Formica bar rails dulled by many rotating drinks.

The Cass Corridor also was Detroit's Skid Row. Faded lettering on flophouses still advertised long-gone dollar-a-day rates, while alcoholics outside hugged brown sacks and shielded their wet brains with stocking caps. A state lottery symbol on one liquor store teased the drunks with dollar signs. Few could spare a buck for a two-way bet. If a gentleman of leisure hadn't hit bottom on Cass, Second, or Third avenues, he'd crashed through it.

The drunks and other indigents made the whores conspicuous, transforming the women into something more tempting than another backdrop might dictate. Beauty, like age, was a matter of perspective and perception in the Cass Corridor. Working girls in their late twenties were considered senior citizens.

A longtime drug-addicted prostitute was a hard sell in the sunlight. More often than not, her body was marred by poor-quality heroin, a neighborhood plague called "mixed jive." The dope was cheap and reliable only for its tendency to cause abscesses when it was cooked and mainlined. The scars were circular. A junkie with a lot of miles on her looked as though a pack of hot cigarettes had been put out one by one on her skin.

The man in the black Buick might have thought twice about the quality of the Corridor's merchandise had he been flagged by one of the older girls. But most past their prime worked the evenings, turning quick tricks in cars, aided by the cosmetic advantages of the night.

Dawn Marie Spens preferred working the noon hour, and she swore she would never let herself deteriorate like that. She stepped from Sabb's Market with a fresh pack of Marlboro menthols and full intentions of getting what she had to do over with before the rush hour emptied downtown that night.

Dawn's appearance fell somewhere between a Wayne State sorority pledge and a newcomer to the sisterhood of the streets. Her skin was largely unblemished, and her shoulder-length auburn hair framed full lips and sleepy chestnut eyes. Other whores called her a "young girl," not because of her eighteen years, but because she was a new face, one who needed hardly a touch of makeup.

That meant good money from the selective tricks, with only a little encouragement from her wardrobe. Her 105 pounds contoured a velour shirt and tight designer jeans but were largely concealed by her full-length leather coat. Her shapely legs would have looked as good in running shoes as in high heels. Her breasts were full, but not lofty.

Dawn Spens didn't need any special effects.

On November 30, that was left to the optical illusion fashioned by the Fisher Building from the prostitute's favorite corner at Second and Peterboro. The Fisher was the only skyscraper to the north on the city's horizon, with Second Avenue running one way dead center into its main doors. It appeared to be only a dozen blocks away, though the black Buick's odometer had measured the distance at nearly two miles.

The car approached in a slow roll, then braked, kissing the curb at her feet. The exchange was an old one, the kind where no one says exactly what each needs or wants.

"Hi, you working?" he began.

He examined her through a pair of tortoiseshell glasses. He had a peculiar grin and slightly squinting eyes.

"Want to go out?" she asked back.

No, he didn't want to go out now. He wanted to go out later.

"Do you have a phone?" he said.

She didn't give her phone number to just anybody.

"Well, my name's Al," he said. "What's yours?"

As she responded she watched him pull out a ten-dollar

bill.

"Here, Dawn, get yourself some lunch."

She first guessed he was an accountant. Then she saw he didn't have a tie. A sport coat and knit shirt peeped out near the collar of his tan overcoat. He wasn't particularly good-looking, nor especially unattractive. Later she would guess his age as forty. But he grinned like a preschooler unable to conceal his mischief. She couldn't remember ever seeing a look quite like that on an older man before.

A vice cop wouldn't be so transparent, she decided. He was just another john. Dawn reached for the ten dollars and recited her phone number.

"I'll call you this afternoon," he said.

Still grinning, he drove off. He might have been nothing more than a dry hustle. As far as Dawn could tell, he'd failed to write her number down.

A few minutes later, John Fry's calf muscle twitched as he heard Dawn's key slide into their apartment door.

The thirty-seven-year-old former biker had passed out smiling the night before, only to be rousted by daylight and the calling of his habit. The twenty-five dollars he'd held back had provided a couple of hours of relief. But a quarter's worth of mixed jive was hardly worth another dope-burned vein in his right leg, and it was certainly not enough to make John civil for the day. He'd sent Dawn out to make some money for more.

Dawn was barely through the door when he realized his girlfriend was returning with little more than a story about a trick with a funny grin.

"But John, this guy gave me money to eat," she said. "He says he's going to call me later."

John's nose was running and his head felt as though it was lined with steel wool.

"Fuck all that," he said. "I'm sick now. There is no fucking later."

He lit a Marlboro menthol. His eyes told her not to even bother taking off her coat.

Chapter 2

I've seen a great many divorced people who burned out very quickly on the singles scene. Too many options make people insecure. They suffer from what psychologists call complexity shock. There is too much out there, too many choices. People want to narrow the field into something simpler and more manageable.

— W. ALAN CANTY,
Detroit Magazine, September 1983; *Modern Bride Magazine,* July 1984

Jan Canty could have imagined spending Al's birthday in bed, but not two thousand miles away from him on a brilliant afternoon in Sun Lakes, Arizona. She still felt bad about leaving him alone.

She set the alarm for 11 P.M. Detroit time, pulled the blankets around her shoulders, and reassured herself with the little talk they had before she left for her parents' house near Phoenix.

"That means I will be gone on November 30, your birthday. You mean that won't bother you?"

"Not at all. Jan, you know that."

She must have asked him five times, five different ways. Al Canty had dismissed every one of his birthdays in their years together, but she thought that might be different this time. He was turning fifty, and she figured that called for something special. In fact, Jan had flirted with the idea of a surprise party.

Then she suspected he would probably dislike all the attention, and she was right. When she mentioned she had entertained the notion, he said, "No, Jan-Jan, I don't want any part of that."

It was so typical of the man she loved. The psychologist who put a formal "W. Alan Canty" on his clinic door preferred life easygoing and uncomplicated on the home front. In his practice he nurtured recovering alcoholics, searching singles, disillusioned divorcées, compulsive personalities, and desperately unhappy neurotics. After a day of helping them untangle their lives, she thought, who wouldn't need some simplicity?

But Jan suffered from her own affliction the week her husband would mark a half century of life. Mononucleosis. Mono—she hated even the sound of the word. It was the second infection that year, and the third bout in a lifetime. This siege had lasted three months.

Jan had tried to rest at home but never really felt sick enough to justify lying in bed all day, every day. Between her work load, Al's schedule, and four thousand square feet of house, it just wasn't practical. Finally, sore throats and fatigue rendered her useless.

"You've got a choice," her physician said. "You're going to have to be hospitalized or just go somewhere and get the bed rest."

She opted for a standing invitation from her parents at their retirement house on the edge of the Arizona desert. Al encouraged her.

"You should go and get well," he said. "Rest up."

He was right. Jan's parents hadn't let her do a thing but sleep since she got off the plane.

Jan suspected Al would be all for the respite the minute she brought it up. They celebrated their ninth anniversary in September, and she easily could say her years with Al Canty had been a pretty smooth ride.

Al seemed to delight in freeing her from pressures during her long pursuit of a career. She'd been a student for most of the marriage. Her quest for a doctorate in psychology had been Al's top priority as well as hers. For years, that Ph.D. had seemed her whole life, and their big, Tudor-style home in Grosse Pointe Park just a place to sleep and do homework between trips to the University of Michigan.

She couldn't have asked for a more understanding partner. He never complained about uncertain meals on nights before finals or about the years the living room went without furniture. Only recently did they buy a TV. There just wasn't time before. Al closed his evenings gently critiquing her papers or giving pep talks when she felt she couldn't take one more day of classes.

It was as good a relationship as she'd seen anywhere, and better than most. Now that she was winding up her postdoctoral program in family counseling, Jan only wished that she and her husband would spend more time together.

The mono aside, at thirty-two Jan Canty was in full bloom. Her toothy smile and turned-up nose blessed her with the good looks of an all-American girl in her twenties. Now they were the makings of a handsome professional woman. A hint of makeup around her green eyes went a long way. In a week, she could find a half-dozen ways to wear her light brown hair. She was just an inch over five feet, but a complement to Al's five-foot-ten frame.

Jan often turned heads, but keeping her husband at her side for extended periods was a more difficult proposition. She'd never met anyone with so much energy for his work. Only in the last year had Jan convinced him to take another day off. For half their marriage he'd worked seven days a week. Finally she'd talked him into Fridays as well as Sundays off. Still he managed to see nearly fifty patients a week and book sixty clinical hours of therapy. He saw patients at the office. He saw patients at home. He dabbled in forensic work in the courts. He supervised other psychologists in Port Huron, nearly forty-five minutes away.

The demanding pace generated a cash flow of more than $150,000 a year. But, Jan wondered, was the money worth days that began at dawn and ended well after sundown?

Some of her frustration, she guessed, had to do with their seventeen-year difference in age. Al didn't socialize much with her younger friends, though with his boyish smile and trim build he could have passed for forty.

The last time they really cut loose together in a big gathering was at a Halloween masquerade. She dressed as a bumblebee, Al as a race car mechanic, a fictitious character he named Al Miller. She guessed he came up with the name from an old Miller race car he was restoring in the garage. She found him a doctor's hospital coat and had the name monogrammed across the back. Al disappeared into the garage and returned with a wrench in his pocket and grease smudged across the smock. She never saw him so outgoing. They partied until 4 A.M. at her friend's.

But that night two years ago was an aberration. With her schedule lighter now, she was disappointed they didn't get out more and do that sort of thing. She liked concerts and Detroit Tigers baseball games. He preferred spending the time with a book.

Well, she reasoned, I can't expect someone his age to like Stevie Wonder. As for baseball, Al just wasn't the type who went for sports, though he never complained when she went to the ballpark with her friends.

In that way, the positives of life with Al Canty offset the negatives. The equation had worked well in June when she had a chance to go abroad as a chaperon for her friend's French class.

"Then Jan, why don't you go?" he said, smiling. "It's a great discount on the airfare. Do it. I'll be fine."

Al had been so comfortable with that trip to France, so why was she worried about this get-well trip to Arizona? He's already told me how he feels, she told herself. He's always been honest about his feelings.

"Are you certain you won't mind?" she'd asked.

"Jan, you go right ahead. I'll be fine. You needn't worry about me."

She remembered his eyes reassuring her through his tortoiseshell glasses. Soon the blankets pressed her into another deep sleep.

Chapter 3

The personality is a product of growth, learning and experience.

— W. ALAN CANTY,
Principles of Counseling and Psychotherapy

"Oh, Ma, you didn't have to do that," he said when she phoned him after his lunch hour.

"Well, Buster," she said, "you're a big boy now."

Gladys Canty was glad she'd marked her son's birthday with a card and five hundred dollars. Al Jr.'s birthdays always warranted one hundred dollars. But a man's fiftieth is a milestone, she told herself when she wrote out the check.

Buster. The nickname was one of those spontaneous things. It came the day her only child was born, Thanksgiving Day 1933, when Al Sr. called her sister to break the news.

"Well, Buster is here," Al Sr. said.

The name had stuck all these years, though no one else called him that. Al Sr., when he was alive, preferred to call him Alan. But it could get pretty confusing with two Alans in the Canty house. Sometimes she called him Alan Jr. But she preferred Buster and, in recent years, had shortened that to Bus.

He was all the family Gladys had left in Detroit. Al Sr. had died in 1976. She had no siblings in the area, and her only surviving sister lived in Cleveland. Buster called her once every day from the Fisher Building. Despite his heavy schedule, he always found time to chat.

That isn't to say that Gladys Foster Canty, at the age of seventy-six, doddered away her days waiting for the phone to ring. In fact, friends often found her difficult to reach

25

at her retirement home on Detroit's far east side. She divided her weekdays between outings with historic groups and visits to a wide circle of friends who clamored for her company. On Saturdays she volunteered in the Detroit Children's Museum—working in its gift shop, selling smart souvenirs to the children. That was her favorite.

"I find it so delightful when the museum fills up with those little faces of innocence," she once explained to a friend.

In the museum or anywhere else, Gladys carried herself upright and took steps that were quick and without hesitation. Gray had yet to dominate her wispy red hair, which she kept up in a loose bun. Age hampered her no more than a lack of academic credentials had held her and her husband back in their prime.

The family hadn't been in Detroit even two full generations, but the Canty name was one of the most respected in the city. Gladys Canty was very proud of that. She and Al Sr. arrived in Detroit from Cleveland in 1929, six months before the crash. Al Sr. had secured a staff position with the first clinic of its kind in the country, a forensic unit originally named the Psychopathic Clinic of Detroit's Recorder's Court.

Bus arrived five years into their marriage and after nine months of daily nausea for Gladys. It was so bad her doctor thought she might lose the baby. She would have liked more children. But Al Sr. made it quite clear he wasn't going to have her go through that again.

She strove to give Bus the best rearing she could in their home near the Detroit River. She kept him smartly dressed, prepared his meals as though he was child royalty, and read him storybooks at night. But Gladys had more to give.

The daughter of an Episcopal minister, Gladys grew up with her father's church across one lot line and her public school across the other. Those dual influences were rekindled by a PTA meeting she attended after she enrolled Buster in first grade. She devoted eighteen years to the organization, rising to citywide president and statewide mental health chairman.

Her son often accompanied her as she met with group

after group around the city. The two of them were on the go together a lot as Al Sr. put in his long hours at the clinic. Buster learned a lot about the city's streets and neighborhoods that way.

After Buster graduated from high school, her organizational skills caught the attention of Detroit voters. She was elected to the Detroit school board, serving twice as president in her fourteen-year board career. If anyone happened to count the headlines, Gladys Canty's unblemished public profile in charitable and community pursuits often exceeded her husband's considerable notoriety.

Their schedules made family life a little less traditional than she would have liked. But Gladys made it a strict rule to be home to greet her son every day when he returned from school. They were a tightly knit trio, she thought. One reason Al Sr. worked so hard was to provide his son with the best education available.

Buster had done far better financially as a psychologist than Al Sr. had with the court. But sometimes she wondered if his practice was taking more than it gave. She could see it under his eyes.

"Oh, Bus, you look so tired," she'd say.

"Oh, Ma, you don't understand. People have so many problems."

"But you're working to help them."

"But Ma, I carry them around on my shoulders, too."

That was one of the differences between father and son. Al Sr. rarely brooded over people he evaluated at the clinic. After a day with cops and criminals, he mixed a highball and discovered more energy as the evening wore on. He spent his nights studying journals or writing for them, often into the early morning hours, invariably causing him to oversleep his morning alarm.

Al Jr. was continuously driven by nervous energy. Bus reminded Mrs. Canty of her brother George. They even looked alike. George Foster's frantic pace contributed to a massive stroke at the age of fifty. He never regained his speech, and he died three years later. The memory worried her.

But Gladys always strove to nurture the bright side. As a child she'd read the book *Pollyanna* and counted it as a major influence in her life. And her son had his hobbies—his collection of antique cars and his bricks. When she thought of cars and Buster, she thought of his old black pedal car and their tightly knit trio at the midget races. Even in his later teens, her son enjoyed watching the racers scamper and bump their way around the oval dirt track.

Now her son had about a half-dozen autos he was restoring in his garage. They looked like piles of parts to her, but Bus pronounced them "choice." The only treasures he valued equally were his antique paving bricks. She wasn't quite sure how that hobby got started, but collecting them by the trunkload from demolition sites had been nearly a seven-year quest. A pile grew behind his garage, had yet to become a driveway, and bordered on an obsession.

Once, when they were visiting Al Sr.'s grave at Elmwood Cemetery, Bus became engrossed by the sight of a wrecking crew working nearby. Laborers were tearing up a brick street. On their way out, he stooped to pick up a couple of the bricks. She scolded him.

"Oh, Ma, it's all right," he said.

"But Bus, it wouldn't look good."

He dropped the bricks but looked hurt. She would have thought she'd told him to put away his play blocks.

Yes, she thought, Buster was a sensitive chap, even at the mature age of fifty. It's what made him a good therapist, she reasoned, and a good husband. He and his wife seemed to be such a happy pair. Jan was such a cute girl she couldn't resist dubbing her Jannie.

"So what are you doing for your birthday, going to dinner with Jannie?" Mrs. Canty inquired near the end of Bus's birthday call.

"No, Ma," he said. "Jan is at a conference in Ann Arbor."

"Oh, and she's not going to be home for your birthday?"

Gladys Canty thought that odd.

"Well, she's at a conference and I have to work late and I have a big day tomorrow," he explained quickly. "Besides, she'll be home later anyway."

Gee, she thought, those two must really understand each other. Besides, who was she to question? Bus was the marriage expert. He'd recently been quoted at length in a Sunday magazine article in the Detroit *Free Press*. It was called "Married Forever—A Good Marriage Is Something You Earn."

She was proud her son had been sought out as a source on the subject. Unlike his father, Al Jr. never sought publicity. Gladys had cut out the article, saving it with a large collection of clippings she had on her late husband.

Bus had served the family name well. She was happy she'd sent him the five hundred dollars. She knew it wouldn't last long. How her son liked to spend money! He could graciously protest all he wanted about the amount, but Gladys Canty could sense his delight.

Chapter 4

*I suppose that at a deeper level, our children, with
their extremely bad self-images, were finally touched
by the awareness that someone so poised and beautiful was performing enthusiastically for them.*
—W. ALAN CANTY, 1976,
Therapeutic Peers, The Story of Project Indianwood

Dawn Spens recognized the resonant voice on the telephone later that Wednesday afternoon.

"Are you busy, Dawn?" he asked.

She would have preferred to be finished for the day. She
liked to get her dates over with early, shooting moves on
the downtown businessmen who cruised the Corridor on
their lunch hours. That left evenings for partying with
John.

But she began to pin the caller down to a price.

"Oh, don't worry about the money," the trick said. "Just
let me take care of that."

Repeatedly John had preached, "First, you take care of
business," but she sensed the date would pay, and probably
pay well. Her customers tipped her more often than not.

The trick agreed to meet her near the White Grove, an
all-night diner only a few doors from where they had met.
It was only a block from the apartment.

Dawn Spens strolled to the rendezvous just after dark.
She could have flagged several quick dates on the way to
the White Grove. But this way there would be no hassles
with the cops. The last thing she needed was to be busted
again.

The black Buick was waiting for her. Its engine hummed
in a parking lot next to the diner, under an old sign for a
defunct Chinese restaurant called Forbidden City.

She could smell the car's interior. It seemed immaculately groomed by a professional garage. They made small talk as the two of them drove to a nearby hotel.

"So what kind of work do you do?"

"I'm a doctor. Actually this is my lunch hour. I work afternoons over here in the Medical Center."

The big medical complex was five minutes away and included the Wayne State medical school and Harper-Grace and Detroit Receiving hospitals.

Dawn anticipated the question a lot of tricks ask: "So how did you end up doing this?" Many men seemed to be as interested in why a woman sold herself as in the sexual pleasures she was selling. Her answer was fabricated and unlikely.

"Actually, I'm from the suburbs, but my parents can't send me to school. I'm just doing this for a while to get the money for college."

But it seemed to satisfy most tricks. At least they stopped asking questions.

The query never came from the man in the Buick. She directed him to the Temple Hotel. The three-story brick residence recently had been painted and was in considerably better shape than most everything else in the Corridor. Two lock buzzers and an iron gate stood between them and the front desk.

In the lobby, stubble-faced men sat on furniture covered with old bedspreads. The room smelled of ethyl alcohol—vapors from the men's lungs as their bodies processed another day's worth of liquor.

They approached the hotel clerk, who booked his business behind a cashier's cage of metal mesh and shatterproof glass. The trick paid five dollars for an hour in the small room with one bed, one table, one light, and one common bathroom down the hall.

The date wanted what every whore knows as a "half and half," fellatio followed by intercourse. After he undressed she held him between her thumb and fingers. What her mouth might not accomplish, her hand would. It sometimes went faster that way.

When they began the second half of their arrangement, he was neither hurried nor forceful like many dates. He was rather ordinary, if there was such a thing in her business.

He was quite pleased afterward.

"Can I call you?" he said. "Can I see you again?"

He handed her a hundred dollars — one hundred top dollars. Some Corridor hookers would work for as low as twenty dollars, and seventy-five dollars was a first-rate date. A hundred bucks transformed a Corridor whore into a call girl.

The trick named Al was grinning again. At first she suspected he was high, but he smelled stone sober. That goofy grin, and he had a funny walk to go with it.

He toddled like Charlie Chaplin as they walked out of the hotel.

"It was as though he thought he was getting something over on somebody," she said later.

But what difference did it make? That was his problem. She looked at him with passive eyes. Of course she would see him again.

John Fry had seen Dawn act that way before. She was sashaying her sweet ass around the apartment while he coveted the comfort of his couch and a night's supply of heroin mix. Then he prompted her for the news.

"How much?"

"I didn't even have to get the money up front."

John cradled his high hairline in his paw and shook his head. He was too stoned to get mad.

John "Lucky" Fry's body looked as though it had been customized to fit a chopped Harley-Davidson. He was two inches short of six feet, 180 pounds, and had tattoos running up arms well developed by years of pumping iron in prison. But when Fry's body chemistry was where he preferred it, he looked as docile as a grizzly darted by a tranquilizer gun.

The best he could do was roll his eyes upward and lecture through his graying red beard.

"I told you about that, man. It's what causes problems. Next thing the guy's got his rocks off and he's gone. Then what are you going to do? Next thing you'll be draggin' your little ass back here and saying '*Aw baby*, I got no money,' "

Dawn stuck out her tongue and unrolled the cash in his face.

"Seventy dollars and a thirty-dollar tip," she said.

She snapped the money once.

"And I think I just found me a sugar daddy."

33

Chapter 5

Emotions are caused from within rather than from without.

— W. Alan Canty,
Henry Ford Community College lectures, 1972

The electronic alarm clock split the bedroom's silence like one of those throbbing police sirens in Europe. Jan Canty strained to push the covers off her body and fought her way to consciousness. She looked around in the darkness, first struggling to remember where she was, then why she was up.

Jan shuffled to a seat at the kitchen table, the room illuminated only by the miniature Christmas lights her parents had strung around the cacti outside a large window. Her head cleared as she gazed at the little lights twinkling on the sharp spikes. Then she picked up the telephone and called her husband Al. She sang softly over her sore throat.

"Happy birthday . . ."

She thought it was long-distance static at first. Then she discerned it. Al was crying. The only time she'd ever heard Alan Canty cry was during a purging moment of grief after his father's funeral seven years ago. It just was not like him. And now she felt a little foolish. She wasn't sure what to say.

"Al . . . Gee, I didn't mean to be that sentimental."

He was quick to respond.

"Well, I just wish you were here because I'm worried about you. You've been so sick, Jan-Jan."

There he goes, she thought, concerned about me again. Jan assured him that the bed rest was producing miraculous results. She wanted to change the subject. She asked

34

him what he had done for himself on his fiftieth birthday.

"I treated myself to dinner at Chung's."

Jan could have guessed it. Then she had to bite her tongue. Al already knew how she felt about that.

Chung's was in the heart of the Cass Corridor, and Al's outings into that area south of Wayne State had always made her nervous. But she also knew Al's love of Chinese food. Chung's servings and its proximity to the Fisher Building made the restaurant too difficult a temptation for her husband to resist.

It was one of his many little quirks she'd noticed over the years. Though he balked at baseball games and other urban outings, often she found herself cautioning him about venturing into Detroit's most dangerous neighborhoods without hesitation. He seemed too relaxed about it, as though he fancied himself really streetwise.

She remembered Al's old habit of stopping at a twenty-four-hour gas station on his way home from work after dark. It was within the Detroit city limits. Another mile and he could gas up in Grosse Pointe. But Al opted to stop where the cashier took his money from behind bulletproof glass. And Al rarely carried his wallet, opting instead to keep a wad of bills in his pants pocket, usually a hundred dollars or more. Many times she had visualized someone clubbing him to death after a fill-up. She got him a Mobil credit card, and he promised he wouldn't stop there anymore.

Al's brick-collecting excursions also concerned her. Sometimes when he returned, she was surprised when he told her where he had found his latest trunkload. The neighborhoods often were Detroit's worst. Sometimes there wasn't any neighborhood left at all. She feared him an easy mark in Hush Puppies and a corduroy jacket as he rummaged among the burned-out houses and demolished warehouses. But Al had to go where nothing was left but bricks, bums, and vacant lots, as though the bricks were worthless unless he pulled them out of the gutter.

"Please don't do that, Al," she would say.

He'd respond in that Shakespearean baritone of his.

"Jan, there's simply no reason to be so concerned."

Al didn't seem to have a healthy respect for danger. But

then she wondered if she was just being classically over-protective. She thought, what am I going to do about it, anyway? Tie him down?

She was glad he was home OK. She wished she was. She told him she loved him very much. After she hung up she gazed for a while at the lights and the cacti.

She found it difficult getting back to sleep.

Chapter 6

*It is the person who is unable to manage his affairs
. . . who is in need of professional help.*
— W. ALAN CANTY,
Principles of Counseling and Psychotherapy

John Mosey's closest friend made his point clear over
lunch.

"You've got several options," he'd said. "One, do nothing, and stay miserable.

"Two, we can go down the street and find a gun shop,
buy a .45, and you can blow your brains out.

"Three, we can go across the street to the bar. I'll buy
the first drink and watch you get shit-faced."

Some choice between two and three, he thought. Die
quickly or spend a lot of time and money trying. Alcoholism had already cost him dearly, including a marriage and
the daily companionship of his two daughters.

Sober for four years, at thirty-three he'd broken the
forty-thousand-dollar barrier in his field, and the door no
longer slammed behind him when he exercised his weekend
visitation rights. Sobriety meant some self-respect, and he
valued it more than a free shopping spree in a liquor store.

But Mosey felt himself slipping. People he respected
were fed up with his moping. Even strangers were noticing
it. "Don't you ever smile?" God, he had heard that one
again. The last time he faced that line of questioning, he
was hoisting five fingers of straight scotch.

"Then," Mosey's friend continued, "There's a fourth option. Why don't you get your butt into therapy? But John,
you're an alcoholic. So let me suggest you don't turn your
head over to just anybody."

"Who did you have in mind?"

Mosey was sure he'd heard the name Alan Canty somewhere before, but he couldn't remember where as he drove to his office a couple of weeks later. He didn't need to ask the psychologist for directions. The Fisher was a Detroit landmark.

The John DeLorean biography was titled *On a Clear Day You Can See General Motors,* but after dark most eyes were captured by the Golden Tower of the Fisher across the street. GM was a squatting bulwark; the Fisher Building reached for loftier heights. At night, gold spotlights illuminated its terracotta roof. The Golden Tower looked like a heaven-bound sanctuary above the city's spotty darkness.

On the lower floors inside, tenants and visitors could bank, dine, buy art, get a shine, be tailored for a suit, and get it cleaned for an evening at the Fisher Theatre, Detroit's Broadway showcase. Cars were kept gassed, washed, and waxed by attendants. The Fisher even had its own historical marker, citing the building as the city's "largest art object." There were 430 tons of bronze, intricate carvings of solid walnut, and forty different types of marble from around the world. Architect Albert Kahn had earned international acclaim with the design in 1928.

Mosey wouldn't argue with that. The building's six-hundred-foot arcade demanded the attention of visitors who arrived for an appointment with a Fisher business executive, doctor, or therapist. The artwork in the barrel-vaulted ceiling was awe-inspiring. Cherubs, eagles, and muses soared above.

Mosey took the elevator to the ninth floor and the Detroit Guidance Center.

"I'm Al Canty," said the man who greeted him in the waiting room.

"Hello, Doctor."

"Oh no, don't call me Doctor. I just won't have it, John. Just call me Al."

Al Canty looked like the archetype of his profession. He was wearing Hush Puppies, tan cords, and a green turtleneck sweater. Mosey guessed him to be in his early forties and was surprised when he later found out Al was fifty. The psychologist reminded him of the actor Michael

Caine.

Al's office seemed out of step with the opulence of the Fisher. Mosey expected to see a big display of degrees and professional memberships on the wall. He noticed only three, tightly grouped in a corner. One proclaimed a doctorate in psychology from the University of Michigan.

There were about two dozen books, all hardcovers. They were held on end by African sculptures in ebony and other hardwoods. They looked like dark muses of the id, put to work propping up all the accumulated knowledge. Later he learned one artifact was a gift from Margaret Mead. One of Al's old mentors was a good friend of the anthropologist.

Al sat in a big overstuffed chair, Mosey in a smaller one. The room felt comfortable, like Al, Mosey decided. He liked the print of a flaming-red vintage Mustang hanging on the wall. He inquired about the auto. The psychologist said he liked old cars. In fact, he had an old Packard he was restoring in his garage. An intellectual who was good with his hands, Mosey thought. He liked exceptions to stereotypes.

It didn't take long for the anger and frustration to come out. Mosey had sat around enough Alcoholics Anonymous meetings to know it didn't do much good to hold back.

Good, Canty said. He said he liked working with AA members because of their openness. Self-honesty was half the battle of therapy. Mosey's AA membership was worth twenty-five dollars off his regular seventy-five-dollar charge for a forty-five-minute session, Al said.

"I've just ended another relationship with a woman and I'm angry as hell," Mosey began. "I get into these goddamn relationships and I've got this inane ability to pick women that aren't worth a damn for me."

He'd helped the last one rebuild her life after she was dumped by a boyfriend, only to find himself turned into her verbal dumping ground. The territory seemed too familiar. After fourteen months he walked out in the middle of their vacation in northern Michigan.

"I tend to pick these women who are always in jams," he continued. "But the payback is always me getting beat up:

39

'Why don't you do this? Why don't you do that?' "

He just couldn't assert himself during the browbeatings, he told Al. Then when he filled up, he blew up, and it was over.

"I'm looking for some answers, Al," he said. "I'd like to know what the hell my problem is."

"Well, self-esteem and guilt often play a role. What kinds of things do you feel guilty about in your life?"

His divorce. How, he thought, could he be a good father to his girls one day a week? That wasn't fatherhood. But he felt as though he'd gotten what he deserved.

"Sometimes back when I was drinking I used to wish my daughters were never born," Mosey explained. "Now look, I don't have the girls. Those thoughts were sick thoughts, but I thought them. Now I'm sober, but I still can't forgive myself for the way I felt about the girls."

"We all suffer from guilt," Al said. "Look, it's natural. I used to feel guilty about the time I saw a prostitute back when I was in college. But it was one of those things young men do. As long as you're not doing it now, it really doesn't count."

Mosey spent a lot of that first session trying to psycho-analyze himself.

"You know, my mother did a lot of crap to my dad," he streamed on. "She always wanted to change him. I grew up hearing it. Maybe that's why I'm so attracted to these—"

Al finally stopped him.

"Your *mother* is not your problem," he said.

Al explained that he was a proponent of rational-emotive therapy, a school of psychotherapy that lends little credence to such notions. The answers were available in the present, not the past, Canty said. In time, he would help Mosey find the answers for himself.

"There's something you're doing right now that gets you into these relationships where you can't pick the people who are good for you. Most people are usually pretty healthy in their lives. But they hit periods of time where they just become disconcerted, confused, lost. We've got to end that confusion and set you back on the right course."

The talk reminded Mosey of books he had read years

earlier by psychologist Albert Ellis. Canty said he had studied under Ellis. Mosey was impressed. Canty suggested *A New Guide to Rational Living* by Ellis and Robert A. Harper. He also gave Mosey a copy of his own *Therapeutic Peers,* Al's account of his work with autistic children.

But it was Al's demeanor, rather than his reading list, that impressed Mosey on that first visit. Mosey never saw him take notes. Al seemed a study in serenity in the big chair.

By December, after eight months of weekly therapy, John Mosey valued Al Canty as an old friend.

"Al just had this aura of comfortability," he later told a friend. "He just seemed to take everything in stride. With Al, the whole damn Fisher Building could have come falling down around him and I don't think he would have gotten shook."

Chapter 7

Their apartment house was called the Homewood Manor. Its address, 644 Charlotte, was well known among those who processed the paperwork at the Wayne County Morgue.

John Fry and Dawn Spens sometimes bitched about the dead intercom, the flaking lime green paint, and the torn hallway carpeting that had ceased to resemble any color. But it was close to work, and it wouldn't always be that way.

They often told each other that.

The couple had already picked out their future address. That happened on a Sunday, just after they hooked up in the summer. John borrowed a Ford Escort from a friend and secured a handful of Dilaudids, 150 milligrams of methadone, and a half-dozen bottles of Asti Spumante for the outing. John wanted Dawn to see Walled Lake, where he grew up.

They mainlined a couple of the Dillies and aimed the Escort north on the Lodge Freeway. It took them past the New Center and the predominantly black neighborhoods between downtown and the city limits at Eight Mile Road. They drove past the mirrored office buildings in Southfield and into the affluent environs of Oakland County. John swigged on the Asti, talking nonstop as he wheeled the Escort along roads that wound through the hills and small lakes of affluent West Bloomfield.

They were nearly twenty years apart in age, but Dawn Spens had fallen in love with the balding former biker. Sometimes she was quite maudlin about it, like a heartsick pubescent girl. Many nights later, during a time when they couldn't be together, she would write:

"My love for you grows stronger with each passing day . . . I love you baby, so much it hurts me deep inside. It feels like someone is tearing my heart out. You *are* and always will be the love and light of my life . . . I yearn to lay in your strong arms. The arms that have protected and supported me . . . You're my *whole* life and you will continue to be my whole life, for as long as you wish."

John was attracted to Dawn's more mature qualities. He considered Dawn Spens exceptionally smart. He told others he'd finally found a partner who could think on his level.

"I guess you could say she was the first woman I met in years that I considered an equal," he'd say of her. "A woman that I could sit down and talk to. None of that simple-time bullshit."

They were following a cattail-lined back road that Sunday when the couple spotted a new custom home sheltered by wild oaks and maples. They found the four-bedroom house for sale, open, and unattended. Dawn ran her hands over the oak-and-white-marble veranda, and John imagined burning logs in the fireplace. They explored the master bedroom upstairs, with its balcony overlooking a woods. When they came in from the upper deck, they had sex on the floor.

Later the realtor arrived. John made small talk with the agent and inquired about a price.

After they drove off, John calculated Dawn's yearly earning power and announced that the home's $160,000 cost was entirely within their reach. All they had to do was save most of what she earned, toss in his miscellaneous deals, and cut down on the drugs. Dawn was quite taken by the idea.

"Babe, I want that house."

Any goal was attainable. At least that's the way John talked. He told Dawn he once owned four gas stations in Oakland County. At the age of twenty-one he was "clearing $7,000 to $8,000 a week." It was an often told story:

"I got married, had a kid," he explained in one version. "I woke up one morning, looked around me, and said, 'What the fuck!' Maybe I'm wrong, but I think it had something to do with all those years of my youth, helping my mom and my brothers.

"I called the company up one morning and said, 'I'm

43

through, man, come check me out.' So they came out, checked me out. I owed them $26,000 or $27,000. I had about $32,000 in the bank . . . I wrote them the check. But I went to the bank, drew all the money out, and got started. I went on a nut. It was my first conviction in Oakland County. I got two years' probation on it."

John told Dawn they could avoid old pitfalls. Besides, she had a "natural talent," as he liked to put it. He had invested considerable time making her believe that after they met.

"If you sell yourself as a $15 whore, you're going to look and act like a $15 whore," he often said. "It's always been my feeling that if you feel you're worth $50, then that's what you're worth. In your heart and in your mind you have to feel qualified to get that money."

Dawn helped her own cause by not letting her dates know she was an addict. Most Cass Corridor johns weren't naive, and they knew a junkie worked at bargain prices. First she aimed for blood vessels in her hands, but in time they swelled. Then one of John's friends offered to mark the vein in her groin with an injection. It became her favorite port of entry.

That Sunday there was as much drug use as there was talk of cutting back. They replaced their planned tour of Walled Lake with a celebration of their dream home and business partnership. The party lasted well into the night.

The evening ended at the Ford-Wyoming Drive In Theatre near an industrial corner of southwest Detroit. They parked the Escort among the pockmarked cars of teens and poor families beating the high price of moviegoing. They pushed down the front buckets and finished off the Asti in the backseat. They ran the last of the Dillies.

Before they passed out, Fry caught the name of the movie. It was *Fort Apache: The Bronx*.

Chapter 8

The last twenty-five years have seen the growth of tremendous popular interest in the field of psychology.

— W. ALAN CANTY,
Principles of Counseling and Psychotherapy

Jan Canty stepped off the December 4 plane from Phoenix with a light step and an agranulocyte count at near normal. Al was waiting for her, grinning widely as she came up the ramp.

"Look at the color back in your face," he said excitedly. "You look ten years younger."

Jan Canty had much catching up to do. She'd let so much slide because of the mono. Her paperwork was piled up at home. And come Monday, she was anxious to get back on track in her postdoctoral program at the University Health Center in Detroit's Medical Center.

Her fellowship was the last phase of her education. She was grateful to be in a program that accepted only three new fellows a year from applicants nationwide. Her training was divided between counseling patients and working with family physicians affiliated with the Wayne State School of Medicine. She was refining her skills in psychotherapy and marital and family counseling.

The program was run by Aaron L. Rutledge, a respected psychologist who used to write a weekly help column for the Detroit *News*. Jan Canty liked Dr. Rutledge's sensible approach to the field. She was always impressed with his definition of professionalism.

"You're not a psychotherapist to your family and friends," he'd say. "Leave it at the office. It's not fair to you and it's not fair to them. Turn it off at the end of the day and just be a spouse, a sister, a daughter."

It was good advice. It took a lot of mental energy to apply her skills. She had no desire to do a free workup on Al, or anybody else. That included herself. She was reasonably sure she hadn't entered the field to exorcise her own demons. She often avoided telling strangers what she did for a living. People at parties sometimes got defensive.

"I don't want to be psychoanalyzed," they'd say.

"Don't worry," she'd say. "I don't work for free."

And it was work. It was not a hobby. It was not a parlor game. Other than her theoretical discussions with her husband, she worked at leaving the mental tools of her trade at the office.

Dr. Rutledge also had supervised Al in the early 1960s. It was just one of several parallels Jan had with her husband. She never really planned to follow W. Alan Canty's career path. Over the years it just seemed to work out that way.

In fact, before she met Al, she would have never thought a bachelor's degree, let alone a doctorate or a big home in Grosse Pointe Park, was in her future. The part of town where she grew up just wasn't known for producing scholars or socialites. Her native northwest Detroit neighborhood bore no resemblance to the affluent suburb known for its mansions along Windmill Pointe Drive. Still, Jan couldn't imagine a better childhood than the one she had on Annchester Street.

Jan Lucille had a twin sister and an older brother. Her parents staked out their share of modest postwar prosperity in a neighborhood where saplings lined the streets and the rows of redbrick bungalows went on forever. Her father's demeanor was as steady as the salary he brought home each week as a products estimator for Ford Motor. Her mother practiced homemaking as an art form.

There were kids everywhere on Annchester, and everyone knew each other. Jan lived right near her school. Her house was a popular stopover for friends. She smelled burning leaves every autumn and wheeled and dealed through several summers in an ongoing Monopoly tournament on a girlfriend's porch. She didn't date a lot as a teen but discovered love with a high school sweetheart.

46

After graduation she felt lost. She was an A student but hadn't applied to a university during her senior year. That was for the daughters of teachers, or the girls who lived in affluent Rosedale Park. Most of her girlfriends planned to marry or find jobs as secretaries. She took a job as one for a branch office of Western Michigan University. For two years she mulled over the idea of doing something more.

Then in the summer of 1972 Jan heard from a friend about a Fisher Building psychologist who was looking for helpers in a therapy program he had developed for autistic children. He was hiring young women her age who could act in short, highly charged plays aimed at bringing the children out of their emotional shells. The job sounded appealing, but Jan took three months to call. She was surprised when the psychologist told her he was still looking for helpers.

Alan Canty had a name for his therapy program—Project Indianwood. He offered Jan a job as an "Indian guide." That's what he called the half-dozen girls who were to put on the skits for the children. They rehearsed frequently in a room on another floor in the Fisher. But as it turned out, Jan wasn't much of an actress. Both she and Al knew it, though he never once told her she wasn't working out. Instead, Al gently steered her into office work, asking her to be the typist for *Therapeutic Peers,* the book he was writing on the project.

Jan liked the bespectacled psychologist from the start. He was bright and quick. But he also had a rich streak of creativity—the kind of colorful imagination not often found in the scientific disciplines. She could also tell he was a romantic from some of the moving passages about the children in his book.

His memory amazed her. Al dictated his book off the top of his head, and she typed the drafts. He never needed notes. Sometimes she made mistakes and lost pages around the office. At first she expected to be lectured about her errors. Instead he gave her gentle advice on the importance of not expecting perfection in everyone and everything. Soon, she found she could make suggestions for the manuscript. And her boss welcomed her ideas to improve his office files.

"You're really college material; you know that, don't you?"

Al told her that several times. Al made her feel good about herself.

After nine months on the job, Jan was flattered when he asked her out. She was twenty-two and he was nearly forty. But he didn't look a day over thirty. He was handsome in a distinguished way. His wavy blond hair fell just over his collar. He looked like a young British actor when he took off his black horn-rim glasses, and sat with his thumb at his chin, cradling a cigarette between his fingers.

On their first date, however, she felt as though she had sneaked into a world she knew nothing about. He took her to a restaurant overlooking Lake St. Clair. She found it difficult to enjoy the view. All she could think about was her dress. She'd made it herself. She felt paralyzed by the prices on the menu. She'd never been in a restaurant where you didn't pay at the front cash register.

Al encouraged her to order an after-dinner drink. He suggested Galliano. It looked like olive oil and tasted as bad to her. She gulped it down to be done with it. On the way out, Al told her she looked as though she was going to get sick. Al was also perceptive. She ran into the bathroom and threw up. She felt guilty that all that money was going down the toilet.

When Al Canty asked her out again, Jan knew he was an extraordinary man. His ability to overlook her shortcomings became one of his most appealing qualities. Once, on a day at Metropolitan Beach with a girlfriend, she locked her keys in her car. She called Al, who was forty-five minutes away at the Fisher Building. He insisted on rescuing them.

"We all make mistakes," he said when he showed up with her extra set of keys. "I'll see you tonight."

Al Canty seemed to have real direction in his life, she thought, both professionally and personally. He was established and working. Back then he had a house on Fisher Road in Grosse Pointe Farms. But he also had an endearing boyish quality. He nicknamed her Jan-Jan. She thought it cute, like the adolescent smile he got when he was embarrassed or when he was trying to hide a surprise.

48

In time, Al explained to her how his first marriage had failed. He had no harsh words for Maggie, his ex-wife, who was ten years his senior. He still admired her intelligence and her administrative career at Wayne State. Their parting after nine years was mutual, he said. They just found they weren't compatible. Jan thought it was refreshing to hear that from someone divorced only two years.

In retrospect, Jan thought it clever how the psychologist prompted her to believe in her abilities. When she questioned whether she could handle university work, he suggested she try one class at a community college. One class turned into a full load. That turned into an apartment on the campus and a full academic scholarship to Wayne State.

Jan decided she wasn't going to let the most sensitive and supportive man she'd ever met get away. After nearly a year of dating, Al was hinting about commitment, talking about what kind of house they might like to live in.

She deliberated about only one thing—their seventeen years' difference in age. She tried to anticipate the scenario years later. One day she'd likely be a relatively young widow.

"I never lost sight that in all probability I would one day be alone," she later told a friend. "But I summed it up in my own mind by saying ten or twenty years with him is worth it, even if I'm alone the rest of my life."

One summer morning, when they were out for breakfast, she decided to propose. Somebody had to do it.

"What do you think about us being married?"

Al was speechless, but he had a look that said, "Well, when?"

Jan took out her pocket calendar, picked up her fork, and stabbed it blindly onto the page.

"How about September 28?" The year was 1974.

"Sounds good to me," he said.

They went house shopping and discovered their big Tudor-style in Grosse Pointe Park. Technically, its architecture was that of an English country house. But most everyone called them Tudors in the Pointes. Al was delirious with the find, though she thought it too large. It did have all the qualities they wanted: Something to fix up.

Something with a fireplace. Something with a home office for Al and his patients. Something with a garage for Al's cars.

Her admiration of Al and his field increased with the miles on her Volkswagen as she commuted to Wayne State. At first she wanted to write children's books. Then, after reading *The Magic Years,* she became interested in child psychology. Finally, hearing Al talk about his practice piqued her interest in adult psychology and marriage counseling.

She plunged into her studies. They nicknamed one of the bedrooms upstairs "the dissertation room," converting it into her study area. She spent years up there with her papers, her typewriter, and her bookshelves. Al was usually seeing patients well after dark anyway.

Her husband was her role model back then. "I just hope one day I can be as good as him," she told her mother once. "If I could be half the psychologist he is, I think I'd be satisfied."

Al's interest in Project Indianwood waned soon after they married. He said he was burned out after nearly twenty years in the field. He hired young professional actresses and recorded the plays on videotape. He sent the tapes to ten autistic programs around the country to be field-tested. He said he'd find his satisfaction in the fact that the work was continuing elsewhere with the videotapes and the techniques he taught through the book.

Therapeutic Peers was published in 1976, and Al gave several lectures to child psychology students at universities, explaining his techniques. There were only a handful of such talks. But she was impressed with his command of the language and his confidence in the subject matter. She carried in the books, selling them to eager students. She knew nothing about book publishing but knew the book was important to him, and to her. Its royalties were paying for her postgraduate tuition, he said.

Al was a superb listener as well as lecturer. He was eager to hear about her classes. Often their discussions were held on their walks to nearby Lake St. Clair along Windmill Pointe Drive. The half-hour strolls just before bed were often the only time they had to really talk on most workdays. Even in winter they'd bundle up and go.

Sometimes he spun detailed monologues about his field. He was well read in the history of psychology and its emergence as a profession in the 1930s. He told her how it grew dramatically following World War II, when the Veterans Administration began providing help to returning servicemen. Most of the men did not have the medical problems that required a psychiatrist, he said. They just needed help to adjust emotionally and socially following the war. Al credited that era with lifting the stigma and mystery that so long had surrounded psychotherapy. Counselors and therapists became the alternative to the parish priest or well-intentioned but often misguided friends that troubled people had sought out in the past.

As Jan's sophistication in the field began to approach her husband's, she filled him in on new treatment methods. He became less a role model and more a colleague. She developed her own conceptions of her work.

Sometimes she and Al debated theory, but usually in a noncompetitive way. Al could not say enough good things about Albert Ellis. The psychologist had helped charge the sexual revolution with such books as *Sex Without Guilt* and *The Case for Sexual Liberty*. But Al admired him as the leading proponent of rational-emotive therapy, or RET, one of the cognitive approaches in their field. In RET, the therapist helps a patient look at his belief structure in the present. For example, if a person feels the world is supposed to be a fair place, they will suffer when anything unfair happens. RET prompts a patient to change his thinking: The world is not always fair; therefore I can expect it to be unfair at times to me.

Like Ellis, Al preferred short-term therapy. He didn't believe most patients required years of analysis on the couch, as required by more classical techniques. Al had attended a number of Ellis workshops and knew the psychologist personally. At a conference they attended several years back in New York, Al took a lot of pride in introducing her to the influential author.

Jan Canty, however, was drawn to the psychodynamic, long-term approach to therapy. She thought a patient's history and unconscious played important roles in behav-

51

ior and perception. Dream interpretation, slips of the tongue, and other dynamics below a person's awareness level had to be examined along with conscious beliefs. The discovery of hidden drives of the psyche, she argued, yielded the kind of long-term changes most patients wanted.

On one point they always agreed: If the patient got better, what difference did it make? Their theoretical debates often ended that way. And their professional differences never stopped them from discussing their field with brainstorming passion.

Other nights they just got silly walking to the lake. Al liked to playact sometimes. He would assume the role of a snob, criticizing the sprawling estates of their neighbors along Lake St. Clair.

"You know, that one would look reasonable if *only* they would put a flagstone sidewalk in," Al would quip, pointing to a forty-room mansion.

"Then why don't you tell them?" she'd say. "You know, just go up and knock on the door and tell them."

The psychological horseplay sometimes sparked romantic moods. They'd return from one of the walks and make love. Al was always gentle, always patient with her on such nights.

On several strolls they found themselves talking about their differences in age, how they might be considered an unlikely pair. The subject had come up again recently.

"You know, one day, Jan-Jan, you'll be alone," he told her on one night. "If that day happens, given the age difference, I definitely want you to remarry."

Jan said such talk was a bit premature. Al's hair did look more grayish red than blond these days, and his hips were spreading with middle age. She wished he'd take time to exercise and not eat so much on the run. But the only thing she could see ailing in Al Canty were the patches of psoriasis that troubled him around his elbows and scalp.

"Nevertheless. I don't want you ever to have second thoughts because we were so happy. I don't ever want you to be alone on my account."

"Al, don't be silly," she said, hugging his arm as they walked.

Their other routine was dinner every Tuesday at an Italian restaurant called the Blue Pointe. It was in its sixth year as a standing date, first nurtured by her graduate school schedule and her work at the nearby Center Point Crisis Center. Al was like that. Once something was established in his schedule, he didn't budge from it. He could be awfully predictable.

Two days after she returned from Arizona they met for dinner. Al was late—delayed, he said, by business at the Fisher. He always kept her waiting at the Blue Pointe. Sometimes she wondered if he even planned tardiness into his routine. Al ordered a Bloody Mary. He didn't drink often. Usually it just made him sleepy. But this evening he was pretty animated. He was still enthused about her recovery and return from Phoenix.

"You are looking so healthy, so good. You know you have been pushing yourself too hard, and I don't want to see you get sick again."

Jan agreed but wished Dr. Canty would take his own advice.

Well, she thought, in another six months they could both ease up. She would be done with her fellowship. Then they could realize their long-term plans. They wanted to practice together in the Fisher Building. Then the "Detroit Guidance Center" sign on Al's office door would take on some significance. Since his father's death, Al was the only psychologist in the suite.

Jan Canty could visualize herself and Al as a good pair of marriage counselors. Al would counsel the husbands. She would see the wives. Then, she thought, who knows? Perhaps we could even write a book together.

She anticipated some good changes soon in their lives.

Chapter 9

A thirty-four-year-old undercover vice cop named Jeff Renshaw was working the day rotation in the Cass Corridor December 7 when he saw the young brunette wave at him from the corner of Second and Charlotte.

The bearded cop was wearing a T-shirt, jeans, and a neck brace behind the wheel of a department surveillance car. He'd also been known to use arm slings, eye patches, and foreign accents in his line of work. He was never quite sure why prostitutes went for such covers. Either it played on their sympathy or made them think they had the upper hand.

Renshaw recognized the girl as she walked from the corner and got into his car. It was 1:45 P.M. He'd seen her before, but obviously she didn't remember him.

"You wanna go out?" she asked.

His nod was restricted by the collar brace.

"What do you wanna spend?"

"I have $30, but I need some of that."

"Could you spend $25?"

"Yep. What for?"

"How 'bout a blow job in the car?"

That satisfied the statute: a price and an act. He produced his badge and arrested Dawn Spens on a charge of accosting and soliciting, a misdemeanor.

She gave Renshaw what he already knew to be her real name. She'd been arrested a half-dozen times that year, three times by Vice. Most hookers had a half-dozen or more aliases. That could make an arrest a real pain in the ass.

The ID hassles, Renshaw once quipped, would cease if the hookers were required to carry Screen Actors Guild cards. Most were natural actresses. Through twelve years of police work, Renshaw never heard more convincing stories or saw more tears than those that came from whores about to be locked up. Their scripts ranged from sick children at home to reservations in drug treatment programs. He had a policy: Don't believe anything a hooker says. Absolutely nothing. He'd been conned one too many times.

Dawn, however, was silent as he took her to Detroit Police Headquarters. When he ran a warrant check, he found she was paid up. Most prostitutes ignored their court dates. They repeatedly jumped bond and worked the streets with anywhere from $200 to $5,000 hanging over their heads.

When Renshaw delivered Dawn to the lockup, she was given a $200 bail. If somebody showed up with cash, she would be out by sundown. Or she could get lucky. When the holding cells got too crowded, judges sometimes turned the whores loose on personal bonds to make room for more serious offenders. By the time a turnkey showed Dawn her cell, Jeff Renshaw was already back on the streets in his neck brace.

Early that evening John Fry watched from the window of the second-floor apartment for the black Buick. He was waiting for Dawn's new customer who always had a pocketful of cash.

Dawn was right about the sugar daddy business. In the past week, the trick named Al had called her three times for dates. Each time he'd picked her up in front of the Homewood, the two of them driving off to nearby motels. Each time she'd returned with $100 or more. One time, John met him in front of the Homewood. She introduced John to the trick as "a good friend."

"It's a *fucking* pleasure to meet you, John," he said, grinning.

People without the proper credentials shouldn't use that word, John muttered later. The man was out of his element. He had a word for assholes like that. He was a "goof."

"With each cussword his eyes seemed to say, 'I said it,' " he said. "And I'll tell you, he don't look like no fucking doctor."

But that wasn't an issue Wednesday evening. Money was. Dawn had called John from the pay phone in the Police Headquarters lockup. Get the bail money from the trick named Al when he showed for his date, she said.

The Buick announced its arrival in front of the Homewood with a blast of its horn sometime between six and seven. Fry scurried down the stairs but fell into a relaxed gait as he approached the car.

"Dawn's not here, *mon,*" Fry said, his dialect taking on a Caribbean quality. Sometimes that happened when he was feeling exceptionally smooth. "She's in jail. She told me to tell you she needs $400 to get out."

The trick reached into his pocket and handed Fry $150 wrapped in a Comerica Bank envelope.

"John, I was going to give this to her tonight, anyway."

John said he probably could raise the remaining $250 himself, but the trick was eager to come to Dawn's rescue.

"I can't get any more money tonight, John," he said before driving off. "First thing in the morning when the bank opens I'll bring the rest.

John could wait. He had $150 and knew one way to put the cash to good use.

Chapter 10

He didn't even know the woman very well. He was just excited about how he would feel that night during the candlelit dinner. He was infatuated, not in love, and when you talk about infatuation, you are talking about yourself.

— W. ALAN CANTY,
Detroit Magazine; Modern Bride Magazine

The bleat of a General Motors horn the next morning sent John Fry into the street to pick up the bail money. Words of gratitude crossed his lips as Al slipped $250 into his hand in another Comerica envelope. John had to resist a smirk.

Not only had he inflated the bond amount. That scam had been replaced by a better one. Dawn Spens was already upstairs in apartment 202, probably watching from the window. A judge had let her out on a personal bond late the night before.

"I'll have the girl out of there by noon," John told the trick. "You can probably reach her after that."

If Dawn Spens had any doubts that she had latched onto her first sugar daddy, they disappeared when he called that afternoon. He wanted to take her shopping.

"Then, would you have dinner with me tonight?" he asked.

Dawn covered the phone with her hand and turned to her boyfriend. She had been working the streets for six months but still sought John Fry's guidance when it came to business.

"John, he wants to have dinner with me. Is it all right?"

"It's better to get paid $100 to eat than get paid $100 to fuck."

John was feeling good. His supply of heroin was already assured for the night.

They went to a mall in Dearborn. She picked out a full-length quilt coat, with matching hat, gloves, and boots. He paid nearly $300 cash for the ensemble. Later she would wonder why he never used credit cards.

"Only cash," he said. "I don't believe in plastic. That created problems for me once."

That wasn't so odd, but the trick did have some quirks. While most dates couldn't wait, he had a spotty sexual appetite. He shunned other forms of physical contact. He never kissed her or even held her hand. The only urgent request the date had made was that she not smoke in his car. He said he was allergic to tobacco.

Now he was paying her to go to dinner. The small Cantonese restaurant was only a few blocks from the Homewood. They sat in a booth under a Chinese lantern, its dragon-lady panel changing colors as a light inside spun around.

Dawn eventually brought the subject up. Heroin glazed her eyes and slowed her speech into a low whiskey voice. Sometime during her vegetable egg fu yung and his pepper steak, she explained how she'd developed a drug habit.

"I had to tell him I was using," she later told another addict. "I figured anybody could tell anyway."

The trick said he knew all about drugs. She listened as he unfolded an elaborate story.

Al said that he had been married, and they had a little girl. His wife was a prostitute. She was working when they met, but she quit after they got married. After their daughter was born she developed a cocaine habit. She began working the streets again to support her habit. He put her in drug treatment centers, but she never stayed straight for long. One day she and their daughter got into a car accident, and his little girl was killed. His wife survived the collision, was on a life-support system for three weeks, then died.

"I still owe a big hospital bill for that," he said.

Later he embellished the story. He didn't use credit cards

because his wife ruined his credit rating. He said he still owned the house in Grosse Pointe where they once lived, but he couldn't live with the memories he associated with the home. He rented it out, staying in a doctor's residence near Detroit Receiving Hospital, where he worked in the emergency room.

Before the evening was over the trick named Al wondered if he could see her from now on in her apartment. John had already advised Dawn that might be a good idea as well, considering the cash he was spending. When he dropped her off at the Homewood, the trick said he would drop by the next day around noon.

Dawn wanted to know his last name. She complained she didn't have his phone number, that she didn't know how to reach him when she was in jail

"Miller," the trick said. "Dr. Al Miller."

Chapter 11

Although psychotherapy is often referred to as a treatment, as though it were some sort of remedy to be applied or administered to a passive patient, it really should be described as an interaction in which both therapist and patient take a very active role.

— W. ALAN CANTY,
Principles of Counseling and Psychotherapy

China red seeped into the dark eastern sky over Lake St. Clair as John Mosey piloted his black Jeep past the mansions on Windmill Pointe Drive. Mosey knew something was changing in his life. He was changing. Here he was up before dawn on a Saturday—not only up, but looking forward to psychotherapy at such a brutal hour.

Mosey owed it all to Al Canty. When he told Al that his unpredictable work schedule made it difficult to make sessions during the day or weekday evenings, Al had suggested Saturday mornings.

"Well, Saturdays are not a problem, but every other weekend I see my daughters," John told him. "I pick them up at 10:00."

"Would you be willing to meet me at my house at 6:45 A.M.?" Al said.

"You've got to be kidding me," Mosey complained.

But he wasn't joking. Al Canty already had a patient booked at 7:30 A.M. on Saturdays.

"If you're willing to be there at 6:45," he said. "I'm willing to get up and see you."

By winter, Mosey found himself getting up even earlier. He took time to drive through the most opulent neighborhoods of the Pointes. He liked to imagine himself lord of one of the castles along the lake. He could picture what they looked like inside. He could see himself in a private library, sitting among books, mahogany, and the stained glass. He could envision himself sipping coffee and reading fiction or Albert Ellis well into the night.

But sometimes that fantasy depressed him. He decided to tell Al about it as they began their session in his den.

"I know these people," Mosey began. "I mean they're buffoons, but they got money. The only thing they know how to do is *make money,* despite themselves. So why do I feel they're successful, and I'm not?"

"Sounds like your definition of success is an unrealistic one," Al said.

"Each generation should do better than the one before it," Mosey continued. "When I think that, I'm a loser. I mean, I come from a successful family. There are expectations involved. My uncle is a vice-president at General Motors. I have another uncle who is a judge. My father owns his own company. Here I am at thirty-three working for somebody else and living in Royal Oak. My dad is brighter than a cat, and I'm certainly no dummy. But I sure feel like a dummy when I'm around him. I mean, for chrisake, I grew up in Birmingham. How the hell do you top Birmingham or Grosse Pointe?"

Al said they came from similar backgrounds.

"My parents expected me to be on the honor roll," he said. "There was lots of pressure. I couldn't even take a shop class. My parents would have thought it appalling if I had gone into the vocational trades."

Al told him he felt insecure for many years. He had wondered for a long time whether he would ever get through his university training.

"I seriously questioned whether I was capable," he said. "But I was. I've also found it's not so much what my parents said, but how I perceived them that was the problem. A lot of this pressure was my own perception.

"John, it all gets back to *self-esteem.*"

How often they had talked about that word. Al said there were a lot of symptoms of low self-worth: People pleasing. The inability to say no.

Low self-esteem was the catalyst for what Al called the rescuer-victim syndrome. What a perfect description of

Mosey's last relationship and every one before it.

"If I put ninety-nine women in a party, I'd find the one fucked-up girl and turn her into a project," he told Al.

"And do you know she would find you, as well," Al said. "Both the rescuer and the victim play their roles well. The victim can sense the rescuer, and manipulate him because of it. The rescuer, in turn, builds up his self-esteem as the savior. Many people, John, spend their entire lives in those roles."

They would work on that, Al said. They would work together. And they did, every Saturday at dawn.

Chapter 12

[The child] gradually develops likes and dislikes of his own which are based not only on his parents' values, but on his own experiences with life as well.
— W. ALAN CANTY,
Principles of Counseling and Psychotherapy

Jan Canty smelled the familiar aroma of Al's coffee brewing in her little country kitchen. It was one of her favorite rooms, though one of the smallest. It made the big Tudor feel like home.

On idle mornings, she liked to sit in the breakfast nook and feel the sun penetrating the two leaded-glass windows overlooking the backyard. By December, virtually all the leaves had fallen from the elms. The few stragglers reminded her of hooked goldfish as they shimmied in the wind.

Al was already working on his second pot of coffee. Never had she seen someone drink so much of the stuff. It remained his only vice. He'd given up cigarettes years ago because she was allergic to the smoke.

Al's addiction to coffee was as much ritual as habit. He bought two or three different kinds of beans, and his patients often gave him new varieties to try. He ground them meticulously, then experimented with various combinations. The mix was brewed, then transferred into a yellow thermos with a tan top. He was probably the only professional in the Fisher Building who arrived carrying a vacuum bottle each day.

Jan Canty had to admit it. Her husband had become somewhat of an eccentric in his prime, and the thermos was one of his most visible oddities. She sometimes wondered what was more important, the coffee or the container. He took it to his mother's and on errands to the grocery store. He toted it on their dinner dates with her best friend, Celia Muir, and her husband, John. He sipped from the plastic cup en route, then set the bottle on the table in fine restaurants, asking waitresses to top it off with more.

Once, he lost the thermos top before a speaking engagement at the University of Michigan. He was so anxious he almost canceled the lecture, until she rushed out and bought a new thermos. It took some time, however, before he became comfortable with the new bottle. He preferred it looking very used and unwashed, and he never left the house without it.

"Al, you're pretty attached to that thermos," her friend Celia once kidded.

"You're right," Al admitted. "It's my blanket."

Jan was surprised when he began to fill the vacuum bottle. They usually waited until the afternoon before going out on his day off.

"Al, you're going somewhere?"

"I have to go to the Wayne County Jail. They want me to do updates on parolees."

"Parolees? This is your day off. Friday. Our day off."

He explained that he'd made a series of psychological reports on prisoners some time back. Now the parole board was adamant that the same psychologist evaluate the prisoners before they were released.

"They want that kind of consistency. I've worked it into my lunch hour."

That's just great, she told herself. And, considering the way he was working lately, she wondered if it was only the beginning. She hated to think what would happen if Fridays became full workdays again. Already Al's clinic schedule was fashioned after a Ford production line, and it seemed to be speeding up. After finishing at 6 P.M. at the Fisher, he came home, ate, and then disappeared into his home office for more patient sessions. He had everything timed to the quarter hour.

"OK," he'd say. "I'm leaving the office at 7:00 tonight and I have a patient at 7:45 at home. Can we eat between 7:15 and 7:30?"

She was beginning to feel like an airline stewardess. Several times Al wanted his dinner in therapy sessions at home. She thought that looked pretty unprofessional, and it wasn't good for his health. She knew he often skipped lunch.

After he sped through a caffeine-driven day like that, she always marveled how Al could shut down, just as though someone had thrown a switch. He became a relaxed, deliberate man with his books and conversations. She wanted him that way on Fridays. And, she had to admit, she was a little hurt he was leaving.

"All right, I'll go with you to the jail," she told him. "I want to be with you. I'll go with you to the jail, then we'll do something together afterwards. I've never been there anyway. I'm sure I'll find it interesting."

Al screwed the cup onto his thermos.

"Jan, you don't. You don't want to go to the Wayne County Jail. It's a crummy place and it stinks. It literally stinks."

He also said he didn't want her subjected to the catcalls from prisoners. The jail was a lot different than their other professional expeditions, such as his college lectures on autism.

He shook his head, concerned.

Maybe he's right, she thought. Maybe I couldn't stand being in that type of atmosphere. Why should I put myself through something like that?

"OK then, go."

She handed him his thermos, kissed him, and pointed him toward the door.

The Wayne County Jail was not Jan Canty's idea of enjoyment, but she suspected it was probably Al's. He always had kept a hand in some criminal work. Earlier in his career, he consulted on criminal cases for the Wayne County Circuit Court. Recently he'd evaluated a teenage murderer in Port Huron.

Jan knew that Al had some of his father's first love in him. On their nightly walks he sometimes spoke of his dad's work with Recorder's Court and the Detroit Police Department. She'd heard a good deal from both father and son.

For Alan Canty, Sr., notoriety began, quite literally, in the streets. In the mid-1930s, he came up with the then novel theory that certain drivers were responsible for an unusually high number of accidents. He backed up his theories with a battery of tests on troublesome drivers, weeding out offenders that ranged from alcoholics to the clinically insane.

His findings drew nationwide attention, spurred systems to detect offenders in other states, and catapulted his career. Later, he wrote on the uses of hypnosis and polygraphs. He taught criminology at Wayne State and the Detroit Police Academy. He lectured at training schools throughout the United States and instructed cops in the art of interrogation. He was commissioned by the CIA in 1954 to conduct experiments on sexual psychopaths using hypnosis and LSD, a drug then thought to be a truth serum.

By then, Al Sr. had excelled in a new area of study—criminals he called "sex deviates." The Recorder's clinic evaluated some five hundred sex offenders a year.

Jan knew that Al Sr. didn't leave all the cases at the office. Once, Al complained that as an adolescent he listened to the sordid details of many cases as his father pontificated about them at the dinner table: Homicides. Rapes. Fetishes. Sexual dysfunctions. Missing children. Child killers. Her husband said he disliked hearing about them but listened to please his dad.

But Al Sr. also was artful in the use of shock value, as in the time he jolted a large downtown assembly hosted by the Detroit Council of the PTA. The organization invited him to speak on sex offenders. He gave the audience more of a lecture than they anticipated.

"Neurotic mothers and frustrated schoolteachers," he began, "do more actual psychological damage to Michigan children than do the small fraction of 1 percent of the state's population who collide every year with the criminal law as sex offenders."

The audience of teachers and civic-minded parents shifted in their seats. The criminologist had more for them to ponder.

"Parents who reject their children, who mistreat them,

overprotect them, or fill them with exaggerated anxieties, even about 'sex fiends,' and teachers who try to work out their own frustrations on the children to whom they stand as parent substitutes do severe damage to unknown thousands of children every year."

The talk made front-page headlines in 1951. Gladys Canty, a PTA leader, got quite a few phone calls.

Al Sr.'s animated speaking style was refined by The Players, an exclusive, men-only theater club in downtown Detroit. Its distinguished members were known for their historic playhouse on Jefferson Avenue, and their all-night drinking sessions following their "frolics." His most memorable role in the troupe was that of neurotic Captain Queeg in *The Caine Mutiny*.

Al Sr. made his sex crime lectures equally compelling. They kept him booked on the criminal justice lecture circuit for fifteen years. Police departments and civic groups around the country clamored for his talks as sex came out of the bedroom into public discussions.

He always closed his lectures the same way. After covering sadism, window peeping, homosexuality, exhibitionism, fetishism, impotence, castration complex, and a half-dozen other disorders, he always said:

"And there, but for the grace of God, go I."

Al saw his father receive many accolades. He was the only non cop to be given a gold badge by the Detroit Police. The University of Louisville awarded him with an honorary doctorate. The state certified him as a psychologist, despite his lack of formal degrees from Syracuse and Western Reserve, the universities he attended.

When he retired from the Recorder's Court Psychiatric Clinic after 19 years as its executive director, the state police tapped him in 1969 to help solve a rash of co-ed killings in Ypsilanti and Ann Arbor. A serial killer named John Norman Collins had eluded police for more than two years.

"I don't know whether I can solve them," Al Sr. told reporters when he joined the hunt. "I'm not God."

Al Sr. could pass an hour richly detailing how the Collins case was solved by basic policework. Jan used to find Al Sr.'s stories captivating. The man's knowledge was formidable, especially for someone with so little formal training. She could see how Al had been influenced. Her husband gave an extemporaneous eulogy at his funeral. The speech covered his career, but said nothing about him as a father.

In that way, Jan felt she really didn't know Al Sr. at all. She didn't perceive him as a very warm man. He reminded her of George C. Scott in one of his more belligerent roles. Toughness was etched into his puffy eyes and pendulous jowls. He could be very opinionated. She figured his jaded world view came from his association with cops.

Maybe that was why Al never chose to devote his entire career to forensic studies, she thought. They had different styles. Al chose his words carefully. His father could swear like an ironworker.

But that didn't diminish her husband's admiration. For years he kept an office for Al Sr. in his Fisher Building suite. Jan began using his sprawling walnut desk for homework. She felt like a dwarf behind the thing. One day, when Al Sr. was still alive, she wondered out loud why it was there anyway.

"Oh, I keep it for Pa," he explained. "He needs a place where he can get away from home and do some writing."

But she had never seen his father use it, and Al had always been somewhat mysterious about his dealings with his father. In fact, he rarely talked about his relationship with either of his parents. The only poignant moment that she could recall was after the funeral. Al broke down crying and said:

"I'm going to miss him so much. I tried to be a good son."

Jan did know, however, that psychology was not Al's first career path. He first wanted to be a paramedic and took some emergency medical training in college. He still had his father's old stethoscope and blood pressure gauge somewhere in the basement.

Then, Al wanted to be an actor. But after taking drama classes and appearing in several college plays, Al succumbed to doubts about making it in that field. She knew he'd sublimated his thespian training with Project Indianwood.

He blended theater and psychology in other ways. He still admired James Dean and the film *Rebel Without a Cause,* the quintessential movie about troubled adolescence in the 1950s. Al was intrigued by the characters and the film's Freudian undertones. He sometimes talked about the tragic nature of the actor's death.

He also cherished the Robert M. Lindner book *Rebel Without a Cause.* Unlike the movie, the book was a true case history of a teenage psychopath. The personality disorder was one of her husband's favorite areas of study. He sometimes thumbed through *The Mask of Sanity,* Hervey Cleckley's definitive work on the disorder. He talked of his father's dealings with them.

Jan always thought of psychopaths as destructive actors. They were not legally insane, nor did they respond to therapy. But Al found intriguing these men, who, void of conscience or true empathy, manipulated others to meet their needs. The psychopath's best role was that of a seemingly normal, often intelligent human being. Behind the mask, however, he plotted antisocial acts ranging from the discounted sale of the Brooklyn Bridge to murder.

Well, the Wayne County Jail was probably full of such seasoned con artists, Jan Canty reasoned. She suspected Al's parolee evaluations were his escape from the daily grind. Maybe I'm being too selfish, she thought, wanting him all to myself for the entire day.

Jan was pleased when his Buick came up the driveway after the lunch hour. She guessed she could live with him missing for a couple of hours on their day off.

Chapter 13

The criminal psychopath, or sociopath, can run the range of crimes from bank robbery to murder. He is without conscience . . . He will do anything to keep from serving in the armed forces. Often he tends to be heavily tattooed.

— W. Alan Canty,
Henry Ford Community College lectures

On his first visit to apartment 202, Dr. Al Miller looked more equipped for an outing to the Detroit Public Library than to the bed of a Cass Corridor prostitute. He carried a yellow thermos and the morning newspaper as he arrived for the Friday lunch hour.

John headed for the White Grove, nodding to the trick on the stairway. The apartment only had three rooms: a bathroom, a small kitchen, and a living room with a fold-out bed. John didn't much care what his girlfriend did with her tricks, as long as they paid in cash. But he had no desire to stick around when she conducted business.

John occasionally gave some thought to the line of work that paid for his drug habit the past three years. Some might call him a pimp, but that word was considered as demeaning around the Corridor as the term "whore." Whores fucked and sucked johns for a living and had to give all their money to their pimps. *Working girls* went on *dates* and got paid by their *tricks*. They received *protection* from their *boyfriends*.

John wasn't proud of his role, but he wasn't ashamed either. He took a rational view of the whole matter.

"Personally, I feel that 99 percent of the people in the world are prostitutes," he often said. "They prostitute themselves to a job or whatever. Therefore, if you got to

70

prostitute yourself anyway, then why make believe you're not, which most people do. The broad, specifically speaking of females, will live with a dude for security, and fuck a man on the side. I'm a realist enough that I'd rather know that she's going out there and getting paid than me going out and prostituting myself and her fucking for free while I'm gone."

"But what makes a girl give her body to a man she doesn't even know?" a friend once asked.

John answered matter-of-factly.

"Money. And if I was a woman I'd be the biggest whore in the world. Because I love money. I'll do anything for money."

John Fry's love of the American dollar had been a costly affair over the latter half of his thirty-seven years. That was one reason he'd gone into prostitution. It gas low-risk crime—for John, at least. He already had marked ten years in six state and federal penitentiaries. Between sentences, he'd married and divorced three times and sired at least five children.

John's tour of prison cells began after he was drafted into the Army in 1965. He was court-martialed twice for desertion. After his discharge, he landed in prisons in Michigan, Minnesota, and Indiana. His felonies included bad checks, counterfeiting, and breaking and entering. He'd never been convicted of a violent crime.

John did well in prison settings. He snagged preferred work details by keeping his institutional record clean. He handed out cell assignments as a clerk He gave advice as a drug counselor in one of the federal pens. In prison, he finished his senior year of high school. He took college-level social science classes, including psychology.

John could pull an average intelligence level on an IQ test. But one forensic psychiatric evaluation also described what was perhaps his best talent: "He can make people feel at ease and has developed the ability to ascertain people's needs and exploit them by fulfilling these needs."

John had a big need not to be locked up. Three times he'd escaped from institutions. When he was paroled from a federal halfway house in 1980, Lucky Fry vowed he'd never go back.

71

The nickname was not intended as satire. John often said he earned it after being severely beaten and left for dead by a rival motorcycle gang. Others said it came from his ability to talk his way out of trouble.

The word "Lucky" soared on a pair of Harley-Davidson motorcycle wings in a tattoo on his left arm. It was only one of seventeen, most of which were penned by prison tattooists.

In a sleeveless shirt, John's brawny limbs put on quite a display. On his left arm was "LBT" (Living on Borrowed Time); "FTW" (Fuck the World); a snarling panther; a "74" for the Harley-Davidson series; a preying eagle; "TWIGGY," a reference to his old girlfriend; and a winged skull in a motorcycle hat.

On his right arm he used to have "Cheryl" over a marijuana leaf, until Dawn crossed out his ex-girlfriend's name with a cousin's tattoo gun. A skull and crossbones bore the words "AS YOU ARE I WAS; AS I AM YOU WILL BE." There was another skull. There also was a yellow tattoo of the cartoon character Tweety Bird.

The most eye-catching of the lot was "WHITE POWER." "WHITE" was printed vertically down Fry's left arm in big block letters, "POWER" down the back of the other. The tattoo was only visible when he was walking away, his back turned to a city that was nearly 70 percent black.

"I guess they figure if I'm crazy enough to have it there," he once said, "I'm crazy enough to back it up."

John's disdain for blacks revealed itself in other ways. He refused to allow Dawn to turn a date with one. Once he put the likes and dislikes of his life in a poem he sent to an old girlfriend. He claimed to be its author:

As I was sitting on my porch one day
Suckin' down a brew,
A nigger rode by on a Harley.
I said this will never do.
I jumped right up and chased it down
With a length of chain,
Then beat the fucker senseless
And squashed its tiny brain,
Then took the bike home with me

72

And freed it from its doom
Of public humiliation, by being
Ridden by a coon.

But John hadn't owned a hog or ridden with any clubs for years. His beard and hair were grown out, unlike those days when he preferred his head and face clean as he mounted the seat of a Harley.

His money was consumed by Cass Corridor drugs, and he complained about the neighborhood frequently. Not only was the dope bad; most of the action was controlled by blacks. John considered the area below his standards.

"I'd always said I'd never live downtown. That's dead," he later told a friend. "I'm not going to get caught up in that."

But John was, and he knew it as he sat in the White Grove. He watched the hustle outside and thought of Dawn servicing the free-spending trick he now knew as Dr. Al Miller.

Already Lucky Fry had made up his mind. He was going to find a way out. Possibly he already had.

Chapter 14

. . . The astonishing power that nearly all psycho-paths and part-psychopaths have to bind forever the devotion of women.

—HERVEY CLECKLEY, M.D.,
The Mask of Sanity

A prostitute by the name of Cheryl Krizanovic cursed what she was about to do. Since the day she met Lucky Fry, her life had unfolded in a series of calamities. But now here she was again, running back to her old boyfriend for help on a cold mid-December night.

But damn if I'm going to spend the winter in the street, she told herself, especially while John and his new girlfriend play house in the Homewood Manor.

Cheryl already had ruined the Ford Escort that had served as her home for four weeks, as well as the regular trick who gave it to her. She totaled the little car on her way to cop dope one night. As for the sugar daddy, the Arab from Dearborn was broke. She'd shut off the sex long before the warehouse worker ran out of cash. But it took an empty bank account to bring him to his senses.

John Fry owed her, she reasoned. He owed her a place to stay until she found something—or someone—else. After all, she thought, I'm the one who kept a roof over his head for all these years. She planned to tell him as much as soon as she got to the Homewood. If that didn't work, she knew a few packs of dope would give John a conscience.

Cheryl Jean Krizanovic didn't wonder anymore how she got into such jams. The prostitute was only two months into her twenty-first year of life, but already, she felt like a worn-out machine.

She met John Fry on a fluke, during an inmate visit at Jackson Prison in 1979. She was fifteen, living with a friend and running from her stepfather and memories of a rape. Two months later, on April Fools' Day, she helped John escape from a work farm.

Since then, she had endured nearly a half-dozen unwanted pregnancies, a miscarriage, a saline abortion, broken ribs, a shattered spleen, several drug overdoses, countless abscesses, and a crippling case of gangrene. She'd been raped by one of John's friends, been train-raped by twenty-nine members of a motorcycle gang, and endured an average of two rapes a month working the streets. John had given her a daughter but then helped her lose it to the courts. She had tried suicide twice. Half of this happened before John ever convinced her to turn her first trick.

But the old machine could still make money, up to five hundred dollars a day if she worked at it. When she first started, her thin shoulders, blond hair, and lashy eyes earned her the nickname Twiggy. Now some of the cops and johns called her the Librarian Hooker because she sometimes wore thick glasses and put her hair up in a tight bun. The dates were nuts for the look.

For two years, Cheryl had turned every trick for John. Now she worked for herself. She didn't know what else to do — at least that's what she told herself. John had always promised her that one day he would find a job; they would kick their drug habits, and she wouldn't have to work the streets. One day did arrive, but it was the day John didn't need her or her money anymore. She was still hurt and angry.

John had been particularly cunning in the way he dumped her, she thought. It was in June, right after she was hospitalized for pneumonia. She came home to their old place off Michigan Avenue finding John had taken in a houseguest. Her name was Dawn Spens, and John said the girl had first been thrown out of her home in Harper Woods by her father, then evicted from her apartment in the Corridor. John had big plans.

"I don't want you to work anymore," he told Cheryl. "Stay in and sleep. This new girl is going to support both me and you. She's our new ticket."

That was if John really meant what he said, and Cheryl knew that could be a fool's assumption. She'd learned there was usually a grand scheme behind whatever he said.

Right off, Cheryl hadn't liked the way John was acting around the new girl. And she didn't like the new girl's attitude. She didn't need to look at the new girl's license to tell she was from the suburbs. The new girl is a snobby bitch, she thought. Dawn acted as though she was too good to talk to anybody but John. One night in bed Cheryl confronted him.

"How come you pay more attention to her than me? Maybe you should invite the bitch into your bed."

That night John moved her stuff out of his room.

"Fuck you, then," Cheryl told him. "Then you ain't gettin' none of my money or none of my drugs."

And he didn't. Cheryl's drug binge ended several weeks later at a stop sign near downtown. The last thing she remembered was using the rear-view mirror to inject heroin into her jugular vein. A squad car found her there, passed out at the wheel. Between that and a slew of outstanding prostitution tickets, she served seventy-one days in jail.

When she got out, it was her twentieth birthday. To hell with John, she told herself. She turned a few tricks and bought herself a cake, the size someone buys for a banquet. She had the baker top it with twenty blue roses and "Happy Birthday Cheryl." She visited a hair stylist and bought a new dress and new set of earrings. She bought a bunch of birthday cards.

"Here, you sign this, and then give it back to me," she said, distributing them to people in the neighborhood.

She thought she was going to spend that night alone with her cards and blue roses. John and Dawn weren't around. They were busy moving to the Homewood. Then John's younger brother, Jim, came over with a friend, a couple of joints, and a bottle of Asti Spumante.

She was glad they did. She was afraid of what she might have done alone that night.

Cheryl knew what her problem was then. She knew what it was now as she walked toward the Homewood. There was a part of her that still loved John. She couldn't understand it, considering the way he had used her. She wished she knew how to make the feelings stop.

When Cheryl reached the apartment building, she resolved she wasn't going to let him see she still cared. John didn't argue about her staying. He said she could have the couch, but she could see Dawn wasn't happy with the idea.

"We're like family anyway," John told both of them. "You know I'd do anything for family, mon. You know me well enough to know that."

Cheryl guessed otherwise. It had little to do with family, friendship, or the love she thought he once had for her. All good ol' Cheryl is to John Fry, she thought, is a couple of extra packs of dope. For now, that would work just fine.

Chapter 15

Bobette Gray was stunned, then furious.

"Come on, Bobbi, everyone knows this *but* you," said her husband's best friend. "You are one of the smartest women I know. You can't figure this out? I'm telling you again, Bobbi, your husband Jeff is *gay*. Homosexual, you know?"

Gay. An ex-drunk. And basically a pain in the ass, she thought. And she had suspected. But the source of her rage wasn't her husband or his sexual preference. It was her psychologist and marriage counselor — W. Alan Canty.

Bobbi Gray punched the buttons on her kitchen phone as though her finger was a sewing machine needle. The words of Jeff's friend filled the pauses between the rings. "Bobbi, Jeff told Alan Canty he was gay at his first session two years ago."

She was a big woman with a wit matched only by her appetite. But she was neither hungry nor in the mood for jokes. She didn't bother to identify herself when Canty answered.

"Dr. Canty, I have just found out what everyone in the world knows. And that includes *you,* and you've known it for damn near two years! My husband is gay, a goddamn homosexual. I feel like a fool, like you two guys have made a fool out of me. I've been acting like an idiot."

There was silence, then that calm, resonant voice she knew so well.

"I can explain this, Bobbi. Can you come on your regularly scheduled time and we'll talk about it? We can handle this problem."

Explain it? She didn't see how. But yes, she'd be there. She wanted to see Alan Canty *handle* this one. And then she was going to tell him where to put the handle.

Bobbi was mad at herself for not following her instincts.

For twenty-five months she had put herself and what was left of her marriage in the hands of the therapist. She should have guessed something like this would happen. She had grown sick of hearing those same words from Canty: "Something is happening between you and Jeff. You have to be patient." Bobbi Gray wished she had fifty dollars for every time he'd said it. She could have moved to Windmill Pointe Drive and walked to see her therapist.

It hadn't started out that way. Al Canty seemed an exception in a profession she suspected was full of oddballs. In fact, that's how she found Canty. Before Al, she and Jeff were seeing an eccentric psychiatrist who had some pretty screwy suggestions. When he told her to "go have an affair" she went shopping for a new therapist. She asked the Michigan Psychological Association for a referral in Grosse Pointe, someone close to home. Alan Canty said he was quite willing to see her at seven o'clock every Wednesday night in his home office. It was only a five-minute drive.

Bobbi liked Canty's unpretentious style, and soon Jeff was going in a separate session. In those first sessions, Canty wanted Bobbi's version of her life. Most of her memories had to do with being fat. She was a zeppelin at two. Her first day of school she learned the meaning of "tub o' lard." Her last year she discovered what it felt like not to be able to shop for a size sixteen prom dress. Weight had been the great constant in her life.

There wasn't anything unique about her obesity. "I eat because I'm unhappy," she told him. "And I'm unhappy because I'm fat." She was sick of diet books and reading about herself in the lifestyle sections of newspapers. She didn't need Canty to tell her she was compulsive and suffered from low self-esteem.

"I have had a lot of success with your type of personality," Canty told her. "Things look really bright for your future."

But then there was Jeff. She knew when they first met at work he was the perfect loser for her.

"Jeff didn't even know his own shoe size when I met him," she told Canty. "And behind every man is a woman who knows his shoe size. It's not like men were banging down my door. I took what was available."

The marriage worked pretty well until the two of them hit their thirties. They pooled their thirty-thousand-dollar incomes and moved into Grosse Pointe Park. They were like a lot of white middle-class couples who worked their way into the smaller homes. They came for the top-flight school system and crime-free streets. They had a girl, aged two, and a boy, aged seven.

Jeff liked to drink. By the time he was thirty, he needed to drink. For a long time, she blamed herself. She took care of him when he got sloppy drunk and covered for him when he was off on a bender. Then one day he left her. He got sober a week later and stayed sober. He moved in with his mother but still showed up every night for dinner, and for support when he got moody.

That was the situation when the two of them began counseling with Canty.

"This marriage *can* be saved," Canty said confidently. "When he comes home make him feel at home. Make it comfortable in *his* home. If he's home for an hour, make it wonderful for that hour."

And Bobbi Gray did. She cooked Jeff's dinners, washed Jeff's clothes, and patted Jeff's back as he walked out the door. She loaned him money. She paid the bills, including the $110 their therapy was costing each week.

"I think he's getting ready to come home, Bobbi," Canty kept saying. "I think he's getting ready. Jeff and you are perfectly matched for each other. He belongs home."

Over time she thought she grew close to Alan Canty. He always gave her a big hug at the end of each appointment.

"Think of me as your good friend," he often said.

Canty also loved her jokes. At times he seemed downright childish about it. If she got off a good one-liner, he would jump up and run out the door of his home office to tell the wife he called Jan-Jan.

"That's so funny, Bobbi," he'd say. "Excuse me. I've got to go tell that to Jan-Jan." She'd hear his voice fading as he scurried off into the big Tudor: "Jan-Jan, listen to what Bobbi just told me . . ."

In some ways, Al Canty seemed an odd duck. He struck Bobbi as the kind of guy who probably got teased to death in school. She could just see him as a scrawny kid with glasses taking crap from his classmates. She knew the feeling well.

And Al had funny little habits. He always brought his thermos of coffee into their sessions and drank the stuff as fast as she chain-smoked her cigarettes. He often was in the same Ban-Lon sport shirt and khaki pants. She watched the shirt fade from green to yellow from repeated washing. She didn't consider Al a good-looking man. But she never questioned why he had such a young, pretty wife.

"In Grosse Pointe, you learn," she told one friend, "the ugly spouse is the one with the money."

Sometimes Canty's obviously fat income bugged her. Often, Al and his Jan-Jan were still eating dinner when she arrived for her session. They ate standing in the kitchen, as though there was no time for a sit-down meal. It seemed they had lamb chops a lot. The aroma irritated Bobbi. She was sick of eating hamburger because Jeff had drained her budget dry.

Once, Canty interrupted a session and unwittingly revealed the kind of spending money he had around. It happened on a particularly bad day.

"I'm going to kill Jeff," she'd told Canty earlier on the telephone. "I'm going to kill him today. The only way to help him is to murder him. There's an old black saying: He needs to be dead, and that's the only thing that's going to help."

At the very least, she was going to file for divorce. Canty was concerned. He summoned her to the Fisher Building to talk. But in the middle of the session he took a long phone call from an antique car agent who had found him a Cord roadster. She listened to him arrange to meet the man at a Chinese restaurant called the Golden Buddha.

"I'll bring you the sixteen thousand dollars," she heard him say. "We'll meet. You bring your wife, and I'll bring mine, and I'll be happy to treat you to dinner."

Then Al ran into another room in his suite and returned with a magazine picture of a white Cord with chrome exhaust pipes.

"This is what it will look like, Bobbi," he said excitedly. "Of course it's just a shell now. Of course you realize it doesn't even work and it's in pieces. Sixteen thousand dollars. But this is what it will eventually look like."

Lamb chops, Cord cars, and hamburger. That night she really laid into Jeff.

"You realize what you're worth to me dead," she told him. "You're worth double the child support in Social Security payments, plus all the life insurance, plus none of this aggravation. I know a dozen kids in the ghetto who will do it for five bucks. It's that easy, sweetheart."

Canty's little office in the big Tudor on Berkshire at one time had served as a good place to cry and carry on. But she'd cried herself out many months ago. She no longer feared being alone. More importantly, Bobbi Gray now knew she wasn't crazy. With two kids, the bills, the house, and her job, she didn't have time to crack up.

She wondered, why hadn't Al Canty told her about Jeff? Why hadn't he saved her two years of marriage counseling, a hundred loads of Jeff Gray's laundry, and the wrenching emotions of hoping for the impossible? Damn it, she thought. I suspected. I asked Al several times if Jeff was gay.

"No, no, no, Bobbi," Al always said.

She'd wanted to believe him. Now that she thought about it, she'd also *wanted* to believe Jeff wasn't an alcoholic, when anyone in his right mind could see he was a drunk. Funny, she thought, how someone can be so blind to bold facts when they think they love someone. Or maybe she was just afraid what the truth would say about her. After all, she picked him as a husband.

Al and Jeff must be some kind of buddies, Bobbi Gray grumbled. Her husband was leading a double life. But she couldn't understand why Al Canty had helped him do it.

Chapter 16

Jan Canty was disappointed Al couldn't meet her for lunch. The proximity between the Fisher and her clinic at the Detroit Medical Center had always made noon get-togethers a nice option. When she pushed him for another day, he made it clear the lunch hour was no longer his own.

"It's the parolee evaluations, Jan," he said. "There's considerably more work than I anticipated. It looks like my lunch hours are going to be filled for some time."

Why, she wondered, would he so easily forfeit the only respite he had in his long days? Had she missed something? Were they having financial troubles?

"Oh no, Jan-Jan, everything is fine," he assured her. "It's just very important they have consistency in these things. It goes with the territory when you take on court work."

She had no reason to think Al would not tell her if they were overextended financially, but for some time she had felt a growing need to be more cognizant of their money matters. For years she'd never protested his handling of the household budget. Al had obviously performed the job well. He was so determined to shoulder the responsibility, and she had so little time. To simplify matters she kept her own checkbook for her fellowship earnings and he kept his own accounts for the practice and the household. Virtually all his bills and statements were mailed to his office. Any time she needed money, Al always had plenty of cash on hand. As for clothes, he enjoyed accompanying her on shopping trips and footing the bill.

But she was beginning to grow uncomfortable with the arrangement. It was time for her to act less like a dependent student and more like a professional. And what if something happened to him? What if there was an emergency? Would she know what to do?

Jan had brought up those questions a couple of times in recent months. Al agreed but said all the paperwork involved would take considerable time to accumulate and explain. He'd get to it when he had "the free time."

That, she suspected, was getting to be a precious commodity in their lives again. For now she would just have to trust him. There was no reason not to. After nine years, she ought to know whether or not she married an honest man. Only a fool, she thought, wouldn't have realized that by now.

Chapter 17

"Listen, Cheryl," John said, "With this trick, we're going to play brother and sister, just over here visiting Dawn."

What else, Cheryl thought. They were roles the two of them knew well. For days she listened to briefings about the new trick named Dr. Al Miller who had fallen in a big way for Dawn Spens.

It started to get real good, John said, when he began coming to the apartment—usually around noon, sometimes in the early evening. Each visit brought a minimum one hundred dollars, but often more.

John got caught up in the research, asking other girls how to milk a sugar daddy. Then he'd pass the expertise on to Dawn, who alone dealt with the trick. She nicked him for rent money, her grocery budget, utility bills, and any other expenditure John and Dawn could inflate or fabricate.

Dr. Miller supposedly wanted Dawn to think of the money as his way of helping. He didn't expect anything in return. With him in the picture, she didn't need to work the streets, he said. Once he got through some financial difficulties, caused by the death of his wife, he wanted to move her out of the Corridor, set her up in an apartment. Then he'd pay for college if she wanted.

"Dawn, you know you're college material," he said.

Soon he planned to have a private practice, he told her. She could come to work as his receptionist. Some days he rambled on about his work, telling hospital stories from the Detroit Medical Center.

On others he was just content to relax at the kitchen table, sip coffee, and read the newspaper. He seemed to be satisfied just being in the same room with her. Dawn later said she often just tuned him out.

Several times he surprised them all in the morning. Dawn took his packages at the door as John scrambled from sight. They were treats like chocolate milk, donuts, and orange juice.

"I just thought you could use some things," he said, grinning. Then he hustled back to his Buick.

One day Dr. Miller brought over what he called his "special blend" of coffee. John had to admit it, the stuff was pretty good. Dawn brewed a fresh pot whenever the trick stopped by.

John theorized the regular was trying to elevate the relationship, at least in his own mind, beyond what it really was. The pattern was all pretty typical, Cheryl thought. Some regulars got quite caught up. It usually never lasted long—a few weeks, sometimes a few months.

"Get all you can right now" was John's advice. "Tricks are unpredictable. You treat every date like it's the first and the last. One day they just don't show, and they're gone—and they don't announce it ahead of time."

But John also wanted to keep a good thing going. He said the trick wasn't to know that he and Dawn were sleeping together. The guy must be stupid or blind, Cheryl thought. John's clothes were in the apartment. But John was adamant. When the black Buick pulled into the Homewood parking lot, Cheryl followed John out of the apartment and they disappeared. It's just good business practice, John said.

By late December, less than a month after Dawn and the doctor first met, Cheryl and John were making their timed exit three or four times a week.

She knew John liked to play hide-and-seek with tricks. Cheryl guessed he came up with such maneuvers to justify the money he received for basically doing nothing.

Protection. There was no protection. All that John Fry, or any other pimp, ever did for a girl was lay a good beating on someone who raped her. But that was after the fact—if he ever found him, that is. Most of the time John got high at home and waited for more money so he could get higher.

Cheryl knew from experience that a girl was largely defenseless when she worked. She had been thrown out of a car naked twenty miles from downtown, fought off a freak wielding a screwdriver, and stabbed a guy in the leg who tried to take what he wanted for free.

Each time John was missing in action, talking "business" with his admirers on the street.

When John did want to hang around their old house off Michigan, they played the sibling charade. He always preached it was bad business to roll tricks. But his professional scruples didn't seem to matter if he was sick and needed quick cash. Then he used to hide in a closet or behind a shower curtain. Just after Cheryl got into bed with the date, John came crashing into the room, shouting:

"What the fuck are you doin' in bed with my sister, man!"

The trick would go soft and run. The date was miles down the road before realizing his wallet had been vacuumed in the excitement.

Now John's playing it slick with Dawn's new regular, Cheryl thought, hoping for long-term gains rather than cash on hand.

She finally met Dr. Al Miller face-to-face one day when they were late getting out the apartment door. At first the man in the green sport coat looked like just another date.

"Hi, Al, my sister Cheryl," John said.

The trick gave her an odd smile. She could have sworn he winked, but his eyelid never moved.

"It's a pleasure to meet you, Cheryl," he said.

Cheryl and John went up a flight of stairs and sat in the hallway. They lit a couple of menthols.

"I told you he was a goof," John said. "It's her first sugar daddy. She's not sure how far she can play him."

Big fucking deal, she thought. He acts as if this is something new.

She had seen a half-dozen regulars just like Al come in and out of her life over the years. Before the Arab, there was the plumber. He was fifty and married. In the end he was endorsing his four-hundred-dollar paycheck and handing it to her every Thursday. They only had sex three times in three months. She would make it a personal challenge: How much can I get without ever dropping my pants? She eventually lost all her regulars that way.

At first she thought it was just the lure of illicit sex that hooked those types. But her own practices changed her mind about that. She figured such men just wanted a young woman at their side who paid attention to them. They were too old to romance one, but too young to forget what the affection of a young girl was like.

Prostitution was the world's oldest masquerade, she thought. It ran on deception as well as desire. All the girl had to do was become whatever the trick wanted her to be, and even the orgasms were fake.

She'd had one gratifying night in two years on the street, but it had nothing to do with sex. He was a sixty-five-year-old guy she'd flagged. He paid her a hundred dollars just to lie next to her in bed for an hour. All he did was hug her.

"It's been so long since I've held somebody young and tender next to me," he told her.

It seemed awfully weepy, but her heart went out to the guy. It was the only night she felt good about the line of work she was in. Cheryl couldn't bring herself to milk a guy like that. She never told John about it. He wouldn't have understood.

Cheryl wondered what kind of moves Dawn was shooting with her new regular in apartment 202. Later, after Dr. Miller left, she asked her.

"He's in love with me," Dawn said. "But he's a goof."

Christ, she thought, she sounds just like John. Well, the goof has been pretty good to her. Dawn's working wardrobe had increased substantially. Al had taken her shopping at the malls several times.

"He's a doctor," Dawn said. "He's my sugar daddy. The rest of you hoes can go out and work the streets. But I've got me a sugar daddy."

And now her shit doesn't stink, Cheryl thought.

"Well, what does he get for all his money?" Cheryl asked.

"Just head. And a lot of days, not even that."

88

Chapter 18

The most pressing topic in apartment 202 was the mixed jive. They talked about when they were getting it, where they were getting it, how good it was, and whose credit was still good at the dope house.

"Getting right" meant getting the first fix. "Bogue" or "sick" was the state of needing one. A successful injection was a "hit." More was one's "do." Fellow addicts were "dope fiends" or just "fiends." They got their "do" at the "dope house" from the "dope man."

Cheryl Krizanovic pretty much had kept her vow not to give John Fry any money. She relished returning from the street with her private stash and shooting up in front of her old boyfriend. But sometimes she felt sorry for him and gave in when he pleaded his need to get right.

Dr. Miller's support, which by Christmas was heading for a thousand dollars a week, wasn't enough to cover Dawn and John's drug costs for two days. Despite Dawn's boasts about a sugar daddy, he was only one trick in many. Despite his plans to help her out, he was little more than a lucrative oddity in the daily flow of dates, cash, and dope.

Habits were paramount to the personalities. The heroin squirrel cage dictated that. John liked to describe dreaded opiate withdrawal as "the flu, pneumonia, and a good ass kicking all rolled into one."

There was no reason to doubt John's expertise on the subject of drugs. He drank his first six-pack at thirteen and smoked his first joint at fifteen. He couldn't remember a day he hadn't lit at least one number through his twenties and early thirties. He acquired his first heroin habit at twenty-one, but unlike weed, hard narcotics were tough to come by in prison.

Now any opiate or opiatelike drug was mandatory. If he wasn't running heroin, he was shooting Dilaudid or swallowing Percodan or Demerol. In a pinch, Jack Daniel's and a couple of handfuls of Somas or Tylenol 4s with codeine would do. John was finding it difficult to mark a decent vein anymore. Many of the accessible blood vessels in his arms and legs had collapsed, a common junkie's dilemma.

Dawn was more delicate, even though she had been using intravenously only six months. Her two-hundred-dollar-a-day habit was dainty by John's standards, but she suffered more debilitating side effects. Her marked groin served her well on dates, but now she was paying the price.

In late October, the area swelled with infection. Two days of chills, headache, and 104-degree fever forced her to the busy emergency room at Detroit Receiving Hospital. Doctors admitted her and administered an IV of antibiotics. By the third day, most of her symptoms were gone. She walked out, against the advice of physicians. They warned her the infection could abscess and create another set of complications.

By Christmas week the problem was back. She told Dr. Al Miller about the increasing pain in her groin. He asked her to remove her jeans and lie down so he could examine the area. He pressed the edge of the small cavity on the inside of her thigh. The exam was brief. She needed antibiotics, he said.

"I've got a friend, a pharmacist. I can get them, no charge."

The next day he brought a physician's sample of pills, telling Dawn to take one every four hours. He didn't seem too concerned. Still, she was uncomfortable with the diagnosis.

"He just acted—different," she later told another addict. "Not like a doctor would."

But Dr. Miller already had talked about a wide range of diseases during previous visits. She wanted his pills to work. She didn't want to spend the holiday in the hospital.

As for Cheryl, the only thing that seemed as predictable as her own drug use over the last three years was John Fry's frequent plans to kick his own habit. When John returned from a visit to his brother's house two days before Christmas, he stuck true to his form.

90

John announced he wanted to go to Gleason, Tennessee, for the holiday to see his dad, Pete. He and Dawn would hitch a ride with John's younger brother Jim. Jim's girlfriend, Janet, and their three-year-old twins were going as well. They were leaving on Christmas Eve.

That's a carload, Cheryl told herself. But for years she had wanted to meet the man that had fathered her old boyfriend. Maybe then she could understand him and free herself from the grip he still had on her.

"John, I'm not spending Christmas alone," Cheryl said.

Her old boyfriend didn't argue. The point was, he said, that Jim, the brother everyone called Six Pack, not be allowed to go south alone.

"Six told me he's going south to see our mother," John said.

Cheryl knew John's mother died in 1967. She suspected Six Pack wasn't talking about her grave.

"The twins' Christmas gifts were stolen," John continued. "He's really been hitting the T and thinks the fucking devil ripped him off."

T—THC, PCP, "angel dust," "hog." Technically it's called phencyclidine. James Dale Fry had been using it for years. While he was on the stuff, Cheryl had seen him ram his head through a plaster wall and string a length of rope for himself.

It was because of Six Pack that John's travel plans included everyone kicking their habits.

"We won't take a thing," he explained. "We can't help Six if we're all fucked up. We're going to get clean. We're going to get clean for Christmas."

But first, John said, they would have to raise money for the trip.

"So you really do want to make the trip down south?" Dawn asked.

"Without a doubt," John said.

Dawn reached for the telephone. She had in her hand the phone number of Dr. Al Miller. He'd instructed her to use it with discretion, saying it was the office suite of a colleague, a place where he took messages.

Cheryl listened as Dawn made the call. It was the first time Cheryl ever heard Dawn work her regular for cash.

"Al, I've got a chance to see some relatives in Tennessee for Christmas. But I need two or three hundred dollars to make the trip."

What a perfect little Miss Priss, Cheryl thought. She sure knew how to sound helpless. Dr. Miller already had paid a visit at noon. If he coughed up another three hundred dollars, that meant a four-hundred-dollar day for the regular.

As she headed out the door to score her share, Cheryl wondered if the trick would comply. When she returned, Dr. Miller had already dropped off the money to Dawn.

"What do you think of my Christmas present?" she said, flashing a handful of bills.

He hadn't brought the three hundred. He brought a thousand.

There was plenty of cash, but Cheryl Krizanovic didn't particularly look forward to a drug-free, eight-hour ride in a car loaded with five adults and two preschoolers. Soon that didn't matter either. John initiated what he called a bon voyage party, a farewell of sorts to drugs and the Cass Corridor.

When the dope ran out the next morning, they had only a few hundred left for the trip.

Chapter 19

Bobbi Gray first considered skipping what she already had decided was to be her last session with W. Alan Canty. Considering the way her therapist had hidden Jeff's homosexuality from her, how could she ever trust him?

Then she decided she had nothing to lose. It was the day before Christmas, and she knew her shrink liked to play Santa. She had a freebie coming. Canty hadn't billed her for therapy during the 1981 and 1982 Christmas holidays.

"It's something I like to do with all my patients at Christmas," he told her the first time. "It's my way of saying thanks."

Bobbi let Canty pour a cup of coffee. She lit a cigarette. Then she let him have it.

"I feel you have represented *him,* my husband Jeff, and not me. It was not in my best interest to keep on with this for *two whole years.* I mean there was never a chance at reconciliation. He's gay, for chrisake!"

Canty was unshaken.

"No, he wasn't when he was married to you. Jeff was on the fence. He was on the fence, and when someone is on the fence and teetering in between, as a therapist it's my job to try to push him over—to the good side. He was teetering between homosexuality and the life that is right for him—the happy, healthy life with a good home and children."

Canty had more theories.

"All this is a result of the process of getting sober," he explained calmly. "Jeff was basically fourteen years old emotionally when he came in here. He started drinking at fourteen, and when an alcoholic starts his drinking career, his mental development stops. In therapy, he can work this out and grow up . . ."

The psychologist continued, but already Bobbi Gray's

mind was wandering. One hundred and ten dollars times a hundred weeks. That was eleven thousand dollars! She started feeling snotty. She could be cruel when she was mad. The things she could have done with that money. What is Al Canty doing with my eleven thousand dollars? His home office was out of the Dark Ages. The carpet was threadbare. Piss yellow walls. Neo-bizarre Danish modern, she labeled it. What crap! If Canty would have hired the cheapest decorator from Sears, he would have told him to throw everything out.

She took a good look at the man she'd trusted for two years. He looked as though he needed a good shower. In fact, she thought, he had always looked dirty. His hair was greasy, and he had dandruff all over his worn-out sport shirt. His skin was sallow. Why doesn't he take a damn vacation and get some sun with all his money? She couldn't imagine anyone having sex with the man. What a nerd he must have been as a kid, she thought.

"You can handle this setback," Canty said near the end of the session. "Bobbi, I'm telling you that you have the strongest mental health of any patient I've ever had."

You bet, she thought. As she got up to leave, he had his hand out.

"Al, this is Christmas, isn't it?"

"What do you mean?"

"I mean, you know, it's always been the last session of the year is free. You know, a gift for your patients. That's the way it was the last two holidays."

Canty looked at her quizzically, as though she was talking Chinese. What the hell is he doing? she thought.

"I don't know what could have led you to believe that," he said in a patronizing pitch. "You must have misunderstood. But I don't know how I could have ever implied that."

He began writing out a receipt. Why, she thought, was he trying to make her feel as though those free sessions were a figment of her imagination? Why is he lying?

"Well, I'm sorry but I don't have any money, Al. I don't have my checkbook with me."

Bobbi Gray couldn't wait to get out of the big Tudor on Berkshire. When she did, she never went back. Her husband Jeff quit going that week as well.

She filed for divorce, but her husband continued his frequent visits to her house, often dining with her and the kids. One night she and Jeff compared notes about their former marriage counselor. They revealed what Canty had told them in individual sessions.

Bobbi told him about Jeff's "teetering" and Canty's promise that he'd soon come home. Jeff listened in disbelief.

"I *wanted* to tell you what I was," Jeff said. "I *wanted* you to know. Every week I said that, damn it. I told him that I'd had enough of this farce. He told me I couldn't do it. He told me he was building you up to be on your own because you were so weak emotionally."

Weak, no. Broke, yes. Bobbi Gray wanted her eleven thousand dollars back.

Chapter 20

Pete Fry had just finished pulling a tanker of prime Tennessee clay across the Carolinas when he got the surprise phone call from his eldest son. John told him of his last-minute plan to accompany his brother on the holiday visit.

"Got room for my old lady and her girlfriend?" John asked.

"I guess we'll find room," Pete said reluctantly.

Pete Fry had been expecting Jim and his family for the holiday. But he hadn't heard from John Carl in five years. The younger of his two sons had kept in touch in the half-dozen years since the sixty-two-year-old trucker had resettled in the South. John, he figured, just didn't give a damn.

Pete Fry was spending the last of his working years in a three-bedroom mobile home out among the rolling bean fields and cow farms of western Tennessee. John was born nearby, just across the Kentucky line in Fulton, before the Fry family migrated to Detroit. But the last they had spent any time together was after John's mother died in 1967. John was booted out of the Army and moved in for a short time. He stole most of Pete's valuables the day he moved out.

They had never gotten along. Most of the time Pete Fry couldn't even bring himself to say John's name, usually referring to him only as "that eldest boy." Pete and Nell Ruth Fry had separated off and on through their marriage. Nell moved in with her mother, and Pete blamed his mother-in-law for spoiling his firstborn son at a young age. John Carl could not sin in his grandmother's eyes, and Pete figured that prevented the boy from understanding the difference between right and wrong. He had always considered John a bad influence on his younger brother Jim.

However, as Pete drove to nearby Gleason to get groceries for his guests, he resolved he would have to put the past behind him. Alter all, this was Christmas, and there was no reason to expect any nonsense. When he returned from town, Jim's rusty Lincoln was parked in his driveway.

"This is Dawn," John said, eager to show off his girlfriend.

Pete Fry couldn't figure out how his son had hooked up with such a young girl. But his attention was more captured by Jim's twins and Cheryl Krizanovic, who later said she had to fend off a pass by the old trucker.

Early that evening the group split up. Jim drove off to visit an aunt. John went to town with Pete, who wanted to buy Western shirts for his guests and teddy bears for the twins. Back at the mobile home, Cheryl looked through a scrapbook with pictures of John and Jim as kids.

Jim returned disoriented. Between lucid periods during the drive from Detroit, he had rambled about "the devil." Everyone wrote it off as flashbacks from the T. Now he was talking crazy again.

Jim picked up his father's twenty-gauge shotgun and started for the door, saying, "It's the devil. I've got to kill the fucking devil."

The girls talked him into putting the gun back on the gun rack and steered him to bed. When John and Pete returned, everyone else soon turned in. Cheryl, Dawn, and John were sick. The effects from the previous night's shooting session were wearing off. John had kept to his plan. They hadn't brought any heroin.

Pete Fry took a foam rubber mattress from his diesel cab and made his bed in the living room. He was exhausted from six days on the road. He was almost asleep when he heard the voice of his son Jim next to him in the dark living room.

"Pop, I want to ask you somethin'," Jim said. "Is it OK if me and the twins move down here and stay with you? I think I'm gonna have to leave Janet."

Pete Fry sat up on his portable mattress.

"Why, you don't even have to ask somethin' like that," he drawled. "Jim Dale, you know the answer to that."

Pete suspected his son and his girlfriend were having problems. Something didn't seem right about the girl.

"And there's something else," Jim said. "I know something that you need to know."

"Jim, can't it wait till mornin'?"

"No, Pop. *This* you need to know *tonight."*

The elder Fry reached for a cigarette. But when he struck a light, the glow of the flame revealed Janet sitting in a nearby chair. She had slipped into the living room as they talked.

Jim held his tongue and shuffled back to his bedroom. Pete Fry figured that whatever his favorite son had to say, he wanted it kept private.

Christmas morning dawned to a dead freeze that stretched from the Rockies to the Deep South, making for the nation's coldest holiday in one hundred years. The temperature was eight below in Detroit, and a minus twenty-five in Chicago.

In Gleason, it was courting zero, and Pete Fry felt an unfamiliar blast of arctic air as his grandson bounced on his chest, waking him at sunrise. What was the front door doing open, Pete complained, especially in this weather?

"Where's your daddy?" he asked the twin.

The boy pointed to the open door. Pete Fry could see his 1974 Ford Gran Torino parked in the driveway. Jim Dale's boots and coat were by the front entrance. He walked into Jim's bedroom, where Janet lay alone in bed.

"Where's Jim?" he asked. "Are you two havin' problems?"

Janet put on her robe.

"I think he's outside," Pete said. "I don't know what's goin' on with you two, but you better get him in here. If you're arguin', he'll stay out there till you make up. I know him. He's gonna freeze to death out there."

Pete Fry pulled on a shirt as he watched Janet go out the front door. She walked directly to his Ford, bent over at the window, and came back inside.

"He's dead," she said. "He's been shot. He's been shot with your *gun."*

Pete Fry thought he was hearing things. What did she mean, shot? Then John emerged, fully dressed, from a bedroom. He walked out the front door, looked in the window of the Torino, and returned.

"Yep, he's dead all right," John said.

Pete Fry ran outside. The windows of the Ford were thick with frost. He couldn't see a damn thing in the car. What were John and Janet talking about? He jerked open the frozen passenger's door.

Jim Dale Fry was slumped under the wheel, his body leaning on the driver's door. He was wearing only a pair of trousers. Blood covered his face and the interior of the Ford. Pete Fry's twenty-gauge shotgun was on the seat next to his dead son.

The patrol cars from the state police and the Weakley County Sheriff's Department were still in the driveway when the ambulance took Jim Fry's body away. After the county coroner examined the Torino, a deputy took the twenty-gauge shotgun from the car and handed it to Pete Fry. He told the father it looked like a suicide, and he later made it official.

"I can't fuckin' handle it, man," John Fry told Cheryl Krizanovic as police radios cracked the cold air. "We have got to go."

She knew how John felt. What a time to be sick, she thought. After the police left, John asked her to clean out his father's Torino. She scrubbed the dashboard and put an old blanket over the bloody seat.

"Me and Six Pack had a deal," Fry told Cheryl and Dawn before they left. "If one of us was to die, we promised not to go to the funeral. We agreed to remember each other as we were."

It wasn't until late Christmas, after a day of shock, phone calls, and funeral arrangements, that Pete Fry realized that his Ford was gone. So were the eyeglasses he'd left on the dashboard. Only Janet and the twins were left in the mobile home. She told him the trio had left for Michigan.

"Why in the hell would they do that?"

Pete Fry paused, then began fuming.

"That goddamn eldest boy has robbed me again," he cursed.

Chapter 21

The snow that dusted the Pointes all week left the Tudor-style homes on Berkshire looking as though they were decorated by Norman Rockwell for Christmas morning. When Jan and Al Canty woke to open their gifts, frost glistened on the diamond-beveled windows that flanked their living room fireplace.

Al was not an extravagant shopper, by Grosse Pointe standards at least. But he'd always given his holiday gifts for Jan a lot of time and thought. One Christmas he hunted down a rare psychological test she wanted. On another, he sent for a sculpture that caught her eye in northern Michigan months back.

There was less effort this year. If Al hadn't pointed it out, she probably wouldn't have noticed. But he kept apologizing as she opened her gifts. She certainly had no complaints. There was a pendulum clock for the kitchen, some perfume, a couple of stereo albums, a stained glass medallion, and a book for her saltwater aquarium. Al, however, remained troubled.

No, Al was *embarrassed*. That was the only way she knew how to describe him when he looked that way. He was blushing, shuffling his feet, and looking at his shoes. She had seen him behave that way before, but only with her. She always felt he was very vulnerable then.

"I'm, um, sorry. They're really not much, are they?"

"Come on, Al, it's no big deal. They're fine."

She knew he was hanging on her every word. She felt very protective of his feelings when he got like that.

"It's the book," Al continued. "The money I was expecting from the book, and the court evaluations. It won't come until January. I thought it would be here by now."

"Al, it's no big thing. The gifts are fine."

Then Al laughed. That was how he usually came out of

one of his boyish spells. Still, it seemed odd that he was so concerned.

Well, she thought, maybe he's feeling overextended with his heavier schedule. She already was anticipating their annual vacation after the holidays. They both needed one.

That afternoon they drove to Gladys Canty's house for Christmas dinner. En route they stopped at a car dealership to take a look at a new car she had ordered. The car had arrived but still had to be prepped.

Jan had spotted the new 1983 red Thunderbird when a friend of her father, a Ford executive, was driving it several months back. He was using it as a company car. She loved the T-bird. The turbocharged five-speed suited her new station in life as a professional. Her Volkswagen days were over. The executive offered to tag the car for her, meaning she could buy it at a substantial discount when he returned it to Ford.

Jan and Al walked across the car lot to eye the car. She brushed off the snow on the windshield and eyed its gray leather interior.

"Al, I can't wait," she said, shivering.

"Jan-Jan, let's let the car be one of your Christmas presents."

He's still thinking about those gifts, she thought. Why does he work so hard to make me happy? His tortoiseshell glasses glistened with the reflection of the red car and the white snow. His mouth was grinning, but his eyes were moist.

"Al, I love you," she said.

They hugged before the temperature sent them scurrying back to Al's black Buick.

Gladys Canty greeted her two guests with the smell of fresh pecans roasting in her hot oven. She went all out on holidays for her son.

She knew Bus had always been very sentimental about tradition. And tradition on Christmas meant turkey, sage dressing, cranberry sauce, rum balls, mincemeat and pumpkin pies—and roasted pecans. How her son loved it when she smothered those warm nuts in butter. She'd always loved to see him eat.

Every year there was enough food to feed a half dozen, though it had only been the three of them every Christmas since Al Sr. died. Bus never liked big gatherings anyway. Gladys Canty knew that Buster was uncomfortable in large groups. He was so unlike his father in that way. Al Sr. always liked to be the center of attention.

Sometimes Gladys Canty thought her son embraced the role of a recluse, as in the time he became enamored with Howard Hughes. It was after his first wife, Maggie, left him. He bought every biography he could find on the billionaire. Buster talked at length about how Hughes's financial empire prospered while its neurotic ruler played in a fantasy world that included private marathon screenings of old Hollywood films in empty movie theaters. Yet, Bus said, the man was a genius. Finally, Al Sr. got sick of hearing about it over dinner every evening.

"To hell with Howard Hughes, goddamnit," he roared one night. "Lay off Howard Hughes, will you?"

Al Sr. rattled her best china when he got that way. But Gladys Canty still missed her husband seven years after his death. Christmas always made his absence more poignant. Al Sr. seemed a tough old character, but she knew a lot of it was just an act. She always thought that deep down he wasn't so sure of himself.

This Christmas their only child seemed to be feeling particularly good about himself as he brought in a big box with a large red sash and bow.

"Ma, this one's for you."

He fidgeted as she opened the gift, a nineteen-inch Sony color TV. It must have cost six hundred dollars or more, she thought. That was Bus, spending money as though his checkbook had no balance column.

"Why, Buster. You didn't have to do this."

But her son was beside himself when she told him she liked the gift. He carried on for a half hour about how great a TV it was.

For her part of the exchange, she gave him a gold Seiko watch. Jan had told her he had his eye on one.

After dinner, Bus began to fidget again. They never stayed very long after the meal. But there was one more

Christmas tradition Bus insisted on each year. After eating they always went for a short walk. Jan invariably stayed inside.

They were gone only a little while. It was very cold as mother and son walked, just the two of them arm in arm.

Chapter 22

A Class of '83 Harper Woods graduate named Dolores Cusmano gazed at the family tree and wondered if the rumors about her old friend Dawn Marie Spens were true.

She thought of past Christmas nights when Dawn and a few of their best friends had gathered in Dee's living room for eggnog. Back in high school, they couldn't wait to be adults. Back then, Dee thought she had a friend for life in Dawn Spens.

Now the Harper Woods rumor mill was grinding overtime. A couple of boys in the neighborhood said they saw Dawn working the streets in the Cass Corridor. Others sniped she was living with a biker. Dee would have to see that for herself to believe.

Yet no one, including Dee Cusmano, had heard from Dawn since she dropped out of school in the spring. It wasn't the first time people had spread dirt about Dawn. Just because she was quiet, some people figured she had an attitude.

Dee knew better. In fact, she figured she was one of the few people who had invested the time to get to know Dawn. For Dee, that was seven years, and even then she didn't totally understand the girl.

Dawn Spens, Dee always thought, was endowed with a curious mixture of brains and bad luck. When they first met in the fifth grade at Tyrone Elementary Dee felt as though she'd found a soul mate. Dee's mother and father had divorced when she was five. She grew up learning how to take care of herself while her mother worked. Though Dawn's mother was home, Dawn met her own needs as well. Dee suspected all was not well in Dawn's bungalow on Elkhart.

Dawn only hinted at family troubles. Then at age twelve she attempted suicide by overdosing on her mother's medication. She spent six weeks in a psychiatric hospital. When Dawn finally began talking, Dee felt she had helped her open up. Dawn's parents weren't divorced then, but Dee guessed they should have been. They fought quite a bit. They split up and reconciled repeatedly.

"I just wish they would make up their mind," Dawn would say.

The Spenses' household was not the kind of home where kids just dropped by. Dawn was quite guarded about who she invited inside. Dawn's father, Roy, was no Ozzie Nelson. Sometimes Dee and Dawn would be sitting in the living room when he came home from his job as a machinist.

"I've got people coming over," he would say coldly. "Why don't you get lost."

Often they went to Harper Woods Memorial Park, across from the high school. Dee shared what it was like before her parents divorced. She tried to bolster Dawn's spirits. Dee suspected Dawn had it a lot rougher at home than she revealed. Dawn envied the stability Dee found after her mother remarried.

"You have the ideal family," she would say.

The Spenses' divorce case two years ago was traumatic on everybody. Roy Spens filed, then his wife, Henrietta, countersued, but they continued living together. Mrs. Spens claimed that her husband had "a violent temper," threatened to shoot her, and gave her fourteen stitches with one beating. A circuit judge ordered Roy Spens to "absolutely refrain from assaulting, beating, molesting, or wounding" his wife.

In a few weeks they were back again in court. Dawn's mother claimed her husband was coming in and out of the house drunk at all hours of the night. The police were called. Mrs. Spens told the court she was under medical care for depression. Roy agreed to leave the home.

But when the divorce was finalized in Dawn's senior year, it was Roy Spens who got custody of Dawn and her younger sister, Patty. Mrs. Spens left Detroit to live with a man in Windsor, Canada. They eventually would marry. It hurt Dawn quite a bit.

Dee remembered an odd proposal Dawn's mother made

after she moved. Henrietta's fiancé had a friend who was serving time in prison. She wanted Dawn to write him. Dee saw some of the letters from the inmate. She could tell he was lonely. But she couldn't understand how a mother could knowingly fix up her daughter with a criminal.

"Dawn, just quit writing him," she said. "You don't need that kind of hassle right now."

Considering all the pressures, Dee never could figure out how Dawn did so well her first two years in high school. Dee had trouble maintaining a C-to-B average. Dawn carried a 3.8 in her sophomore year with little effort. She was naturally bright, and a quick study if there ever was one. She seemed the perfect student. As a junior she managed the school's bookstore. The yearbook photographer captured her in all-American poses at pep rallies.

Her choice in boyfriends, however, wasn't so wholesome, and there were many undesirables to choose from. The high school had a big drug problem. The school had its jocks and its burnouts, but Dee always thought Harper High was equipped with more of the latter. A lot of the kids got their drug money from naive parents. Others stole for it. Some fenced clothes snatched from a nearby shopping mall during their lunch hour.

Dawn was attracted to questionable characters. The first was the son of a Detroit police inspector, but he wasn't headed for a career in law enforcement. Dee wasn't sure what he liked more, drugs or stealing. Once, on a dare, he walked into a J. C. Penney store and lifted a miniature TV.

"What do you see in someone like that?" she asked Dawn.

"He's nice to me," Dawn said. "He takes me places. He pays a lot of attention to me."

Dee suspected Dawn craved a lot of love. But Dee wondered if she really knew what it was. Dawn seemed to think love simply was someone making her the center of attention.

Her last boyfriend, a Detroit dropout named Donnie Carlton, wasn't bad-looking, but that was about all Dee could say good about him. Dee thought Donnie was a transparent con artist. To Dawn, he was salvation.

Dawn started dating him during her senior year. She had

saved up her money from working at a pizza parlor and bought herself an old Plymouth Duster. In a few months Donnie had ravaged the car in accidents. Roy Spens accused Donnie of stealing some jewelry and banned him from his home.

Dee began seeing less of Dawn, who started missing classes. She didn't see her much after school either. She was always with Donnie. Then, one night, Dawn and Donnie snagged Dee's boyfriend.

They couldn't have had worse timing. Dee and her boyfriend were considering marriage after graduation, and they had made dinner plans with her father so he could meet him. The night of the dinner, however, her boyfriend came up missing. He'd been at her house but left with Dawn and Donnie Carlton, who stopped by while Dee was gone. When he didn't return, she met her father at the restaurant, alone and humiliated.

It was nearly midnight the following evening when the trio returned. They pulled up wasted in front of her house in Dawn's Duster. Later Dee learned they had stolen from her room the pain medication her doctor had prescribed for her back. They had gobbled the pills and drunk two cases of beer. Her boyfriend lay in the front seat, barely breathing. She couldn't wake him up. Dee was furious as her mom emerged from the house to investigate.

"Dawn Spens, if anything happens to him I'm going to hold you responsible," Dee yelled.

Dawn just stared at her. She'd seen that blank look before. Dawn had a way of turning to a passive silence when she was in trouble. She'd seen her work people for sympathy that way, but Dee wasn't feeling very charitable.

"I'm not kidding, Dawn," she raved. "I cannot believe you subjected me to this knowing how important that dinner was, then brought him home in this state in front of my mom."

Dawn later apologized.

"We were just out and about doing our thing," she said. "They talked me into staying out and partying."

All Dee wanted was a phone call. She didn't expect one from Donnie Carlton. And she eventually dumped her boyfriend. But Dawn was her best friend. She felt betrayed, conned. What, she thought, were all those talks in Memorial Park about? Maybe she really didn't know Dawn after all.

They saw even less of each other after that. Two months before graduation she heard from Patty Spens that her sister was thinking of dropping out. She saw Dawn that night at Memorial Park.

"I'm thinking about leaving," Dawn said. "I think I'm going to move in with Donnie."

Dee did everything she could to dissuade her.

"You only got a little while to go. With your average, you've got a chance at a scholarship. You always wanted to go to college. Why do you want to stop now?"

"Things are too tough, all the way around. It's something I've got to do. I've got to get out of here."

"Dawn, you're going to get messed up with the wrong kind of people and the wrong kind of atmosphere and something is going to happen. You can't run from your problems."

Dawn said she'd phone her the next day. The call never came. Dee heard Dawn moved in with Donnie, who had an apartment near downtown Detroit.

It had been eight months. Dee Cusmano wondered where her old friend was living and what she was doing now. Those old high school traumas seemed pretty stupid now, she thought.

Dee Cusmano wondered if Dawn Spens felt the same way.

Chapter 23

John Fry concocted the scam as he looked at his father's Torino, parked outside the Homewood, the day after Christmas. Cheryl Krizanovic watched Dawn Spens dial up Dr. Al Miller.

"Hey, Al, guess what? I found a car," Dawn said. "Yes. It's here now. But he wants the money right away."

Then Dawn looked as though she was going to cry.

"Aw, Al," she said. "I need eight hundred dollars *real* bad. I need this car *really* bad and this guy is going to sell it to somebody else if I don't get it."

Cheryl had used the same plaintive little girl's voice with her regulars. She never understood why men bought it, but they did. Dawn was adept at playing the role. With her deep-set brown eyes and slightly pouting lips, the word "helpless" was written all over her face. Dawn, she thought, could make a trick feel sorry for her and never say a word.

Dawn met Dr. Miller in front of the Homewood early that afternoon, showing him the car as she accepted the eight hundred dollars. When she returned to apartment 202 she handed the money over to John.

But Dawn would never own the car. The Torino later would be dropped off with one of Pete Fry's cousins in Detroit for return to the South. Later, Dr. Miller would accept Dawn's excuse that the car deal fell through. He wouldn't ask for his money back.

Later that night Dawn asked John for one hundred dollars.

"I don't have any money."

"I just fuckin' gave you eight hundred dollars this afternoon."

Fry smirked and squeezed the yellow tattoo of the cartoon character on his right arm.

"Tweety Bird got drunk," he cracked.

Then John began adding up the totals. Lunch, one hundred dollars. Christmas Eve trip money and gift, one thousand dollars. Car scam, eight hundred dollars. Holiday total: nineteen hundred dollars.

"I mean, we're talking about this much in a three-day period," Fry later told a friend. "He was actually giving her more money than I could understand.

"I mean, the girl is getting a hundred dollars a day, and he's only spending a half hour with her. He takes her to the shopping mall and buys her a three-hundred-dollar coat. All cash. No credit cards.

"By this time I'm thinking, yeah. This guy is a fuckin' gold mine."

Chapter 24

A Detroit cop named Mark Bando had waited months for the opportunity to roust Lucky Fry. Now he had one.

"I knew he'd eventually fuck up," he said. "It's his destiny."

A routine record check had shown Fry was wanted on an assault and battery warrant. The thirty-three-year-old Bando and his partner, John Woodington, noted the A&B for their next call to the Homewood Manor. It would only be a couple of days.

Bando first learned of Fry two years ago when Fry and Cheryl Krizanovic were staying at the Travler Motel on Cass Avenue. On three successive nights, the motel's guests — most of them dubious characters themselves — had complained:

"She turns tricks day and night. He comes home every evening, picks up his money, then beats her for about forty-five minutes straight. You can hear her screaming all over the motel and just why the fuck don't somebody do something about it?"

Fry and Miss Krizanovic had earned a place in what Bando called his "whore book" — a three-volume directory of twelve hundred Corridor girls and street types. Bando shot pictures of John and Cheryl from his squad car for their entries in one of the eight-by-fourteen-inch bookkeeping ledgers:

> *Cheryl Krizanovic — "Twiggy" 7108 Clayton. Pimp: John "Lucky" Fry. John Carl Fry — "Lucky" — fiend/pimp/punk.*

The book tracked the turnover and helped flag false IDs. The ledger rode in the squad car with other items Bando kept in a doctor's valise: A 35mm single-lens reflex for detailed photography. A 110 camera for quick photos. A flashlight and binoculars. A stack of three-by-five cards for notes. And a pair of "bum gloves" for handling derelicts.

Mark Bando had been working the neighborhoods near downtown for five years, but he already was legendary in the neighborhood he and Woodington called "the sewer hole." They navigated the Thirteenth Precinct's "whore car," a patrol devoted exclusively to busting prostitutes, pimps, and johns.

When he first joined the force ten years ago, the former Wayne State history major barely passed the department physical with his five-foot-seven, 140-pound frame. His parents met in a U.S. detention camp in Utah during the Second World War. The street life often made note of his Japanese roots. He was the "rice-eating bitch," the "slant-eyed mothafucker" whose "Nip ass should have been nuked in Hiroshima."

Off duty, the cop was writing a nonfiction book about an American company in the European theater of World War II. Bando was pounding out the historical narrative in a home office decorated with war memorabilia—including a mannequin of a fully outfitted GI. The story was about 122 GIs who were surrounded in the Battle of the Bulge. They were men in the 101st Airborne who died by the dozens and jumped out of airplanes until their feet bled.

"If they're on the other side, you'd call them fanatics," he once told a friend. "If they're on yours, they're *dedicated*. The country today is full of artificial heroes. Sports stars are not heroes. Nor are actors. But people who actually risk their lives." Bando loathed the TV show "Entertainment Tonight."

The way the cop looked at it, when the Thirteenth Precinct commander assigned him and Woodington to the whore car nearly two years ago, he wanted them to bust whores. Most cops in the Thirteenth made five to ten arrests a month and wrote as many tickets. Bando and Woodington were arresting fifty and writing a hundred. Many cops considered bringing a girl into the Thirteenth in handcuffs unbecoming to police work.

Bando, however, remembered how bad it was in the Corridor before enforcement was increased. One night he took a girlfriend to the opera at the Masonic Temple, and he couldn't get his car down Second Avenue. The girls were three lanes deep flagging dates. He couldn't see letting them rule the streets unchecked.

The sewer hole, Bando resolved, was ruled by predators. The weapon of choice for many punks and pimps was the baseball bat. The law had no control over the Louisville Slugger, but it was as deadly as Mace.

"Just goin' to play a little ball, Bando" was a common line from someone on the street on their way to even a score.

Bando grimaced when people talked about prostitution as a victimless crime. Some of the johns may have thought they were spending time with sexually liberated party girls, but the cop never saw any such emancipation. He saw girls as young as eight turned out by local pimps. He arrested one pimp who had cut off his whore's finger and kept it iced in the refrigerator. Another time he recorded a bloody prostitute who ran up to his squad car, screaming.

"Look, Offitha, I'm bleeding from where he hit me!"

"Shut the fuck up, bitch, you bleed more than that on your period," the pimp said.

"Quit lyin', mothafucker, you hit me upside my haid!"

"You two-dollar punk bitch, I didn't do nothing but use your ass . . . got them abscesses all over you. Stankin' bitch! Go on out and turn tricks! That what she *want* to do."

Some girls were second-generation whores. Bando once copied a note left by a prostitute dead from an overdose:

"It's so fucking sick in this neighborhood, it's sickening. Everybody I know is a stone dope fiend to the max. I'm going to try to get some good friend tricks of mine to co-sign a car for me and get the fuck out of Detroit altogether. My baby is not going to go through what I went through. I'll get a better life for my baby if I have to kill a motherfucker to get it."

But most of the whores in Bando's book came from everywhere and most of them were going nowhere. There was no pattern to their backgrounds. One girl was the daughter of a Grosse Pointe doctor. Another's father was a police chief in Kansas. Many started without drug habits. The closest he'd heard to a logical reason for the career choice came from a reformed prostitute he knew.

"I just wanted to be loved," she told him. "My father never loved me. So I said, 'I'll show you, Daddy, I'll get love from the johns.' "

Bando decided early on that if he ticketed the girls enough times and struck fear into their pimps, a few might just wake up and get out. At least they got clean in jail. He'd received Christmas gifts from some of the girls, those he'd taken to emergency rooms after they were brutalized by dates or their boyfriends. Those who didn't lie usually got a break. The rapport had paid off. Bando had solved two murders with his connections.

But most girls were bent on destroying themselves.

"Some of these whores look like they're studying for parts in *The Night of the Living Dead*," he said one night.

"It's the teeth," said Woodington. "Always the teeth are the first to go. They turn yellow, then begin to fall out."

"Why's that?"

"It's the semen. The semen creates a new kind of plaque that rots their teeth."

The black humor helped for a while. The pair had improvised a number of gags the previous summer. They played Wagner's "Ride of the Valkyries" on the squad car's public address system as they swept the streets, or Bando's favorite, "Man Eater," by Hall & Oates. He piped the lyrics as the squad car flew out of an alley, spotlighting negotiating johns.

But the predators fought back. Some of the pimps tried to track their patrol schedule. Bando and Woodington worked odd shifts. When Bando went on furlough, they spread rumors about the cop:

"Bando got caught screwing a fifteen-year-old hooker in the backseat of a police car."

"Bando locked up a girl who wasn't a whore and got fired."

"Bando got promoted to inspector."

On Bando's last vacation, Woodington fought back with another gag. He told people his partner had tried to kill himself and "botched the job." When he returned, Bando put bruises on his forehead with theater makeup. Woodington drove him around. Bando was seemingly dazed and speechless. When a group of prostitutes gathered around the squad car, Woodington explained Bando was nearly brain dead.

"I feel bad," said one. "Bando wasn't that bad. He was just doing his job."

By the end of the year, however, Mark Bando was finding the job more difficult and the humor harder to come by. Three prostitutes he had some hope for had died of drug overdoses. He was fed up with local hoodlums he called the Cass Corridor Commandos. They were Southern white families who for years committed a wide variety of the crimes in the Corridor.

Lucky Fry ranked right at the top with the rest of the predators, he thought. On New Year's Day Bando and Woodington decided to do a little stalking themselves. The pair was called to the Homewood Manor on a routine gun complaint. Fry's apartment was just down the hall.

Lucky Fry was alone when he opened the door of apartment 202. The two cops surrounded the pimp. They were looking for an excuse to give him what they liked to call "a tune-up."

"Woman beater. You wouldn't resist arrest, would you, faggot?" Bando spat.

But Lucky Fry wouldn't take the bait. He just glared.

They cuffed him and took him to the Thirteenth Precinct. After more than two thousand arrests, Bando could tell a standout when he saw one.

"That guy is destined for bigger and better things," he told his partner. "Did you see that look in his eyes?

"Lucky Fry's a goddamn killer."

Part Two
1984

Chapter 25

Jan Canty always looked forward to their yearly trip to Sun Lakes the first week of January. But this year she felt Al needed the Arizona vacation more than she did.

Not that Al was so eager to go. He never was. It wouldn't be the first time she would have to pry him from his practice. Al's concern for his patients often exceeded his own best interests, and she thought he was looking tired and drawn. The prosecutor's office, he'd said, had increased his work load at the jail. She had little knowledge of forensic work, or even the court system itself. But she did know he couldn't keep up the pace, whatever the work entailed.

Lately, he seemed more interested in her work at the University Health Center, which was part of the Detroit Receiving Hospital and Medical Center complex. He wondered who ran the psychiatric unit and emergency-room admissions. He wanted to know how hospital records were kept. He was curious about what the hospital looked like inside.

That's all he needs, she thought. How could he possibly have any mental energy left to get involved in my career?

Always a deep sleeper, Al now was tossing and turning some nights. His psoriasis was flaring up. It has to be work-related stress, she concluded.

As he complained about the trip, Jan packed both their bags. Sun Lakes was the ideal rest spot. Her parents had relocated from Detroit to the small retirement community for the dry air and the perennial Arizona sun. In January, the weather was like April in Michigan, without the rain. There were few distractions. A post office, a small grocery store, a golf course, and a travel agency made up the heart of the town.

Al complained all the way to the airport, but, predictably, his attitude changed once they got to her parents' house. They stayed in the guest room, in the same bed that had cured Jan of her mono. Al spent the first day in bed, sleeping. He emerged unshaven and made sure everyone in the house knew he'd put his new watch away for the week.

"For us, a vacation is any place without a schedule," Jan said. Al agreed.

They had a lazy week together. Jan's mother pulled out her best recipes for dinners. Another night they ate out at one of the good Mexican restaurants nearby. Al spent a lot of time on the patio reading a stack of custom car magazines he'd brought. Several times she noticed him sitting out there alone. He seemed preoccupied with his thoughts as he cleaned his nails with a pocketknife he always carried. At night, he watched TV and was less vocal than on past trips to her parents.

One night a local station carried a special on the Grand Canyon. Al became quite interested in the program. It was a documentary about a rescue project for burros in the canyon. The animals were descendants of donkeys brought by nineteenth-century miners. The program detailed the rich history of the bearded explorers with big appetites for gold and straight whiskey. The men were gone, but the burros they left behind had multiplied in the wild and now were in danger of starving.

That year, the four of them decided to visit the Grand Canyon National Park. Every year they liked to go on one sight-seeing trip. Jan, Al, and her parents drove the six hours north to the park but found many of the roads, lodges, and activities closed for the winter. They stopped at a lookout. Jan's father took a picture as she and Al posed.

Al and Jan Canty were standing on the edge of the great precipice.

Jan later chuckled about the photo. She was wearing a ski jacket and knit cap, Al a light winter jacket. They looked as though they had been roughing it for days, when it had to be one of the shortest canyon visits on record. They lingered along the edge of the picturesque drop-off for about an hour, then drove home that night.

When they returned to Sun Lakes, Al was anxious to get

back to Detroit. He never stayed more than a week, while she usually remained for two.

Al was talking about his practice and the prosecutor again as Jan and her father drove him to the Phoenix airport. But after a week on the bum, he looked refreshed. Jan had no doubt he'd put his recharged cells right to work once he got back to Detroit.

Chapter 26

Dr. Al Miller's antibiotics provided only temporary relief for Dawn Spens's infected groin. Two days after her return from Tennessee, she hardly could walk. Now she was in the hospital.

On December 28, John and a couple of friends had carried her down the stairs of the Homewood Manor and taken her to Detroit Receiving Hospital, Dr. Al Miller's supposed employer. He sure knew the right people at the hospital, John later said. Dr. Miller smoothed the way for her admission. When Dawn arrived in the emergency room, the receptionist was expecting her. She didn't have to wait like many other walk-ins who weren't dying on the spot.

Receiving, the city's leading trauma center, specialized in gunshot victims and other urban casualties. Physicians wasted no time with Dawn. The abscess had tunneled into her leg and was threatening her femoral vein. As they prepared her for surgery, Dawn signed a release giving surgeons permission to amputate her leg if necessary. Then she changed her mind. She'd take her chances on the table.

The surgical team cleaned the abscess. They found the femoral vein damaged, but not permeated. If she would have waited another night, she probably would have bled to death. They repaired the blood vessel but left the leg open to drain. Dawn would have to pack her own dressings for many weeks to come. She was in the hospital ten days and regularly received Demerol, a drug similar to morphine, for pain.

Money was in short supply back at the Homewood as John Fry's young money-maker was undergoing repairs. After a night in jail, John's warrant problems were temporarily behind him. Cheryl Krizanovic turned tricks but kept the proceeds for herself.

Dr. Al Miller was on vacation.

When he returned, he visited Dawn every day in the hospital. He said that he had left Receiving and been transferred to an administrative job at the psychiatric unit in nearby Harper-Grace Hospitals.

Dr. Miller had a predictable routine on his visits. He eyed her hospital chart and told her she was "making good progress." Dawn later commented his bedside manner seemed somewhat staged.

Near the end of Dawn's stay, hospital staff began decreasing her pain killer. The Demerol had warded off heroin withdrawal after the surgery, but now the young drug addict felt the calling of her habit.

Finally, Dawn asked Al to drop off some money to Cheryl or John. John was to get heroin, Dilaudid—anything—and bring it to her in the hospital. She was bogue. She was sick.

Cheryl Krizanovic met Dr. Miller in front of the Homewood. He grinned behind the wheel and handed Cheryl a Comerica Bank envelope for the drugs.

"You know, Cheryl, sometimes I wish we would have met before I met Dawn," he said. "I think you and I could have gotten real close."

Cheryl accepted the compliment without protest but had no plans to make time. She still was angry at John Fry for leaving her, and she wished Dawn would go back to Harper Woods. But she wasn't about to break a rule of the streets. Cheryl Krizanovic did not shoot moves on another girl's sugar daddy.

Then Al asked, "How long have you known Dawn?"

"A while. A few months."

The regular wanted to know more. Where was Dawn from? What "type" of girl was she? Was she "nice"?

Cheryl gave him one-word answers. If Dawn wanted him to know anything, she figured, she could tell him herself.

"Well, Cheryl, tell me about this guy John," Dr. Miller continued. "Dawn's in love with him, isn't she? How long have they been living together?"

"I don't know anything about it, Al."

This guy John, she thought. You mean, my brother?

She knew John Fry's sibling scam wasn't as believable as her old boyfriend thought. Sometimes John thought he was so clever, but he was transparent.

This trick Al, Cheryl thought, knows what's going on. He's not as gullible as John thinks.

On another night Dawn Spens came up with a different plan. She called John Fry and told him Al was dropping by with some money. John said the dealer down the hall was out of dope.

"Then have Al take you to the dope house and drop you off with it here," she said.

Fry protested. The trick was a goof, he said.

"This is taking the date relationship too far. I don't like the idea of a trick knowing my business."

Dawn pleaded with him on the telephone. It was OK, she said. Al knew all about drugs. Al could be trusted.

Later that night John Fry jumped into the passenger's seat of the black Buick and the two men drove off into the night. Dr. Miller told John Fry he liked to be called Al. He didn't like the formal title of "doctor."

"Al, you look like you got some sun on your vacation," John said. "Your complexion looks real good."

"John, its the canyon. I do it every year."

His vacation was an annual ritual, Al said. He met his brother in Arizona and the two of them hiked deep into the Grand Canyon. There they met an old miner who kept a pack of mules. They took the mule team into isolated parts of the canyon.

"We spent a lot of nights just listening to his stories and drinking Jack Daniel's around the campfire."

Al said he had been doing it for years to get away from the pressures of medicine.

"It's kind of like a purging process I have to go through."

Fry later told a friend, "I could almost hear the 20 Mule Team Borax theme playing."

Then Al began talking about a drug-smuggling problem

at Harper-Grace Hospitals. He'd been telling Dawn the same story. He knew of a group of physician's assistants who were stealing morphine from stock. They were supplying it to street sources through a network of cabdrivers.

"Here, John, I'll show you," he said.

Al turned up Second Avenue in the direction of Wayne State University and then came back toward downtown on Third. He pointed out what he said were unmarked cars parked near Jumbo's and the Sweetheart Bar, two hooker hangouts.

"Those are cops, John. They're watching the cab deliveries from Harper."

John had some friendly advice, though he later found out the story was completely fabricated.

"Don't you get involved in that shit, Al. I've been around this kind of thing all my life, and you definitely don't want to do time."

"Oh, no, no. But I do know a lot about it."

When Al finished his tour, he handed Lucky Fry a hundred dollars. They stopped in front of a dope house a half mile from the Homewood. John went inside and returned with ten packs of mixed jive.

Dr. Miller dropped John off at the hospital. Fry gave three packs of heroin to Dawn and kept seven for himself. John cooked Dawn's in the bathroom. The rest was made easy by her hospital IV line.

"It didn't make sense," John said later. "The trick said he lost his wife because she was a dope fiend. Now he's helping Dawn cop drugs."

Chapter 27

"Dawn Marie Spens! Like where have you been, girl!"

Jackie Brown couldn't believe it. She had found her old girlfriend, who had been missing for nearly nine months. She'd heard through the grapevine that Dawn Spens was in the hospital. It was true. There she was, and she looked in pretty bad shape.

"What *happened* to you?"

"An aneurism."

Jackie had no idea what that was, but Dawn said the problem started when she fell on the ice. She pulled back the bandage on her leg. Jackie saw a hole as big a silver dollar. God, she thought. You've got to be kidding.

"They've got me on morphine," she said.

Her old girlfriend looked stoned, or worse. She hadn't shampooed in days. She was chain-smoking Marlboro menthols. It was all too predictable, Jackie Brown thought. Dawn Spens had found the shit end of the stick again.

Jackie had heard the recent rumors in Harper Woods, but she wasn't about to interrogate her old friend. She wondered about Dawn's boyfriend, Donnie Carlton.

"I've got a new boyfriend," Dawn said. "Oh, and he's thirty-eight."

"He is?"

She seemed proud of her acquisition but quickly switched subjects.

The two shared a lot of memories. They began when Dawn's family moved just down the block when Jackie was four. At eight, they smoked their first cigarettes to-gether—a pack of True Blues Dawn stole from her mother. They smoked themselves sick.

Dawn got away with that one. But most of the time she wasn't so lucky. She was always getting grounded—for stupid things, Jackie thought. Dawn's younger sister Patty had asthma and got all the attention. Dawn got attention, but the wrong kind. All Dawn had to do was give her sister a surly look and the Spens household went into a seven-day lock-down.

For thirteen years Jackie lived only a few houses away. But she never did figure out how that Spens household operated. She rarely saw Dawn's mother and had no idea what she did with her days. Her father was gone a lot. When the parents were both away Dawn invited her to visit. It wasn't her idea of home. The place always was strewn with clothes. Full ashtrays were everywhere. Dirty dishes filled the sink.

Jackie recalled Dawn's adolescence unfolding in a predictable cycle of slight ups and heavy downs. But Jackie could never get her friend to talk about it. She gave up trying. Dawn Spens was just that way—quiet, self-contained, but always disturbed about *something*.

The two of them cut loose for a while. Jackie liked to call those early teen years their "experimentation with delinquency." Dawn earned the distinction of being the first student in their class to be suspended for smoking cigarettes in school. Then they discovered drugs—marijuana mainly, then downers and hallucinogens such as mescaline. They smoked joints on their way to class in seventh and eighth grades.

Dawn even smoked up a couple of times during movies in science class. Once she set her desk papers on fire. The science teacher was livid, demanding to know how it started. Jackie figured her girlfriend would be suspended. But after class Dawn had a talk with the instructor, and nothing happened. Dawn had always been good at identifying and tapping compassion in people.

And here I am, Jackie thought, feeling sorry for her again as she puffs her Marlboros. There were no flowers or cards. Where was her family? Where was her boyfriend?

Jackie would have liked to know what happened after Dawn left Harper Woods to live with Donnie Carlton. Jackie couldn't bring herself to probe for the details, though she visited Dawn three times.

"So what are you going to do when you get out of here?" she asked during the last.

Dawn said her boyfriend was from Tennessee and they would probably move there. But first, she might spend some time at her mother's place in Windsor.

"I'll probably be at my mother's," Dawn said.

When she left, Jackie Brown suspected she might not see her friend again for a long time.

Chapter 28

Donald Scott Carlton, a young prisoner with the cocky, glazed-eyed looks of actor Sean Penn, was bumming cigarettes from a visitor in the Macomb County Jail one afternoon and talking about his old girlfriend Dawn Spens.

"Like, the first night we went out I was high on mescaline, weed, cocaine, and was drinkin'. I just sat there against the door of her car. I just leaned up against it all night long and just stared. Like, I practically stared a hole right through her head. I knew right away we were meant for each other.

"The first time Dawn's dad seen me, me and Dawn were sittin' in the living room watching TV.

"He came walkin' in and said, 'You ain't good enough for my daughter, get the fuck out of my house.'

"Me, I was just into getting high and going out with the guys. I was shooting dope from the time I was fifteen. I was singin' in a rock band, and a lot of it was going around. Dawn did a lot of pills—Valium, downers, Tylenol 4s, whatever she could get.

"Whenever we got high we just went nuts. Once I was behind the wheel, and me and Dawn got into an argument. The car got up to seventy miles an hour and we were flyin' down this street.

"I said, 'Quit it, bitch!' and slapped her.

"We hit the curb and went up on the grass and had a flat tire. She was wild.

"Well, there were a lot of problems going down with her dad. He used to beat her and didn't let her talk on the phone. He'd hang up the phone while she was talkin' to me and smack her. She finally got sick of it and decided to get out.

"I really didn't have anything to do with it. I'd moved downtown. She said she'd rather be with me than her family.

"At the time I was runnin' an arcade at Woodward and Montcalm and makin' pretty good money. I'm skimming a little off the top, too. That's how the criminal mind works. There's a lot of scams downtown.

"She was freaking out because people down there were always coming up to me for drugs. She was real confused, and I just told her not to worry about it.

"She'd say, 'How can you live down here? Let's move somewhere else.'

"But I didn't want to because the money was good down there. All the time we were together, I didn't let her know I was shooting dope. So when she moved down, she found out—I think from Monica, a hooker down there.

"So Dawn says, 'If you're goin' to do it, why can't I?'

"And we fought because I didn't want her doin' it. Mixed jive and Dilaudids. Dawn had Monica cop for her.

"So I said, 'You might as well not do it behind my back.'

"And we started gettin' high together. The money we had would go to that. Instead of going out for food, she'd want to stay in and get high.

"And I said, 'If you want money to eat, go get some money.'

"She was real good at it. Her looks for one. She just used to talk, kind of lead a guy on and talk him out of some money. It was mostly on a borrowing basis. And then she'd come up with this 'poor innocent me' bit: *I don't have this and that. We can't eat and we can't get that.*'

"And they'd give her money—the guys who hung around down there. She once got two hundred dollars from this guy Pat, who was a carpenter.

"She'd say, 'I got kicked out of my house.'

"Dawn could rap. She really had a mouth on her. But I wasn't saying, 'Go sell yourself.'

"One day we had a party of about six people in our apartment at Montcalm and Park.

"This guy said, 'I know a couple of guys who would pay her.'

"And I thought about it, and she heard it. But I said no.

"She said, 'Why not? It can't be that bad.'

"And we fought about that. Finally, one day we were broke, and I wanted to get high, and she wanted to get high.

"And I said, 'Fine, go ahead and do it.'

"It was a guy I knew from the arcade. He drove a nice car, an Imperial, I think. He was about thirty-five. I'd seen him doing tricks with girls. And I waved him over and said, 'My girl's looking for some action.' So I told him to drive around the block and pick her up.

"She acted like it was nothin'. That kind of freaked me out. She didn't say she didn't want to do it again, or like, yuk. But then I told her she had to take a bath before she got in bed with me, you know, to wash the guy off. And that freaked her out.

"She started getting close to Monica. Then I got her a job at this store and I know she was turnin' tricks with guys at the store. She was getting pretty good money at first, fifty to sixty dollars.

"The drugs and prostitution really made us get along bad. We got into some fights, and I smacked her around . . . It was something that would go on between us. We'd get in an argument, and she'd just keep it up and keep it up until I got so aggravated I'd smack her . . . All we did is fight . . . She wouldn't go to bed with me.

"One day I was walking down the street and calling these queers all kinds of names—fags, bitches—and that really got them mad. Later on they came running after us with brand-new baseball bats. I got hit. And they beat the shit out of me in the street and dragged me into the building and beat the shit out of me in there.

"They finally quit 'cause somebody was beating on the door. But I went to the hospital, and Dawn never came and seen me or nothin'.

"Lucky came into the picture before that. I saw him a couple of times before that. Lucky and a guy named Russ seemed to think they would take over for Dawn.

"I said, 'No way, you're crazy.'

"But every time they'd see Dawn, they'd try to talk her into going with them.

"So then after I got out of the hospital me and Lucky and Russ made friends. This was their little plan, and I fell for it. They said they had this house, and they—wanted me to be the house manager for them. You know, when the girls bring their tricks to the house, make sure nothing funny goes on. Dawn would come in with a guy and go to the room, and I'd just sit there. I hated it.

"Then Lucky would come back and con her out of some money, but actually he was tryin' to pimp her. And she'd bring me one Dilaudid and buy Lucky four.

"So I told her, 'Fuck it, let's leave.'

"And she said, 'I don't want to go. I'm making lots of money.'

"I said, 'Yeah, but you're giving it to him. You ain't spending it on me or on us.'

"And she said, 'But I'm making money for me.'

"Anyway, then she asked Lucky to take me back downtown because I was beating her ass a lot. He took me for a ride back to the apartment downtown.

"He said, 'Don't come around, or I'll kill you.' I haven't seen her since."

When he was finished with his story, Donnie Carlton held out his right arm, displaying a crude jail tattoo: "Dawn." He was serving four months for car theft. He'd just turned twenty-two. Before he was twenty-three, he would be doing time for murder.

Chapter 29

Dawn Spens was released from Detroit Receiving Hospital January 10, just in time for her nineteenth birthday the next day and another shopping trip with Dr. Al Miller.

She returned to apartment 202 lugging a load of new boots, sandals, designer jeans, and a purse with a 1984 daily pocket calendar tucked inside. She'd also bought John a gray leather jacket. He tried it on, then slouched on the couch to examine the calendar.

Soon Dawn had drifted off into a crossword. Ever since he'd known her, his girlfriend had filled her spare time with a pencil and puzzle.

"Hey," John said as he thumbed through the new daily reminder. "Why don't you use that fucking pencil and this calendar to track how much this goof spends on you every day."

John Fry needed some kind of new angle on the trick. He knew he wouldn't be able to maintain his diligence in anticipating the trick's visits. Dr. Al Miller had told Dawn he wanted to see her every day.

Later that week, John decided to test Al's tolerance. He stayed put rather than bolting for the door when the black Buick pulled up outside the Homewood. Al arrived in the apartment, then watched as John slipped on his new leather coat for a walk.

"That's a nice coat, John."

"Like it? Dawn bought it for me."

John winced. He hadn't intended on pushing the point that far. But Al remained undaunted. He was grinning.

"She has very fine taste, John. Look what she got for me, John."

Al was wearing a new suede coat, with a sheepskin lining.

Later Dawn explained she bought both coats at the same

133

time, sort of. She told Al, "You're always buying me things, but I never get you anything."

"So he gives me five hundred dollars and I got him the coat," she explained. "We got it at Sears. I bought yours right there with the rest of the money."

John cautioned Dawn not to be so obvious. He already figured Al knew the score. But why make the trick jealous by rubbing their relationship in his face?

"It just isn't good business," John said.

Chapter 30

When Jan Canty returned from Arizona, not only was she surprised that her husband had bought himself a sheepskin-lined coat, she thought it even more out of character that he was wearing it.

Not that it didn't look good on Al. The suede was fashionable, and that too was unlike him. Others might call his appearance rumpled. She called it functional, at best.

Al had acquired some pretty peculiar grooming habits over the years. His hair was much shorter than the long, wavy look he sported through his forties. He'd discovered he didn't have to comb it as much, and he didn't. His dandruff added to the overall effect.

"Al, you look dusty to me," she'd say.

Al never showered. He took baths. Lately, she'd noticed he was taking them more often and was staying in the tub longer. She guessed it was more for relaxation than for hygiene. He was soaking every night for an hour or more.

As for clothes, first and foremost, Al loathed ties, and he didn't own one, preferring turtlenecks in the winter and sport shirts in the warmer months. On their wedding day she wore a flowing white gown. Al wore a dark pin-striped suit — and a light gray turtleneck.

Al also preferred everything well worn. He had two dozen old shirts in the closet, half of them missing a button or two. As fast as she sewed them on, others fell off. But when she bought him a new shirt — or trousers or a sport jacket, for that matter — the clothing would remain in the package for months. She teased him about it sometimes.

"What are you doing, Al? Letting them season for a while?"

She had learned over the years that Al was reluctant to make changes of any sort. His appearance was as predictable as his clinic schedule. In twenty years, he'd only had two pairs of glasses—first a pair of black horn-rims when she met him, and then the tortoiseshells he currently wore.

When Jan inquired about the winter coat, he answered her with a question.

"Well, do you like it?"

She nodded. He looked at her as if to say, "Aren't you proud of me? I cleaned up."

He was beaming.

Wow, Jan thought, what in the world has come over him?

Gladys Canty was complimentary the night Buster dropped by to show off his new winter coat.

"Oh, Bus, did Jan get that for you in Arizona? It looks very good on you."

"No, Ma, I bought it at Sears the other day."

Mrs. Canty looked at him quizzically. She'd always known him to dislike shopping. Now he was becoming clothes-conscious.

A few days earlier he bought a nylon jacket for himself as well, right after they had conducted some business at a nearby bank. Buster made quite a scene with the manager that day. The bank had failed to notify her that her CD had matured.

"What kind of business are you running here?" Bus demanded. "What kind of incompetence kept her from being notified?"

Mrs. Canty was shocked by his belligerence and was compelled to defend the bank-official herself. After they left, she told him how he had embarrassed her so.

"Alan, you sounded *just like Pa*."

"I guess I did, didn't I?"

He grinned widely, delighted by the comparison.

Then, as they walked back to her house, they passed a sporting goods store. Alan spotted the blue jacket hanging in the front window. He dashed inside, saying he had to have it.

Mrs. Canty later inquired about that new garment.

"Well, Bus, how do you like that new jacket?"

"Oh, Ma, I took it back. I'm having them sew a monogram."

He said he was having the store put "Cadieux Bar" across the back. She was perplexed. Cadieux was a well-known street nearby, but she'd never heard of the bar. And he didn't belong to a bowling league or any sort of sports team sponsored by a bar anyway. He didn't even go to bars.

"Well, Bus, why would you do that?"

"Oh, Ma, I just really like those things."

She asked herself, why was he trying to act like one of the boys? My Lord, he's changing, she thought. She wouldn't have thought it possible at his age.

Chapter 31

Six days after she got out of the hospital, Dawn Spens was in jail again after being picked up on an unpaid prostitution ticket. That night Dr. Al Miller dropped by the Homewood Manor looking not for Dawn, but for John Fry.

"I've got some time to kill, John," Al said. "You doing anything? Let me buy you a drink."

Al was dressed more casually than usual. He had on a pair of jeans, a sport shirt, and a blue jacket with "Cadieux Bar" monogrammed across the back. The two men went to the Gaiety Bar, located only a block and a half from the Homewood.

One of the favorite tunes on the Gaiety jukebox was "Whiskey Bent and Hell Bound" by Hank Williams, Jr. Often the customers took the lyrics literally. The bar went through an average of five cue sticks a week, most of them splintered in fights stemming from the action on the bar's pool table. Lit by a fluorescent canopy in the middle of the saloon, the table's green felt was the only plush amenity in the Gaiety Bar.

Fry ordered a beer and a shot of Jack Daniel's. Al asked for the same. At the pool table two patrons were engaged in a game of eight ball. Fry walked over and placed a quarter on the table railing, challenging the winner to the next contest.

When Fry returned to the bar rail, Al had already thrown down the shot of bourbon and ordered another round.

"So how did you get into the prostitution game, John?" Al said.

Fry had already suspected the trick had invited him to the bar for questioning. He gave his dissertation on the business. Al listened carefully.

"True, we all do prostitute ourselves at one time or another," Al said. "I gave it all up for medicine. You sell out. But it's still there. That's why I like to come down here. You don't just give it up."

Al pointed at the pool table.

"Used to play a lot of pool myself, John. As a matter of fact, I supported myself through college one year with a pool stick."

"Is that right, mon," Fry said.

Al said his parents weren't happy with his lifestyle in college. He kept fooling around with hot rods and motorcycles, so they shut off the funds. One summer, he said, he lived out of his car, circulating from pool hall to pool hall. He developed a drug habit, shooting heroin for several months.

The story had little basis in fact, but at that point John could only suspect as much. Lucky Fry tossed down his shot and kept a straight face.

Al ordered a third round. He told John the same story he'd told Dawn about his cocaine-crazed late wife. He appeared disturbed by the memory.

By then it was John's turn at the pool table. After he won the game, he looked up to find that Al had placed a quarter on the railing. Now he'd know for sure whether the college pool story was bullshit.

The two of them played six games in all, downing more bourbon and beer as they played. Al was quite the sight, toddling around the table as he chalked up his stick. But between the whiskey and the heroin habit, John wasn't exactly at the top of his game.

"The trick was no great pool player," he would later recall of that night. "But he knew enough shots to win."

The series ended in a draw. They each won three games.

In time, Al's voice deepened as he drank, falling into a booming, condescending tone. A prostitute in the bar propositioned him, but he laughed loudly and steered her to Fry.

"Hey, here's another one for you, John."

Just about the time the song by Hank Williams, Jr., was making another of many spins on the jukebox, Fry left the bar rail and went to the bathroom. When he came out Al

139

was in a shouting match with a sloppy drunk who had been hovering around the pool table.

Fry rushed toward the dispute, protective of a major source of his income. Just as the drunk cocked his fist, Al kicked the lush in the shin, doubling him over. By the time John reached the fracas, Al had pulled out a small buck knife.

"Come on, let's get the fuck out of here before the cops come," John said. He pulled his drinking partner away from the table and out the door.

Al was laughing wildly by the time they reached his Buick. The trick walked as though his center of gravity was square between his hips rather than swinging from east to west.

"Man, what the hell happened in there?" John asked.

"The guy said he knew my wife. He said he used to fuck her when she was working the streets."

John was eager to send Al on his way. It wasn't even nine o'clock, but he could see the doctor already had too much to drink.

That same night Jan Canty gave a lecture to parents and teenagers at the Center Point Crisis Center as part of a series by the Family Life Education Council. By the time she was finished it was nearly ten o'clock.

Earlier that day, she'd told Al she was giving the talk. Her husband thought her topic was an appropriate one — alcoholism and its effect on the family. When she got home that night Al was already asleep in bed. She figured he was exhausted from another one of his long days at work.

Chapter 32

We're getting a success rate somewhere between 60 and 70 percent. These are children previously diagnosed as hopeless . . . I wouldn't be too surprised if within the next year or so, we're talking about a real viable therapy for autism that has grown out of the work we have done here on the Indianwood Project.

— W. ALAN CANTY,
Autism lecture at Concordia College, 1978

Ever since he'd chanced on *Therapeutic Peers: The Story of Project Indianwood* in a used bookstore near Wayne State, *Bob Willing* had been enchanted by W. Alan Canty's little paperback about autistic children.

Now the aspiring psychologist needed a fully licensed therapist to supervise two thousand hours of clinical training before he could be certified by the state. He had just the person in mind.

Therapeutic Peers was a heartfelt, colorfully written book, quite unlike most jargon-ridden academic publications on autism. He'd read the seventy-two-page paperback several times but had never been able to find another copy at bookstores anywhere.

W. Alan Canty wrote that his interest in autism began in 1959 when he was a clinical trainee at the Birmingham Psychiatric Clinic. As a young intake worker, he was the first contact with the facility's upscale clientele. The clinic did not treat psychotic children, but requests for that kind of help frequently crossed the young Canty's desk. Often, the children were autistic.

"Our answer was always the same," he wrote. "The cause was unknown and there was no local therapy available."

Canty was particularly moved by one hopeless five-year-old girl named Dawn. Dawn's first symptoms were tantrumlike tirades in her crib. Her mother used increasing doses of paregoric-based cough syrup to quiet her. Dawn then took to rocking endlessly until her buttocks bled and holding her breath until she turned blue.

At the same time Alan Canty became interested in antisocial adolescents. The young psychologist supervised group therapy for troubled high school boys.

Encouraged by good results with the teens, Canty reflected on the girl named Dawn. There must be a way to help such children, he wrote. He secured permission from James Clark Maloney, the clinic's director, to try group techniques with autistic children in a day camp setting.

Canty plunged into books on childhood schizophrenia, believing the condition was similar to autism. The psychologist found that researchers had stressed that in many cases there were early difficulties between mother and child.

"Maternal immaturity and perfectionism was highlighted with her inflexibility, generating tension in the child," Canty wrote. "These mothers tended to subtly shape the child's behavior along lines which communicated that only socially acceptable acts made them worthy of love."

Such children had deep anger toward their parents, Canty surmised. He wondered if that applied to autistic children as well. He reviewed fifty-five cases in one autism study group, reporting:

"I learned that these parents were also found to be 'cold and humorless perfectionists,' whose behavior towards their children had been frigid and mechanical . . . Some of the fathers even admitted that they hardly knew their autistic offspring. These parents treated marriage like a business meeting . . ."

Eventually, Canty came up with his hypothesis of autism. The child, he reasoned, had a vast well of suppressed anger toward his parents. But he "split off" his anger or rage because his fear of parental disapproval was so strong. This froze emotional development. There was no more rage. No more fear. No more joy. Nothing.

Canty employed his theater training from Wayne State in his therapy program. He would present skits to a test group of children in an attempt to unleash their hidden rage. Perhaps live drama could shatter their rigid shells of self-confinement.

He called it Project Indianwood. High school girls were the most likely choice as helpers, he wrote. They would serve as actresses for the psychodramas. Such girls had experience as baby-sitters, and children often became attached to adolescent girls, he reasoned. He wanted to avoid mother figures.

Canty chose three camp uniforms for his "Indianwood guides." In one, he had the girls dress in cutoff jeans, sweatshirts, and sneakers. Another was the "teenage hoodlum look," composed of black boots, a denim skirt, and dark turtleneck top. The third was the "campus cheerleader look," composed of knee socks, rally skirt, and crew neck sweater.

Canty dreamt up a series of violent fairy tales as skits. They featured villainous young women and evil men. One was about a princess who directed the murder of her husband. Another was about a psychopathic ballerina. There was much dying and many parental figures "destroyed with great sadism and relish."

After weeks of trial and error, the skits began to get results, he wrote. Canty reported his young actresses got laughter and tears from children whom he once described as his "wooden Indians." Their emotional responses were infectious—thus the title of his book.

Canty wrote that he nurtured the project through graduate school and his doctoral program, improving it with time. One later refinement was in the appearance of his "guides." By the early 1970s, his teenage guides were exceptionally beautiful girls. Most had slim, shapely figures and long brown hair. He wrote:

"Physical attractiveness and actual facial beauty turned out to be unusually important. As the years passed and we worked with more groups, I noted again and again that the prettiest guides on the staff invariably brought the first response from the children."

Bob Willing didn't quite buy all of it. Autism remained

one of the most baffling and stubborn of all mental disorders. Effective treatment had eluded everyone. Willing knew that recent studies showed the disorder was probably biochemical and not caused by "anger at Mother" as Canty believed.

But Willing did believe that the emotional intensity Canty was shooting for with his skits did work to some extent. Willing had been using psychodrama techniques in a day camp for troubled children where he worked.

"I'm going to tear out your heart and squish it in my fingers," Willing would say, distorting his face and his body. "I'm going to cut off your head and rip off your arms."

It sparked reactions from one normally stone-faced child. As Canty had written, play violence seemed to be the pipeline to their hearts.

At forty, Bob Willing finally had charted some direction after a bumpy trip through psychedelia and the Me Decade. Stops along the way included the family tool business, a Colorado commune, and a job in stringed-instrument repair. He'd studied painting, sculpture, and improvisational music. His under-graduate degree was in fine arts. Finally, he'd found clinical psychology and the world of disturbed children.

Though he'd never met him, Willing suspected Alan Canty also possessed an intellectual mix of the arts and social sciences. He was the perfect choice for a supervisor. Willing called him for an appointment one day in late January.

"I'm awfully busy," Canty said. "I've got an awfully full schedule, but if you want to come in, we can talk."

Willing made an impassioned pitch in Canty's Fisher Building office. He told Canty about the results he was getting at the day camp. He talked about his background in the fine arts and his twelve-year quest for a bachelor's degree. Willing said he needed a supervisor who knew about autistic children. There just weren't many around. And he asked where he could find more copies of *Therapeutic Peers*. There weren't any of those around, either.

"I've got to distribute some more," Canty said. "I've been awfully busy warking on another book. I've been so darn busy my body chemistry has been out of whack lately."

Canty appeared so straight, so established, Willing thought. He had imagined Canty living like him, among artists and students in the city's cultural center north of the Cass Corridor.

Canty explained what supervision entailed. They would have a forty-five minute session once a month. They would discuss professional approach, specific cases, and personal problems affecting his work.

Then Canty handed him two copies of *Therapeutic Peers*. Willing could tell the psychologist was flattered.

"You know, when you first came in here I was going to try and tell you no—politely. But I'm real interested in your work with children. I can't do it myself anymore. It's just too draining."

Canty said he had ceased Indianwood therapy sessions in the Fisher several years back. But he had made videotapes of the psychodramas, however. They were being field-tested in children's programs around the country.

"I can't do it myself anymore," Canty said. "But I'm going to try and keep in contact with the children through you. What do you think you can pay me?"

Willing already knew a supervisor received a fee. But he was embarrassed. His day camp job paid little, and he was barely getting by as it was.

"I have very little money. I could, uh, scrape ten dollars together."

"Fine. But just so you know, I normally charge twenty dollars for fifteen minutes of consultation. Normally you would pay sixty dollars."

They shook on it. When he left, Bob Willing felt as though it was his lucky day.

Chapter 33

Cheryl Krizanovic had entertained a slim hope that she might win back John Fry by moving into the Homewood Manor. Instead she'd only made herself more miserable.

As the days passed, she became certain her old boyfriend was thoroughly bewitched by his young whore from the suburbs. Cheryl had never seen John Fry treat another human being so well. She was jealous of all the attention he gave Dawn.

One night when she and Dawn were alone, Dawn complained about their lifestyle. She said she was growing sick of the prostitution, the drugs, and John's temper.

"I can get enough money from Al to leave John. Al says John's a bad influence."

"So then, why don't you leave him? You *should* leave him."

"But I *love* John," she said.

Cheryl wondered why Dawn even bothered to tell her. She figured Dawn was just showing off. Compared to my four years with John Fry, Cheryl thought, this girl is living a fairy tale. She still was virtually unscathed. Cheryl had seen John slap her only twice, when she got right up in his face and downright mouthy. If Cheryl would have tried that, she would have ended up hospitalized.

In fact, John had put Cheryl in a hospital bed for six weeks nearly two years ago. Someone had told him Cheryl was shooting dope behind his back, holding out on him. He caught up with her on Second Avenue, then marched her behind the White Grove. There were only two punches, one to her side and an uppercut under her ribs. He had more abuse planned for her at a friend's house, but she started throwing up.

Doctors discovered two sets of broken ribs and a shattered spleen. A surgeon removed the organ. Cheryl showed

Dawn Spens the long scar on her side.

"All over a couple of packs of dope," Cheryl said.

But Cheryl also owed John Fry for saving a limb, her right leg, the time an abscess turned into gangrene. He'd always kept her guessing with those kind of contradictions. John didn't force the tattoo "Lucky" on her left thigh, but he vowed he'd "cut it out" if she ever left. He used to warm her heart by talking about honesty, but he never let her forget it when she told him she'd been raped by one of his friends. He once saved her from a fatal overdose but then told his brother he was going to put her in a garbage dumpster if she died. He convinced her to leave the only man who she guessed really cared about her, then he left her for Dawn when she did.

The man's name was Dale McMasters. He picked her up nearly two years ago while she was hitchhiking to the Cass Corridor from their old place off Michigan Avenue. Cheryl told him she was "a social worker and sex therapist." He laughed and told her he went by the name of Frank. He was in his early thirties and was hauling rigs out of Dearborn between stays at his home in northern Michigan.

The meeting started a friendship, one she kept concealed for months from John. Frank was the first man she ever met that didn't want something from her. When he found out she was a prostitute he said, "I don't pay for it," but he offered her money so she could rest from the streets. He said he was a former addict and wanted to help her get off drugs.

At first she and John played the brother and sister routine. Cheryl let John think Frank was a regular trick. But John didn't like him.

"Twiggy, end this," he kept saying.

Then Frank McMasters befriended John Fry. He had them as guests in his house in northern Michigan—in Alanson, near Petoskey. He wanted to help them both kick their habits, but it had never worked.

Cheryl Krizanovic knew Frank McMasters had fallen in love with her, but the big trucker had given up long ago. Twice she'd left John and stayed with Frank up north a few days. He never took advantage of her. She found some

147

peace in the Lake Michigan surf and the still northern nights. She spent hours watching the water off the long pier in Petoskey.

But inevitably John Fry came begging, promising to get clean. They always ended up high and back in the Motor City. Frank finally became disgusted with the routine. She hadn't seen him in nearly a year.

Now Cheryl knew only one way to deal with her resentments. She turned as many tricks as she could snare and shot the profits into her veins as fast as she could score. By February, even John Fry appeared alarmed. One night he called Frank McMasters in Alanson.

"Frank," he said. "I know you had feelings for Cheryl, man. It's over between me and her. She's killing herself down here. How would you like to come and get her?"

Frank said he would think about it.

Dr. Al Miller, meanwhile, had an open wallet for Dawn Spens. He continued urging her not to turn tricks on the streets. When she complained she had to make money somehow, his payments increased. He wanted her out of the Corridor. John Fry bragged to fellow addicts that she could squeeze her sugar daddy for a half a grand at a time.

"I think he felt guilty that he'd almost cost Dawn her fuckin' leg," John later told one. "He was starting to get really possessive and protective of her. Didn't bother me a bit. He could be possessive and protective all he wanted — for one hour a day."

Cheryl Krizanovic wondered how long the doctor could hold out. He must not have been hurting too bad yet. He'd bought himself a new car, a 1984 Buick Regal. The color was black. "A royal ride for a royal trick," Cheryl quipped. His daily visits were more predictable than the Detroit bus schedules. But he never came on Sundays.

One day Dawn asked him why. Al said he often had business in Port Huron that day, and if not, he visited his mother. Mother Miller was old, lived alone, and could barely walk, he said.

"I'm all she has in Detroit," he said. "And she's virtually blind."

John Fry was shooting himself sightless with mixed jive. He spent days at a time in the Homewood. If he wasn't in his own apartment, he was with other addicts down the hall. Cheryl noticed he had lost a lot of his swagger since his brother's death. With her and Dawn in and out between tricks, the doctor showing up, and John squabbling about money, life in apartment 202 was suited for a study of combat stress.

Often the only order in the day was Al's visit. Everyone became civilized so he could relax with his newspaper, drink his special blend, and have his little chats with Dawn. About once a week, if he was lucky, Dawn said, he got a blow job.

But Dr. Miller represented only an hour in a twenty-four-hour day. The rest of the time was divided between bitching and drug-induced apathy.

The routine changed for ten days when Cheryl was jailed on outstanding prostitution warrants. But after her release, she tangled with a neighborhood junkie over a pack of dope. She had survived the worst of her heroin withdrawal in custody, only to come out with plans of starting again.

John Fry called Frank McMasters.

"Frank," he pleaded. "She's virtually clean, mon. I'm telling you, mon, she's clean. Can you come and get her?"

Frank said he'd think about it.

The day after she was released from jail, Cheryl Krizanovic complained to Dr. Al Miller on his visit that she wasn't feeling well. She had missed her period. Her abdomen was swollen.

"I don't have the money to go to a doctor, Al. Can you tell me if I'm pregnant?"

"Well, I don't know about that, but let's see."

Cheryl was about to strip when he told her just to lie down on the couch. He poked around on her abdomen with his fingers. Only a lab test could tell for sure, he said. When she left the apartment with John she was convinced he wasn't a doctor.

"A doctor would go up inside you, John," she said. "He'd feel around."

A week later she would be hospitalized for a severe case

of gonorrhea, but not before Frank McMasters showed up at the Homewood Manor unannounced at four in the morning. It was the day before Valentine's Day, and he was on his way to Pennsylvania to visit relatives. Then he planned to return home to Alanson.

"Don't argue with me, Cheryl, but you're goin' with me," he said. "Pack your things."

Cheryl was never so happy to see him. They spent a day in Pennsylvania, then drove back to the north. She asked Frank to take her to Lake Michigan on their way to Alanson.

"But its the middle of February, Cheryl."

He drove to the Petoskey pier anyway. It jutted a quarter mile into the bay. Cheryl jumped out of the car and ran the best she could with her swollen tummy. The pier was covered with ice and the temperature was nearly zero.

When she reached the end, Cheryl let the horizon fill both edges of her peripheral vision. The lake was frozen. But Cheryl Krizanovic wasn't complaining. She held up her arms, gave a shout to the big lake, and borrowed a deep breath from the clean northern wind.

Chapter 34

The child now begins to react to, and interact with, the mother and to experiment with her reactions to his behavior. His ever-increasing attempts at interaction are based on his past experience, and the positive or negative feelings which have resulted.
— W. ALAN CANTY,
Principles of Counseling and Psychotherapy

Gladys Canty had thought that the days of being her son's banker had stopped a couple of years ago. She was troubled when she found out otherwise one day in late February.

Buster dropped by in a rush, saying he needed nine hundred dollars. He needed nine hundred dollars right away. He had a cash flow problem. The shortage had been caused, he said, by the Wayne County Circuit Court. They owed him money for his case evaluations.

"They haven't paid me in a couple of years. Ma, they owe me a bunch."

"Oh, Bus, how come?"

"The county is in dire straits. You know that, Ma. You've read about it. They're having payless paydays. You know how it is with a bureaucracy."

Yes she did, but she also knew about her son's ways with the money. She had often warned him that he lived beyond his means. Repeatedly, in the years after he had remarried, she had bailed him out with checks in five figures. Their disagreements on money had reoccurred with the predictability of a dunning notice that kept arriving in the mail.

Bus always called his requests "loans." But he never paid her back. Of course, she never pestered him for payment.

She had plenty of money. It was the principle of the thing.

She sometimes wondered where he got that streak of irresponsibility. She'd noticed it in several areas of his life over the years. She and Al Sr. had done their best to give him the most progressive upbringing available. When he was a baby, they even wrote away to Washington, D.C., for books from the government on child rearing. The pamphlets covered everything from health to discipline.

"I was good about telling him when I was proud of him and when I wasn't," she would later recall.

Early on, Gladys Canty improvised a way to let her son know when he was being good or bad. She and Bus found the expression together in a children's book she was reading to him one night in his preschool years. The book talked about a boy who could "stand tall."

When he was bad she would say, "Oh, Buster, you weren't standing tall then."

He picked right up on the expression. When he knew his behavior was unacceptable, he'd come to her saying, "Well, Mommy, I guess I wasn't standing tall when I did that."

But her son also let her know when he'd been good. He used to throw his little shoulders back, sport a big smile, and practically march into the room.

"I was standing very tall, wasn't I, Mommy," he'd say.

As he grew, she and Al Sr. sometimes disagreed on methods. She worried about him when he wanted to play out in the neighborhood, or stay out past dark. Al Sr. was more permissive.

"You don't understand," her husband would say. "Boys have to do that. You don't understand, you're not a boy."

Al Sr. himself was not a punctual man. Often he would sleep in on weekdays, not rising until well after he should have been at work. Sometimes he didn't get up until noon. She often found herself at the foot of the stairs shouting time bulletins through the morning. Often she would be stewing.

"It used to bother me greatly," she later complained. "I took my responsibility very seriously. And I suppose I was irritated because I was an early riser and he was asleep when he should have been up doing his chores."

Still, she couldn't complain about her husband as a provider. He let Gladys amass quite a nest egg for her retirement. When she and her husband were both working, Alan Sr. insisted she bank every dime of her salary for the future. Those savings went untapped for years. In fact, she and Al Sr. often went without. Much of her husband's salary went to Alan Jr.'s education.

It was more expensive than they anticipated, again because of her son's inability to discipline himself. First he enrolled in Hillsdale College, a small school three hours west of Detroit. But he flunked out after a year. He complained he didn't like being away from home in a small, conservative city. Then he explored the idea of being an osteopath, visiting a school Al Sr. recommended in Kansas City. He returned saying the place was not for him. Finally, he decided he'd enroll at Wayne University, then a budding urban college.

He began in liberal arts, then became enchanted by the theater. It seemed a natural progression to her. In his teens they had season tickets to a theater and opera series. In high school he'd played the lead in *The Royal Family,* his high school's senior play. The part was the extent of his extracurricular activities in high school, and he studied it with a passion. She helped him with the lines. Sometimes he sang around the house. His voice was rich, but always about a half step off-key.

At Wayne he dove into theater with vigor. He spent hours hanging around the Bonstelle Theatre. He couldn't say enough about James Dean, his favorite actor. He took up smoking, holding his cigarette like the young star, but he never inhaled. He dressed like James Dean, wore his hair like James Dean, and mimicked James Dean's lines at the dinner table.

Al Sr., however, thought his son was making a chancy investment of his time and energy.

"Alan, if you want to go into acting, fine," he said. "But you have to have something else. Acting can be so—temporary. Take some education classes, at least. At least you'll have something to fall back on."

Bus took his advice, but "something" was a long time coming. He received his bachelor's in psychology at twenty-six, his master's at twenty-eight, and his Ph.D. at thirty-five. Al Sr. paid for the entire journey, not to mention a host of miscellaneous living expenses.

Sometimes Gladys Canty thought she'd become so protective of her own money because of all those costly years with Bus. She'd sewn her holdings into CDs in banks around Detroit and Grosse Pointe. She hadn't driven a car in years, so now she depended on her son to shuttle the money from bank to bank, reinvesting the certificates as they matured.

Gladys Canty also had put Al Jr.'s name as a coholder on all of her largest accounts, as well as on the title to her house. She wanted her son to have the right of survivorship in the event of her demise.

Bus had been helpful along the way. He'd passed on sound advice on several investments from professionals at the Fisher Building. She only wished he could be more diligent about his own budget. He reminded her of an adolescent with an unlimited allowance. It used to irk her when he'd get a wedding or birthday invitation from someone he hadn't seen in years.

"I sent them a check for $100," he'd say proudly.

"Why, Buster, it doesn't call for that kind of gift."

"Ma, let me do it the way I want to," he'd snap back.

Now he needed $900. She thought of the new black Buick Regal he'd bought recently, and the cleaning lady Bus and Jan had coming to the house twice a week. She figured the housekeeper was worth $320 a month alone. They'd argued about that before.

"Ma, you don't understand," her son would say. "That's our lifestyle."

The dispute would continue along these lines:

"Oh, Bus, you're living beyond your means."

"Do you realize how much money I make, Ma?"

"Then why can't you meet your expenses?"

"Do you have any idea what my expenses are at the Fisher Building?"

"Bus, I think I do."

Then he would angrily say, "Forget it. I'll get it someplace else."

"Oh, you know I'm going to give it to you."

She knew there was no *someplace else*.

Gladys Canty wrote him a check for $900. Then he left. He was in a hurry. Buster always was in a hurry when he needed money.

Chapter 35

Mark Bando bailed out of the squad car and sprinted toward the Homewood Manor after Dawn Spens. The cop caught the front door just before it locked shut and raced toward the sound of high heels clicking down the basement steps. He caught her on the landing, pinning the prostitute against the wall as he cuffed her.

Bando wasn't sure why she fled when he and John Woodington drove up Charlotte from Third. But they had a standing policy about such situations: You approach someone in the car; they run; you catch them first; you worry about what they're wanted for later.

Back at the squad car they found she was wanted for $400 in outstanding warrants.

"Time for a ride downtown, Dawn," Bando said.

The prostitute squinted her eyes, glaring at some spot in space. Capricorns could be like that, he thought, like robots or something. He wasn't surprised when her birthday put her square under the sign. He pulled out his whore book.

Dawn Marie Spens 20082 Elkhart, 7112 Clayton; 5'4" — brn/brn. "Dumb Donnie Carlton's protégé."

Bando felt like adding "lost cause" this Friday, March 23.

Almost a year ago the cop welcomed her to the Cass Corridor with her first arrest. Bando and Woodington had heard a whorehouse was operating above a market on Park and Montcalm, its main attraction a young girl named Dawn. They eventually caught up with her on the streets. When they checked Dawn's handbag they found a set of works.

Bando was disappointed. She hadn't been in the neighborhood two months. He booked her for possession of narcotics paraphernalia, then he called her father. He was hoping to get her back to Harper Woods before she destroyed herself. If she didn't, he knew the neighborhood would.

"We're concerned that something should be done before it's too late," Bando told Roy Spens over the telephone. "What do you think? Can she come back and live with you?"

Then Dawn got on the phone. Bando remembered it as a somewhat sentimental scene. Tears rolled down her cheeks. The sewer didn't stink so bad that night.

Roy Spens seemed eager to do what he could. The father agreed to meet Bando and Woodington the following night at Chris And Carl's Cafe on Cass. Dawn promised she would meet them there, too. Her father would pick up her things and take her back to Harper Woods. Bando and Woodington would be there as a kind of stabilizing influence, just in case Dumb Donnie or anybody else tried to make trouble.

They met Roy Spens at the restaurant. The three of them sipped coffee and waited. Roy seemed like an OK guy, Bando thought. They talked about what kind of work he did. He said he appreciated them trying to help. They waited for more than a half hour, but Dawn never showed up.

Several days later Bando and Woodington heard that Dawn had hooked up with Lucky Fry.

"What could she possibly see in that sick, sadistic, sociopathic gnome?" Bando asked his partner. Lucky Fry had always reminded him of a twisted version of the trademark character on the Vernors ginger ale bottle.

Then he heard from the vice squad that Dawn was turning tricks on Michigan Avenue. Dates were lined up around the block for her, they said.

Bando arrested her again in November. There were no tears that time.

Now, as he processed Dawn Spens on the warrants, he didn't much care what happened to her. By then he knew that talking to Dawn Spens was like having a conversation with a wall. She was quite unlike the verbal Cheryl Krizanovic, Fry's old punching bag. Dawn Spens was spooky, he thought. Bando remembered Fry's icy stare the day he arrested him in the Homewood.

"Dawn Spens and Lucky Fry deserved each other," he later said. "They both seemed cold-blooded, heartless. There was something missing. He was ruthless. She just didn't give a shit. They complemented each other perfectly. Together they formed a third personality of their own."

When he heard the news during his visit to the Homewood, Dr. Al Miller told John Fry he didn't have the money to post Dawn's bond. She would have to spend the weekend in jail, waiting for the courts to open on Monday morning.

What was she doing in jail, anyway? She wasn't supposed to be working the streets, Al said. John tried to explain the ways of the Japanese cop.

"Bando, man," John said. "He's death on whores."

Al toddled to his Buick and sped off, seemingly irritated.

Early the next evening Dawn's sugar daddy made a visit to Police Headquarters. The building at 1300 Beaubien had hardly changed since it was built in the Roaring Twenties. The ambience inside would make Kojak feel at home. Visits to the eighth-floor lockup were as intimate as those in most jails. Prisoner and visitor talked over a telephone, eyeing each other through a small window of shatterproof glass. Visits were restricted to lawyers, immediate family, and medical personnel. But on slow nights, the cops working the desk on the first floor relaxed the rules.

Dr. Miller didn't need an M.D.'s credentials to make the visit. At the precinct desk, an officer wrote down the name he gave for the March 24 pass. The cop filed a copy, then directed Dawn's visitor to the elevator to the lockup above.

On the pass he wrote: "Alan Canty, a friend."

Chapter 36

. . . The now potentially-disturbed individual literally convinces himself of the validity of his own thinking. He is actually making himself emotionally disturbed, since his difficulty is growing, not out of the specific behavior of others, but rather out of his reactions to their behavior and the way he has allowed himself to experience them.

— W. ALAN CANTY,
Principles of Counseling and Psychotherapy

John Fry and Dawn Spens were stirred from their sleep by the pleading car horn outside the Homewood Manor. It was the morning of April 8, a Sunday. Dawn shuffled to the window.

"Damn. Al's out there."

"Fuck it," John mumbled. "I ain't gettin' up."

The next series of bleats from the Buick raised John upright. Then he realized what day it was.

"Fuck, I don't even have time to get right," he grumbled. "What the fuck ever happened to never on Sunday?"

John pulled on his clothes and ambled downstairs to let the trick in. Dawn scurried around the apartment, picking up. When the two men reached the door of apartment 202, John started down the hall to wake up a friend.

"No, John," Al said. "Come in. I want to talk."

Dawn went to the kitchen to fire up a pot of Al's special blend. She explored a bag of juices and chocolates that Al had brought her for Sunday brunch. John sat on one end of the couch and Al on the other as they waited for the coffee.

"John," he began. "I know you and Dawn are boyfriend and girlfriend."

"Who, me? What?"

159

"Let's stop the games, John. I've been around."

They talked for only a few minutes. Dawn seemed to be giving them time to talk. She lingered over the treats in the kitchen.

Al said he had developed some "strong feelings" for Dawn.

"OK," John said. "You're saying *that* to say what?"

"What would it cost for you to bow out of the picture?"

John explained he was not the kind of man who just walked out of somebody's life for money. He'd have to think about it. It would not be easy—or cheap—to reestablish himself.

"The girl means a lot to me, too," he said. "Like I said, Al. I'll have to think about it."

Al looked as though he was ready to deal right there, but John Fry had no intention of letting a trick personally hand him a large sum of cash. He considered the drug purchase for Dawn when she was in the hospital a risky enough venture. He knew too little about Dr. Al Miller. What he did know just didn't make sense. Al was too aloof to be the basic middle-class trick looking for thrills in the Cass Corridor, but too much of a goof to be an undercover cop. Plus, there was something about the proposal that just plain pissed him off.

John decided to let Al make his next move through Dawn. He left the apartment so she could be with her juice, her chocolates, and her sugar daddy. When he returned, John and Dawn discussed the trick's offer.

"What the fuck is goin' on?" John said. "Where does he come off, coming to me like that?"

"That's just the way he is," Dawn said. "He wants you to bow out of the picture."

"Is that what *you* want?"

"Don't even try it, John. You know me better than that."

But that did not mean, Fry added, that they had to pass up such an opportunity.

"Can we squeeze him?" she asked.

"If that's what he wants to do, it can be done."

Now they were thinking as one.

The negotiations were conducted as Al visited that week, with Dawn relaying the offers back and forth. Al first offered two thousand dollars and a plane ticket to a destination of John's choice.

"I couldn't believe it," she told John. "It was that easy."

"But I'm not," John said.

He knew Al was willing to pay more. He countered with ten thousand dollars and a plane ticket. By midweek, they appeared to have an agreement.

"Tell him five thousand dollars," John said, "and he'll never see me with you again."

Al bought the package. The plane ticket was left as an option once John decided where he wanted to go. Al said he would deliver the payoff in cash on Friday. Lucky Fry, meanwhile, was already making plans for himself.

None of them included a trip to the airport.

161

Chapter 37

The patient whose mental disturbance has reached psychotic [insane] proportions is no longer in contact with the external world . . . These patients have suffered a complete breakdown . . . There are specific techniques for treating psychotics but these are usually carried on in a hospital setting . . .

— W. ALAN CANTY,
Principles of Counseling and Psychotherapy

Jan Canty was hardly through the doorway after a lunch date with a neighbor when her cleaning woman pressed the message into her hand: "Call your mother-in-law. Emergency!" When she reached her, Gladys Canty's voice was breaking.

"Jannie, something has happened to Alan. I don't know what. He won't talk. He's calling for you. Jannie, I know something terrible has happened."

It was Thursday, April 12, the day Dr. Al Miller would have been looking for ways to raise five thousand dollars.

Jan dialed Al at the Fisher Building. She called a half-dozen times. Each time someone picked up the phone.

"Al? Al? Al? Is that you?"

Each time there was only silence.

She buckled herself into her new Thunderbird and made quick use of the five-speed. Her anxiety raced with the Ford turbo on the freeway. Finally the Golden Tower of the Fisher appeared ahead on the cityscape. She hoped her mother-in-law had overreacted. I hope I'm overreacting, she thought.

Jan canceled the notion when she reached her husband's suite. Something was very wrong. Two patients were in the waiting room. Al never let that happen. He had a separate exit door from his counseling office so patients never had to

162

meet.

The patients looked at her with anticipation. She walked right past them, heading directly to Al's inner office. There she found her husband.

She was shocked. There was no sign of the comfortable, rational man who had left for work that morning. Al was pressed deep into his big chair, his head nearly touching the wall. His face was a study in terror. His body was frozen with it. In all her life — in all the cases she'd seen in the university clinic — Jan Canty had never seen anyone look so horrified.

"Al. Honey. *What's wrong?*"

He didn't seem to hear her. Alan Canty appeared enraptured by the vision of some dreaded act, as though someone was just about to blow off his head.

"Al . . . Al," she said. "Al . . ."

He was mute. His mouth moved, but only because his tongue was swabbing the inside of his lower lip. Next to his chair he'd scrawled something on notepaper. Jan picked it up and read it. At the time it didn't make sense.

The patients, she thought. She raced back to the waiting room, composing herself along the way.

"Excuse me, there's been a family crisis and I need to help Al," she said.

They rose. They wanted to help.

"No, please," she said. "Please leave, everything is under control. I'll contact you as soon as I can."

She hurried back to Al. He was cold to the touch. He was perspiring heavily. Her clinical mind raced through a dozen university lectures and a thousand pages of text. *State of shock.* No. *Insulin rush.* No. Wait, *this is Al.*

Jan Canty started to cry. Her brain was locking up, like a computer trying to run two different programs at once. She was thinking like a clinical psychologist. She was feeling like a wife.

Then one program crashed. *Pychotic break.* My God, she thought, my husband is having a psychotic break. His schedule. The coffee. The sleepless nights. The work at the jail. The load has finally caught up with him and pushed him over the edge.

Jan had to get help. Al needed help. He needed a hospital, and judging from that look on his face, he needed one now. The University of Michigan, her alma mater. She would take him to University Hospital.

Her newfound purpose steadied her. She began talking to Al in a calm, rational voice, as with a crisis call back at the Center Point Crisis Center. She gently took Al by the arm and led him from the office to the parking garage. She would take him first to Dr. Aaron Rutledge. He had connections at University Hospital, and she trusted him.

Al seemed to stabilize once they arrived at Dr. Rutledge's office ten minutes later, but he remained severely withdrawn. His responses were limited to little more than a nod of the head. Jan felt more stable, too, in the company of the therapist who had supervised her for three years. Together they tried to secure a bed at University Hospital, but the psychiatric unit was booked. He would have to be admitted the following day through the hospital's emergency room. Jan decided she could contain the situation herself for twenty-four hours. After all, she told herself, I'm a psychologist.

She might as well have hooked Al up to a remote control once she got him back to the big Tudor. He was compliant, meek. He did anything she said. Here and there he would try to act normal. He laughed at things she said, but she knew he hadn't understood a word. When she served dinner, he ate mechanically, but she could tell he wasn't hungry. From time to time he looked frightened.

She knew a psychotic break was like that. Al's symptoms were textbook: loss of touch with reality—times, places, dates, faces, names. Sometimes the patient comes in and out.

Jan tucked him into bed. She lay down but didn't sleep.

The next morning Jan Canty decided to seek some help for herself. She called her closest friend, Celia Muir. They'd known each other twenty years. Ces, as Jan called her, and her husband John were the only couple that could lure Al out of the house for a dinner date. She knew Al liked John.

John Muir offered to drive all of them to Ann Arbor to get Al admitted. They met at the couple's house in the western suburbs. Al had been quiet all day. But when they arrived at the Muirs' home, he got out of the car and stood with his back against their garage door. That frightened look was back.

By the time they got on the road, it was late in the afternoon and raining.

Al sat in the front with John. Jan heard him mumbling during the forty-mile drive. In between disjointed phrases she heard him say, "I'm in over my head." And later, "The Cass Corridor."

Al's shoulders hunched together. When the car hit a bump, he jerked. He's so frightened, Jan thought.

"Are you comfortable, Al?" John said softly. "Are you cold?"

John patted him on the leg.

"Am I going to be OK?" Al began.

"You'll be fine, honey," Jan said.

"Am I going to be OK? *Am I going to be OK?* Am I going to be a bad boy? *I'm a bad boy.* Am I going to be OK? I've been bad. I've been bad. I am a bad boy."

She thought, what is he talking about? She wished they were at the hospital.

Then she thought she heard him crying. His shoulders got even closer together, as though they were trying to touch his breastbone.

"Do you still love me, Jan?"

"Of course I do, honey."

"Do you still love me, Jan? Do you love me, Jan? You're so good. You're so good to me, Jan. Jan, you've never done anything wrong. I'm so bad. *I'm so bad.* Am I going to be OK?"

"Al, of course I love you. You know I love you."

It went on for thirty miles. Al seemed to find comfort by leaning next to John, who often patted him on the leg. Her best friend's husband was such a steady, warm man, Jan thought. She was glad she had called her friends.

When they got to the emergency room Al cowered under the fluorescent lights. He wouldn't make eye contact with anyone. He sat down and shook. He was cold to the touch.

The wait dragged on. Eventually, tears began to stream down Al's cheeks. Doctors and nurses were scurrying about in response to a car accident case. A young child with a lacerated hand was crying. A man limped through the door

165

with a broken foot.

At first Jan thought the emergencies were upsetting her husband. Then she knew better. She thought, I've fooled myself into believing the hospital simply will give Al a big dose of psychotropic medication and release him in twenty-four hours. No, it isn't going to be that easy.

Neither was the admitting process. Eventually the four of them were escorted to a small interview room with a window. Al's behavior was getting stranger. At one point he marched, standing tall as he swung his arms mechanically. But most of the time he walked with his shoulders hunched. He clasped his hands in front of him as a four-year-old would do while exploring a room full of objects he was told not to touch.

Jan wanted her friends along during the intake, and John seemed to have a calming influence on Al. A psychiatrist came in and began asking Jan questions about Al's episode. She responded like a diagnostician.

"Dilated pupils, rapid breathing . . . labile emotions. Mute . . . Yes, it was acute onset . . . No, no suspicion of drugs."

When she saw the psychiatrist was scribbling down her answers she became tongue-tied. God, she thought, I'm acting like I'm conducting an intake interview again. This is my husband, not a patient. And her husband was crying again. Damn it, she thought, what are you, Janis Lucille Canty — his psychologist or his wife?

She turned to Al and comforted him. The psychiatrist's voice became distant. She found it hard to concentrate on his questions. One word kept coming to her mind.

"Preoccupied. I've never seen a man so *preoccupied*."

When the intake interview was over, the four of them were left alone. By then it was well after dark and storming heavily. The wind pelted the window glass with rain so loudly she had to look to see if it was hail.

Outside she noticed flashing lights, oscillating colors descending from the black above. One was flashing bright red, like some kind of ambulance in the sky. Then came a pulsating sound, as though massive amounts of air were being hurled against the hospital by a great bird's wing.

That noise. It was a helicopter, she realized. The hospital

heliport was right outside the window.

"I never knew this was here," Jan said, turning to her friends.

Al had been crying quietly. Now he began to weep loudly. She'd never seen Al weep like that. He took off his glasses. He began rubbing his face with his palms, as though he was trying to clean his skin of some kind of acid-laced dirt.

He began speaking between sobs, but she could hear only a few words. Later Celia and John would report what he was saying. The choppers were getting louder.

"They're coming," Al sobbed. "They're coming to take us all. They are coming to take the wicked and the evil. But they won't take the pure, the pure as snow."

He fell to his knees on the floor in front of the chair where Jan sat.

"I could have never done this to you," he told his wife. "You're so pure and they're so bad. I've been such a bad, bad boy. And you're so pure."

What in God's name, Jan thought, is he talking about? She looked quizzically at her friends. The choppers kept drowning Al out. There wasn't one, but two or three. They were arriving in succession. It must be some kind of big emergency.

"They're coming for the wicked and the evil. *They're coming.*"

His sobs escalated with the noise. The rain was hitting the window in sheets. She moved from the chair to the examining table. She had to move. She couldn't be still or be near him.

Al followed her, walking on his knees. He was frantic, pleading, trying to explain to her. Trying to tell her.

"I've been a bad, bad boy," he cried. "The things I've done. My birthday. *A fraud.* You're so pure. As pure as snow. *A fraud.* Everything I've done is *a fraud.* They'll find out Indianwood is *a fraud.* But you're so pure, as pure as snow."

He looked like a condemned man. She tried to calm him.

"No, honey. You're not bad. You're confused. You know Indianwood wasn't a fraud. I know it wasn't a fraud. I was there. I typed it, remember?"

Then he began stroking her body with his palms as

167

though she was some kind of pagan idol.

"I've been so very bad . . . And you're so pure . . . As pure as snow. As pure as snow . . . As pure as snow . . ."

It was a chant, like a call and response. His stroking began to frighten her. It was almost sexual.

"*As pure as snow* . . . As pure as snow . . . *As pure as snow* . . . As pure as snow . . . *As pure as snow.*"

Damn that noise, she cursed. She wanted to soothe him. How? She couldn't hear herself think. The helicopters were hacking the air to pieces. The window glass shook. She could feel herself beginning to unravel. My God, she thought, what is happening to my husband? *What is happening to me?*

"MOMMY," Al shouted. "MOMMY . . . You will take care of me. You'll never leave me. No matter what. Mommy. No matter what I've done. You'll never leave me. *Don't leave me, Mommy.* Don't leave me, Mommy. *Don't leave me, Mommy.*"

Jan Canty felt Celia Muir's hand on her arm. Her friend pulled her out of the interview room.

"Let John be alone with Al," Celia said. "Jan, let John be with Al."

"Ces, he's so sick," she began to sob. "I don't know what he's doing. I looked at him and I didn't even know him."

Once the paperwork was processed, Jan and her friends walked Al to his room in the psychiatric unit. He lay down on his bed. He didn't want to take off his shoes.

"Honey, want me to take them off?"

Al shook his head no. He didn't want to be covered with a blanket either.

"I don't want to stay here," Al said. "I just want to go home."

"You've been working way too hard," she said. "Now you can get some rest. Everything's going to be OK."

She paused to take a last look at him. He was completely spent.

"I love you," she said. "I'll be close. I'll come back tomorrow."

"God," Jan told Celia and John on the drive home.

168

"Maybe I should check in and book a bed right alongside Al. I'm exhausted."

It was the only light moment of the night. That evening Jan planned to sleep on her friend's couch. She didn't have the energy to drive herself home. It was well after midnight.

It had been some Friday the thirteenth.

Chapter 38

Celia and John Muir lay exhausted, but awake, trying to find some order in the disorderly events of the night.

"Do you think there's some truth to what he was saying?" John asked his wife.

They went over Al's ramblings again. They suspected Jan Canty comprehended only fragments. She was so worried she couldn't seem to connect with what he was saying. And what they'd heard was disjointed as well.

But on the drive out to the hospital, John heard Al talk about meeting some prostitute in the Cass Corridor on his birthday. Al said he had to help her.

"She really needs me," he'd whispered. "But I haven't told Jan. I haven't told Jan. I haven't told Jan."

The Muirs decided the scenario was feasible. They had heard Al Canty talk recently about Detroit's street life during an outing to a Mexican restaurant on the south side. He pointed out a couple of prostitutes on the street as the four of them rode to the restaurant in his new Buick Regal.

"See, that's how they do it, pick up their johns," he said. "Most of these girls are severely addicted to drugs."

But such offbeat subjects were not unexplored territory for Al. He often fascinated them with stories about patients and his father's criminal work in the courts. He had a vivid memory for detail. It was one of his entertaining qualities.

Celia and John felt as though they were in the classic Ann Landers dilemma. How, Celia said, do you tell your best friend that her husband may have screwed a whore on his fiftieth?

The question was too trying to even ponder at this hour. And Jan needed stability, not mystery. John walked into the kitchen at 3 A.M. and found her wide awake, making up a list at the table. That was Jan, John later said, organized and orderly. It was her way of coping. As for the prostitute, maybe Celia could talk with Jan about it some time.

But it would be many weeks before Celia Muir would be able to exorcise the mental picture of Al in that interview room.

"My God, John, did you see what he looked like?" Celia asked.

"He acted like somebody with brain-stem damage, repeating that stuff over and over," John said. "You know, after you two left, I told him I loved him. He was obviously very desperate and frightened. I wanted to give him something to hang on to.

"I said, 'Al, you know I really love you.' It seemed to soothe him."

Several days later Celia Muir picked up her ringing telephone and lost her breath.

"I'm looking for Jan," Al said. "I'm coming home. They're letting me out of here tomorrow. I'm looking for Jan."

She told Al that Jan had already left, then ended the call gracefully. She thought, what if he comes here looking for her? What am I going to do? I can't handle seeing him that way again.

Celia Muir was scared. She saw Al as unpredictable. *That was it.* That was what was so disturbing about the waiting room, the phone call. Al Canty, out of control. It was so foreign to his nature.

Celia and John talked about that point quite a bit one night. They decided they had come to know him pretty well over the years, as well as anyone *could* know Al Canty. Al had always been so analytical about everything, so aloof. John remarked that he talked with Al many times at length but never really knew how he felt.

"Everything he said was so censored, guarded. I've never actually felt like I knew him to the core."

Al always seemed uncomfortable when he and Jan dropped by their house. He couldn't sit in the living room more than a few minutes before saying, "Well, where *are* we going?"

Sometimes Celia and John thought that was because their

171

lifestyles were so different. Celia and Jan were steadfast friends but had pursued entirely separate life paths. Jan had chosen a career, while Celia embraced the work of home-making. She and John had a modest colonial, two daughters, and plans to adopt a third. Celia and Jan had a standing line about their differences.

"I come to your house for the noise," Jan would say. "I love it. You come to mine for the quiet. We ought to switch for a while."

But not for more than a couple of hours, Celia thought. She'd stick with the cookie batter and the paw marks of children. Celia and John saw themselves as independent, but at the same time *dependent* on each other. "When one of us is down, the other pulls up," Celia said. Sometimes they found serenity; other times they clashed. But their failings always balanced out.

Jan and Al never showed that kind of blood-and-guts unity, John and Celia agreed. They never had arguments. They had *disagreements* on *issues*. Their lives seemed so clearly split. She had her car. He had his. She had her schedule. He had his. She planned to have her practice. He had his. Time wasn't shared—it was delegated.

"How do you make it with these kids?" Jan said once. "With our lifestyle, we just couldn't fit it in."

Al acted as though he liked kids. Actually, he only *tolerated* them. Al Canty always wanted to be the center of attention. Celia thought that made him incompatible with children. Little ones have a way of upstaging most adults. She thought they'd made a wise decision to remain childless

John Muir, however, wondered if the decision was really Jan's to make. He saw her metamorphosis on the subject as a classic example of the way Al Canty delicately shaped his wife. When they first married, Jan was excited about one day being a mother. Al said he was all for fatherhood, but John suspected his heart was elsewhere.

Then Jan began questioning having children. John was convinced Al was cleverly spoon-feeding her: Her career was more important. Children didn't fit their lifestyle. She would have to make sacrifices.

Al never had to say he didn't want children. Finally, it was *Jan* that didn't want them. It was Jan that made Al get a vasectomy.

"Gee, you really changed your feelings about that, Jan," John commented one night.

"No," Jan said. "I never really did want children."

Al Canty, Celia and John agreed, liked control. They'd seen a prime example of that over the winter, when Jan and Al had a disagreement over where to park her new car. Al had that five-car garage, but she was forced to park her new Thunderbird in the driveway. Al said he needed the space. Al told her, "Well, if you really need a garage, you could keep your car over at my mother's."

That was four miles away.

"Ces, I told him, 'What am I supposed to do, Al? Walk over there in the snow?' "

John was flabbergasted she had to fight for a stall. But he knew Al catered to himself and was thrilled when others catered to him. Al talked of the best house, the best car, the best coffee, the best office address—the *best*. Not that he was materialistic. For Al, saying he had the best seemed more important than possessing it.

"Choice," another of his favorite words. "That dinner was very *choice*."

Al manipulated all of them when they went out as couples. They ended up at his choice of films. They dined at the restaurant of his choice. But rather than go through the hassle of outwitting him, everyone went along with the program. Al liked eateries where they knew him, where he got special attention. When they dined at a new place, he always made a rather evident effort to charm the waitress.

"Now what *is* your name?" he would say. "My, now that *is* a lovely uniform you have. I'm sure you're a very fine waitress."

If she bought the bullshit, Al was quite delighted with the restaurant. If she didn't, which often was the case, Al complained all night how the place fell below his standards.

Al, in fact, expected to be served most everywhere. He'd been coming to the Muir household for years, but he still insisted his coffee be brought to him as he sat in the chair.

"Oh, Celia, more coffee please, would you?"

Then he showered Celia with compliments.

"Celia, you're such a good mother," he'd say.

173

She knew he just wanted another cup of coffee.

Al rarely did anything menial. Home maintenance was foreign to him. Better to pay somebody else to do it, he'd say. He never labored over his cars. Better to hire somebody to do it.

Yet Al was always buying things for his garage.

"John, I better get a set of tools," he'd say.

Al and John then rushed to Sears for tools, but Al never opened the box when they returned. Al had three boxes of the same set sitting in the garage. And he never finished his cars. Just as one automobile was a small job away from full restoration, he abandoned it and started on the next. The appearance of undertaking a project seemed more important than the project itself.

Project Indianwood had those overtones. Jan once expressed puzzlement in their dating years that on some days Al's Indianwood guides didn't seem to do much. Al paid them by the hour often to just sit around in his suite all day and wait for his next move.

One day, after Al was admitted to the hospital, Celia and Jan talked about his babbling about the Indianwood program.

"Celia, Indianwood couldn't be a fraud because I typed the thing," Jan said. "He stayed awake well after midnight many times working on it."

"Maybe he copied it from somebody else," Celia offered.

"Couldn't have. It came out of his head. His memory isn't *that* good. He just must have been confused."

Celia knew Jan had a lot of trust in her husband. How could she not trust him? On the surface, at least, he always appeared to be putting her first. Jan had always been Al's star pupil, Celia thought, and she suspected he wanted to keep her in that role. Celia was shocked when she found out one day that Jan still did his typing at night. It was the same job he hired her for ten years ago. Why should a Ph.D., she thought, do his secretarial work?

But Celia knew Jan was dedicated and warmhearted. She was dedicated to Al, perhaps to a fault.

Celia and John reasoned Jan probably saw beyond Al's veneer. And despite Al's self-centered ways, the Muirs too had grown fond of the eccentric psychologist. John suspected that in a lot of ways, Al just was socially inept on a personal level. He often said the same superficial things over and over.

"How are you, Al?" John would ask, greeting him.

"I'm doing well. *Real* well. How about you?"

"Good, Al."

"You look like you're doing good. You look well. You look like you're doing *real* well."

It was as though Al didn't know what else to say, without risking an emotional revelation. But the Muirs felt there was a good man inside. He'd given John many rousing pep talks as John switched careers from car painter to stockbroker. One year he showed up at their doorstep bearing a Christmas tree.

There was a lot of child in him, too. Al once took an entire afternoon playing tea party with the Muirs' daughter. Halloween was more of a holiday than Christmas. He set out a half-dozen pumpkins for trick-or-treaters at his door. He delighted in telling ghost and murder stories on rainy nights and windy walks to Lake St. Clair.

"If only he didn't have to pump himself up so much," Celia said. "He really isn't fooling anybody."

"In fact," John said, "it makes him easier to be had."

The Muirs felt concerned for him. During several visits they made to University Hospital in the following weeks, they could see he was being forced to do things he'd never done. He had to fold his laundry. He had to make his own bed. He had to take part in soccer games for recreation.

Al appeared angry at his predicament.

"A psychologist being treated by psychiatrists," John said later. "And no doubt Al doesn't think they're anywhere near as talented as him."

Celia and John Muir found Al Canty's crisis embarrassing. They felt embarrassed for Al.

Chapter 39

Jan Canty drove directly from the Muirs' house back to the psych ward, taking a toothbrush and some clothes of John's that might fit Al.

"Now these are some things from John," Jan said.

Al was sitting on the edge of the bed. At first she thought he looked better.

"This is *his* shirt?" Al asked. "This is *John's* shirt?"

He caressed the flannel as though he'd waited a lifetime for it. Then he put it on, right over his bathrobe.

"This is *John's* shirt? This is *John's* shirt?"

He wore John's shirt for nearly two weeks — sometimes in the shower with the rest of his clothes. Jan would visit and find him under a baptism of spray. He couldn't get clean enough.

"I'm cleansing," he'd say.

On another visit he pointed to a room of an elderly fellow patient and said:

"My dad, Jan. My dad's in there."

"I guess Al's a lot sicker than I thought," Jan later admitted to Celia.

University psychiatrists told Jan Canty her husband needed an extensive evaluation. They suspected mind-altering drugs, because of the acute onset of his strange behavior.

That makes sense, Jan thought. It was a typical clinical course for someone his age with no prior history of hospitalization. The psychiatrists had questioned her repeatedly about that.

"Are you sure he's never had another episode like this?" one kept asking. "It's highly unusual for this to be the first at his age."

Yes, I know that, she thought, but she was sure he hadn't. Al certainly would have told her if something like this had happened before. She'd even called Gladys Canty about it. His mother was adamant. No, nothing like this had ever happened to her Buster before.

But Jan wasn't surprised when Al's drug screen came up negative. More than ever, she was convinced exhaustion was the culprit. And she could see why.

Back at the Fisher Building she was swamped. She was discovering how much she really didn't know about his practice and what it took to maintain their lifestyle. Both needed immediate attention. Al could lose everything in a couple of weeks. Contacting his patients took days. His appointment book was difficult to read. Finding patient phone numbers was complicated by a file system that should have been cleaned out and updated years ago. If his patients asked, she told them he was in the hospital for exhaustion.

The paper chase got worse. Al's idea of clinic organization was a cluttered conference table in one of the suite's rooms. The table was stacked with professional publications, unopened mail, grocery lists, and just plain junk. She wondered, how can anyone make any sense of this?

At first she was reluctant to open mail. She respected Al's privacy. He had always respected hers. But then when she found he'd be hospitalized longer than a week, she had to act. Someone has to pay the bills, she thought.

There was a pile of them. As she arranged the envelopes, one in particular jumped out at her. It was for their health insurance policy. She tore it open. It was $576—and overdue. My God, she thought, Al's in the hospital and they're going to cancel his policy.

She ripped through several more envelopes: office rent, an electric bill, the answering service—all overdue. These must be paid now, she thought. But how? There was a zero balance in Al's checking account. There were only a few dollars in hers. She couldn't find a savings account. She wasn't even sure if he had one.

Jan knew of only one place to go, though the proposition of approaching Al's mother struck her as humiliating. As it turned out, she'd have to make three such trips in April. For all practical purposes, Jan realized, Al was broke without his caseload.

Gladys Canty wrote more than $6,000 in checks to get

them through the month. Even then, Jan wasn't sure the office and household budgets were sound. Many of the bills had past-due amounts. She wasn't sure which ones might have been brought up to date by Al after the billing date.

This all has to change, she told herself. She didn't know whom to be more angry at — Al for failing to take her into his confidence, or herself for being so trusting. Nothing in her life, she thought, could top the embarrassment of asking for that money from Gladys Canty.

"As soon as Al gets better, all this is going to have to change," she told her mother-in-law. "This marriage can't last on those kind of terms."

Gladys Canty agreed.

"That's no way to live," Mrs. Canty said. "Alan Sr. and I had everything jointly owned and shared the knowledge of everything else."

But Jan Canty would have to wait. By the end of April, the University of Michigan psychiatrists had made their diagnosis: a major depressive reaction. True, Al had worked too hard for too long, they said. Stress was a factor. But also Al appeared to be holding in too many feelings.

She wondered what they were. But none of the hospital therapists had been able to penetrate his shell. The diagnosis made sense. What she'd seen as preoccupation had probably been withdrawal, a major symptom of depression.

The hospital staff suggested outpatient therapy once he was released. Al had already made his wishes known in that department. The day Jan found him incoherent in the office, Al had scribbled a name on his notepad: "Dr. Awes" — Dr. Lorraine Awes.

Jan had heard Al use the name, pronouncing it as in the Wizard of. She knew he'd gone to Dr. Awes for therapy as a young man. He had spoken highly of her. He told Jan she'd helped him deal with the pressures of becoming a psychologist.

Jan also had found something else scrawled on the notepad next to his desk that day: "Mother is the ultimate passive-aggressor." She knew the psychological term described someone who vents anger with nonassertive but annoying behavior, like someone habitually late for appointments.

Something was amiss between mother and son, Jan

178

thought. She'd sensed conflict in recent years but had never been able to discern it because both of them were so guarded about one another. Whatever it was, whoever treats my husband should know about that and a few other things as well, she decided.

Jan was thinking like his psychologist again. She decided the only way to shut it off was to type out everything she'd observed about Al before and during the breakdown:

Preoccupation. It had escalated. She'd found him alone in the den on several nights, looking as though he was outlining a new thesis without the benefit of paper and pen. It was difficult to get and keep his attention.

Insomnia. Psychomotor retardation. Apathy. Loss of appetite. Loss of interest in cars.

She let her mind drift further back. Al has never gotten over his father's death, she thought. He's never really let out his feelings. He's never really grieved over his loss.

The next day she delivered the list to Dr. Awes at her office in West Bloomfield. The psychiatrist was soft-spoken and, she guessed, was in her late sixties.

"I thought this might help you," Jan told her.

Dr. Awes accepted the paper politely. Jan wasn't expecting much more than that. She knew all about confidentiality. When Al got out, he would be in the psychiatrist's hands. Jan reasoned she had done everything she could. Maybe she could just be his wife now.

Gladys Canty did not speak with Dr. Awes, but with one of the psychiatrists treating her son at University Hospital. She wanted information on Buster but found herself answering questions rather than asking them.

The psychiatrist wanted to know how long Alan had been depressed, how often he had such spells. It was a routine she'd heard before. She hated the way psychiatrists were so evasive. No, she said, he'd never had anything like this happen before.

Gladys Canty didn't consider it important enough to reveal what she wrote off long ago as "a bad case of the nerves." But, in fact, her son had been hospitalized before for emotional troubles. The first episode was when her Bus was starting college. He got a notice from the draft board to appear for a physical. He completely fell apart.

"I can't go in the Army," he sobbed. "I just can't . . ."

She couldn't understand. He wasn't upset about military service when he was at ROTC camp just after high school. He was just a little homesick. She still had the letter he wrote to her. He was eighteen years old, and it began:

Dear Mommy,

Before I went to bed, I thought I better get a letter off to my . . . best girl . . . I don't mind this Army life too much, but it's not like being home . . .

But the draft-board letter made Bus so anxious he could hardly function. Al Sr. called his good friend, psychologist James Clark Maloney. Dr. Maloney recommended Al Sr. take his son to the Haven, a private sanitarium in Oakland County. Meanwhile, Dr. Maloney would find a top psychiatrist.

Al Sr., however, couldn't drive him to the Haven. He had an out-of-town speaking engagement. So on a Sunday afternoon, Mrs. Canty drove him out there herself. On Monday, she also appeared at the draft board and explained her son had been hospitalized. He was classified 4-F.

A week later Dr. Maloney had him released under the care of a Dr. Awes. He went for sessions several times a week.

Back then, she thought Bus's therapy would never end. She recalled it as lasting several years. The drain on Al Sr.'s salary was substantial. Dr. Awes's office was located nearly an hour away in rural Clarkston. Sometimes she drove him herself and waited in the car.

One particular trip always stood in her memory. Bus came skipping from the office, grinning widely.

"Why, Buster, what are you grinning for?" she said.

"Well, Ma, I had a good session," he said.

"What was so good about it?"

"Oh, I told her what a witch you were."

"Alan, *you did?*" She hoped he wasn't serious.

"No, Ma, you know I wouldn't say that."

"Well, you're feeling awful good about something. Did you really talk about me?"

"Oh, sure. I talked about both you and Pa."

Gladys Canty disliked all the mystery.

Later, Alan met Maggie. After they were married, Gladys Canty assumed the sessions had stopped. He didn't come to them anymore for the money, at least.

She thought her son's emotional troubles were behind him. Bus and Maggie began their marriage in a townhouse downtown. His first wife, then a teacher at Wayne State, apparently covered most of the bills. Bus was engrossed in his internship at Merrill-Palmer Institute. Later they bought the house on Fisher Road in Grosse Pointe. For years everything seemed fine.

Then one day he came over terribly upset. Maggie was leaving him, he said. She wasn't happy with their financial arrangements, he said. Gladys Canty knew her son's first wife as an independent woman not afraid to speak her mind.

The day she left, Buster again went into a real tailspin. He sobbed and blamed himself. Then over a period of days he became listless and morose. He couldn't work. Al Sr. took over his practice for several weeks. Bus said he was seeing Dr. Awes.

But the divorce continued to generate trauma, for Gladys Canty's husband as well as her son. Bus and Maggie had been married nine years, and her son had to have a witness testify that the marriage was not salvageable. She'd assumed Al Sr. would take that role. In fact, she sensed her husband was excited at the prospect of returning to a Detroit court where he was so well known.

A few days before the hearing, however, Bus came to her with a request: Could she tell Pa that she was going to be his witness?

"Ma, I just know if Pa goes down there he's going to see Maggie and say something—work her over and do something embarrassing," he said. "Ma, we don't want anything like that."

That, she insisted, would be a request he would have to make for himself. And her son did, very reluctantly.

Al Sr. never let his son know it, but Mrs. Canty could tell her husband was upset. The day she and Bus went to court, Al Sr. stayed in bed well into the afternoon. He brooded about it for days.

After the divorce in 1972, Bus seemed to find new purpose, especially after he met Jan. She remembered her son bringing Jan over the first time.

"Ma, isn't she beautiful?" he kept saying. "Isn't she just beautiful?"

Now, Gladys Canty couldn't imagine what might prompt a breakdown. She couldn't help but think of Dr. Awes as the University Hospital psychiatrist skirted her inquiries with expressions she knew all too well.

"We're doing a complete evaluation," the psychiatrist said.

Why, she thought, do they always have to be so secretive?

Chapter 40

By May 9, the dogwood blossoms in Ann Arbor were so thick they would fall any day. Jan Canty noticed them through the window as she waited for final paperwork on her husband's discharge.

Only then did it occur to her. It was spring. She wondered to herself, how long have the trees been in bloom? How could I not have noticed? That's right, she thought, I haven't needed an overcoat in quite a while.

What a four weeks it had been, the last few spent trying to convince Al to remain in the hospital. By late April, he not only was on the rebound, he was anxious to get back to work. But he needed *rest,* she told him. After all, work put him under in the first place, a notion Al himself readily agreed was true.

But Jan also could tell her husband wasn't comfortable discussing his breakdown. He seemed embarrassed by it. If she brought it up, he began to get that little-boy look she knew so well. He couldn't look her in the eye when he got that way. She suspected that Al felt as though he had let her down by falling apart.

She wished he wasn't so concerned about her. He needs to look after himself, she thought. He works too hard at trying to please me.

Well, she thought, that's got to change, along with a few other things. She had questions that needed answers. She was worried about their finances and her ignorance of their budget.

But she also decided now was not the time to confront her husband. He seemed so fragile. He was compliant and hesitant. As they waited for the discharge, she noticed his back was slightly slumped. Even his posture looked submissive.

Jan was anxious about the discharge. The psychiatrist emphasized that Al not return to work immediately. He

183

should avoid stress. She heartily agreed. But she knew her husband. On several visits Al had brought up money.

"I'm sure I've run up a lot of bills, and I've got to get them paid," he'd said. "We need the money."

"Al, I don't think you're ready," she'd said.

Jan held his arm as they walked out the hospital's door. Al took a deep breath of the spring air. Then they noticed some sort of celebration under way on the hospital grounds.

"Let's go see what they're doing over there," he said.

A big tent had been set up. Dozens of people were milling about. Hospital staffers were pouring coffee and dishing out ice cream and cake. Jan and Al looked at a big banner strung across the front of the tent. It said "Patient Appreciation Week."

The atmosphere was festive, but Jan Canty felt awkward as she and Al made small talk. The world seemed superficial. They seemed superficial. There Al was, trying to minimize what had happened to him. Here she was, watching her every word, worried that she might upset him. How everything had changed in just one winter!

On the way back to Detroit Al insisted they stop at the Fisher Building before going home to the big Tudor. She hoped he would be pleased by what he found. She'd organized the big, cluttered conference table. She'd thrown out the notices of conferences he'd never go to or books he'd never buy. That way there would be less of a backlog for him to plow through.

"What happened to all my stuff?" he asked.

She smiled, explaining the new order.

"This pile is for this, that pile is for that . . ."

But he became unsettled by the arrangement. A few minutes later she found him sitting in the big leather chair in his counseling room. He was thumbing through his appointment book.

"Don't think you're going back to work right away, Al Canty," she said. "It's not a good idea."

They had a discussion about it right then and there. They agreed he would wait several weeks before seeing patients, and then it would only be a few at home. There would be fewer hours and more vacations. Saturdays would be half days, instead of eight to eight. And the coffee. He was going to have to switch to decaffeinated coffee.

"OK, Jan," Al said. "I won't go right back to work."

He was saying exactly what she wanted to hear. For some reason, she had the nagging suspicion he really didn't mean it.

Chapter 41

Downtown attorney *Ted White* had mixed feelings when Al Canty called him to say he should come in for his regular 3:30 P.M. appointment at the Fisher Building. He hadn't seen his therapist in nearly five weeks.

Now he wasn't sure he really wanted to make the May 15 appointment. Not that he didn't need the help. He just couldn't decide whether therapy was doing him any good.

White wanted a cure to his mental turmoil — and he wanted it quick. That's why he had gone to W. Alan Canty in the first place, following a thirty-two-day stay in a psychiatric ward of a private hospital in Grosse Pointe for severe depression.

White saw his indecision about resuming therapy with Canty as typical of his own neurotic personality. At forty-five, Ted White was a vice-president in one of the largest banks in the state. But the title was more impressive on his business card than on his tax return. By white-collar standards, his income was as modest as his Harper Woods address.

Financial insecurity had lured him into trouble in the first place. The previous summer, following an internal Armageddon, he made The Big Decision. He took a second mortgage and sank twenty-five thousand dollars into a speedy film development franchise. He bought the seventy-seventh store in the national chain and planned to buy two or three more.

But the seventy-seventh store was the franchise's last. The parent company folded. In less than five months Ted White was broke. When he couldn't shave in the morning without sobbing, he checked himself into the psychiatric unit. There he also found out he was an alcoholic, and he began attending AA meetings.

One day after his release, a friend handed White an excerpt from a book by psychiatrist David D. Burns. It was called

Feeling Good: The New Mood Therapy. Dr. Burns wrote about a new "cognitive therapy" that was effective, practical, and, most importantly, short-term.

White wrote Dr. Burns at the University of Pennsylvania, asking for a list of cognitive therapy specialists in Detroit. He received the name of W. Alan Canty.

"They say this kind of therapy is fast," he told Canty on his first visit in early January.

"Can be three to six months," Canty said.

The psychologist said he usually found it counterproductive spending month after month psychoanalyzing parental conflicts and flaws in childhood development.

"What's important is what we're doing in the here and now," Canty said. "And, we're going to stay in the here and now."

White explained his recent financial disaster, his hospitalization, and his membership in AA.

"I recommend you stay with AA, Ted," he said. "It's a good program, though I tend to think there's too much reliance on God. I like to put my faith in my own reasoning."

And rational thinking was what cognitive therapy was all about, Canty said. He added that he'd studied under Dr. Burns. But he preferred the works of Albert Ellis, another former teacher.

He assigned a lengthy reading list for White: *Feeling Good, How to Be Your Own Best Friend, The Psychology of Self-Esteem, The Neurotic Personality of Our Time, Our Inner Conflicts, When I Say No, I Feel Guilty,* and *A New Guide to Rational Living.*

White bought all of them except for a copy of the Ellis and Harper rational-living book, which Canty handed him.

"I read it at least once a year," he said. "And you should too, for the rest of your life. It really has kept my thinking straight."

White found *A New Guide to Rational Living* compelling reading. He underlined pertinent paragraphs and sentences with pencil. One chapter quoted a self-help group called the Associated Rational Thinkers on the benefits of rational-emotive thinking:

Rational thinking has the following four characteristics: (1) It [bases itself] primarily on objective fact as opposed to subjective opinion. (2) If acted upon, it most likely will result in the preservation of your life and limb rather than premature death or injury. (3) If acted upon, it produces your personally defined life's goals more quickly. (4) If acted upon, it prevents undesirable personal and/or environmental conflict.

White and Canty had begun to discuss RET in their sessions before the psychologist became ill. At first White suspected Canty was a psychologist accustomed to getting results. Early on, the therapist offered him a fast cure for cigarettes. He had a couple dozen cartons of nicotine-free cigarettes in his office. He handed White a carton. White tried a couple but couldn't stand the smell. His wife smoked the rest and quit. But eventually she was smoking again.

Before his psychologist's hospitalization, White was growing discouraged by Canty's therapy as well. He had read that in the cognitive approach the therapist took an active role in sessions. But he hadn't seen Canty get that involved. If he wasn't pouring one cup of coffee after another, he was answering the telephone. Without a secretary, he took a lot of calls.

Often Canty was late for the three-thirty appointment. He'd come down the hall apologizing, offering various excuses. He was tied up in court evaluations. He had work at the county prosecutor's office. He was helping a Cass Corridor prostitute in the hospital.

Ted White could see how Canty had worked himself into physical collapse. Listening to him make those appointments, White had determined that the therapist was taking patients during every waking hour. He couldn't understand why anyone would need to work that much, especially at rates approaching one hundred dollars an hour.

Well, White thought, maybe the sessions will improve now that his psychologist was rested up.

When he arrived for the May 15 session, Ted White would find the psychologist on time, exuding confidence, and more at ease. Canty would tell him that he had lightened his work load, switched to decaffeinated coffee, and was "learning to relax" a little more.

"I guess, more or less," Canty would say, "I've got to start practicing what I preach."

Chapter 42

There are also those persons who optimistically think that emotional problems are just temporary, or situational, in nature. Unfortunately, this is seldom the case.

— W. ALAN CANTY,
Principles Of Counseling and Psychotherapy.

John Fry and Dawn Spens had accepted the inevitable. Dr. Al Miller wasn't coming back. When Dawn tried to telephone him, she got a female voice. "Dr. Canty's office." That was his colleague, Al once told her. She wasn't to leave messages. She should hang up if he didn't answer. Before, Al himself often answered with a simple "hello."

They had expected the five thousand dollars on Friday the thirteenth. Fry said it was the wrong move on the wrong day. "It's over — too much pressure too quick. It was good while it lasted. But we pushed him too far."

Dawn hustled to finance two drug habits ballooned by four months of prosperity. She went from collecting Comerica envelopes filled with crisp cash to squeezing johns for tips of worn ten- and twenty-dollar bills. Her workday was no longer limited to the lunch hour. There was no talk between her and John about the house in West Bloomfield.

On May 6 Dawn Spens was arrested again by the vice squad. After she was released, they got into an argument over drugs and money. It seemed as though John always got a bear's share of both. The argument ended when John swung a broomstick across her thighs.

Later Dawn complained she was coming down with the flu. She had a fever, chills, and sweats. She kept working nonetheless.

Lucky Fry was sprawled on the sofa when Dawn returned from the streets May 10 just after the lunch hour. She sashayed into the apartment and left the door wide open behind her.

"What the fuck are you so happy about?" John said.

"Look who's here!"

John looked up to see someone's head poking around the edge of the doorway. He focused on a familiar grin, wide as ever.

"Hi, John," said Dr. Al Miller.

Al walked over to the couch in his Chaplin toddle and shook John's hand. He eyed the small apartment like a man returning to his boyhood home.

Al was eager to explain his absence. He said he'd gone to a medical conference in Ann Arbor with a colleague and crashed in an automobile accident on the way back. He spent four weeks in University Hospital, two of them in a coma. He just was released yesterday. Al went on a good five minutes with the story. Fry forgot most of the details, but he wouldn't forget his first impression.

"I didn't think the punk was in no hospital," he later said. "I figured he had tried to get away. He had tried to deal Dawn out of his life, but realized he couldn't do it. For some reason, he couldn't live without her. The next move was up to him."

The trick already had made it. He already had asked Dawn Spens if the five-thousand-dollar deal still stood.

Chapter 43

The psychopath should never be trusted.
> — W. ALAN CANTY,
> Henry Ford Community College lectures

Dr. Al Miller brought a stethoscope on his next visit to the Homewood Manor. He also brought five thousand dollars in cash, most of it in hundred-dollar bills.

Dawn Spens was suffering shortness of breath. Al listened to her chest and back with the instrument. She asked him if she should go to the hospital. He pulled off the earpieces and told her to get plenty of bed rest. She really didn't have much choice. She was so weak she could hardly walk. She threw up anything she ate.

As for the five thousand dollars, the cash prompted John Fry to move his clothes to a friend's apartment down the hall. John said he was still making arrangements to leave town — but he had moved out. Before that could be pursued, however, the two men had a more pressing concern. Dawn was gasping for air and had a temperature of 104 degrees. She wanted Al to take her to the hospital.

"Are you sure you want to go?" he said.

"*Yes,* I'm sure," she said.

Al drove Dawn and John to the emergency room at Detroit Receiving Hospital. He didn't accompany them into the facility. He said he had a full schedule that day. But again, she didn't have to wait for admission. It was May 11.

Physicians diagnosed Dawn as suffering from bacterial endocarditis — a blood infection in the heart, common among IV drug addicts. Doctors had no difficulty determining she was one. Her groin abscess still was open from her hospital stay in January. She had it packed with a fine-mesh

192

gauze. She confessed to doctors she'd been using the area for injections.

The bacterial endocarditis was a bigger concern. It was potentially fatal. With the disease, bacteria build up on the valves of the heart, forming clots that could break loose and flow to the brain and other organs. Her physicians ordered heart tests. She would have to stay in the hospital at least twenty-eight days while they gave her an intravenous antibiotic.

John Fry, meanwhile, would have no problem keeping himself occupied. In the Cass Corridor, five thousand dollars made him a wealthy man. He could stay high for weeks. He planned on keeping a low profile, but Dr. Al Miller and Dawn Spens had other plans for him.

Though Dawn was getting fifty milligrams of hospital Demerol three times a day, she wanted more drugs. A couple of times Al drove to the Homewood to see John, who gave heroin to Al for Dawn. Then Dawn had Fry introduce Al to one of his drug connections, a small-time Corridor dealer who lived in the Homewood named *Gene Johnson*. Some days Al brought Johnson to her room with the drugs. On others he visited Johnson and brought the heroin himself, smuggling in one to four packs and syringes she could use with the IV.

She spent a lot of time just watching TV and staying stoned.

"Basically it was my own fault that I kept doing it," she later told another addict. "But I seriously think the man wanted to watch me kill myself."

Al also said he knew all the doctors who were treating her. He had discussed her case with them, he said. One day, Dawn watched him step into the hall with a third-year medical student who was assigned to her case. When Al returned, he said he knew her from a class he once taught. Dawn would forget the student's name but remembered that she had a large diamond engagement ring.

Al also had some ongoing stories about himself. He said that while he was in the hospital, the home he owned in Grosse Pointe had been burglarized. Thieves had trashed every room. He had a crew of workers repairing the damages.

193

Then one day, after a visit, Al complained that his new Buick Regal had been stolen from the hospital parking lot.

Back at the Homewood Manor, John Fry was shooting a hundred dollars' worth of mixed jive and Dilaudid at a sitting, while trying to dodge his own series of bad breaks. Street creditors were after him for a three-hundred-dollar outstanding debt. He'd borrowed the money to get Dawn out of jail earlier in the month. Fry planned to pay them off with part of the eighteen hundred he had left from Dr. Miller's payoff money. One night his creditors threatened to send over a wrecking crew. It was the same group that one time clubbed a friend senseless with a baseball bat. He told them they'd get their money that evening.

That night Fry made a drug purchase at one of the Homewood's dope pads. He had the eighteen hundred in his wallet. He pulled off his pants so another addict could hit him in the leg. Later he found that his wallet was missing. He suspected another junkie stole it when his pants were down. He returned to the apartment and a fight ensued. Another addict shot him in the hand with a pistol, he later told friends. The bullet cut away the flesh of the middle finger. He wrapped the hand with gauze but didn't seek medical treatment.

The third week in May John called Frank McMasters in Alanson. He told him he had to get out of Detroit. Then he went to Detroit Receiving and visited Dawn to tell her his plans.

He made Dawn promise she would taper her habit and ultimately quit using in the hospital. John said he would get medical care in the north and kick his habit. When she was released, he would send for her from Alanson. Maybe he could get a job there.

They had lived in the Homewood Manor for nearly eight months. Eight months was too long, John Fry said.

"I've got to get out of here and get clean," he told her. "I'm going to Frank and Cheryl's. It's got to change. If you keep using you're going to end up dead from the dope. And I'm going to end up dead because these motherfuckers in the street are going to kill me."

Then he headed north, leaving Dawn in the care of Receiving Hospital and Dr. Al Miller.

Chapter 44

As she looked at the records of Dawn Marie Spens, third-year medical student Barbara Tacoma found the prospect of treating yet another addict depressing.

Her twelve-week rotation in internal medicine at Receiving Hospital had offered a lot of medical knowledge, but not a lot of hope. So many of the hospital's ample caseload of addicts had thick hospital files that told the same story. They received medical attention for drug complications only to return to the streets and end up admitted again from further abuse.

The twenty-four-year-old aspiring doctor just wanted to finish her studies and return home to western Michigan. She had a fiancé and internship waiting for her in Grand Rapids — her kind of town, where family values were practiced as though they were on the endangered species list.

Tacoma could see Dawn Spens was in serious trouble, and it wasn't only her endocarditis. She had an open abscess on her leg. Her admission chart said it all: a "deep, foul-smelling sinus track draining purulent exudate."

Tacoma was moved that someone five years her junior was so physically spent. She expected Dawn, with her medical file of a hard-core addict, to be indifferent to her bedside manner. That impression changed when they began to talk.

"Oh . . . let me see your ring," Dawn said.

The young addict complimented her on her three-quarter-karat solitaire. Barbara held out her hand and told her about her fiancé and their wedding later that year.

"What are you going to do?" Dawn asked. "Tell me about your wedding."

She was surprised to find Dawn so pleasant. Dawn had the vocabulary of a college freshman, rather than the street vernacular Tacoma had grown accustomed to hearing. Dawn asked intelligent questions. She gave articulate answers.

Over the next three weeks Tacoma found herself spending more time with the young addict than with any of her other patients. She sensed Dawn liked her, and she liked Dawn. She found their visits uplifting. Her heart went out to her. Here, she thought, is someone who would respond to help.

One day she asked Dawn if there was anyone special in her life. She said she had her boyfriend John, but she didn't seem all that enthused.

On another day, they talked about her drug addiction.

"You know there is help available," she told her.

"I know, I know," Dawn said. "I should get help. I should. It's all the people I've been around."

At first, Barbara Tacoma had the feeling Dawn was just appeasing her. She made it a point to do a little digging. Where was her family?

"My parents don't care what I do," she said. "My parents don't care where I am."

Then an ultrasound examination was made of Dawn Spens's heart. It showed an abnormal mass of echoes in the right atrium. There was the possibility of a clot. Tacoma was there when a resident delivered the news.

"You're not just fooling around with anything here," he said. "This is for real. With a thrombus sitting on your heart, it could be any moment and you're gone."

For the first time Dawn seemed to take seriously what Tacoma had been telling her about her habit. She wanted to know all the possible medical scenarios. She said she was going to seek treatment. A number of options were available through hospital social services.

"You're right," Dawn told her in one heart-to-heart talk. "I need help. I can't do it alone."

One day, early in her stay, Tacoma saw Dawn entertaining a visit by a casual-looking but professionally dressed man. Dawn was excited, even proud, when she introduced him.

"This is Dr. Al Miller, from Harper-Grace Hospitals. He's a psychiatrist — an M.D."

Dr. Miller extended his hand and grinned, downplaying his credentials with a self-disparaging remark. Later Dawn explained he was a friend of the family. Her family had deserted her, but Dr. Miller hadn't. He was trying to help her out, she said.

That day, Barbara and Dr. Miller went into the hall outside Dawn's room and chatted. The psychiatrist wanted to know all the details of her condition. He wanted to know her progress. He had a good grasp of medical terminology. Tacoma didn't have to clarify any of her statements, at least.

Tacoma asked him a couple of questions about his work, but he was evasive. She had done a six-week tour in psychiatry at Harper-Grace but couldn't recall seeing his name. But that wasn't unusual. Psychiatrists often spent a lot of time in their offices.

Dr. Miller also had a strange demeanor, she thought. Maybe it was his all-knowing smile, as though he knew something she didn't. She hated to stereotype his specialty, but he wasn't the first shrink she'd met with that kind of look. A lot of them were secretive. It seemed to go with the field. After he left, it struck her that she'd learned little about him, though they talked a good five minutes or more.

In time she noticed Dr. Miller visited every day at lunch. Tacoma was impressed that an M.D. was taking that kind of time from his practice. She knew few who would make that kind of sacrifice, even for a nice girl like Dawn who really needed the help.

Two other things struck her as odd. When Dr. Miller was around, Dawn seemed quite carefree about her body. Hospital gowns could be quite revealing, and Dawn made no effort at modesty. She would casually walk around the room, her bare buttocks showing in the back. Also, Dr. Miller always arrived with a reddish brown overnight bag made of parachute material. It was not the kind of valise she'd expect to see with a physician. It looked very unprofessional.

One day during a break a thought struck her. She remembered other addicts caught using street drugs in the hospital. Dawn had never been screened because nothing led anyone to believe she was using; she was making progress. Plus, her room was close to the nurses' station. But that bag of Dr. Miller's got Tacoma wondering.

"You know," she told a resident, "I wonder if that guy has a bag of goodies with him."

197

Then she felt silly for saying anything. She'd seen too many movies. She'd been in Detroit too long.

In early June, Dawn got good news. Follow-up ultrasounds showed no sign of a thrombus on her heart. Doctors planned to release her on June 10, but Barbara Tacoma wouldn't be there for the discharge. She was returning to Grand Rapids.

The medical student stopped by Dawn's room to say goodbye. She was happy the girl finally had gotten serious about getting help. Barbara Tacoma wished her well. It was nice, she thought, to leave Detroit on a good note.

Later it soured considerably. Dawn Spens, she was told, refused help when the hospital's social services department offered her treatment for drug addiction.

Chapter 45

Jan Canty wondered if there wasn't some kind of springtime conspiracy afoot to foil her husband's recovery. And Al wasn't helping his own cause either. Already he was back to work.

"We need the money," he said. "And it will be good for me to get back into my routine. I really feel, you know, at loose ends without my schedule."

Then, only five days after his discharge, she got a disturbing call at home. It was Al. He wanted her to pick him up at the Fisher.

"Jan, my car's been stolen."

She was upset. Al mistook her anger as being directed at him.

"It's not my fault," he said.

"That's not the point," she said. "You just don't need this kind of pressure right now . . . What happened?"

He said that the Regal had been snatched on West Grand Boulevard, right outside the Fisher. Running late from a visit to the prosecutor's office, he'd left it at a meter instead of parking the car in the building's garage.

She guessed something about the car made it attractive to thieves. When he first got the Buick, the wire wheel covers were stolen. He complained about that for weeks. It was uncharacteristic of him to be so irritated that long about anything.

They had a good talk when she picked him up. A little rational-emotive thinking was in order. They lived in a large urban area, she and Al reasoned, and statistically these things were bound to happen. It was just a matter of time before they too would be victimized. They could get by without the car. Al could use her new Thunderbird.

Police eventually recovered the Buick. It had been stripped

of its radio, battery, wheel covers, and other easily fenced items. It was repaired in three weeks and returned.

But the second week in June, the Regal was stolen again. They had just finished processing the paperwork on the first claim. This time, Al said, the car had been taken outside Detroit Receiving Hospital, where Jan worked. Al said he'd stopped there on his lunch hour to visit one of his patients, who was ill after recent surgery. The car was recovered a few days later. The same items were stripped.

Al seemed more accepting. They tried to joke about it.

"Well, we sure know the claim routine," he said.

But Jan felt something was closing in on her. She couldn't put her finger on it, but she felt more vulnerable than at any time in her life. On Good Friday her parents' home in Arizona had been burglarized. Now the car, twice. All this on top of Al's hospitalization. It was as though some hidden force was at work in their lives. She felt compelled to act.

She urged Al to have alarm systems installed on both the cars and the house. The home security system cost three thousand dollars, but she saw it as a good investment. With Al's hours and her coming and going, the big Tudor was too easy a mark for thieves.

Jan also decided to document their valuables. She'd made photography her hobby since she got out of postgraduate school. Now she put it to some practical use. She loaded up her Pentax and shot photos of every room in the house and each office in the Fisher suite. She arranged the pictures, by room, in a small album listing furniture, valuables, and their worth on an adjacent page. She stored the album in the Fisher, the negatives in a dining room cabinet. Al was impressed by the effort.

While Jan fought paranoia, Al eased day by day into his predictable patterns. She could see he still wasn't sleeping well. Sometimes he sweat heavily in the night. He said he'd switched to decaffeinated coffee. But then she discovered he'd compromised on that promise. He had concocted a new blend of half and half.

Within a month after his release he was filling his days with work again and his spare time alone with his own thoughts. He lingered alone in his home office or headed directly from a late patient session to his tub. There were fewer walks to Lake St. Clair and more time spent in front of the TV. Several times she cozied up to him, rubbed his shoulder, and asked him what was bothering him.

"I'm working on it in therapy," he said.

Al was seeing Dr. Awes once a week, and for that she was grateful. He never talked about his therapy, but she sensed it was doing him some good. The psychiatrist had tapered him off the lithium prescribed by doctors at University Hospital. And though Al was approaching the same stressful pace Jan felt had gotten him into trouble in the first place, he was doing much better than during those first awkward days after his release.

One night, when she felt he was ready, Jan told him about the trauma she'd gone through with the bills during his absence.

"Al," she said. "I need to know about the money, where it is, you know?"

"Well, what do you need, Jan?" he said. "How much? Let me see what I can come up with."

No, she didn't want money, she told him. She wanted to know their financial standing. Did they have savings? Were they overextended? Shouldn't she have a list of his accounts?

"Well, Jan," he said. "We've got an IRA. We're set. You don't need to worry about that."

"Al, its just not a very wise way to do things," she countered. "I have to be included. What if you got into a car accident?"

The discussion ended as others had on that subject many times before. He promised he'd show her his financial system when he got time. It was all very complex, he said.

She thought, what's the big deal? It's not as though I'm some gold digger preparing to take a steam shovel to his net worth. But she felt uncomfortable pushing the point.

Once Jan realized she couldn't keep him from working, she urged him to pursue some diversions, to take some time for his hobbies. As for his quest for paving bricks, he had all he would ever need. She suggested he work on his cars.

Through the years Al had usually disappeared into the garage on his day off to tinker. Even more, he enjoyed being around car buffs. They went to meets at the fairgrounds and the shows at Cobo Hall. They had seats for the Detroit Grand Prix. On Friday afternoons he used to go to one of several classic car shops on the east side and shoot the breeze with its owner.

But that all stopped when he turned fifty.

Jan was pleased when one Friday afternoon he followed her suggestion. He put on a pair of blue jeans, saying he was going to trade some parts. That's what he liked best — wheeling and dealing the rare parts back and forth with other collectors. He would sell quite a few in the next few months.

Jan saw it as a good sign. She knew his enchantment with automobiles went back many years. A child's car called a Jeep Junior he'd built at twelve was in the garage collecting dust. He had carted it with him over the years from one residence to another. Now he had five adult toys. Most of them were classics in various stages of restoration: an old Studebaker, a '32 Miller Indianapolis race car, a '41 Hollywood Graham, and a '32 Ford Cabriolet, the one they'd been chauffeured around in on their wedding day.

Then there was the red Porsche, the only one that ran well enough to drive. Al said it was a replica of the sports car James Dean was driving at high speed when he was killed. He never let Jan behind its wheel, though he knew it was her favorite.

"Jan-Jan, the car is too dangerous," he always said.

Yet Al often took it out. Sometimes he even sped off in the rain with the top down, though the wipers didn't work.

That didn't make much sense. If it's so damned dangerous, she thought, why does he keep getting behind the wheel?

Chapter 46

Frank McMasters looked at the man in the fetal position on the floor of his living room and wondered if maybe he had judged his old nemesis too harshly.

At first he doubted John Fry really wanted to get clean. Before, such proclamations were nothing more than diversionary tactics. They bought him time — time to figure out a new angle on Cheryl, time to come up with some face-saving move.

"Frank, everything is just coming apart around me, man," he'd said when he telephoned from Detroit. "Does the offer still stand? Can I come up to your place to clean up?"

"Sure, it still stands," Frank had said. "But no fuckin' around this time."

And John hadn't tried to leave, even when his body was paying him back for every fix. Frank never saw him in worse shape than on May 23, the day a friend drove him to Alanson from Detroit. An open cavity ran down his middle finger into the web of his swollen left hand. It looked like a drug abscess to Frank and Cheryl. But John said he had been shot. He also had an infected abscess in his foot.

"Mixed jive — in pusher packs of ten every hour," John said. "My body's burned up, man."

Frank and Cheryl wanted to take him to the hospital. But John had insisted on kicking first. They put a small mattress on the living room floor. John gave Frank thirty of his last thirty-five dollars. He asked Frank to buy three bottles of Jack Daniel's. As he withdrew from the heroin, John drank nearly a fifth a day. The rest he poured on his infected hand. Frank couldn't help but laugh. Even while going cold turkey, Lucky Fry had a flair for drama.

But Frank knew exactly what John was enduring. Frank

203

had been addicted to morphine as a teenager. He still got deep satisfaction from the knowledge that he hadn't shoved a dope spike through his skin in more than fifteen years, or even smoked a joint. Seeing John on his floor reminded him again why.

Frank's house in Alanson was as good a place as any to detox. The two-bedroom was built on the edge of the vacation village known for its nearby hunting and fishing. The house was left to him by his late father. Except for the flow of tourist traffic between Petoskey and the Mackinac Bridge, nothing much ever happened in Alanson. Frank liked it that way. He'd driven trucks out of Detroit but preferred the construction jobs that came and went with the seasons in the north.

What a junkie's soap opera it had been since he met Cheryl and John. Frank sometimes wondered why he put up with it. But he sensed a basic decency in Cheryl. If only she could stay away from John and the dope. Her old boyfriend seemed to have cast some kind of spell over her. He'd given up trying to understand.

Several times Frank and John almost came to blows when they first met. Once Frank told John if he ever hit Cheryl again, he would show him what a real ass kicking was like. Another time John suggested they take their difference outside. Frank walked out into the middle of the street. "I'm out here, John, waiting for you," he said. John never came out.

But those tensions left when John met Dawn. Now John seemed to have a genuine concern for Cheryl. That was the important word—*seemed*. It was part of the enigma of Lucky Fry. Only John knew what John was thinking, and Frank wasn't even sure about that.

Frank did know that John, among other things, was a habitual bullshitter. But there was something about John he liked. If only he didn't expend so much energy substituting BS for what he possessed in real talent. John could be a captivating conversationalist. He had a philosophical approach to life. But often it was convoluted.

John lived by a self-defined code of ethics—subject to change if the situation required it. "You know that's not me,

Frank" and "That's not my way, mon" were favorite expressions. The big question was: What was his way?

Lucky Fry would be the first to admit he was a pimp, a junkie, a thief, and a con artist. But this, John always reasoned, was not entirely of his own choosing. It was generated by the failings of those around him. Every time he tried to free himself from the lifestyle with a grand plan — invariably an illegal one — it backfired and he ended up back in prison. The streets were the only place he could cope.

Frank had seen John try to go cold turkey once before, more than a year ago. On the second day Frank had handed John a weed whip and put him to work on a two-foot growth of grass out front. John spent the day hacking away, trying to sweat the dope out. He almost stumbled into a bog on the edge of the property.

"I wouldn't go in there if I was you," Frank yelled, half kidding.

"Why?" Fry asked.

"It's quicksand and stuff in there, and I'm not sure where it's at."

"Oh yeah," John said. "Good place to bury somebody, ain't it?"

That was quintessential Lucky Fry, always scheming about something he never really planned to do. The next day John headed back to his own trap. He couldn't take the withdrawal and went back to Detroit and the drugs.

But there were no plans like that this time. After John was up and about, he talked about the last three months. He told Frank all about Dr. Al Miller and the five-thousand-dollar payoff. The money hadn't even lasted a full two weeks.

"Its just as well I'm up here while Dawn's in the hospital," he said. "The man paid me to be somewhere else, didn't he? But we were doing a thing behind his back."

John talked about his brother's death. He broke down and cried. "My father hates my fuckin' guts," he said. "And I hate his. Jim was all the family I had."

Later, Frank and Cheryl drove him to Northern Michigan Hospital in Petoskey for his hand. He was admitted immediately.

John Fry called Dawn Spens at least daily from Frank's house and later his hospital room. He made six hundred dollars in long-distance calls, all charged to Frank's number. John wanted to make sure she was getting clean back in Detroit.

Soon John was boasting to Frank and Cheryl that Dawn had kicked her habit. He seemed pleased that all was going well for Cheryl as well. John wondered how much work was available in the north. He talked about relocating.

When Dawn was released from Receiving Hospital, she told John she didn't want to stay alone at the Homewood Manor. John agreed. It was better she put some distance between herself and the drugs in the Cass Corridor. Dr. Al Miller, Dawn said, would pay for a room for her at the Congress Inn, a motel popular with truckers on the border of Detroit and Dearborn.

"Well, when I get back things are going to be different," John told her as he sipped on a Jack Daniel's and Coke that Cheryl had smuggled into his hospital room. "I'm clean. You're clean. We don't have to go through all this horseshit no more."

John was released from Northern Michigan Hospital on a Monday in mid-June. Doctors had saved his hand with a skin graft that connected his third and fourth fingers. Healed, it looked like a mutant hand, as though two fingers grew together.

Fry was supposed to rest a few days, then return to the hospital on Friday so a surgeon could remove the graft. Frank was working a nearby construction job. John and Cheryl spent the day alone talking about old times. John Fry was clean, and Cheryl felt some of his old magic stirring inside her again.

Later that day, John called Dawn at the Congress Inn and asked her to catch a bus to Petoskey. She told him she would telephone him later. The call never came. That evening, John telephoned Dawn a half-dozen times. There was no answer in her room. He quit trying after 2 A.M.

At breakfast the next morning he still wasn't getting an answer. John decided to do some investigating. Cheryl watched him make the calls as she cooked eggs for her old boyfriend. First he called a friend in the Homewood Manor.

"Cheryl, she was downtown last night," he said after hanging up.

John was dialing another number, that of a heroin dealer across the hall from apartment 202. He had Cheryl speak to him.

"Dawn was in and out of there all night last night," she told John. "He thinks she still might be in your apartment."

"Put her on, man," Fry barked.

Cheryl watched as Fry's face turned a dark shade of red as she handed him the telephone. It always scared her when he got like that.

"What the fuck are you doin'?" he said when Dawn got on the line.

". . . You're supposed to be clean.

". . . What's all this bullshit you been layin' on me?

". . . I don't give a fuck if you don't want to talk about it.

". . . You're gonna talk about it.

". . . You bitch.

". . . No, don't even try it. It's too late for that. Don't move. I'll be home tonight."

John Fry slammed the phone and paced like a caged grizzly in heat. Cheryl kept frying eggs. Then he made another flurry of calls. Afterward, he explained to Cheryl what had happened: Dawn had been using since the day she got out of the hospital. Dr. Al Miller had picked up three packs of dope himself that day and had taken it to her at the Congress Inn.

"I'd like to beat that motherfucker until he can't walk," he said. "Cheryl, I need money."

He wanted to catch a bus to Detroit. Cheryl reminded him of his doctor's appointment. His fingers were still hooked together. He was in no condition to travel with that heavily bandaged hand, she said.

"Please, Cheryl," he said. "Give it to me. I've got to get

back to Detroit."

Cheryl had never heard John beg her quite like that for anything. She'd never seen him so helpless. She would have thought his mother was still alive, calling him from her deathbed in Detroit. She wished John had given her the kind of love and concern he was showing for Dawn.

Cheryl fetched the only money they had, forty dollars in rolled quarters on Frank's dresser. Later that day she took him to the bus station in Petoskey. When he boarded the Greyhound, John Fry was still clean.

Chapter 47

The psychopath is egocentric.

> — W. Alan Canty,
> Henry Ford Community College lectures

Many times John Fry would explain what happened after he returned to Detroit and found Dawn Spens at the Congress Inn. The basic story never varied.

"A friend had picked me up and dropped me off at the motel," Fry recalled in one detailed version. "When I got there she was sittin' and waitin' on me. I was hot.

"She had told me after the second week in the hospital she wasn't using anymore — just strictly Tylenols and what they were giving her in the hospital. I found out different about that, too.

"Come to find out — and I verified this through other people, not just her — Al is picking up dope for her from the day she got out of the hospital. It was like he wanted to keep her strung out, have a hold on her. I also later found out that Gene Johnson had tried to shoot a move on her. His name was on the motel room bill. He knew what kind of money we were getting from Al.

"When I confronted her she said, 'Aw, baby, I'm sorry.' She started crying.

"I said, 'What the fuck happened?'

"She said, 'You not being here . . . I was depressed.'

"She claimed she thought I left her.

"She said, 'Al came out here one day and brought me three packs of dope, and I started hitting it.'

"I said, 'Wait till I get my hands on this punk.' I said, 'Is

209

this how it's going to be? I did you a favor by going to Frank's. I went through all these changes to get clean. Frank was going to get me a job. I gave all that up to come back, because you start using.'

"She said, 'I'm sorry.'

"I said, 'Fuck that. It's too late now for that. We can't change what has already happened.'

"Then she said, 'I want to quit.'

"I said, 'Good, I got seventy-five Tylenols.'

"The doctor had prescribed them for my hand and they make it easier to kick. And, at the time she was only doing three packs of mix a day. Al had come out that day. He gave her five hundred dollars. He wasn't going to be back until the following Tuesday. It was the weekend of the Grand Prix. So I kept her away from the drugs all weekend. I fed her the Tylenols.

"The day he came back out, they left. They were gone about an hour. I'm laying out by the pool. I was still not supposed to be around. When I went back to the room she had three or four packs of dope.

"I said, 'What's the point of me going through all these changes, giving you my Tylenol 4s? And I need them for the pain in my hand. I thought you wanted to quit. Get out of it. Quit working.'

"Then, I don't know why I did it, but I did. And, I *was clean* I said, 'If you want to be dope fiends, we'll be dope fiends. If you want to be a dope fiend, I'll be a dope fiend with you.'

"I'm tellin' you, man, that's how much I was in love with this fuckin' chick. She had the dope, so I took off all my clothes and laid back in the chair.

" 'Hit me,' I said. 'Come on, hit me.'

"So then we started back into it . . ."

Chapter 48

They didn't argue this time about the money. Gladys Canty, she told herself, you're not going to play that old, cracked record again. She dated the check July 2 and noted "loan to Alan." Then she handed her son the check for $1,650.

He'd said his stay at University Hospital put him behind in his fees from patients, and his own doctor bills were coming due. The last thing he needed, she thought, was more pressure. Gladys Canty was worried about Bus's practice. If her husband was alive, she thought, he'd be worried as well.

Al Sr. had taken such an interest in their son's career when he was alive, she would have thought it was his own. First he complained about Al Jr.'s thesis revisions for his doctorate at the University of Michigan. "What in the hell do they want from him?" he said as Al Jr. struggled for several years to satisfy the committee.

Then he wanted to spearhead the fight with the Lansing bureaucracy to get Al Jr. licensed by the state board of psychology. In 1970 he endorsed Al Jr.'s application. He informed them he'd personally supervised Bus for nine years, writing:

"The applicant is my son. As director of the Psychiatric Clinic of the Recorder's Court in Detroit for the past twenty-one years, I have had ten psychologists under daily supervision. My standards are high. This applicant was expected to and did meet these standards."

When the state refused to certify Al Jr. at the top level of "consulting psychologist," Al Sr. exploded. The board claimed Al Jr. lacked enough postdoctoral experience and even ordered him to cease his private practice.

But Al Sr. suspected otherwise. He was always very sensitive about the fact that he headed the court clinic without a Ph.D. He suspected some of his colleagues talked about it behind his back.

"They're doing this to Alan to get at me," he stormed.

He urged his son to appeal the ruling. Al Jr. went to the capitol in Lansing, alone. She suspected he was afraid of what his father might say to the bureaucrats. Bus struck a compromise that allowed him to practice at the lower certification level until he received the higher ranking two years later.

But Al Sr. remained unsatisfied. He urged Bus to be certified by the American Board of Professional Psychologists — the top credential available, one that would give him a national standing. After much work and testing, the results came in.

She remembered that day as one of the most significant in Al Sr.'s life. He toasted his son at a Thanksgiving dinner in front of Jan and her parents.

"This is a great day," said Al Sr., lifting his glass. "My son has passed his boards."

Everyone at the table was impressed. She couldn't remember how Buster reacted, but she knew his father was quite moved by the moment. He was sliding into ill health. He didn't have long to live.

Mrs. Canty didn't want to see all that effort by the two of them sabotaged by illness. She couldn't believe what a stroke of misfortune he'd had with his health. Then his car was stolen. No wonder his moods had become so unpredictable.

On some of his regular visits Buster was exuberant. One day they took a walk around the block, and he spotted a man playing with his dog in his backyard.

"Hello, sir, how are you?" he yelled out. "It's sure a wonderful day, isn't it?"

His spontaneity caught Mrs. Canty off guard.

"Why, Bus, you don't even know the man," she said. "Why are you so friendly today?"

"Oh, Ma, I'm friendly to everyone," he said. He grinned

like a young boy who'd just caught the biggest fish at summer camp.

On other visits he was largely silent, absorbed in thought. She wondered if he was troubled about something besides his recent misfortunes. Several times she had asked him, "Buster, are you and Jannie getting along OK?"

"Oh sure, Ma, you know we get along great," he said.

But often she caught him daydreaming. It would happen right in the middle of one of their conversations.

"Bus . . . Bus, are you listening?" she would ask.

"Sure, Ma," he'd say. Then he'd come up with the right response. He'd heard every word she'd said.

It was as though that active mind of his was divided in two, she thought. One side kept track of the present and the other was off somewhere else. Gladys Canty had no idea where.

Maybe the $1,650 would ease the stress and help him get back on track.

Chapter 49

Dawn Spens and Dr. Al Miller picked out the car together at a used car lot on Detroit's east side. It was a 1975 white Thunderbird, but in good shape for its age. Al paid for it in cash following the Fourth of July weekend. The cost was $1,600 and some change.

John Fry made a mental note. Dawn's new car wasn't the first Thunderbird that had commanded the trick's attention. Once, after his Buick Regal was stolen, Al arrived in a 1983 red Thunderbird to pick up drugs for Dawn in the hospital. John noticed the car's immaculate gray leather interior. His nostrils detected a hint of perfume. John had been skeptical of Al's story that he was a widower since the day he heard it.

"He said it belonged to the daughter of the guy he worked with," he later told a friend. "But I figured it might be his old lady's car."

One of the first uses of Dawn's T-bird was a quick trip up to Alanson. Cheryl and Frank hadn't been getting along since John's visit. When Cheryl offered to cover the gas, John and Dawn drove up and got her. She booked herself into a room at the Congress Inn.

John and Cheryl often took off in the Thunderbird to avoid Al during his lunchtime visits to Dawn's room. His routine was as predictable as his support. He paid her daily for her company. He tipped her more often than not. He never showed on Sunday. Every Monday he paid her room and telephone charges, which ran nearly $200 a week.

But by putting Dawn up in the Congress Inn, Al had succeeded in distancing Dawn from Cass Corridor prostitution only to locate her in a better-paying market. The motel, located near I-94, drew plenty of road-weary truckers with its

214

large parking lot built for their big rigs. The girls could snag dates right outside the room. If action was slow there, a "ho stroll" waited just across the nearby Detroit city limits on a stretch of Michigan Avenue dotted with topless bars. Pressure from Mark Bando and others in the Cass Corridor already had prompted many of the better-looking women to relocate there. Tricks were paying in the $50- $75 range.

On her first night back in Detroit, Cheryl Krizanovic made a half-hearted attempt to flag a date on Michigan but couldn't go through with it. Clean, she found herself too timid to work. The next day she found herself in Dawn's room with a syringe of cooked heroin in her arm. She complained the high wasn't all it was cracked up to be. Then she went out and got herself another pack of dope.

One week later, Frank McMasters showed up at the motel in his pickup truck. When Cheryl refused to return to Alanson, he booked a room. Over the next two months he would make the five-hour drive between Alanson and Detroit a half-dozen times, trying to persuade Cheryl to return.

On his first stay, Frank finally got his first look at the doctor he'd heard so much about. At first he'd wondered whether John had exaggerated Dr. Miller's role in supplying Dawn's habit. Then one day Frank, John, and Cheryl sat in his truck and watched as Al arrived in his Buick to visit Dawn. John had been complaining all morning, waiting for money and drugs. After Al left, they went back to her room. Dawn had $80 and three packs of heroin. The two of them hadn't left the motel. He decided John wasn't bullshitting.

Others witnessed Al's readiness to supply Dawn's habit. He often accompanied her when she copped Dillies from a small-time dealer working out of a room at the motel. One time, when Dawn was short on money, she used Al as a credit reference. She called him at his office and handed the phone to the dealer.

"Give her anything she wants," Al said. "I'll pay you tomorrow."

John had vowed they would no longer use the mixed jive that had perforated their bodies in the Cass Corridor. They would shoot prescription Dilaudid or a better-quality heroin.

"If we're going to do drugs, it ain't gonna be no fuckin' garbage," he told Dawn.

John secured a connection in Hamtramck for so-called "raw heroin." It was not as pure as the name implied but had a higher opiate content and fewer pollutants. Impressed with the quality, John planned to do a little dealing himself.

Al's plans included moving Dawn from the motel to an apartment. He had a building in mind near the Fisher Building, one that he'd lived in himself during college, he said. Dawn stalled him. She searched through newspapers for something else. John had yet to formulate his next move.

In late July, Dawn picked out a flat in a quiet Polish neighborhood in Hamtramck. She and Al looked at the apartment together one lunch hour. Then he brought a Comerica money order to her for a $250 security deposit. The next day he brought her another $250 money order for the first month's rent. He left the payee's line blank.

It was the only time Al had ever given her anything but cash. John Fry noticed a woman's signature on the checks when she showed them to him. It was Jan Canty.

"Who's the broad?" he asked.

Dawn said she had asked Al the same question. "He says it's the woman who sometimes answers his phone and does a little typing in the office."

Financially, at least, it was turning into a very good summer for Dawn Spens, now that Dr. Al Miller was led to believe he had her to himself. She had her own car, a place of her own waiting in Hamtramck, and—at a conservative $100 a day—a $31,000 annual income, delivered six days a week tax-free. All she needed was some furniture.

Her sugar daddy had been urging such a setup since he first started seeing Dawn regularly. Finally, Dr. Al Miller had everything in place.

Chapter 50

Such a person may want to enslave others or to enslave the partner in particular . . . This tendency may take the form of molding or educating the victim, as Professor Higgins in Pygmalion *molds Eliza . . . It is particular to sadistic relationships of this kind that keeping a hold over the victim is of more absorbing interest than the person's own life.*

— KAREN HORNEY,
Our Inner Conflicts

An executive secretary named Betty Noble and her husband, Ed, were driving through the New Center one Sunday in July when she noticed the pedestrian walking near the Fisher Building.

"My God, Ed, that looks like Alan Canty," she said, pointing.

"Do you want me to go back?" Ed asked.

A dozen mental snapshots from her late teens, not all of them pleasant, came to her mind. Alan Canty, she thought — what a lesson he had been in the wily ways of a spellbound man. More than thirty years had passed since they dated, but still she'd never met another man so cleverly determined to secure her affection.

They met one winter at a YMCA dance. She was a slim junior with auburn hair at Denby High School. Al was a senior at Southeastern. She was intrigued by his outstanding manners, stylish clothes, and his automobile. Car ownership was uncommon among the boys she knew.

They lived only a few miles from each other, but in much

217

different worlds. Al's Jefferson-Chalmers neighborhood was called "little Venice" because of its boat canals and custom homes just across the border from Grosse Pointe Park. It was a neighborhood of professionals, and she knew from the newspapers that his father was a big shot in Recorder's Court. Betty's turf was blue-collar, and her father an hourly worker at General Motors.

He never did like Al, and she should have listened to her dad. He said he had "a look that couldn't be trusted." But Betty found him boyishly charming on the first date. They went to the Woods Theater in Grosse Pointe to see a movie. But when it came time to buy the ticket, Al had no money.

"My mom gave me five bucks," he apologized. "But I left it in the pocket of my other shirt."

He praised her for putting up with his forgetfulness, and they hit it off from there. They dated for more than a year. At first everything was normal enough. He took her home to meet his parents. She was very nervous that day. The home was quite stylish, full of paintings and antiques. She had the feeling his father was psychoanalyzing everything she said. She felt ill at ease in the presence of such a well-known psychologist. His mother was quite proper, giving some of the history behind the art objects in her home during the visit.

"And this," Betty remembered her saying as Mrs. Canty held up one, "is one of Alan's favorite antiques."

Betty thought it appropriate he had a lead part in *The Royal Family,* his high school play. He even took fencing lessons to prepare for the part.

Al made the typical advances of most teenage boys. They parked near the Detroit River but never got farther than necking in his car. But Betty saw him as a loner. He didn't seem to have any friends. She also saw his temper. Once, when he was delayed by slow service at a gas station, he tried to run down the attendant.

She suspected he was spoiled. When he went off to Hillsdale College, he often wrote of opulent parties and the large allowances students got from their parents. Often he made the three-hour drive from Hillsdale to see her on school

218

nights. She typed his term papers for him, but he didn't put much effort into his schoolwork. He frequently was late with his assignments, but it was no wonder, with all the time he was spending on the road.

She began to feel uncomfortable around him. In time it became clear to her that Al Canty had designs on something other than her body. It started subtly at first, then accelerated.

He insisted on determining in detail where they went, when they would get there, and what they would do when they did. He corrected her diction and suggested impressive words for her to use. He told her how she should carry herself and how to wear her hair. He insisted she wear certain clothes. He was particularly adamant about her shoes, forbidding her to wear high heels.

Eventually she felt as though he was trying to fashion her into a woman of higher social status. She started feeling like an object, like one of his mother's prized antiques.

"I mean, he was focusing his whole life on me," she later recalled. "As though I was his only purpose in life."

Then one day a neighbor reported to her father that Al broke into their house one night while the family was gone. The neighbor spotted Al in their basement, rearranging the laundry on the clothesline. When he was confronted, Al denied it.

"This boy has to go," her father said.

And Betty Noble was sick of trying to live up to Al's standards. One day she told him it was over. She returned his graduation picture, his gifts, and all the letters he wrote. She assumed that would be it, but she misjudged him. He pulled out the biggest diamond ring she'd ever seen. At least it looked like a diamond. To this day she wondered if it was real or fake.

"I was going to marry you," he said. "I even bought the ring."

She stuck to her intentions. He returned the following weekend from college. He had a lump on his arm. He said it was cancer. He begged for pity, again asking her not to break off their relationship. The following week she got a telegram. The return address was from Mayo Clinic. He said he was there. He was dying. The cancer had been confirmed by doctors.

Betty showed the telegram to her father, who promptly relieved her feelings of guilt. Her dad pointed out Mayo Clinic was in Rochester, Minnesota. Al had put the return address in New York.

Then Al Canty frightened her. He showed up in her school parking lot and stood at odd hours outside her house. One day he walked into her school while she was at her locker between classes. He threatened to make a scene unless she left with him. He grabbed her by the arm. It hurt as he pulled her from the school.

For three hours he drove her all around Detroit in his car, trying one argument after another to win her back. Secretly, she only disliked him more. Betty begged him to take her to her after-school job. She was already late. Finally, he did.

Her dad was livid.

"Alan Canty's father needs to do a little work on his own son," he said. Then he called Al Sr. up.

"You're going to have to keep your son away from my daughter," he told him. "Are you aware your son has been driving home from college every night to see her?"

The senior Canty was very polite. He said he would take care of the problem. Betty hadn't seen Al since—until this day, walking across West Grand Boulevard.

"*Betty,* do you want me to go back?" her husband Ed asked again.

I wonder what Al's up to these days, she thought. But Betty Noble decided she didn't want to find out.

"No, that's OK," she said. "Just keep driving."

Chapter 51

Jan Canty didn't know what to make of it. For years, everywhere she looked in and around the big Tudor there were unfinished projects. Now, in just one summer, she would have thought the crew of "This Old House" had arrived to film an episode.

Following the burglar alarm crew came the painters . . . and the landscapers . . . and the window installers . . . then the painters again . . . and the furniture deliveries and the bricklayers. At the center of the undertaking was W. Alan Canty, who after years of indifference to needed improvements was attacking the home-beautiful production like a director with a hot new script.

But the focal point was Al's antique-brick driveway. Two brick masons had been on their hands and knees for weeks, carefully placing the precious stones in a precise pattern stretching from the garage to the street. For seven years the pile of bricks had grown behind the garage as Al brought them home by the trunkload. Before he called the masons, weeds were growing through the middle of the mound.

It was one of the eyesores that started the recent disagreement they had about the house. For years Jan did what she could to bring the big Tudor back to its original elegance. She'd painted and wallpapered. She'd hunted for antiques to complement the decor, buying an antique gas stove and an old oak icebox for the kitchen. She'd installed new electric outlets. She'd removed paint from hardwood doors and trim until she smelled the stripper in her food.

But Jan felt as though she was refilling Lake St. Clair one drop at a time. Only two bedrooms were done—their master suite and a guest room. The living room wasn't fully furnished. Al's home office was outdated, featuring what she once quipped was "early basement decor."

The basic upkeep was impossible for a working couple. One Friday she decided to trim the eight-foot-high hedge that enveloped the wrought-iron fence around their corner lot. She had an electric trimmer, but still it took her two full days. By Sunday night, her arms felt as though she had been pumping iron all weekend with Arnold Schwarzenegger.

She began questioning the wisdom of owning the place back in 1981 after she got her doctorate. She approached Al about selling it back then. It would simplify their lifestyle, she said. They would have more free time to travel. But he balked completely. Several times since, they had discussed it. Then it turned into their only standing argument.

When she brought it up again several weeks after he got out of the hospital, Al was not only more determined than ever to keep it, he was offended by the proposal.

"I'll have no part of that," he said.

"But its just *too* big. We really don't need it, Al. And, it's never going to get done."

Sure, it was designed by Albert Kahn, the architect of the Fisher. Sure it was beautiful.

"But Al, you're hardly ever home to enjoy it anyway," she continued. "This is *crazy*. Let's just sell it and get something we can manage—just you and me."

"I'll have no part of that," he said.

Jan thought, why is he being so damned obstinate? She was tempted to take a firm stand right then and there. She knew if she really showed displeasure with him, he would wither into that embarrassed, boyish demeanor. She felt he'd probably do anything to please her when he got like that. But she knew her conscience wouldn't tolerate it. After all, she was trying to take pressure off him, not heap it on.

Now Al had responded with the home-beautiful effort. As she watched him directing the brick masons one Friday, Jan began to realize what a bundle of contradictions her husband was. For years he'd done nothing around the house. Now he was masterminding every project in sight. One minute he could be aloof, the next as childish as a preadolescent boy. He kept the most disorganized office records she'd ever seen. But he maintained a clinic schedule so rigid that it determined within the quarter hour when he ate and slept. He insisted on such exact timing, but then he was always ten minutes late.

She thought of others: He was a disheveled dresser, but he had other meticulous habits, like his coffee brewing. He made a ritual of washing the coffeepot but got upset if she washed the stained thermos cup. He liked to buy and sell old car parts but wouldn't lay a wrench to them himself. He came from one of the most proper families she'd ever met. But he himself didn't own a tie. He preached openness and understanding, but he guarded his financial matters like Fort Knox. He was often rushed and hurried. But then he would soak in the bathtub for hours. Even her mother had noticed the baths on a recent visit.

"Where's Al? It's time to eat," her friend Celia Muir said when their backyard barbecue was ready.

"Celia, Al's in the bathtub," Jan's mother said. "He's taking a bath—again."

God, she thought, the contradictions were everywhere. He fancied himself an intellectual, yet he couldn't wait for his copy of *People Magazine*. He was a vocal critic of TV entertainment who knew all the latest Hollywood gossip. He was a psychologist, a proponent of short-term cognitive therapy. But Al Canty himself was seeing a *psychiatrist* who practiced the long-term therapy of free association.

The thought led her back to University Hospital, and the horrifying scene in the admission room. That's it, she thought. He's trying to prove to me—to himself—that he's capable. I should have guessed it. Maybe I'm judging him too harshly.

Her theory seemed more logical as she watched him return from work every evening. Each night he examined the handiwork of the bricklayers. He seemed to find satisfaction in each freshly laid row. She remembered how he'd kept lists in the basement of each brick's urban origin. He had a half-

223

dozen or so samples labeled, too, their printed histories available upon request.

What a crazy, eccentric hobby that was, she thought. It had all started after his father died. He got the idea from the redbrick streets around Elmwood Cemetery, where Al Sr. was buried. When workers began ripping them up and trucking everything away, Al began his pilgrimages to the old cemetery to fill up his trunk.

"I'm not stealing them, Jan," he said once. "They're just going to use them for landfill anyway."

Finally, he was getting them all in place. She sensed it gave him a great deal of satisfaction.

Chapter 52

The psychopath is potentially dangerous.
> — W. Alan Canty,
> Henry Ford Community College lectures

"GET UP, PUNK! I got somethin' for you!"

Lucky Fry's voice shook the house like a big clap of thunder. His Western shirt strained at the snaps as blood pumped his chest and biceps and flooded his face bright red.

The guy named Ike was in his underwear, sprawled on the couch for the late movie. He turned just in time to take John's right paw flat across his face.

"I said get up, bitch! You like to fuck with women and kids. Come on, *fuck with me!*"

The guy named Ike lunged for his pants. John went for a nearby table. It groaned and snapped as John tried to break off a leg for a club.

Frank McMasters wanted to run for shelter when he saw Lucky Fry get like that. Ike was running too, across the room for the door. He was still in his jockey shorts when he bolted into the hot August night.

All John would have needed was a baseball bat, Frank thought. He hated to think what John would have done to the man with his favorite toy.

John was on a mission when he asked Frank to accompany him to his late brother's house on Clayton that night. Earlier he'd discovered that Jim's old girlfriend Janet was living there with the twins and turning tricks for Ike. John found the refrigerator empty, the twins dirty, and Janet crying in the living room. He pressed her until she told him what happened: Ike had locked the twins in their bedroom during a two-day bender. Unable to get to the bathroom, the twins had messed their pants. Ike rubbed their faces in their soiled underwear as punishment. When she complained, he punched her in the eye.

"I should have killed that dirty slimy sonovabitch," John said. He still was pacing around the living room.

Frank had no doubt John would have if Ike had made the wrong move. John often spoke about the "uncontaminated personalities" of children, and most gravitated to him as to a balding teddy bear. They liked his funny faces and smirky smile, and he was especially protective of his twin niece and nephew since Jim died.

Most of the time, Frank knew Lucky Fry to be pretty laid-back. In fact, often he'd seen John embrace the role of peacemaker when other dope fiends got irrational. His rapport with kids added to the image. People that didn't really know him, people like Ike or the trick Al Miller, could easily misjudge him as just another stoned, aging hippie living out his years on the street.

But Frank McMasters knew John also had a temper that could strike without warning, like a cyclone when the atmospheric conditions were just right. Frank wondered if Ike realized how close he'd come to booking a drawer in the Wayne County Morgue. A slight shove or a casual insult would have done it.

Once Frank saw a simple slap in the face from Cheryl turn the tornado loose. She hit him during an argument back at their old house off Michigan Avenue. That was the first time Frank saw the bulging chest and crimson face. John picked up a baseball bat. He bypassed Cheryl in favor of the entire house. He swatted the Louisville Slugger through two lamps, then turned a couple of wooden chairs to kindling. He pounded a jewelry box into a pile of splinters. He was working on the plaster and wall lath when Frank ran over to get John's brother. It took three men to tackle John and hold him down. On the floor he came to his senses.

"Boy, I guess I fucked up, didn't I," he said.

John explained later that he couldn't stand to be hit. "My old man hit me with anything he could get his hands on. Axe handles. Sledgehammer handles. You name it. Ever since, I just go out when any motherfucker lays a hand on me."

But Frank also had seen an offhand attack on John's self-styled sense of dignity push him over the edge. Once they were sitting in a diner off Michigan, waiting for Cheryl to return from the streets. When she walked in the door a man patted her rear on his way out. The guy was at least six feet and over two hundred pounds. That time John's shirt button flew across the table.

"She deserves respect," he cursed. "Motherfucker should not put his fuckin' hands on her unless he's payin' for it."

John stalked out of the restaurant, walked up behind the lug, and slapped him on the ass. When he turned, John boosted him off the cement with one uppercut. He was already unconscious when he hit the sidewalk.

Frank knew never to challenge John Fry when he blew up like a blowfish. Otherwise, John was harmless, though he frequently talked tough, made homicidal threats, and reminisced about past battles. According to John, he'd single-handedly taken on rival motorcycle gangs, wasted Vietcong in Nam, and worked under contract for the Mafia as a hit man. Frank had heard a dozen or more stories from John about the men he'd supposedly killed. Frank figured he told such tales to command respect from others on the street. The dope fiends bought it, but he didn't.

The stories also were ploys to control his girls, Frank had decided some time back. The first time Cheryl ever left him and stayed in Alanson she was convinced John would kill her. She said she had once watched him carve up a black dude for insulting a friend outside a bar. He ran off bleeding, but later they heard he died. That seemed feasible, considering John's hatred for blacks.

But then Cheryl told him that John had served ten years in Jackson for murder. She said John had killed a state's witness right in the courtroom. Frank thought it all a little farfetched. He asked a county sheriff's deputy to run a record check. John Carl Fry had served at least ten years all right, but all for small-time, nonviolent crimes. From then on, Frank saw John's ongoing body count as just another one of his fantasies.

"Frank, I've got to spend a few days laying low at your place," he said one time when he showed up in Alanson unexpectedly. "I killed a guy the other night."

"Right, John," Frank said. "Who was it this time?"

Chapter 53

By summer's end, there seemed no limit to Dr. Al Miller's gullibility. The Hamtramck apartment for Dawn Spens was only another "squeeze play," as John Fry was fond of calling their schemes to extract cash from Dawn's sugar daddy.

The first $250 of Al's apartment deposit money went to groceries. John Fry wanted the refrigerator and cupboards well stocked for his late brother's twins. When a friend asked what happened to the second $250, John Fry chuckled and pointed to the tattoo on his arm.

"Tweety Bird got drunk."

Following John's eviction of Ike, John and Dawn left the Congress Inn and moved into Janet's house. The two-story sat on a shabby block of Clayton bordering a south-side warehouse district. Even then, Dawn talked Al into providing $1,200 for furniture for the apartment she would never occupy. The move to Clayton was only temporary, she told Al. Her girlfriend Janet couldn't take care of her kids and a four-bedroom house alone.

But Al never complained, even when the twins disappeared one day. John paid a south-side mother to take care of the preschoolers in her home. He didn't want them around the operation he was planning to set up.

"No more fuckin' around," he told Dawn. "You wanna be a whore, then I'll be you're pimp. But we're gonna do it right."

In two weeks, John transformed the house into a prospering dope and trick pad. John dealt heroin in one bedroom. In the others Dawn, Janet, Cheryl, and other prostitutes turned tricks. Fry rented rooms to other Michigan Avenue prostitutes for five dollars a date, but he wasn't after the five spot.

229

He knew once the johns paid the girls, the money would end up in his hands for dope.

Over the next two months Cheryl Krizanovic would alternate her residence between the Congress Inn and the home on Clayton. In another effort to convince her to return to Alanson, Frank McMasters came to Detroit for a week in late August.

One day Frank was visiting Cheryl when Dawn yelled through the house, "Hey, fuckin' Al's comin' over." Frank had always wanted to meet the doctor face-to-face. He knew Dawn had to be milking the man for very large sums of money. Frank had watched John repeatedly give Dawn the choice: Get money from Al, or work Michigan Avenue. Dawn always preferred the former. John told Frank privately he would just as soon have Dawn Spens on the street. Frank could tell John resented Al. He still blamed the trick for providing her with drugs while he was cleaning up in Alanson.

When Dawn made the announcement, a half-dozen drug addicts in the house responded in a well-practiced drill. Paraphernalia was put away. Empty beer cans were picked up. Bedroom doors were closed. Everyone took seats in the living room.

Al came in the back door. Frank, John, and Cheryl were hiding in a bedroom off the kitchen. Frank, dressed in a well-creased pair of dress pants and sports shirt, put on a businessman's demeanor and pretended he was one of Cheryl's tricks.

"Baby, don't be in such a hurry to leave," Cheryl called as Frank left the bedroom. He was face-to-face with Al, startling the trick somewhat.

"This is Al Miller, Dr. Al Miller," Dawn said sweetly. "He's a real good friend of my family."

Al relaxed with the introduction.

"Frank, its very nice to meet you," he said. He was very formal.

Frank watched as Al headed toward the stairway with Dawn. But when the doctor made a point of stopping in the

230

living room, Frank couldn't help but notice a personality change. Al stopped and struck what appeared to be a pose. As the doctor looked over the half-dozen addicts, he nodded his head up and down slowly. He reminded Frank of James Dean.

"What's happenin'," he said.

Frank never had seen anything quite like it. He thought, what is this, *The Strange Case of Dr. Jekyll and Mr. Hyde?* The man actually thinks he's part of this — part of the action. He obviously doesn't realize how foolish he looks.

"Frank, I told you the fuckin' guy was a goof," John said later.

But John, Frank soon found out, could look pretty comical himself during Al's visits. He went to any length to avoid him. Periodically the doctor would drop by without calling. When his Buick Regal was spotted out front, John hovered like a baseball runner in the middle of the house, waiting to see which door Al chose to enter that day. As Al knocked on one, John would run out the other.

One day Al caught John by surprise, strolling into the house before he could escape. John squatted under a living room table, while Frank and others crowded around as the trick came through. Frank later had a good laugh. But John didn't think it humorous.

"That motherfucker's a pain in the ass," he said.

When Frank returned to Detroit for nine days in mid-September, he could see the routine was wearing on John, and that John and Dawn weren't getting along very well.

Frank had always seen Dawn as a prima donna. She snubbed most of John's friends. She ignored people when they tried to strike up a conversation with her. She referred to the other prostitutes as "two-bit whores" and other addicts as "junkies." When she did join a conversation, she was condescending, often flaunting her suburban upbringing.

Al shows up and she turns into the queen of the nest, Frank thought. "I got a sugar daddy that beats all them whores on the street" was one of her favorite expressions. Once Frank watched her demean everyone in the house. A large group of

231

people were gathered in the living room when she launched a verbal barrage.

"Goddamnit, John," she bitched. "I don't like this. All these fuckin' whores comin' in here and junkies gettin' drugs and all this shit. We live here. Can't we get some kind of peace?"

John Fry laughed. Then he looked her dead in the eyes and said, "Bitch, just what in the fuck do you think you are?"

A few days later, when Frank and John were riding alone up Michigan Avenue in Frank's pickup truck, John talked about leaving his hooker from Harper Woods.

"That girl's driving me nuts," he said. "It's this snotty attitude she has towards everything. Frank, I think I gotta dump her."

"If you do, don't make any moves on Cheryl," Frank said. "Try that again, my friend, and we're enemies."

"No problem," John said. "But I just can't put up with the girl's mouth no more."

They talked for quite a while that day. John said he felt as though the streets were closing in on him again. He recalled the clean days he had up in Alanson.

"Frank, man, I was clean," he said. *"I was clean."*

Now John estimated he and Dawn were going through more than a thousand dollars a day in high-quality heroin. They paid for it from his dealing and from money from Al and Dawn's other tricks.

"I'm goin' nowhere, Frank."

"All you have to do is quit and run away. It's not like you can't get out of here. You know you got my place. It's not like you don't have someplace to go.'"

Frank had never known John Fry to be so out of sorts over a woman. Dawn Spens, he thought, must possess a little magic of her own. John seemed to lack the confident control he'd had all those years with Cheryl. John was silent as the pickup bounced and swayed down Michigan Avenue.

"Frank," he said, finally. "I got a bad feeling. If I stay in Detroit and stay with this broad, one of two things are gonna happen."

"Yeah, what's that?"

"I'm gonna die a dope fiend. Or, I'm gonna end up back in the penitentiary."

Frank didn't say anything. But neither one seemed out of the question to him.

Chapter 54

*Love is an exchange of vulnerabilities It is kind of
frightening because you have to let yourself be open. A
lot of people don't want to take that risk.*
— W. Alan Canty,
Detroit Magazine; Modern Bride Magazine

One cool September evening Jan Canty found herself de-
bating whether to ask her husband the question she had held
inside on many warmer nights. She could hear the water running for another one of Al's baths, then only silence as he
soaked. She sat alone on their bed, trying to put her anxiety
into perspective.

Much of the unsettling aftermath of his hospitalization
had passed, and his manic interest in the house went as fast as
it came. Now he was back in the daily clinical grind she
thought had weakened him in the first place. But he wasn't
the man she married. The supportive, spontaneous intellectual she had known until a year ago had been replaced by a
intensely private man who wrestled nightly with his own
thoughts.

His time in front of the TV was steadily increasing. That
was as foreign to his character as the show he liked the most,
"Mike Hammer." Sometimes he watched "Hill Street Blues"
or "St. Elsewhere." But she noticed he often remained unaf-
fected by the plots. Sometimes she wondered if he was really
watching, though the volume was often quite loud. She suspected he tuned the shows in only so he could tune her out.

Other nights she found him alone in his easy chair sipping

on liqueurs—Amaretto or Drambuie. They were his favorites, but Al never had been a heavy drinker. Usually he only had one or two, and only when they were out. Now he was having three or four at home, sliding deeper into himself with each drink. She'd try to inspire conversation, but his attention span never lasted more than a few minutes.

"What, Jan?" he'd say after she asked a question.

"Al, is something wrong, something bothering you?"

"No, I'm just tired. It's nothing. I've had some difficult patients, lately."

And the work. Damn the work, she thought. Wouldn't he ever learn? He was nearly fifty-one years old. What was the point? They had everything they would ever need. They had too much. She still wished they could dump the house, find a nice condo, and spend the difference on vacations.

But Jan knew better than to push that point anymore. Al was dead set on keeping a full clinical schedule and finishing the parolee updates for the prosecutor's office. He'd even reneged on the Saturdays. He'd cut the day in half for a few months but now was back to a twelve-hour shift.

She was worried the stress might cause him to do something irrational. She feared he already had. Over the latter part of the summer Jan had made some sense out of Al's fragmented monologue during the admission process at University Hospital in April. She and her girlfriend Celia Muir had talked about it over lunch one day. Celia told her what she heard under the roar of the emergency helicopters.

"Jan, he kept saying, 'I'm so very bad, and you are so pure.' Do you have any idea what he was talking about?"

Jan thought about his rambling during the ride to the hospital. She'd heard him say "Cass Corridor" and "prostitute."

Could this, she thought, be what all this was about? The depression. Was Al suffering from the guilt over a one-night stand with a prostitute?

She had to face it. Their sexual relationship had gone the way of their evening walks. Even before his illness, it had been in serious trouble. Al had always been a patient, sensitive lover. But when she got her Ph.D., he lost all interest.

235

After his advances stopped, he greeted hers with moodiness or excuses of being too tired. Usually he didn't have to say a thing. She could tell by his body language he was unwilling.

At first she thought it was something about her. But then she realized other shows of affection, such as holding hands or hugging, hadn't waned at all. Well, she thought initially, maybe it's his age. Then she realized how ridiculous that notion was. Male menopause was one thing, she thought, but men didn't just one day stop having sex altogether.

Jan had been trying to discuss the problem delicately. She always prided herself in not being a nagger, and she certainly wasn't going to nag him about sex. In fact, as his work schedule increased in recent months, she tried a bit of humor.

"Al, now that you're back working," she said, "does that mean we can stop playing brother and sister?"

"I'm working on that in therapy," Al said.

The response was beginning to serve the same purpose as his TV shows. Well, she thought, I guess I can't expect him to regain his sexuality overnight.

But Jan remained troubled that he might have sought an outlet before his breakdown. For months she held back asking him about the prostitute when it popped up in her mind now and again. He already was embarrassed about his hospitalization, and she didn't want to add to his anxiety right afterward. But now, she told herself, there's just no reason not to ask him what that Cass Corridor stuff was all about.

She was waiting for him in the hallway when he got out of the bathtub. Al paused outside the bathroom door momentarily to towel off his face.

"I'm bushed," he said. "I think I'm going to lay down for a while."

"Al," she began. "There's been something I've been wanting to ask you about for a long time. Let's sit down and talk about it."

He walked to the guest room instead of their bedroom. She thought it odd. He rarely went into that room.

She began by recalling the scene—the breakdown, the drive out, the hospital.

Buster and Ma in a
family photo taken in 1984.
(Credit: The Detroit *News*.)

Alan Canty, Sr., shortly
before his retirement as
executive director of the
Detroit Recorder's
Court Psychiatric Clinic.
(Credit: The Detroit *News*.)

Alan Canty and wife Jan
on a vacation at
the Grand Canyon.

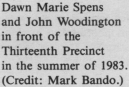

Dawn Marie Spens
and John Woodington
in front of the
Thirteenth Precinct
in the summer of 1983.
(Credit: Mark Bando.)

A partying John Fry
just after moving
into the bungalow
on Casper
in March 1985.

John Carl Fry poses in the window of Mark Bando's
whore car shortly after moving into the Cass Corridor
in the fall of 1983. (Credit: Mark Bando.)

Dawn Spens when she was still living in Harper Woods.

Dawn Spens in front of the Thirteenth Precinct station in the summer of 1983. (Credit: Mark Bando.)

Dawn Spens in Harper Woods.

The south-side Detroit bungalow on Casper where Al Canty was killed and his body mutilated. (Credit: Michael Green, The Detroit *News*.)

Al and Jan Canty's Tudor-style home in Grosse Point Park. (Credit: Michael Green, The Detroit *News*.)

Police photo of Alan Canty's 1984 Buick Regal the night it was found torched near a pair of south-side Detroit railroad tracks. (Credit: The Detroit Police Department.)

Detroit policemen Mark Bando and John Woodington in 1983. (Credit: The Detroit *News*.)

Robert Agacinski,
the Wayne County
assistant prosecutor who
tried the Fry-Spens
murder and mutilation case.

Jay Nolan, John Fry's
defense attorney.
(Credit: Harrol Robinson.)

Recorder's Court Judge
Michael F. Sapala.
(Credit: David Coates,
The Detroit *News*.)

Robert Ziolkowski,
Dawn Spen's
defense attorney.
(Credit: Russ Pfeiffer.)

Homicide inspector
Gilbert Hill.
(Credit: Michelle
Andonian.)

Detective Gerald Tibaldi leading John Fry to his arraignment on murder and mutilation charges. (Credit: Edwin C. Lombardo, The Detroit *News*.)

Dawn Spens and John Fry being led by detective Marlyss Landeros to their arraignment on murder and mutilation charges. (Credit: Edwin C. Lombardo, The Detroit *News*.)

"You remember you were talking in and out on the way out to Ann Arbor?"

Al nodded his head.

"Al, do you remember saying you were in the Cass Corridor with a prostitute?"

There, she finally said it.

"That you'd gotten in over your head," she added.

Momentarily Al seemed to lose his breath. Then he looked at her very quizzically, as though he was searching his own mind for some kind of misplaced thought.

"You did, Al, and I want to know what you meant by that, honey."

"Aw, Jan-Jan," he said.

She saw that boyish look of embarrassment she knew so well. He bowed his head, shaking it slowly, as though he'd really let her down.

"Before you answer me," Jan continued, "let me tell you that I think that everybody is human, and these things happen. What's more important right now is honesty, not, you know, worrying about my reaction."

"But Jan-Jan."

"Because everybody makes mistakes. And I do, too. I mean, a one-night stand isn't going to make a difference. I mean, you've always been very good about helping me when I'm in a jam, and what's bugging me now more than anything is: Is it true or false?"

She was offering him full forgiveness if he needed it. She was offering him a way out. She just needed to know the truth, for the sake of his own conscience as well as her peace of mind.

He was very matter-of-fact.

"Confused," Al said. "I must have been very confused. I might have thought it was me because of my fatigued state."

His amplification was quite elaborate. A female therapist he was supervising was trying to rehabilitate a Cass Corridor prostitute and had "gotten in over her head," he said.

"She didn't know her limitations. And I was trying to steer her back to her professional role. She was overinvolved with this patient. She was seeing her outside the clinical setting. But you don't leave your office. You know that. It's unethical. You don't try and rescue people like that. But I was very worried about her at the time, so I must have confused myself with her. I couldn't see myself doing anything like that. It's just plain unethical."

"You're asking me to believe that?" Jan said, studying his eyes.

"Yes," he said, looking right back into hers. Then he looked hurt that she'd carried around the question so long.

Jan thought carefully about his response. She'd already weighed his behavior. Al didn't fit the profile of the wayward husband. She'd seen plenty of them in marriage counseling and heard the stories from other women. Every hour of his day was accounted for. Al didn't hang out in bars. He never stayed out all night. He never leered at other women. He had never abused her, verbally or physically. As far as she knew, Al had no resentments against her.

At times the notion even seemed preposterous. Al cruising for a prostitute in downtown Detroit? God, she thought, I can't even get him out of the house to see a Tigers baseball game.

Well then, she decided, I'll believe him. Until he proves otherwise, she thought, I have to believe him. I *want* to believe him. If he's lying, she thought, then he's the one who has to live with it. She resolved right then she could not spend the rest of their marriage worrying about something he may have done one night. She hoped she wasn't fooling herself.

Afterward they went downstairs to watch television. Al turned up the volume. This time she was glad the TV was there. She felt very awkward the rest of the night.

Chapter 55

Every day, Cheryl Krizanovic found herself walking the mile up Parkinson Street from the house on Clayton to Michigan Avenue, where she flagged dates outside a topless bar called Dirty Harry's.

Some days she saw Dr. Al Miller's Buick Regal cruise by — the doctor heading for another date with Dawn. Then one afternoon when the October chill had transformed green trees to orange and red, Al stopped to give her a lift. As they headed to the house, he complimented Cheryl on her appearance. She still looked pretty healthy from her sabbatical in Alanson.

"I've been clean for four months," she said.

"I'm so happy for you, Cheryl," he said. "I really am."

Cheryl was lying. She had been dipping into the raw heroin John was dealing on Clayton. But several times before, Al had encouraged her when she spoke of staying clean.

Cheryl always found that odd. She wondered to herself why he didn't feel the same way about Dawn. He appeared to prefer her strung out. His only concern was the presence of other men. Again it was on Al's mind as they drove down Parkinson.

"Cheryl," he said. "Who else is Dawn seeing? Is Dawn still seeing that guy John?" He said it as though he already knew the answer.

"Not to my knowledge," she said.

Cheryl didn't want to get in the middle of that triangle. Al dropped the subject as fast as he brought it up. He steered the conversation to the colors of the maples and elms.

Al was slick that way, Cheryl had observed over the past ten months. He could slide in and out of a touchy subject gracefully. From the beginning she had suspected he was a student of human behavior. She'd noticed how he often sat quietly with his coffee, seemingly studying all of them on his visits.

Cheryl could see why John called him a goof. But she always felt her old boyfriend underestimated Dr. Al Miller. Now, she guessed, Al had detected John was still in the picture.

But Al, Cheryl thought, was selling John short as well. She suspected Al had no sense of how calculating her old boyfriend could be when it came to ensuring an adequate supply of cash. In fact, she already knew that John Fry had taken out a policy on Al. She learned that the afternoon Dawn, John, and she took the white Thunderbird to get some cash from the trick. Al had suggested Dawn meet him outside his office at Harper Hospital. Dawn dropped Cheryl and John off across the street, then drove to the hospital entrance to wait for her sugar daddy. When Al emerged, John started talking.

"This is all bullshit. The man don't fuckin' work here. He's got a place in the Fisher Building."

John was smirking. She'd seen that expression many times over the years. When he looked like that, John couldn't resist serving up some information.

"And, besides, the punk ain't no doctor."

"Well, John, I told you that exam he gave me was kind of funny."

"Yeah, he ain't no real doctor. And, the punk's *married*."

If it was true, she knew John considered the information priceless. She wondered what he'd done — followed Al home? Followed him to his office? Or maybe he was just running another line of intrigue. She'd always found it difficult discerning fact from fiction with her old boyfriend.

John smirked again. He wouldn't say anything else.

Cheryl had seen him play private eye before with regulars, such as the one-armed plumber she dated for three months. When she couldn't milk any more money out of the man with sweet talk, John stepped in. He asked her to check the

240

plumber's license and probe him for details about his income. One night John followed the guy right to his house, threatening to tell his wife. John squeezed him for $350 in all. Later John lost interest, complaining he wasn't worth the effort.

The plumber's cash flow was minor league compared to Al's. Cheryl guessed it would only be a matter of time before John would make a move on Dawn's date. She knew one thing for certain about Lucky Fry: When it came to money, nobody just walked out on the man. Before John met Dawn, Cheryl had tried. But he had always found a way to get her back — whether it was by bullshit or brawn.

The little chat between Cheryl and Al would be their last. On October 23 she left Detroit for good. The exact date would stick in her mind for a long time. She would consider it an important anniversary.

Frank McMasters had headed back to Alanson. He'd given up trying to get her back. The day he left they had an argument over her drug habit outside of the house on Clayton. Frank pulled her leather coat off her shoulders.

"I'm not leaving this crap just so you can hock it for dope," he said.

She screamed for help and John came running out of the house. John showed her that day just how much he really cared about her.

"Hey, man," John yelled from the porch. "You guys are gonna attract the police."

The month she spent living with John and Dawn on Clayton reminded her of the days at the Homewood Manor. She came back to Detroit thinking her old boyfriend John Fry had changed. The only difference in John was he had switched to a better-quality dope.

John still blamed his downfall on Dawn and Al. It sounded all too familiar. She remembered all the times John had told her she had let him down — "hurt him" was the way he always put it. She'd let him down by getting raped by one of his friends. She let him down when she refused to turn tricks. She wondered, but what about my feelings? I was the one who was raped. I'm the one who has to turn the dates.

Cheryl finally was beginning to see how her old boyfriend operated. He had no conscience. He had no real feelings for anyone. He had only an array of realistic disguises he used to cover those flaws. She'd spent five years looking at nothing but masks—the caring philosopher, the prideful protector, the hurt little boy. But everything he touched told another story.

"The little boy," she'd conclude later, "had the devil inside him."

Turning twenty-one in late September started it all. Even the heroin couldn't numb the truth. She couldn't look at her own body in the mirror. She'd sold herself in pieces to a thousand men, but the parts of her she valued most she'd given away no charge to John Fry. Cheryl wondered if she had a year left, let alone a normal lifetime.

One day, Cheryl remembered seeing a place in Petoskey called the Women's Resource Center that advertised a safe house for battered women. She decided she would have no trouble proving she met the criteria. All she had to do was take off her blouse.

On the morning of October 23 she found herself in the Cass Corridor one last time. She had a couple of hours to kill before catching the Greyhound to Petoskey. She spent them sitting in the White Grove, gazing through the wiremesh windows at everyone caught in one form of slavery or another on the street. Mark Bando spotted her there, came inside, and arrested her on an outstanding warrant. She had enough money on her to cover the $150 bond.

"I'm leaving, Bando," she said as she walked out of Police Headquarters. "I'm leaving Detroit and I'm going to get clean."

"Whatever you say, Cheryl," the cop said.

She knew he didn't believe her. But as she boarded the Greyhound later, she really didn't care. She knew she was going to go to the safe house in Petoskey. She knew she was going to get clean — not for Mark Bando, for Lucky Fry, or for Frank McMasters.

Not for anyone else.

As the Greyhound left the Detroit skyline in a blast of black diesel exhaust, Cheryl Krizanovic leaned into the backseat and closed her eyes.

This time, she thought, I'm going to do it for myself.

Chapter 56

The two addicts timed their approach with the Buick's arrival at the curb. They made their move when the driver got out of the car.

John Fry could see the shakedown unfolding through the kitchen window as Dawn went outside to meet Al. When one of the junkies held a blade under Al's rib cage, John shoved a kitchen knife in his back pocket and headed out the door. He decoyed his intentions by approaching in a lazy gait.

"Hey, what's happening, mon."

"Nothing that concerns you."

"Any fucking thing that happens in this yard concerns me. You gonna do somethin' with that knife, motherfucker, you better do it to me."

One of the men didn't like what he saw, spun, and sprinted up the street. The other walked away slowly. John still was glaring when he looked back.

"I'm glad you were here, John," Al said.

He wasn't grinning. Dawn got in the Regal and the two of them drove off. Less than an hour later the three of them sat around the kitchen table, sipping coffee. Al said that he and Dawn had a good talk.

"John, she tells me she's had problems with those two guys before," he said. "Are you doing anything right now?"

John said he'd been working as a truck driver for the past few months, but now he was laid off.

"Would you consider hanging around and making sure nothing happens to her? I can't be here all the time. My job keeps me away."

"Don't have nothin' better to do," John said.

After Al left, Dawn told John that she had laid the groundwork to get him back in the picture. She told Al the entire neighborhood knew he was bringing her money. That made her an easy mark for thieves. If he couldn't be there to protect her, somebody should.

"Well, I guess you could say that it was a setup," John later told a friend. "The robber was real, OK? But at the time I didn't really know she had buzzed him up about all this. Let me tell you somethin' about this girl. She's good, mon. I can't take credit for it. I take credit for some of it, but she was a con artist when I met her. I'm not knocking her. It paid off for both of us."

Chapter 57

Part of a child's ability to develop feelings of trust and mistrust are based on his ability to have a tantrum and have his mother go along with the tantrum or accept the fact the child has normal emotions of anger and rage.

— W. ALAN CANTY,
Concordia College lecture

Jan Canty hated to admit it, but she really wasn't looking forward to another Thanksgiving at Al's mother's house. She'd never felt comfortable with her husband's family. With her own parents in Arizona, she would have loved to have another parental homestead nearby where she could kick off her shoes. But the Canty home had never been that kind of place.

The bungalow always felt like a museum to her. It wasn't only the antique square grand piano and the pristine knick-knacks in the living room. The house was always uncomfortably quiet. She wished someone would turn on a stereo, or even the TV. Instead she knew the three of them would sit quietly in straight-backed chairs in a semicircle. There was a casual family room in the back, but the door was always closed. There was a screened-in porch, but she'd never seen it used, even on summer's hottest days. Everyone just stayed in the living room and perspired.

When Al Sr. was alive she'd often sat in one of those chairs and sweat through what seemed like interrogations. Where are you working now? Aren't you glad Al supports you in school? How much does your tuition cost? Is that a new sweater? Did Al buy it for you?

"What kind of car do you drive?" Al Sr. once asked.

"An old Volkswagen bug, a convertible."

At first he seemed relieved; then came the follow-up.

"I suppose you want to get a Cadillac now, huh?"

She tried to fight back. She always suspected they thought she'd married Al for his money.

"I have no interest in Cadillacs. I don't even like them. I mean, they're big hogs." Then she realized Al Sr. drove one.

Even with Al Sr. gone, his presence still seemed to dominate the household. There was much talk about the family's professional stature and the good Canty name. But Jan also sensed underlying conflicts that never really surfaced. She was never really sure how mother and son felt about Al Sr. They seemed to idolize him but have underlying negative feelings. They seemed incapable of resolving their ambivalence.

Typical of that was an odd conversation she watched them have one afternoon about Al Sr.'s contribution to an athletic scholarship fund at Syracuse University. She recalled it along these lines.

"Oh, Ma, you know Pa was a very generous kind of person."

"He certainly was, Bus."

"And, Ma, that's why he endowed the scholarship fund for athletics."

"But Bus, I never was aware of that."

"But Ma, that's why he did it, out of generosity. Don't you think it was good?"

"No, Bus, I don't. I never did approve of it."

"But Ma."

"I was *livid* with him, Buster."

And that would be it. Subject dropped. They often seemed to be criticizing Al Sr. and protecting him at the same time.

Mother and son often had little spats like that. They had a singsong way of bickering. "Oh, Ma" and "Now, Bus" signaled something was cooking. One Thanksgiving they argued about where the turkey should be carved. Mother wanted it on the table. Son wanted it on the stove. It started with "I'll help."

"No, Ma, I'll do it."

"No, Bus, I'll do it."

"Oh, Ma."

"Now, Buster . . ."

The dispute escalated as the two of them tugged at the turkey. Their tension was mutually contagious, but their anger was always restrained. There was never any shouting or profanity. That day they did let go as they bickered—of the bird. The turkey thudded to the floor. Al started to raise his voice.

"Now, Buster," Mrs. Canty snapped. "That's no way to talk to your mother."

Their disputes often ended with that line. It always stopped Al cold, sending his shoulders into a hunch. Why, Jan thought, doesn't he just *stand tall* and tell her he's madder than hell? He seemed no more capable of that kind of natural response than a preschool child.

Despite the proper veneer, Gladys Canty in many ways still infantilized her son, Jan had observed over the years. Jan's first hint came when they bought the big Tudor. When Gladys toured the home she noticed they had moved their things into the master bedroom.

"Why, Bus, you're not going to sleep in here, are you?" she said.

Who, Jan thought, did she think she was?

His mother's perception of him—of both of them—revealed itself in other ways. She was always pushing children's food on them—sweets such as cookies, cakes, and chocolates. Not only was there the nickname Buster, but Gladys was fond of calling her Jannie, or "little Jannie." Once Gladys bought Jan a sweater. When she returned it because of her allergy to wool, she found it came from the children's department.

"Does she see me as a child?" she asked Al.

"Oh, you know how Ma is," he said. He often dismissed

248

any of his parents' quirks as insignificant.

But she could tell he had some uncomfortable memories. When Jan took up photography as a hobby she discovered her husband had an aversion to the camera.

"I love what you're doing," he said. "But do me a favor. Please don't take pictures of me."

"Why?" she asked.

" 'Cause every time I turned around I was getting my picture taken as a kid. I was so sick of it."

One night they watched a half-dozen 8mm movies taken of Al in intervals from age nine months to six years. The black-and-white films were full of what were now classic cars and scenes taken in the backyard of the family's old place on Chalmers. Some were filmed at outside parties. One thing struck Jan in all of them. Al usually was the only child, even at the backyard parties. He looked out of place in close-ups as he toddled among the skirts and pant legs of adult giants.

Al Sr. always was impeccably dressed in tailored three-piece suits in the films. Gladys had a fondness for modest dresses and flats instead of heels. Her tastes in grooming and clothes for her son, however, were more elaborate.

In one film, at the age of three, Al had long golden curls that fell to his shoulders. Such was boys' fashion at the turn of the century, but the year was 1936. Al was embarrassed by the image. Later he told Jan that Al Sr. finally ordered his wife to "cut those goddamn things off."

As he approached school age, young Al sported the look of a proper English schoolboy rather than the typical Detroit youngster in dungarees and T-shirts. She saw photos of shorts-and-blouse ensembles with white embroidered collars. Al told her once that on his first day of school his mother dressed him literally like Buster Brown—the lad in the shoe with the round hat, big silk bow tie, and long Dutch-boy haircut. Al even had a bulldog for a pet.

"My God," she said. "What a way to send a boy to school in Detroit. This isn't the early 1900s. That's kind of insensitive."

"Well, you know Ma."

"Well, I wouldn't do that to my kid at five."

"Yeah, it was kind of weird."

Then Al fell into a very strange kind of laugh, as though he was outside of himself, chuckling at a secret memory.

Where, she thought, was Al's father's influence in his childhood? The only input he ever seemed to have concerned Al's quest for a Ph.D. Jan could easily imagine how her own dad would have reacted if her mother had emasculated her brother that way.

But she knew Al's mother's influence in clothes continued well into later life. When Al moved from his old house on Fisher Road, Jan helped him pack. She came across one box that she thought had been left by his ex-wife. It contained a bright green-and-black plaid jacket and a plaid smock in bright yellow, red, and black. All looked as though they belonged to a woman.

"Here, Maggie left some of her clothes, Al," she said.

He had a chilled look on his face.

"Those . . . are my clothes," he stammered.

"I've never seen you wear those."

"No, I never did."

She knew he was embarrassed.

"They sure are ugly for a man," she said, trying to back out of her previous words.

"Well, *my mother* bought them for me."

Then he changed the subject. He usually did anytime Jan tried to initiate a meaningful discussion about his childhood. However, through his veiled complaints over the years she detected her husband had spent a lot of time listening to lectures on what was proper and what was not.

Jan detected little of that tone on this Thanksgiving visit, but she couldn't help but notice how tense her husband was as they waited for the holiday turkey. He spent less time talking and more within himself. The house seemed more silent than ever. Jan might have welcomed even one of their tiffs to liven everything up.

At one point Jan felt sorry for him. He seemed almost pathetic as he hunched in one of the living room chairs, his body slanted away from her and his mother He was nibbling on a cookie and staring out a window.

"Al, what's wrong, honey?" she asked him after they left.

"Jan-Jan, I'm working on it in therapy," he said.

Chapter 58

Compensation is the choice of an equal, but different goal. For example, the 5-foot-4 teenager who can't make the football team, so he becomes captain of the school debate team. Overcompensation, such as doing it to feel superior, is a symptom of neurosis.

— W. Alan Canty,
Henry Ford Community College lectures

A computer room supervisor named Ray Danford glanced at the calendar and decided to phone his old friend Alan Canty. No matter where their lives took them over the past thirty-five years, they always found a way to get in touch in late November, when their birthdays fell only five days apart. Al suggested they meet on a Saturday for lunch.

"Where?"

"How 'bout Marcus? It's still there, you know."

"The Original" Marcus Hamburgers, Ray thought, one of the old hangouts from their late teens. That would be nostalgic. He wondered if the food was still the same.

Not only was the diner dishing up the same small burgers when they met two weeks later, the place looked as though it hadn't been redecorated since 1949. They sat on stools at the counter and ordered up a bunch.

"The waitress even looks the same," Al said.

"She may be the same one," Ray joked.

The two friends had covered a lot of life's territory since the summer of '49, when they met. They could have spent the whole lunch reminiscing, but Al's mind was on current affairs.

"By the way, Ray, I've met this girl named Dawn," he began. "Yeah, a prostitute. She's from Harper Woods, in fact, but I found her in the Cass Corridor living in an apartment with her boyfriend."

Al offered up a few more sketchy details of the relationship. He saw this girl frequently. Dawn and her boyfriend were drug addicts. He said he'd worked out a pretty sophisticated schedule to enable the escapade. He'd been seeing her a year.

As the story unfolded, Ray felt as though the oxygen was being sucked from his chest. He sometimes got those attacks. A doctor once told him it was hyperventilation. Finally he had to interrupt.

"Uh-oh, Al," he said. "I've lost my breath."

When Al saw the frightened look on Ray's face he started laughing. Soon he was cackling like hell, while Ray struggled to put the brakes on the panic attack. Seeing Al's reaction helped him pull himself back together.

"What's so goddamn funny about me losing my breath?" Ray asked.

"Nothing," he said. "Nothing."

Al Canty always did have an odd sense of humor, Ray thought. But his laughter had a manic ring to it, as though from someone under heavy stress. Then Al jumped back into his story.

"Ray," he continued, "they think I'm *Al Miller,* Dr. Al Miller."

Al grinned widely. It was an inside joke. Ray knew Al Miller as the race driver Al Canty used to cheer on at the old track at Schoenherr and Eight Mile Road. Miller and his black stocker won most of the races they saw in their teens on the quarter-mile oval. Back then it was billed as the fastest dirt track in the country.

Marcus Hamburgers wasn't the only thing that hadn't changed over all these years, Ray thought. He and Al had talked about that as psychology majors at Wayne University.

"Nobody ever really changes that much, even in analysis,"

Al used to say. "The basics are still there."

And the way Ray saw it, the Dr. Al Miller masquerade was basic Al Canty, another in a series of many charades. In their early years, Al had always compensated for what he lacked in basic masculine bravado with scams of intrigue and psychological daring. But Ray could only think of one that involved a hooker.

Then they were both college students in their early twenties. One Friday afternoon, Al came by with two hundred dollars he said he'd stolen from a girlfriend. He'd heard about a place in Chicago called Rush Street. In no time the two of them were off to see it in Ray's black Volkswagen bug.

They booked into a Chicago hotel. Al procured a prostitute and brought her back to their room. Actually, soliciting her was one of the more normal aspects of the trip. At least he paid her. Al blew most of the stolen money on food and drink. When they left the hotel, Al distracted the clerk so Ray could sneak out with their suitcases without paying. Then Al sent a postcard from the Chicago YMCA to his mother, writing they were staying there.

But Al overlooked something. He'd put his home address on the hotel's registration. When the hotel bill arrived at his parents' house, he wrote "not at this address" and sent it back.

"If you're going to break some rules, you should use a fictitious name," Al later said.

Most people would have written that off as a youthful prank if it was his only one as a young man. But there were many others. With women, especially, Al seemed to be more intrigued by his schemes to seduce girls than by sex itself. Ray spent hours listening to Al analyze ways to find angles on attractive girls in bars, but his friend never once left his seat to make an introduction. Once Al posed as a veterinarian to secure a drug believed to be an aphrodisiac from a druggist. He rented and furnished an apartment to try it out on the date. Another time he assumed the role of a private eye to find out about a girl he liked. He tailed her, kept logs of her daily schedule, but never did ask her out. Once he stuffed his

254

cheeks with cotton and told a girl he was dating he was terminally ill. As a dying man's request, he asked her to make love. She caught on and dumped him.

Then there was a film he made in college called *Wire Home*. It served two purposes: It was a serious Freudian drama. It was also an effort by Al to seduce the high school homecoming queen. She was a stunning girl with long chestnut hair. Al hired her as the lead actress. Ray was the cameraman.

As for the Freudian theme, *Wire Home* referred to a house held together by wire — the weak structure of the family. The plot featured a young man whose father was always out of town on business while his mother scurried about the city from one bingo game to another. The main character, the son, kills his girlfriend, or she ends up slaying him. Ray wasn't sure. Al had been promising to show him the film for years.

As for the homecoming queen, Al got nowhere. Most of his charades failed because of transparency or miscalculation, like his plan to dodge the draft. A couple of nights before his physical, they rented a motel room on Jefferson and filled him full of blackberry brandy. Ray would never forget propping Al's arm on a telephone and, at his insistence, trying to break it with three stomps of his boot. He only bruised it badly. Ray just couldn't bring himself to put his weight into it. Al was anxious about what his mother would think, so he came up with some kind of story about the injury.

Scruples were never an issue in such ventures. Back then Al Canty envisioned himself following a higher order of conduct than common morality. Society's rules were part of what their intellectual mentor, Sigmund Freud, called the superego. Ray had to admit he felt the same way back then.

As young men, Ray Danford and Al Canty concocted a chemistry that bonded their friendship and set their worldview. While Ray was raised in a blue-collar household and Al in one of middle-class sophistication, they had much in common. Ray was painfully shy, and he stammered. Al was ostracized as an aloof odd duck. Together, they found deliverance in the essays of Sigmund Freud.

Back then, they guarded the newfound knowledge as though it was their own private stock. Freud not only gave them a new way of looking at everyone, he'd taken away the world's sting. Everything could no longer be measured in the black-and-white standards they'd always found troubling. The higher order was the ability to see and analyze the varying shades of gray.

They developed nicknames for the unenlightened. Freud once called religion "mass obsession with neurosis." Ray and Al called churchgoers MONs. High school heroes could be as easily discerned. They called swaggering macho types Chuck Need. Ray and Al knew that they *needed* to be that way.

They fancied themselves sophisticated intellectuals. They talked with Al Sr. about human behavior and were intrigued by his demonstrations of hypnosis. They saw themselves on the leading edge of the trends of the day. Freudian psychology was invading American culture. Filmmakers had discovered the unconscious. Directors such as Elia Kazan buried Oedipal allegories and other Freudian concepts in films such as *East of Eden* and *On the Waterfront*.

It carried into their studies. Ray took thirty-nine hours of psychology at Wayne State but eventually had to drop out to go to work. Now he had a daughter and son, lived in a Harper Woods bungalow, and cleaned carpets for a second income. Ray had married his high school sweetheart, Jeannie. In fact he met Al at the party where he asked Jeannie to go steady. It was August 4. They still observed the date with an annual gathering of old east-side friends.

Al took psychology to the limit. He was the only one of the old gang who had really done it, turned his college training into a way of life. Their friendship had fluctuated over the years. They drifted apart when he was with his first wife Maggie. Al was running with a pretty sophisticated crowd. With Jan, he'd become more accessible, throwing a couple of August 4 parties himself at his big Tudor.

What a shame about this prostitute, Ray thought. He found Jan Canty exceptionally attractive with an unpretentious personality to match. Al had pulled some secret maneuvers on his first wife Maggie. But as far as Ray knew, they all revolved around hiding a half-dozen antique cars in garages around the city. Ray thought Al had settled down after meeting Jan. Now he had this escapade going. Ray guessed his old friend knew what he was doing.

Al was eager to meet again as they walked out of their old hangout.

"Ray, let's meet like this once a month for lunch," he said.

Ray Danford agreed. He knew full well that through the years he had been Al's only close friend and confidant.

Later that day Ray remembered his daughter, April, talking about a girl named Dawn who had dropped out of sight several weeks before the 1983 graduation. He asked her about the dropout.

"Didn't you say there was a girl in the high school named Dawn, who just disappeared?"

"Yep."

"What was her name?"

"Dawn Spens. Nobody has heard from her since. Why?"

"It's nothing."

He wondered if she was the same one.

Part Three
1985-86

Chapter 59

*No matter how hard you try there will be people who
will not like you.*

— W. ALAN CANTY,
Henry Ford Community College lectures

Dawn Spens ushered in the new year with another trip to
the hospital. She took a few swallows of champagne at a
party thrown by a cousin, complained of pain in her side,
then passed out. When she awoke to 1985, she was jaun-
diced.

Dr. Al Miller had cautioned her that her recurring dizzy
spells and nausea during the holidays were caused by her
drug habit. She and John were not only shooting heroin, they
were dabbling in intravenous cocaine as well. Muscle strains
from vomiting caused the pain under her right ribs, Al said.
He suggested she go easy for a couple of days, and the problem would clear up.

The advice may have been good, but Al's diagnosis left his
physician's skills in serious question. When John took his
girlfriend to Southwest Detroit Hospital near downtown Detroit, doctors admitted her for chronic hepatitis. It was her
third major hospitalization in twelve months.

That week, Al was scheduled to leave for Arizona for another yearly purging session with the old miner and his
mules. But Dawn tried to reach her sugar daddy before he left
to let him know she was in the hospital. She got the answering
service for Dr. Alan Canty.

Dawn and John decided to do a little investigating. John

261

looked up the listings for Canty in the telephone book. There was a Dr. W. Alan Canty in the Fisher Building and a residential listing in Grosse Pointe Park. Dawn remembered that on one of their lunch hour drives Al showed her the outside of the house he owned in Grosse Pointe Park, but had been renting out since his wife's death. The street, Berkshire, matched the listing for Dr. Canty in the phone book.

"If that's him, call the punk's house," Dawn said.

The parallels became more intriguing when John dialed the number. A woman answered the phone, saying Dr. Canty wasn't home. John identified himself as a friend trying to reach the doctor.

"It's kind of important," he said. "Where can I get a message to him?"

"Well, this is the housekeeper," the woman said. "And he and Mrs. Canty are out of town for a week."

John hung up.

When Al returned the next week, he was eager to show off a new pair of engineer boots he said he bought in Arizona. They had steel toes.

"Thought I might need 'em," he quipped to John. "Just in case we go back to the Gaiety Bar."

Al also brought a photo album to Dawn's hospital room. It contained pictures of his house in Grosse Pointe Park. Since claiming the home was burglarized and trashed in the summer, he had spun an ongoing narrative about the house being repaired and renovated. Now the work was done, and he wanted to show Dawn the results. He left the album for her to peruse.

Later, John and Dawn studied the collection of photos and peeked into a lifestyle they'd only seen in magazines. There was much carpet, wallpaper, and wainscoting. There were windows of leaded glass and carved cove moldings meeting the home's ten-foot-high ceilings. John and Dawn gazed at Japanese art and Oriental furnishings in brass and black lacquer. Room after room featured well-kept antiques: dark armoire with a long oval mirror, a nineteenth-century ice chest, a double bed of brass and wrought iron. They saw a country kitchen in solid oak and an airy sun-room with ceramic tile flooring. They saw a living room larger than their entire apartment back at the Homewood Manor. A leather couch and easy chair faced the fireplace. There was only one exterior picture in the collection, that of a walkway made of squarely laid bricks.

The album looked as though someone was trying to record all the owner's belongings. Unaware of their research in the phone book, Al had unwittingly furnished John Fry and Dawn Spens with a tantalizing documentary of his wealth.

Dawn Spens didn't last a full two weeks in Southwest Detroit Hospital. She walked out when physicians restricted her visits. John told friends her urine had tested dirty with street drugs.

On January 13, Al drove her to Receiving Hospital, where again she was admitted for hepatitis. They ordered a subclavian IV line to supply her with nourishment and Demerol. Nurses were told to keep a close watch, but she wasn't given drug screens.

Dawn would spend fifteen days in Receiving. John Fry left the trick pad on Clayton and moved into a cousin's house on the southwest side. Every noon hour except Sunday, Al picked him up there, and the two visited Dawn. Al usually stopped at the gift shop. He still would do anything for the hooker.

"Whatya doin'?" John asked Dawn one night on the telephone.

"I'm making up Al's list. I want to see what I can get."

Al took her fingernail kits, makeup kits, coloring books, comic books, cartons of Marlboro menthols, and her beloved crossword puzzles. She spent hours doing crosswords, and staying high.

Al also provided money for heroin and transportation to the dope house. He always waited in the car while John copped. Dawn complained frequently about the shortcomings of the hospital's doses of Demerol. John made up the difference in her IV.

John and Al began to talk quite a bit during their excursions. For the time being, at least, they seemed to be tolerating one another's roles in Dawn's life.

The subjects varied widely. Al expounded on Detroit history, pointing out local landmarks and explaining ethnic origins of various neighborhoods. John told him about his family's roots in the South. After seeing a TV documentary on James Dean, Al analyzed the actor, adding how much he admired him. John had a lot of memories from the fifties as well. Al talked about old cars, John about vintage bikes. He showed John a picture of a Cord convertible he was having restored. He said he sometimes made trips to Boston and New York to find parts. John remembered Al telling Dawn he used to ride a Harley.

"If that guy rides a Harley-Davidson, Popeye is a punk, man," John said at first.

Now he wasn't so sure. Al was a bundle of contradictions, John began telling his friends. The affluent intellectual obviously was out of his territory but also had a believable grasp of Detroit's lawless element. Sometimes he even took on a bit of an accent, as though he was trying to get the hang of street jive.

One trip they made together particularly intrigued the former biker. The two of them drove to Detroit's Brightmore district, a west-side enclave known for its mix of lower-income white families and motorcycle clubs. While they waited in Al's Buick for another drug addict to cop in a dope house, Al talked about motorcycle clubs.

"John, I used to party with some of the clubs. Forbidden Wheels was my favorite."

He named others: Renegades, Scorpions, Huns.

"He knew the language that only a person who had been there or done their homework could know," Fry later told a friend.

Another time Al revealed he almost got caught committing an armed robbery of a gas station when he was young.

"I can identify with some of the things you do, John. Me and a couple of buddies. They got caught, but I got away."

Fry later tried to explain to his friends the seeming clash between the bespectacled, duckfooted doctor with the funny grin and the stories he told.

"This guy is such a contradiction that he makes me look like an asshole when I start trying to explain it."

Nothing, however, had Lucky Fry's attention more than

the kind of money Al was spending. One night, John used Dawn's date book to calculate the amount for the year 1984.

"Moneywise, he'd bought her six cars—though only two were actually bought," he would later recall. "The rest were squeeze plays. Counting the lump sums and the money every day the total was between $130,000 and $140,000."

At times John inflated that figure to as high as $300,000. The amount changed depending on whom he was trying to impress or what mood-altering substances were swirling in his circulatory system. But among his closest friends, the $140,000 figure remained constant.

John knew the money just didn't fit the merchandise. For that kind of cash Al could have the most expensive call girl in Detroit catering to him in a suite on the seventy-fifth floor of the Westin Hotel. He asked Dawn about it one night.

"Just what is this guy getting?"

"John, I swear to God. I've screwed the guy less than a half-dozen times."

Then, she said, after a week or two of no physical contact, Al usually put in a formal request, saying, "Well, are you going to take care of me?"

Then she gave him oral sex.

"There's got to be something this guy wants," John later said. "At first I thought it was an attraction to Dawn. But she really ain't *that* great—not for *that* kind of money. And the way she treats him, it's just not normal. If you're giving a broad $200 to $300 a day and just spending an hour with her, that girl is supposed to say nothing wrong to you in that hour."

That wasn't the case either. Since late fall, John had been watching his girlfriend cop an attitude. The sugar daddy who once was her source of pride now was a source of disgust. "The way she put it. She hated him—hated what he represented."

Dawn Spens nicknamed Al "The Pinhead" behind his back, a slur that stuck from the day she conceived it. Her attitude crept into the ways she requested larger sums of money. If Al stalled, Dawn pouted. She might speak to him. She might not. She might go to lunch with him. She might refuse to leave the house. "As far as sex, he could forget it," John said.

But Al kept coming back. One day John watched her storm out of the house with Al sitting at the kitchen table.

"What about Al?" John said.

"Fuck him," she said. "He'll go home when it gets time."

Once she brought her sugar daddy to tears over the white Thunderbird he bought her. When the engine began knocking John told her to sell it. Earlier, Al had told a dope dealer named Stumpy who frequented the trick pad on Clayton that he would back Dawn's line of credit.

John came home one day to discover Dawn browbeating her regular. Al was sobbing as he walked with slumped shoulders to his Buick.

"It's your fault that the car is gone," she shouted at him. "You told the dope man to give me anything I want. But you didn't fuckin' pay him and I had to give him the car."

"Please, Dawn," Al begged. "I'll get you another car. *I will.*"

Later, when Al didn't produce money for another automobile, she waited until John was present before squeezing him again.

"You said you could get me a car," she told him.

Al looked embarrassed. Then Dawn looked at John.

"Fuck it," she said. "I'll get *John* to get me a car."

The tactic produced more cash. John found a well-used gold Thunderbird to give the squeeze credence. The car didn't last a month. It was hot and was eventually sold for dope money.

By late January, as John watched Al run a daily shuttle from the southwest side to the dope house to the gift shop to Dawn's hospital bed, where he was often met with indifference, John had no doubt Al was hooked. But he couldn't understand the nature of the bait.

"So when I started lookin' at all of this, I said there's got to be somethin' more somewhere," he said later. "I told Dawn, 'I think the punk is writing a book — *The Life of Dope Fiends,* or whatever.' Because nobody puts up with all that and keeps coming back."

Chapter 60

We also see many people who are disturbed by feelings of insecurity and inferiority. They sometimes attempt to compensate for their inferiority feelings by attempting to speed, to outwit the police or showing off in some other manner . . . The Detroit Traffic Clinic unmasks these people for what they really are—social misfits.

— ALAN CANTY, SR.
"The Detroit Traffic Clinic," 1959

In other cases we find the youth who violates because, as a result of a hatred for the father, he now commits an aggression against authority or against the police who to him represent a father substitute.

— ALAN CANTY, SR.
"The Youthful Problem Driver," 1942

Ray Danford recognized the melody under the lunchtime chatter of the Cadieux Cafe. He was surprised Al Canty hadn't already acknowledged the old hit from *My Fair Lady* called "On the Street Where You Live."

"Hey, Al, listen," he said, gesturing to a speaker. "They're playing your song."

He teased his old friend about how he'd worn out his record of the sound track in their midtwenties. Al used to rave about *Pygmalion,* the Bernard Shaw play that inspired first a movie, then the musical. He was fascinated with the story of the aloof English professor who wagers that he can take a

267

young flower girl out of the gutter, dress her up, and transform her into a sophisticated lady. Everyone else was playing rhythm-and-blues records and going to drive-ins. Young Al Canty saw the musical, hummed the "The Rain in Spain," and mused about Henry Higgins's efforts to control the wily Eliza Doolittle. The old gang thought his taste a bit odd.

As they waited for a couple of orders of steamed mussels, Ray could see why his old friend missed the song. Al was troubled over the young prostitute that he had lightly called his "latest thing" only a month ago.

"This is really getting to be a drain on my finances, Ray," he said. "The thing is really getting to be a pain in general."

"How much of a pain?"

"Large amounts."

"You see her every day, or something?"

"Six days a week. A couple hundred at a time."

"You mean a couple hundred every time you see her? Christ, Al. That's twelve hundred a week."

"It's been more than that. And the time. It's taking too much time from what I should be doing. And her boyfriend is a real pain in the ass."

Al told him about the tattooed pimp named John. But Ray wasn't surprised that a character like that was around. Al's interest in street types went way back.

Ray remembered a time in high school when Al always had the latest information on neighborhood thieves, con artists, and motorcycle clubs. Al thought a few of them really had a lot on the ball. Ray remembered one in particular named Harold. Harold could take an Oldsmobile and refit it with a Cadillac's body, turning the cheaper auto into an imitation of the real thing. Al studied under him to learn the switch. Al bragged how Harold also showed him how to snap a padlock. Then one night, he went with Harold on a gas station burglary on Jefferson. Al engaged the attendant in a conversation while Harold picked the safe. They got three hundred dollars.

Al was attracted to psychopaths, even before they discovered the personality disorder in college textbooks. They had quite a few discussions about it. As Freudians, they believed the psychopath lacked development of the superego. In layman's terms, the psychopath didn't have a conscience.

Ray Danford sometimes wondered about Al's superego as well in those days. When Al drove, he ignored red lights and other traffic laws. Once he deliberately turned the wrong way down a one-way street in front of a squad car. He handled that cop as he did the others. First he wouldn't roll down the window. Then he'd crack it, and the line was always the same.

"Well, my dad is Al Canty. You know him. He works at the psychopathic clinic."

The name often got him off. Then Al laughed wildly as they drove away. Later Ray would learn that Al, as a teenager, accumulated scores of traffic and parking tickets. His embarrassed father paid some and got others dismissed. Finally one judge suggested to Al Sr. that they let him serve five days in the county jail. Al did the time but continued amassing violations.

Al liked attention and often emulated people who were at the center of it. In high school, he spent one summer imitating a classmate popular with the girls at the YMCA dances. Al worked for weeks rehearsing all his moves — his lines, his physical mannerisms, his pattern of speech — and ended up looking foolish on the dance floor.

Ray sometimes wondered why Al didn't just be himself. Then he wondered if there really was an Al Canty. He was always posing back then. Al had dozens of theatrical postures he could summon at will. When he was still, he sat or stood, holding a cigarette between vertical fingers, his elbow resting on his waist. When someone in the old gang told a funny story, Al would lean back in his chair, toss his head way back, and cackle. It was a hollow, unconnected laugh.

Then, in his early twenties, Al discovered James Dean. He was intrigued by the actor's search for his own identity, in his lives on the screen and off. Dean could very well have suffered from an Oedipus complex, they decided as young Freudians. His deep attachment to his late mother was well publicized. Dean only made three films, and all of them fascinated Al.

Al thought the actor was brilliant as the young man trying to win a demanding father's love in *East of Eden*. The character finally received it, but only because the father discovers the real nature of love on his deathbed.

Al decided Dean stole *Giant* from Rock Hudson and Elizabeth Taylor. He played a self-condemning oil tycoon who had it all — except the woman he wants. The self-destructive character ended up disgracing himself in front of a national audience.

When *Rebel Without a Cause* hit the screens, Al bought a red jacket like the one Dean's lead character wore and began dangling a cigarette from his lip. For months they analyzed *Rebel Without a Cause* from the first scene to the last. It was high Freudian drama, and brain food for the two of them.

They agreed that Dean's awkward and shy hero, Jim Stark, was filled with confusion about his role in life. The movie introduced Stark drunk and curled in the fetal position in the street, clutching a toy monkey he wouldn't give up.

Stark was both an infant and an adult, lost in his own hidden fantasies. He couldn't find direction from his mother, who complained how she suffered giving him birth, or from the father who bought him everything. In one scene Stark's smoldering resentments drove him to nearly choke his dad to death.

Sometimes, out of the blue, Al used to grab his temples and recite Stark's classic line to the film character's bickering parents:

"You're tearing me apart."

Al knew all the dialogue. In one early scene the troubled Stark found some empathy from a police officer named Ray. Al had a lot of fun with that one. He used to turn to Ray Danford, hit a Dean pose, then say Stark's line from that scene:

"You can see right through me."

In the film, Stark met the teenage tramp Judy, played by Natalie Wood. She was promiscuous in order to punish her emotionally estranged father. Stark's alter ego is Plato,

270

played by Sal Mineo. He was a weak, neurotic teen, too unstable to survive an adolescent society dominated by bullies. He was an only child with an absentee father and a mother always away on trips or at social functions.

Then, Jim Stark won over Judy. With Plato in tow and the bullies on their trail, they holed up in an abandoned mansion and acted out their own imaginary family. Plato found some temporary satisfaction in the masquerade. But in the film's climax, Plato was killed, while Stark found his manhood.

Adults criticized *Rebel* for inflaming a teenage population into delinquency. For Al and Ray, the film was a tragedy about families paralyzed by hypocrisy and the denial of feeling.

The movie was Al's favorite actor's epitaph. Ray remembered them hearing the news on the radio on September 30, 1955. He was driving Al out to Clarkston for a session with his psychiatrist. James Dean was dead, killed in a car crash. At the time, the actor was writing a script for a film he wanted to star in and direct — *Dr. Jekyll and Mr. Hyde*. Was it a reckless accident or a suicide?

Like his film hero, Al Canty kept searching for something to latch onto well into his late twenties. Once Al complained about his inability to connect with himself. He described one of his earliest recollections, from the age of eight.

"We built a fort and I hit another kid with a snowball," Al said. "The only thing that kept going through my mind was *is this all there is?* It was like the Peggy Lee song."

Al always seemed to have only a peripheral interest in most things; his inability to get his hands dirty with his cars was a classic example. Psychology was the first and only entity that Ray Danford had ever seen bring total commitment. It obviously had served Al well on the material level. But now Ray could see that his clinical knowledge was little help with his attraction to the hooker and her pimp.

"Well, maybe you just better get out of this thing," Ray said as they cracked their mussels.

"It's pretty bad. You ought to see her. She's yellow. She's in the hospital now with hepatitis. She's virtually killing herself

271

with drugs."

"That bad?"

"Yeah, if she died there my troubles would be over."

"Well, that would be one way out," Ray said.

Al thought the proposition was funny. The two old friends had a good laugh, but it provided only temporary relief of Ray Danford's concern.

Chapter 61

Christine Duchene Messmann was weary of the controversy over the twenty-year-old drug addict with the long medical history. By late January, Dawn Spens had become the most challenging case in the third-year medical student's rotation at Detroit Receiving Hospital.

Messmann found much promise in the young woman who talked repeatedly of turning her life around. A resident of Harper Woods, she saw Dawn as a neighbor.

"Lookit," she told Dawn. "Age twenty is young. But thirty comes up real fast. But if you don't reform, I don't even think you're going to make it to thirty."

They spent a lot of time talking, and Dawn spent a lot of time agreeing. Her friend John, she said, was a reformed addict and was going to help her get straight. There was the older man in tortoiseshell glasses who visited her as well. He also was concerned. Messmann assumed he was a friend of the family.

"It seems you've really taken an interest in Dawn," he said once, taking her aside. "I want to thank you for that. That's nice 'cause she needs help. She's really a good girl."

Messmann felt good about the holistic approach she'd taken with the entire case. She offered to refer Dawn to a drug program, but Dawn wanted to move in with her mother in Windsor. Messmann had talked to the mother twice and she seemed eager to have Dawn. Dawn's father also had visited several times.

Messmann had a lot of hope for Dawn. The intern on her team, however, didn't see it that way.

"You're wasting your energy on an addict," he said. "Nothing ever comes of them."

They'd had a running dispute over the case. Messmann wasn't naive. She could see Dawn had a knack for keying on people's weak spots. One night Dawn had dropped Messmann's name to get more Demerol from a compliant nurse.

Dawn's pain — or lack of it — was the most debated subject on her team. Dawn complained of discomfort, though her chart documented a steady recovery from hepatitis. The intern wanted to cut off her Demerol; Messmann wanted to taper it.

"Yeah, yeah," he'd say. "You know these patients are manipulators, don't you? She's a drug addict and shouldn't get anything."

Messmann put her reputation on the line against the senior team member.

"When we have an alcoholic suffering from pancreatitis you don't just say, 'Tough. You did it to yourself,' " she argued.

It came to a head the last week in January. The Demerol was discontinued January 25, while her subclavian line remained in for nourishment. When Messmann talked to her two days later, Dawn said she was finalizing her plans to go to her mother's. On the morning of the 29th, Christine Messmann arrived for her rounds and found her patient missing.

Dawn had signed out the evening before against medical advice, then fled the hospital with her subclavian line still in place. Messmann knew what that was for. She already knew the value of a subclavian hit on the street.

"Did you hear what happened to our young patient?" the intern gloated.

Messmann felt as though Dawn Spens had kicked her in the stomach.

About four weeks later Christine Messmann was dining at the Blue Pointe when she saw the man in the tortoiseshell glasses again. She would see him there several times, always sitting with an attractive young woman. One Tuesday night she walked right past their booth. The man looked up and grinned. They exchanged a "hello." His companion looked up.

Messmann felt like asking him about Dawn Spens, maybe adding what she'd gone through with the addict he visited so often. But she sensed he didn't want to talk.

That's fine, she thought. Why spoil a good meal with a bad memory?

Chapter 62

A former topless dancer named Linda Sue Stennett was wondering whether it had been such a good idea to give her third cousin John Fry a place to stay while Dawn Spens was in the hospital. Since Dawn had left Receiving Hospital, the scene in her south-side house reminded her of an ex-husband's nine-hundred-dollar-a-day heroin habit.

Not that Sue didn't like to party. She'd do a little coke or smoke some weed if it came her way. But she had four young daughters in her south-side home. The thirty-year-old welfare mother didn't want any trouble, and she thought it might be brewing with Al, the physician John sometimes called The Doc.

The way Sue understood it, Al was trying to get Dawn off the streets, and now off drugs. When Dawn was in the hospital, he sometimes came in with his thermos of coffee and chatted. Al was going to refer both Dawn and John to a methadone program.

John had treated Sue pretty well while Dawn was in the hospital. He bought groceries with money from Al. He played a lot with her two youngest. John always did have a way with children. Her six-year-old, Tonya Sue, adored her "Uncle John."

Al, too, had tried to help out. One day her nine-year-old, Tony, had pains in her stomach. When The Doc dropped by, John asked him to examine her. He pressed on her stomach and her side.

"To be on the safe side, you better have her examined at a hospital," he said. "She could have appendicitis."

It turned out to be a bad case of gas. Despite his missed diagnosis, she still liked Al's demeanor. Sue couldn't under-

276

stand why he provided Dawn with so much money, considering she'd once said they didn't have sex.

Sue Stennett knew that Dawn and John were curious about The Doc as well, and that they weren't satisfied entirely with only daily support. Lately, Dawn and John had been talking about ways to cash in. Dawn brought it up one night as they were sitting around her kitchen table.

"Al knows more than he lets on," Dawn said. "I'd like to know exactly what he's into."

She and John tried to pinpoint it, speculating he was involved in a drug ring or "something big."

"We know he's married," Dawn said. "But there's something else he's hiding. There's something he's into and something he knows. I think we could get a lot of money out of him if we knew what it was. We could blackmail him. We could blackmail him good."

Dawn was excited by the proposition, and John was all for it too. What people do is their business, Sue thought.

But by late February, John and Dawn were making her uncomfortable. She felt as though the two of them were taking advantage of her. John no longer bought groceries or even an occasional six-pack. She suspected Dawn got money every day from Al when he came by and picked her up for a lunch hour drive, but all of it was going to dope.

One morning Sue woke to find Tonya Sue wrapped in a bath towel and standing with wet hair in the living room.

"Tonya, what are you doing?"

"I was taking a bath and Dawn and Uncle John chased me out."

Sue wondered how the two of them could even find room to use her tiny bathroom together. But when she opened the door, three dope fiends, as well as Dawn and John, came out. They'd all been shooting up.

"John, I'm not going to live the way I did," she said.

John said it wasn't his fault. Dawn had gone out to score drugs that morning and brought the three men back.

"I don't give a damn who did. I'm not going to put my kids through this garbage. You and Dawn are going to have to find someplace else to stay."

They left later that day.

Chapter 63

As soon as she saw the icy look on Gladys Canty's face, Jan wished she'd never brought up the new office furniture.

"Why, Bus, I was never informed of this," Gladys said. "How in the world can you afford that?"

Jan asked herself, what business is it of hers, anyway? Al's fifty-one years old. Mother doesn't have son on an allowance. Jan couldn't understand why Gladys was acting as though her husband had been tapping his mother for regular handouts.

"Buster," Mrs. Canty continued. "Why, that furniture you already have is perfectly suitable. I don't see why you need to buy new furnishings."

He wasn't buying it, Jan thought. I *am,* damn it.

Al hung his head. He was stammering, struggling to change the subject. Jan was glad when they left.

"Even if you were paying for it, why does she care what you do with *your* money?" she asked Al in the car.

"Well, Jan-Jan," he said, "you know how Ma is."

Jan had saved for three years to decorate her office the way she wanted it, now that she was hanging out her shingle with Al's. She knew the limits of her own budget. She wished she could say the same for her husband's. Instead of learning about their holdings as Al had promised many times, she felt the money mystery was deepening. Once she asked him if her doctorate tuition had put them in bad straits.

"Oh no, Jan," he said. *"Therapeutic Peers* is in its seventh printing."

But she suspected the book hadn't done as well as he claimed. Recently, she proposed they get a full accounting of the book's sales. Al said he didn't have time. She'd also suggested they combine a vacation with visits to some of the ten hospitals where he said his videotapes were being tested.

"Let's do an update and see how they're doing," she said.

"No, Jan, this is not a good time for that," he said.

She couldn't understand why he was being so evasive about the financial and research aspects of the project. On the other hand, he was opening up more about what inspired the book. He admitted to her one night it was somewhat autobiographical, that he himself had experienced some of the parental conflicts and childhood anger he documented in the book.

There were other signs of financial stress. Recently she'd opened a letter mailed to their home from the state treasury department. Al was delinquent for about five hundred dollars in estimated tax payments for 1984. She handed him the notice.

"Oh, I've taken care of that," he said. "It was an oversight on their part."

When a couple of more state envelopes arrived in the mail, Al snatched them up before she could open them. When she tried to question him about the household budget, he became embarrassed and quiet.

Maybe his practice had suffered more than he let on during his breakdown, she thought. Damn, I wish he would quit trying to shelter me. What had been a luxury for so many years was now a source of irritation. Well, she figured, that's *his problem*. I have my own career to attend to, my own office budget to worry about.

It had taken nine months, but Jan's steady effort to build her own practice was paying off by early March. She started with only a handful of referrals and two workdays per week. Now her practice was blossoming by word of mouth.

When Burroughs Corporation secured the ninth floor of the Fisher Building, requiring her and Al to move, Jan looked at the change as an opportunity for a fresh start. They'd picked out a suite on the tenth floor that would be ready by early April.

Jan reasoned that the move would be good for both of them. Al seemed to be stirring from the preoccupation that had plagued him through 1984. He was enthusiastic about his own therapy with Dr. Awes, and he even was finding time for lunch dates with Ray Danford. Al spoke so highly of him that she'd always encouraged their friendship. Now if Jan could only get him to break away from the Wayne County Jail and the prosecutor's office, maybe they could start having lunch together again.

"Soon, Jan-Jan," Al said. "I'm wrapping that up."

But she sensed something else was brewing in her husband's psyche. He seemed to be hurt, even resentful, that she was stepping out in her own career. Her first hint came more than a year ago, when she was invited to be the keynote speaker at the spring conference of the Michigan Association of Marriage Counselors and Therapists. It was after her bout with mono.

Al had told her friend Celia Muir: "I don't think Jan should go. She's been so sick."

Then a few breaths later, he told Celia, "You know, they've never invited me to speak."

Jan thought it an odd statement. Al never went to professional conferences. She thought he'd at least be eager to share his knowledge on autism, a specialty with which she had little contact among child psychologists. She found conferences educational, but Al balked at all invitations.

There were other signs. Their friendly discussions about approaches to psychotherapy had turned into vindictive debates. He became defensive when she suggested that a father and daughter he was treating be brought in for joint counseling. He was offended when she made improvements on reports he asked her to type.

"I can handle it," he snapped.

Jan was beginning to wonder if what she had interpreted as Al's supportive nature in past years had in fact been paternalism. He seemed more gracious when she was carrying an armful of college texts.

On their recent Arizona vacation Jan's mother had noticed him brooding about his role. As the family watched TV in one room, Al sat alone in another next to the fireplace. He spent a couple of hours gazing at the flames, getting up only to poke the logs. Jan's mother went in the room to chat. He turned to her and said:

"I can't thank you enough for taking care of Jan when I couldn't. I don't like it when I can't take care of Jan-Jan."

Her mother later said, "Jan, it was as though he was in mourning. I really felt sorry for him."

Jan knew Al fancied himself to be protective of younger women. She remembered how proud he was when he became the hero of the agency that supplied the young actresses for Project Indianwood. A businessman returning from a martini-soaked lunch made a crude pass at one of them in a Fisher elevator. Al procured his card by engaging him in a business conversation. Then he called his boss.

"I want you to know what your employee did in the Fisher Building, and I won't have it," he told him.

Later he told Jan, "You know, she's tired of men leering at her. This guy pulls this crap in the elevator and I handled him. It's too bad she can't be recognized for her talent or her brains because she is so pretty."

Back then Jan was impressed. Now she wondered if Al really was the liberal thinker he perceived himself to be. When she told him she was going to practice under her maiden name, he stewed for days. She only wanted to eliminate confusion now that they both carried the title of "doctor." Everything else had always been segregated—their files, their billings, their telephones, their answering services. She never even answered his phone, and he wanted it that way.

So, Jan wondered, why is he being so cold about the name change? Jan had also insisted she pay for her share of the rental of the suite. He didn't like that idea either.

They seemed to have grown so distant from one another in the past couple of years. And their sex life still showed no signs of revival. Maybe it was no coincidence that they'd stopped making love shortly after she received her Ph.D. Maybe I've become a threat to him, she thought.

Several times she tried to talk to him about that and other problems. He always had the same response.

"Jan-Jan, I'm working on that in therapy."

She hoped he worked everything out soon.

Chapter 64

Anne Fordyce concluded that lying was the only graceful way to end her therapy with Alan Canty. The attractive twenty-five-year-old graphic designer wanted out.

In the first place, Anne had wanted a *hypnotherapist*. She found Dr. Canty under that heading in the Yellow Pages when her chronic insomnia forced her to seek professional help.

Her ever skeptical mother was suspicious from the start. She called Dr. Canty to question his credentials. He cited degrees from the University of Michigan, the University of Chicago, and several other colleges.

"Haven't I seen your name somewhere?" she asked.

"Well, of course you would know my name. I've written for the Detroit *News,* the Detroit *Free Press.* I've written books and done articles for all the syndicated papers."

By the time Dr. Canty was through ten minutes later, Anne's mother said she felt like a dummy. Months later they would find out he was puffing, as he did with Anne.

"I have a 90 percent success rate with sleep disorders," he told her right off. "I specialize in them. It shouldn't take more than ten sessions."

That was twenty-four sessions and six months ago, and she'd yet to be hypnotized. Dr. Canty told her the source of her sleeplessness was her mother. They were too close, he said, and Anne was acting out her mother's own complaints of insomnia.

In some ways, the therapist appeared to care about her. She was his last patient every Tuesday. When they were done, he always walked her to the elevator and shook her hand. He told her he missed her when he returned from vacation. Several times he'd complimented her on her shape. It first came up during a conversation they had about women's insecurity about breast size.

"Well, you have nothing to be ashamed of," he said. "You're very well proportioned."

But it was Dr. Canty's unsettling demeanor, rather than his awareness of her figure, that bothered Anne. He fidgeted quite a bit. His hands always were busy during their sessions. He never had much eye contact with her. When they did he seemed to get more nervous. On the table next to his chair he had a sculpture of a polished brass sphere imprisoned in a wooden cube. It reminded her of his uptight personality. His fingers toyed with the thing, as though he was trying to pull the brass ball out of one of the holes in the cube.

A couple of times Dr. Canty introduced his wife. She was attractive and dressed in the smart professional fashions that Anne liked to wear. Dr. Canty seemed a rumpled remnant of the early sixties. He struck her as a lonely intellectual who had only books waiting for him at home each night.

What a contrasting pair, she thought. But her therapist often spoke highly of their marriage, and matrimony in general. A few months earlier Anne had married, a move Dr. Canty praised.

"Your husband is the most important person in your life and you've got to commit yourself to him totally," he said.

Another time he said, "Jan and I have a good understanding with each other. Any time I'm late, I'll call and tell her. Marriage requires that kind of commitment and consideration."

But Anne Fordyce wasn't there for marriage counseling or mental disorders. Even Canty told her "you have no mental disorders whatsoever." She just wanted to sleep.

So Anne had been telling her therapist she was sleeping six to eight hours a night, though she was hardly getting half that. She didn't want to be manipulated into more therapy. She didn't trust him anymore and often found him intolerant.

"No, that's not what I'm asking you," he'd snap if he was unsatisfied with her answers.

By late winter, he was buying her lies about sleeping. He even agreed to hypnotize her during her last session. She had been bugging him to do that for six months.

Finally, the day came. She followed him to a couch in another room in his suite. She was uncomfortable from the start. Anne had worn a short skirt. She felt it hike up well above her knees as she lay down.

What a time to be in a stupid miniskirt, she thought. Dr. Canty sat behind her head. She didn't know if it was because she was self-conscious or her general mistrust, but she could feel his eyes on her legs. He asked her to count from one hundred backward and relax her muscles limb by limb.

By the time she reached zero she was more tense than when she began. Dr. Canty told her to use the relaxation technique each night before she slept.

"That's all there is to it?"

"Most people have misconceptions about hypnosis."

Dr. Canty shook her hand and wished her well. He told her to come back for follow-up if she had any more sleepless nights.

"You'll do well, though," he said. "You're well on your way out of this."

I certainly am, she thought.

Chapter 65

*Another character disorder is nomadism. These people
are always on the move.*

— W. ALAN CANTY,
Henry Ford Community College lectures

The aluminum-clad bungalow on Casper bore no resemblance to the custom home in West Bloomfield that John Fry and Dawn Spens once fantasized about owning. But it was luxurious compared to the living standards they had known since hooking up in the summer of 1983.

Between their stays at the Homewood Manor, the Congress Inn, and the trick pad on Clayton, they had crashed at a half-dozen cheap motels, dope houses, and cramped homes of friends and distant relatives. The bungalow at 2518 Casper had a hearty lawn and a porch with a wrought-iron railing. The two-bedroom was a good hundred feet off the street, hidden behind a two-story duplex, abutting the backyard lot line at the alley.

Through all the moves, drugs and the trick Al were the two constants in their lives. His daily visits — except Sundays — never let up. Neither did his support wane when they found the house on Casper. He covered the $450 security deposit and the $225 monthly rent. The Doc was pleased they had found the house, the referral coming from one of Fry's old friends from Jackson Prison. The old south-side Detroit neighborhood was a lovely suburb compared to the gritty Cass Corridor.

The bungalow was one long city block off the Vernor-

Springwells business district. The area was lined with family-owned businesses and small restaurants catering to a neighborhood mixed with Poles, Italians, Hungarians, and Southerners, who settled it to be close to the Ford Motor Rouge complex and other smokestack industries nearby. Jackets monogrammed with "United Auto Workers — Local 22" were a common sight. Suits and ties were not. The Doc, with his sparkling Buick Regal, his trademark thermos, and his dress slacks and sport coats, would soon stand out as a neighborhood oddity.

Longtime residents of Vernor-Springwells had been seeing a number of unfamiliar sights in recent years. Crime was on the increase, and undesirables were taking over the once well-kept duplexes and aging single-family homes. John Fry and Dawn Spens, however, appeared to be taking steps to keep from contributing to the crime rate.

They signed the lease for 2518 Casper and the same day enrolled in a westside methadone program called Private Health Systems. Nearly two years of intravenous drug use had inflicted much damage on Dawn. Her skin was sallow. Circular scars dotted her legs above heavily swollen ankles. Her abscess had healed, but it had marred her groin as though she'd been hit with a hatchet there.

Al would take Dawn and John to the clinic daily and cover the $100-a-week cost so the pair could get decreasing daily dosages of methadone. But Dawn Spens would not mention Al in a questionnaire she took home with her from the drug program.

The psychological history asked Dawn to list family members and other people she deemed important in her life. She described her relationship with her father as "poor," but "those with her mother and sister as "good." She listed "John C. Fry" as her fiancé and described him as the "most significant person" she knew. Then she gave her reasons:

"Because I love him, he loves me, we have a very good and open relationship, we make each other happy when we are not around drugs, and he helps me [with] my drug problems and other problems I have."

Dawn answered more questions concerning her boyfriend, the only person she indicated was aware of her drug habit.

How did he perceive the problem?

"A serious problem that I can overcome if I really want to and I try hard enough."

What were John's expectations of her?

"Only that I try my best, but [he expects] me to try."

The questionnaire continued:

"Are any of the people listed willing to become involved in your treatment?"

"Fiancé—John Fry."

"How do you perceive problems that are presently faced by family members . . . ?"

"My fiancé's employment problems are due to past drug use, which is now coming under control."

Dawn answered questions concerning sex:

"What were your impressions of sex during your early life?"

"I wanted to wait until I was married to have sex."

"From whom did you learn about sex?"

"Parents."

"Have your impressions about sex changed?"

"Yes."

"In what way?"

The space was left blank. Then the questionnaire asked her about money management.

"How do you generally handle money when you have it?"

"Good, because I budget for necessities—except where drugs are concerned."

The questionnaire wanted to know Dawn Spens's "recreational activities."

"How do you currently spend your leisure time?"

"Shopping, reading, crossword puzzles, decorating my house, watching TV, talking to my fiancé."

Finally, it probed possible causes for her habit.

"Were you an abused child?"

Dawn indicated no.

"Have you been abused since you have been an adult?"

Dawn indicated no.

"Do you think you have the potential for abusing others?"

Dawn indicated no.

"Do you have any serious problems?"

She indicated yes, adding, "My desire for abusing drugs."

"If yes or maybe, do you believe that you need help for these problems?"

"Maybe," she answered.

A twenty-four-year-old unemployed barmaid named Juanita Deckoff wondered what her new neighbors would be like as she watched them move into the bungalow in her back-yard on March 15. The brawny man with the beard and the young brunette were unloading boxes from a black Buick. She also watched an older man in a sports coat carry a potted rubber tree into the house.

Later she introduced herself to Dawn and John. They seemed nice enough. John said he ran a landscaping business and had all kinds of plans for the lawn and shrubbery. John was gregarious, outgoing, and sometimes spoke in a black street dialect.

"Yeah," he later said. "People often accuse me of sounding like a nigger."

The Ides of March was also moving day for Jan and Al Canty. Their new suite on the tenth floor of the Fisher Building was ready. Jan thought the day an opportune time to get rid of some of the junk they'd accumulated in the old office. One item that she'd noticed was already gone was a gaudy artificial rubber tree. Al had hung on to it for ages.

"I've got a patient who has always admired it," Al said. "I gave it to her."

Jan laughed.

"You've got to be kidding, Al. That thing is dinosaur quality. I can't believe anybody would want it."

But Jan didn't find it too humorous when Al left her alone with the Fisher Building moving crew shortly before lunch.

"Got to go to the court," he said, grabbing his thermos.

She protested.

"Jan, you know how lawyers and judges are. I've got to go down there."

She knew he scheduled a couple of hours every day at the

jail, the courts, or the prosecutor's office. But she was irritated he hadn't budgeted his time for their Friday move. She listened in disbelief as he made another comment on his way out the door.

"Could you have my office together, I've got to start seeing patients on Saturday."

He wouldn't return for four hours.

How, she thought, can he do this to me with so much yet to do? The Fisher Building provided the movers, but someone had to direct them, pack and unpack the files, and arrange all the furniture. She would have to shuttle back and forth from floor to floor. That left no one to watch for the telephone installers. Without an office exchange, Al's patients would start phoning their home. For weeks, she already had been getting disturbed at all hours of the night. Usually it was the same person, someone who kept dialing wrong. Jan couldn't understand how the caller could keep making the same mistake.

When she answered the phone, he sounded like a black man, always asking in a slurred voice for some woman.

Chapter 66

*Children who have angry fantasies will have this kind
of fantasy: They'll wish they could be on a big elephant
and that the elephant could go through a community
and tromp the heads of all the bad guys.*
— W. ALAN CANTY,
Concordia College lecture

By their third lunch, Ray Danford was finding his old
friend's situation with the hooker and her boyfriend rather
ironic. There Al Canty was, using the title of "doctor" on the
south side. For years Al vowed he'd never make an issue out
of the designation before his own name.

Ray knew why. Alan Canty Sr. had pushed Al relentlessly
for his Ph.D., while Al respected his dad for accomplishing
so much without one. He admired his father's hard-bitten
approach to the profession, which included the old man's
penchant for knocking out research articles deep into the
night over a fifth of bourbon.

As they looked over the German menu at The Little Cafe,
Al stirred up a batch of old memories about his early conflicts with his parents.

"Hey, I'm seeing Dr. Awes again for help with this problem
I'm having."

"Awes! She's still practicing?"

Ray was surprised the psychiatrist hadn't retired by now.
They recalled the scores of trips they'd made together to the
psychiatrist's office in the 1950s. They put a lot of miles on
his black Beetle driving out to Clarkston. Al gave Ray the

five dollars his father provided for the trip, but they never used more than a dollar in gas. It took an hour to get there, an hour for therapy, and an hour to get back. They made the trip two or three times a week.

Ray's wife Jeannie used to complain about how they were gone most of the night. A girl Al was dating accused him of being gay because they spent so much time together. Then Al worried that he was a latent homosexual. Ray remembered Al's relief when Dr. Awes told him no, she didn't think he was gay.

Their public explanation for Al's sessions was that he was studying to be a therapist, but Ray knew otherwise. Sometimes they used to talk about his psychoanalysis on the drive back. A lot of it had to do with his relationship with his parents.

"Ray, I keep having this funny recurring dream," Al told him once. "I'm on the back of a big elephant, and the elephant is crushing Ma and Pa with its feet."

They really talked quite a bit that night in light of everything they'd learned from Freud. Ray knew Al suffered from what they dubbed "momism" when they were young. Anyone could see that mother and son were very attached to one another. Most of the day, Al's mother was gone on school and club business. But when she was home she hovered over Al, often pampering him with food.

"Now, Buster, you just sit right down and let me fix you something very good to eat," Mrs. Canty said when Ray and Al dropped by Al's house after classes.

It was all pretty foreign to Ray. Al's old place on Chalmers was the first house he'd ever seen with a pantry. Ray's family was poor, and he'd never seen a sandwich with lettuce on it until he left home. Al inspected every leaf. Often Al picked at dishes when they stopped at restaurants on the way home from his sessions with Dr. Awes.

"This just isn't right," he'd say.

"Not as good as Ma's, huh?" Ray would tease.

"Yeah, Ma pampers me so.

But Al also resented his reputation as a mama's boy. Once Ray and a couple of guys in the old gang teased him about being homesick when he came back from Hillsdale College for vacation. It was the only time he ever saw Al rise up and want to fight.

Now Ray could see Al was trying to stand up and face the situation with the hooker, but typically he was making a procedure out of it.

"So how's that going, with the girl?" Ray asked.

"I'm trying to get out of this thing," Al said. "I'm going to taper them, you know, wean them from my support."

Al also had a new physical regimen to accompany his plan to eliminate the girl named Dawn from his life. He insisted on a Perrier and lime after Ray ordered a beer with his lunch. Ray never knew Al, unlike Al Sr., to be much of a drinker, though he sometimes used to treat alcohol as though he was experimenting with LSD. Al got plastered with the sole intent of releasing his internal conflicts, a good drunk turning into a session of weepy name-calling and other soul-purgings.

But this lunch in mid-March Al was looking for ways to regain control of himself, not lose it.

"You know I was in the hospital earlier this year because of my metabolism," Al said. "I'm trying to watch what I eat and drink. I've got to stay sharp, especially for a court evaluation I have this afternoon."

Chapter 67

On April Fool's Day, Dawn Spens put on a white uniform, walked into the Central Outfitting furniture store on Vernor Highway with John Fry, and bought a $269 kitchen dinette set on credit. She told the store manager she had beed employed as a nurse for two years for a Dr. Al Miller.

A man answering a call to the number she provided for the doctor's office verified Dawn's employment at $275 a week. Dawn paid a $129 down payment on delivery of the furniture to the bungalow on Casper, but the store never received one payment on the balance.

"April Fool's has always been my favorite day," John Fry later said. "It's the day I escaped from prison."

Thirteen days later Dawn and John went shopping again, this time at Albert's Furniture, and with one important difference in Dawn's list of credit references.

Robert Saleh, Albert's thirty-four-year-old manager, was anxious for a sale in the new store his family had just opened on Fort Street. The business was in one of the south side's tougher neighborhoods, but the former Michigan State University linebacker had yet to be intimidated by any of his customers. That included the imposing man in the beard, white coat, and white broad brim hat who was browsing through the store with the girl in the tight jeans and freshly curled permanent.

She picked out a $429 nineteen-inch color TV and a $50 stand and then asked if she could secure some credit. As he filled out Dawn Spens's credit application, Saleh found himself eyeing her full lips and hoping for a glimpse of her breasts between the buttons of her shirt. He decided her hairstyle added a wild flair to the way she had sashayed around the store.

"Where do you work?" he asked.

"I'm a receptionist at the Fisher Building for Dr. W. Alan Canty."

"Can I have the phone number and the address?"

Dawn didn't know the street address or zip code, but she had the phone number.

"Spell the doctor's name."

Dawn stuttered with the letters. Saleh filled it out phonetically — "Cantee." A receptionist who doesn't know her boss's address, he thought, or the spelling of his name? But Dawn provided other references, including her mother, father, sister, grandfather, and her friend in the white coat and hat, John Fry.

Saleh took $50 in down payment and told her he would deliver the TV himself if her application checked out. She insisted on an ambitious payment plan for herself, pledging to pay him $25 a week. After she left he called only one reference, the doctor. He got an answering service. It was a Saturday. On Monday, the doctor called him back.

"This is Dr. Canty. I believe Dawn Spens came in there and is applying for credit on a TV."

"Right, does she work for you?"

"Lookit, give her anything she wants. If she can't handle paying for anything, don't worry. I'll cover her in any way."

Saleh figured if this doctor was going to go that far, perhaps he should come in the store and co-sign.

"Can you come in and sign something?"

"Lookit, I don't have that kind of time, do you understand? Just give it to her. She's covered."

Later in the day Dawn showed up at the store with another $50.

"Your doctor seems like a nice guy," Saleh told her. "Especially for him to give you a reference like that."

"Yeah," she said. "He's worked with me quite a bit."

Obviously, Saleh thought, she wasn't a receptionist. Maybe she was his patient, or his concubine. The distinction seemed irrelevant. Saleh had the doctor's word, his phone

294

number, and his address. Later that day he delivered the merchandise to her bungalow on Casper.

From the start Dawn was delinquent with her weekly payments. Saleh himself drove to the bungalow to collect. He didn't mind at first, as the visits gave him another peek at the intriguing girl with the wild hair.

Dawn had an array of hard-luck excuses for her late installments. Other times John answered the door. He was polite, easygoing, and said he liked to be called Lucky. Saleh didn't trust him. Nobody can look like such a hard-ass, he thought, and be that gracious.

One day the doctor himself came into the store while Saleh was busy taking a credit application.

"Who's Bob?" said the guy in the glasses and loud checkered sports coat.

"I am. Who are you?"

"I'm here to make a payment for Dawn Spens. And what difference does it make who I am? I'm giving you her payment, aren't I?"

He appeared in a hurry. He handed Saleh $25, then flashed an arrogant grin.

"I'm the doctor," he said.

If Saleh hadn't been occupied, he would have asked him to co-sign right there. But he'd already decided Dawn's line of credit was closed. Soon he would be making two or three trips a week to get his $25 installment. One balmy spring day, Dawn came to the door in a tank top, and Lucky in a T-shirt. When he saw the scars up and down both their arms, Robert Saleh knew the account was in serious trouble.

Jan Canty couldn't remember a time when she'd seen her husband as agitated as on that afternoon in late April when he returned to the Fisher an hour late from his daily visit to the jail.

"Al, what's wrong? You look so upset."

"The Fisher Building is squeezing me," he snapped. "The Fisher is putting the squeeze on me for back rent."

They must have made some kind of mistake, she thought. We've only been in the new suite a month. How could the rent be behind?

"Well, they've always been reasonable people," she said. "Let's go down there together and work it out."

Al took a deep breath and collected himself.

"No, it's OK. Don't worry about it. I overreacted."

He became preoccupied as he walked back to his office. Gee, she thought, solved just like that.

Jan shook her head. *Putting the squeeze on me.* That was the first time she'd ever heard Al use the phrase. He must have picked that one up at the jail, she thought.

Chapter 68

The psychiatrist watched her patient try to steady his limbs by locking his fingers and placing his hands in his shifting lap. He'd sped out to her home from his office after discovering the truth.

"Wow, that was a close one," he said. "They *know*. They do know who I am."

Dr. Lorraine Awes listened as he told her what he found scrawled on a sheet of notebook paper lying in a pile of odds and ends in the south-side bungalow. There it was: "Canty, W. Alan, Ph.D.," his office address, his office number, his home phone number.

"They must have gone outside, damn it," he stammered. "Gone through my glove compartment where I kept my wallet."

Missing was the self-assurance the psychiatrist had been hearing for eleven months. Al had been so adamant that his identity was his secret.

"It's not a concern," he said more than once. "They only know me as Al, or The Doc."

Dr. Awes suspected all along her patient was only trying to keep her at bay with such rationalizations. Finally he was faced with the realization that what he was doing was not without potential consequences.

"I guess I've only been kidding myself, haven't I?" he said.

He trembled for most of the one-hour session, but the psychiatrist welcomed his fear like the warmer days of late April. Now maybe they really could get some work done.

Lorraine Awes had always been very fond of the patient

with the introspective talents of a psychologist and the smile of a young boy. She remembered when he first showed up for therapy at her office more than thirty years ago. He was twenty, but as emotionally frail as his willowy frame and as misdirected as his wavy hair. Two years of college and he had yet to compile a course credit. His father would not have that sort of thing. Something had to be done with the boy, he demanded.

Dr. Awes expected to find the son of the flamboyant Recorder's Court clinic director apathetic and unmotivated. She misjudged him. Alan turned out to be bright and eager, but shackled by an exceedingly complex personality. It took them more than fifteen years of intermittent analysis to sort it all out. He emerged from therapy with the elusive doctorate his father was so determined he should have, while gaining a healthy admiration for his dad. Without help, Dr. Awes believed, Al might have never held up as his father battled his own demons through his son.

The psychiatrist only wished they hadn't left this bit of unfinished business the first time around. Obviously they had overlooked something. She knew unresolved conflicts could hide like that, remaining dormant as long as certain needs were met.

Other things hadn't changed with time. Dr. Awes still fielded comments about her strong resemblance to Bette Davis and the pronunciation of her last name. Some of her patients reported dreams about the Wizard of Oz, but most never made the connection. She, too, wished psychiatry could be as cut and dry as reaching into a wizard's bag for new hearts and minds. Long-term analysis dominated her field when she began her residency at Pontiac State Hospital and Lafayette Clinic. Now drugs effectively treated some forms of mental illness. She welcomed the breakthroughs. Not every patient was inspired or introspective enough for psychotherapy.

She knew Alan Canty was. Al's own realization of the depth of his compulsion had driven him into a temporary paranoid state and a psychiatric ward, but she didn't consider him psychotic. Upon his release he was confused, but searching for deliverance from his neurosis. When they began therapy again it seemed as though they had only missed a couple of sessions, though a decade had passed since their last appointment.

Al had been seduced by his own psyche before. They recalled the drama student he fell for in college days. He would have dived into a handstand for that girl. They both agreed she was neurotic, possibly schizophrenic. But that made her all the more the temptress. When Al perceived her as helpless, he was powerless to resist her frequent demands.

Maggie, his first wife, Al misjudged completely. He envisioned her as a single mother in trouble, but in a few years reality took over. She was a free spirit with a will and career of her own. When he realized she could get along very well without his psychological nurturing, the marriage was destined to fail.

Dr. Awes saw many parallels as Al told her about his fiftieth birthday and the young prostitute he saw that day on the corner.

"She looked so young, so helpless," he said.

Dr. Awes knew Al was alone that week in more ways than one. In his mind, his isolation began the day Jan received her Ph.D. He believed he no longer needed him in the role of a mentor that had satisfied him for so many years.

Dr. Awes preferred to analyze the human psyche in terms of its simple needs rather than psychological jargon. Alan Canty, she believed, had a ravenous need to be needed. This time that want had disguised itself in the form of the girl he called Dawn.

Maybe the whole affair might never have begun if he could have told Jan he was hurt that she was going to Arizona the week of his birthday. But such risky displays of emotion were foreign to Al's makeup.

From the beginning, Dr. Awes never doubted Al's parents were determined to raise a good son. Maybe they were too determined. She remembered when his mother dropped off a diary of his upbringing, one that revealed she began toilet training the boy in his first few months. Dr. Awes decided that revealed what kind of self-control was expected in the Canty household.

Through the years, psychiatrist and patient had talked

about many things: a father he could never satisfy, a mother who treated him like a child, his lavishing of gifts on others to buy love and respect, the playing of many roles in a solitary search for self-esteem. That and more had inspired his destructive masquerade.

When he showed up for therapy in May, Al had even disguised his real intentions from himself. Right off, her patient was anxious about his hospitalization. He worried that Dawn would think he had abandoned her, rejected her like people in her past. He entertained the fantasy that if he could instill confidence in the prostitute, she would get off heroin and make something of herself.

Al's outward concern was a comfortable disguise, all for the benefit of his conscience. Dr. Awes urged him to look at the reality of his actions. They peeled off the masks one by one. Underneath generosity was control. Underneath affection, conquest. Underneath sacrifice, domination. Yes, the more dependent Dawn was on him, he finally admitted, the better.

Still Al kept going back, even when he later complained that Dawn was taking advantage of him. He detailed Dawn's frequent attempts to humiliate him and rumors that she called her best customer degrading names behind his back.

"When I arrive she often has her hand out," he said once. "She says, 'Well, how much did you bring me today?'"

Yet he only desired her company more. Dr. Awes pointed out that Dawn was unwittingly soothing him. Her punishment helped ease the guilt for his control over her life, temporarily freeing him to control some more. Some charitable treatment by the prostitute might even help terminate the affair, the psychiatrist decided.

Al also went into depth about John but dismissed him as a manageable character. He explained how John had tried to remain in the background at first but eventually he came forward as her pimp. Al said his pathology was obvious; John was a textbook psychopath. Al was convinced there was no love between Dawn and John, only a business relationship.

"Oh, he's only done time for petty crimes," Al said.

Dr. Awes thought he was being naive.

"But this is a situation that is potentially dangerous," she said. "His type of personality is potentially explosive."

Dr. Awes already was concerned about the extent of drug use involved by the pair. At first, Al said, they pestered him to bring prescription drugs.

"I pointed out to them I wasn't that kind of doctor," he maintained.

Al rationalized that their lifestyle was a chance to satisfy his scientific curiosity. He reported their binges in great detail, adding he'd more than once had to rebuff their efforts to persuade him to join them. He realized his financial support alone wasn't enough for the couple's insatiable appetite for narcotics. He detailed the pair's other illegal activities, from kiting bad checks to furnishing their new house with stolen goods.

"They repeatedly amaze me," Al said. "These people are thoroughly rotten through and through. I mean, nothing they do is good."

Al chronicled Dawn's physical deterioration and was amazed that her heroin use in hospitals went undetected by medical staff. He was astonished that John thought his prostitute had some kind of sexual hold on Al, the pimp usually leaving them alone when he visited. Al said he had no desire to have intercourse with Dawn. He said she suffered from venereal warts.

For months Dr. Awes had been hammering away at her patient's resilient delusion of invulnerability. But often the psychiatrist found it difficult to get him to focus when he found so many aspects of his scenario entertaining.

Al was amused by the game of deception the hooker and her pimp had played for many months. He was intrigued by the plethora of hard-luck stories Dawn created early on to get money. He played along, knowing it all went to drugs. He found laughable John's attempts to disguise the fact he lived with Dawn while leaving hints of his presence throughout the house. He chuckled at Dawn's excuses for the days her car was gone. Many times he'd seen the car leaving, with John planted behind the wheel.

By April, however, Al was disgusted with the entire situation, but even more disgusted with himself. He worried about his marriage and was suffering from massive amounts of guilt. He admitted he might as well be throwing money away, money that should be going to his life with Jan.

Dr. Awes herself was amazed how clever her patient had been in keeping everything from his wife. When the psychiatrist questioned Al about the financial strains that might be showing at home, he dismissed any cause for alarm.

"She watched me spend sixteen thousand dollars once on an antique car that arrived in pieces," he said. "She's very understanding about my finances."

But Al condemned himself for betraying her, and he was adamant about protecting her from his secret. She must never know, he said. Dr. Awes believed her patient was on the verge of discovering genuine affection for his wife. Al and Jan's time together could form the foundation for a healthy relationship.

Dr. Awes felt Al had made considerable progress. He realized he could cut off his own blond curls and didn't have to fear ridicule at the thought of dressing up. He didn't have to be the surrogate Ph.D. unafraid to go eye to eye with a psychopath. If he was lonely, he could say it. If he was angry, he could show it. But only Alan Canty could put away the disguises. If he didn't work it out for himself, the psychiatrist believed, her therapy hadn't accomplished anything.

Recently, Al had devised a plan to wean Dawn and John from his financial support. He said they were taking methadone, and he felt obligated to support the effort for a while, considering the way he'd enabled their drug habits for so long. Dr. Awes was concerned he was looking for leniency, like an alcoholic switching to beer in a last attempt to control his drinking and get everyone off his back.

But now both psychiatrist and patient were running out of time. Al remained her only patient, and she was seeing him at home. She had closed her West Bloomfield office in January. Dr. Lorraine Awes planned in one month to relocate in Anchorage, Alaska. She had family waiting there. She'd delayed the move already for Al. Understanding his problem was step one. Now he needed to act.

"Al, you know what you have to do," she said.

She hoped finally he had all the motivation he needed.

Chapter 69

Juanita Deckoff thought the transformation was pretty astounding. So much had changed with her new neighbors in just a matter of weeks.

Dawn was as busy as a newlywed with a new home when they first moved in—scrubbing down every room, putting up new wallpaper in the kitchen. She returned one day from shopping with several bags of new household items, including a hundred-dollar gray marble canister set.

She boasted to Juanita, "Hey lookit, I blew four hundred dollars at K Mart."

"Wow, wish I could do things like that," Juanita said. "Have four hundred dollars just to blow."

Next came the furniture—an early American living room ensemble, a new color TV, a new dinette. Juanita wondered where they got the money. She never saw either one of them go to work. She guessed they were on general assistance, and she suspected John was dealing in stolen goods.

Right off, Juanita's three-year-old daughter took to John, who often brought her candy from the beer store, and the older man who visited every day but Sunday. As he toted his thermos through the backyard on his way to the bungalow she always ran to give him a hug.

"My new neighbor, my new neighbor," she'd say.

For several weeks Juanita had assumed the man named Al was Dawn's dad—they acted so much like father and daughter. Then Dawn explained one day that he was just a good friend of the family.

At first Al was their only frequent visitor. Then after a month, the bungalow began drawing a crowd. A young blonde named Tammy Becker stayed with them a while, and people started coming and going at odd hours.

Juanita considered herself pretty streetwise. She grew up in Dearborn Heights, hitchhiked through forty-three states, and married in California. When she left her husband, she returned to Michigan and hooked up with Mike, an old classmate who now was her live-in boyfriend. Mike Oliver worked days at a local car wash but was around enough to recognize what was happening in the gray bungalow. Mike said their neighbors were dope fiends and he wanted nothing to do with the place.

By May, Juanita could see he was right. One by one items were disappearing from the bungalow. First the living room furniture, then the color TV. One day she walked into the house to chat with Dawn and saw it hadn't been cleaned in two weeks. Dishes were piled high all over the kitchen. Newspapers and junk littered the living room. In the middle of the mess sat Dawn, working a crossword puzzle.

"My God, girl, don't you think of anything else to do?" Juanita said. "You're going to go cross-eyed with those things."

As Dawn pondered words for her puzzles, creditors began calling on 2518 Casper. A man from a local furniture store was relentless in his pursuit. Sometimes he came to Juanita's door, inquiring of her neighbor's whereabouts. Later, the telephone was shut off. Dawn had talked to her mother long distance to Windsor nearly daily for two months. The phone bill was four hundred dollars delinquent when Ma Bell turned off service. Dawn's mother began visiting her daughter on occasion, bringing along her boyfriend to just sit around and chat.

John finally admitted to Juanita that Al had hooked them up with a treatment program. But Juanita could see that another drug besides methadone was fast taking the place of their old heroin habits. Dawn and John were crazy for cocaine.

Juanita didn't want anything to do with needles, but she'd snort a line or two if it was around. Dawn sometimes invited her in to get high. By June, Dawn and John were making three or four trips a day to buy coke, usually copping in twenty-five-dollar to hundred-dollar amounts. Al often gave

Dawn a ride to the dope dealer at the lunch hour.

Juanita and Dawn began to have regular chats. One afternoon in early June, Dawn dropped by to use Juanita's telephone to call Al, and afterward they had a conversation about her son. She told Dawn he was throwing frequent tantrums and sometimes acted withdrawn.

"Well, Al is a psychologist," Dawn said. "And he specializes in children. He's dealt with autistic kids. Give him a half hour with him and he'll tell you whether he needs special care."

Juanita made a mental note to ask Al the next time she saw him. She wasn't even sure what the term "autistic" meant.

Other days they just complained about their men. Dawn and John sometimes got into spats over little things. As items were sold from the house for coke the tension seemed to increase. Once John ordered her to trade their AM-FM radio to their coke connection.

"I already called over there and they said they don't want the damn thing," she told him.

"Take it anyway," John ordered.

Dawn threw the radio but calmed down shortly. Their fights never lasted long. They always were over dope or money. Juanita suspected the latter was increasingly in short supply.

Chapter 70

The central purpose of all psychotherapy is to help the patient grow to the point where he can make his own decisions, act upon them, and live comfortably with the results.

— W. ALAN CANTY,
Principles of Counseling and Psychotherapy

Dr. Lorraine Awes felt optimistic about her patient as she prepared to move to Alaska on June 5. Al gave her the impression he'd confronted Dawn and John with what everyone already knew about the Dr. Al Miller ruse.

"I've also reduced the money considerably," he said. "But they are pretty angry about the money."

Their calls for cash had been coming to his home, Al said, adding he often had to scramble to get to the ringing phone before Jan. There were no threats of blackmail, and Al hoped that wouldn't be the next step. Nevertheless, he changed to an unlisted number. Jan was complaining about the "wrong numbers" coming at all hours of the night.

Dr. Awes couldn't shake Al's determination to see Dawn through the methadone program. He said he drove them to the clinic and paid their bill on Friday afternoons. But, he said, the program would run its course in a couple of weeks. Then he was finished.

Al revealed the couple had found a new drug of choice in cocaine. He was curious about their animated behavior while on the drug. He described one scene where they smoked it through a water pipe. But he said usually they took it intravenously, with Dawn's first response always a sprint to the bathroom to throw up. Dr. Awes repeated her warnings about his safety.

But Al couldn't shake his guilt about the effect he'd had on Dawn's life. In recent sessions, Dr. Awes watched her patient create a new role for the pimp. As long as Dawn had John, Al reasoned, he wouldn't have to condemn himself for leaving her. It was crucial that John be there to catch Dawn when Al dropped her. And with his identity known, Al wanted to end the affair as uneventfully as he could.

Their last session was the week the psychiatrist left for Anchorage. Al seemed exceptionally upbeat. There were few signs of the mystified man who had come to her thirteen months ago. He wanted to get on with his life, devoting his time and energies to his wife and their practice. His psychiatrist felt confident he was motivated.

"I'll write you and let you know how I'm getting along," Al said as he left. "I know what I have to do and I'm going to do it. I'm sure I have everything under control."

She hoped he was right.

Chapter 71

Gladys Canty liked her son's suggestion. Buster wanted to take her to lunch, and he'd never been in the habit of doing that sort of thing.

Mrs. Canty had a meeting that Friday in June with the Sorosis Club, one of the oldest women's clubs in the state. Its membership had dwindled from one hundred to two dozen over the years, and she'd already committed herself to meet with four or five of them at a friend's house.

"Well, Ma, I'll pick you up there," Bus said. "At noon."

Her son showed up exactly on time, then spoke briefly to her friends, shaking hands with every one. He was glowing, and her friends were quite pleased with the way he livened the room. Gladys Canty was proud.

"Well, Ma, where shall it be for lunch?"

"Oh," she said. "I've had coffee and donuts and I'm really not that hungry now."

Bus suggested they go to Sanders confectionery in Grosse Pointe. When he finished his tuna casserole there he asked, "Are you in a hurry to get home?"

"Why, no, Bus, you know I'm not exactly booked up these days."

"Come on. Let's take a drive."

Bus drove her all the way to downtown Detroit, then headed back toward the east side out Jefferson Avenue. They passed the Renaissance Center and the new development under way nearby. They drove past Elmwood Cemetery, where Al Sr. was buried. As the Buick headed east, he pointed out buildings slated for demolition and talked of the city's plans to rebuild the riverfront. The city, he said, was looking better than it had in years.

Her son fascinated her with his little tour. He seemed so relaxed—his old self, she thought. Over many months she had tracked his moodiness. And a week earlier he'd come to her for another one of his loans.

"I keep getting these bills for my time in the hospital," he said. "Just when I think they're over, I get another."

They didn't argue about the money. She thought, he must have really fallen behind when he was sick. The check was for twenty-five hundred dollars. He vowed it would be the last.

Soon Bus reached Chalmers and wheeled the Buick onto the street where he'd grown up. He reminisced as they drove the mile toward their old neighborhood near the river. They remembered the big elms and the neat lawns. Now they saw houses boarded up under open sky, and weeds choking vacant lots.

Buster parked the Buick Regal in front of their old home. It was the site of many memories. She cherished the photographs of him pedaling his toy car up the driveway. What a head of curls he had! she thought. How she hated to cut them!

Now their once grand Dutch colonial was painted gaudy pink, trimmed with a tasteless green. There was no hint of the garden she once nurtured. The front siding of the house was heavily soiled. One of the two Roman pillars that held up the porch was tilted.

The only sturdy sight was the tree planted by Al Sr. It was called a Five Way Apple Tree and was supposed to produce a mix of several distinctly different types of the fruit. It bore a bountiful crop, but the apples were always wormy. She wondered how it was doing at full maturity.

"It's a shame what has happened, isn't it?" said her son, staring at the house and yard. He was quite silent for a while.

Then, quite suddenly, something jolted him from his gaze. He looked at the Seiko watch she'd bought him for Christmas.

"What time is it?" he asked himself. It was past one o'clock.

"I've got to go. I've got to be somewhere."

"Why, Bus, I thought this was your day off."

"Yes, it is. But I've got to be at the courts."

309

"You're still doing *that?*"

"Yeah, Ma, but not for long. Finally, I've almost got that wound up."

In a few minutes he'd dropped her off at her home. Gladys Canty watched through the screen door as he sped off down the street.

Chapter 72

Keith Bjerke pushed his coffee cup across the table to the man he knew as Al but preferred to call The Doc Known to his friends as BJ, the thirty-four-year-old ex-convict had always enjoyed Al's coffee and his company.

"Well, BJ, you look a little pale today," The Doc said. "Are you feeling all right?"

He felt fine now, sitting in Lucky Fry's kitchen. A week ago he was in a hospital bed, suffering from kidney failure. The Doc knew it and wanted to give him another checkup, his fourth in as many days. The Doc reached for the stethoscope and blood pressure gauge he kept at Fry's house and began wrapping the device around BJ's arm.

Fry and Dawn were in the bedroom with a syringe full of cocaine. The Doc had just taken the three of them to the dope house and waited outside while they copped.

"You know, BJ, you're going to have to watch your health," he said, pumping the hand bulb. "Renal failure is nothing to mess with."

"You're right, Doc."

He finished by timing his pulse, then tapping along BJ's back with his fingertips. When The Doc returned to his thermos, BJ picked up the front page of the morning newspaper and scanned the headlines. By mid-June, the rioting in South Africa still showed no signs of letting up.

"Ain't this some shit, Doc," BJ said. "As far as I'm concerned they can kill all the fuckin' niggers down there. In fact, what they ought to do is just annex Madagascar and give *them* all the niggers"

"Now, BJ," The Doc said. "They should have their rights. They are 90 percent of the population. They have 0 percent representation."

He went on for a good five minutes. He gave the history of the country, cited reasons for the unrest, and finished with a stirring plea as to why most Americans should give a damn. BJ wasn't surprised The Doc was so idealistic.

But at least he can articulate his ideas, BJ decided after The Doc drove off in his Buick. Most in Lucky Fry's cadre couldn't put together a simple declarative sentence and had interests that didn't go much beyond the quality of their latest score. Trick or no trick, The Doc always got BJ's due respect. He figured he had it coming.

BJ had seen it before, a straight type hanging out with criminals and fiends. But unlike the others, The Doc wasn't there to get high. Sometimes BJ had the feeling he was studying all of them as he sat with his coffee and his paper. He was so quiet that most of Fry's friends didn't even notice anymore that he was in the room.

But BJ also felt The Doc was concerned about some of the people in Lucky Fry's circle. He'd watched The Doc buy groceries, jump dead batteries, take dope fiends to the hospital, and make his car available for most anybody in a jam. Once he gave BJ a ride to the pawnshop. He'd seen The Doc console Dawn many times when she was depressed.

"One of the nicest fuckers you'd ever want to meet in your life," BJ later told a friend. "The Doc was a hell of a guy."

BJ always figured The Doc would be capable of a lot more charity if Dawn hadn't abused his generosity so much. She talked as though she hated the motherfucker, often employing her favorite line: "The fuckin' pinhead. I wouldn't fuck him. He's lucky I suck his dick."

BJ also watched Dawn play The Doc against Fry. She'd been squeezing her boyfriend about the regular date's standing offer to set her up in the suburbs.

"I don't need you, John," she said when they bickered. "Al said he would take care of everything."

"Well then, bitch, go with Al," John always countered.

BJ sensed a growing animosity from Fry toward The Doc, a dislike that had started months ago. BJ remembered how his Buick Regal was stolen right after Fry complained about The Doc's money falling short about a year ago. BJ suspected that that and other rip-offs were Fry's way of retaliating. Lately BJ often found his neighbor stewing as he waited for The Doc and his cash.

"Where's The Doc?" BJ would ask.

"That motherfucker is a pain in the ass," Fry would say.

Fry was far more forgiving of his girlfriend, and he often bragged about Dawn's talents as a hooker.

"She's good, mon," he'd say. "The best."

But BJ knew she hardly worked the streets anymore, depending only on The Doc and a couple of longtime regulars for cash. Fry also had other things working for him, including a pile of blank payroll checks and a bonding machine. BJ knew firsthand that Fry and a couple of other dope fiends had kited about eight thousand dollars' worth of bad paper all over the city. Fry had used the same slippery delivery on merchants that BJ first discovered when he met him seven years ago in Jackson Prison. Fry was the head man in Quarantine, and new inmates had to see him for their cell assignments. He acted like everybody's buddy, but he was always looking for an angle.

"Lucky Fry knows how to stroke your ego and pat you on the back," BJ said later. "Rah, rah for the home team and all that. But John Fry is a chameleon. He can be whatever the situation calls for."

He was equally deceiving as a drug source. Fry took perfectly good bags of cocaine and turned it into garbage with cut, saving the best for himself. He wasn't any more generous with his money. He had made a lot of enemies by shafting dealers on the south side who gave him credit. Fry was fortunate he had The Doc to shuttle Dawn to a connection in the Morrell Apartments a couple of miles away, BJ thought. The middleman took her money and scored the coke from the dope house. The dealer didn't want anything to do with Fry or his girlfriend.

BJ knew the pair's routine so well because that was how he timed his visits to their bungalow from his house down the street. When BJ saw The Doc's black Buick glide up Casper, he knew Fry and his girlfriend would be into the cash and the coke. If The Doc didn't take them to score, BJ would offer his wheels and usually get some of the spoils. There were ample opportunities Fry and Dawn were shooting at least three hundred dollars' worth of cocaine a day, and they'd been at it like that for a month.

BJ knew from experience that the pair's bender could go on as long as money and metabolisms held out. BJ's last coke binge had lasted six months, before his kidneys went to hell. Withdrawals weren't a factor as with heroin. It just felt too good to stop. Cocaine-induced feelings of power and control usually prompted racing minds to devise all kinds of grand schemes for money to buy more. Then, after a couple of months of many sleepless nights, the nervous system began to feel as though it was charged with static electricity. Coke fiends could get pretty testy and paranoid. One spark and they were kicking somebody's ass. But most of the time, Coke stimulated a lot of chatter and camaraderie, especially when a few six-packs or a fifth of whiskey were employed to help lower the voltage.

A couple of nights later, BJ, Dawn, and Fry were nurtured by that very combination as they partied in front of the living room TV at 2518 Casper. A little black-and-white with a coat hanger for an aerial had replaced their new color television. BJ didn't even have to ask what had happened to the big set.

Late into the evening they found themselves staring at a commercial for an item called The Ginsu Knife. Fry sucked on a beer and poked fun as an announcer pitched the kitchen blade at a carnival barker's pace. They watched a TV chef wield the wonder knife, cutting an old rubber boot and a beer can. Then he sliced up a tomato.

"Fuck you, man," Fry said. "That's a bunch of bullshit."

"OK, smart-ass," Dawn said. "If you think so, why don't you try it? We've got one."

She went to the kitchen and returned with a long, serrated blade bearing the Ginsu trademark on its black handle. Fry smirked as he held up the knife before going to work on a beer can. In a few seconds he held up both halves of the Budweiser.

"Well, I'll be fuckin' goddamned," he said.

Everyone had a good laugh.

Chapter 73

With a cacophony of honks, beeps, and *aaoooogaaas* the cavalcade of more than two hundred antique cars rolled down West Grand Boulevard. Then the Wheels of Freedom parade chugged to a stop as the drivers positioned their cars all about the base of the Fisher Building.

A retired Ford Motor engineer named Dan Hall parked his 1929 Chrysler roadster at the curb as the boulevard was cordoned off for spectators. Next to the fireworks, the procession was the most colorful event of Detroit's Freedom Festival week.

Hall was surprised when a beaming Al Canty came toddling out the brass doors of the Fisher. They'd hunted down several old cars together, and Hall had always had his eye on that 1932 Ford Cabriolet of Al's. But the therapist hadn't been around old-car circles in more than a year. Hall had missed his fellow auto buff.

"Where the hell have you been, Al?" he asked.

"Well, Dan, I've got problems," he said, eying Hall's roadster. "But I should have them all straightened around in a couple of weeks."

Hall wanted to inquire if he could help, but he could see Al was rushed.

"Dan, I've got a couple of patients sitting upstairs," Al said.

The psychologist suggested they have lunch and wanted to set a time right then and there. They'd meet Friday, July 19. He'd have his problems solved by July 13.

Celia and John Muir couldn't help but notice Al Canty's

new demeanor over the past few months. It showed no signs of letting up as they joined the Cantys for dinner the first Saturday in July. They all were sitting at a window table in a downtown restaurant called Floods, listening to Jan talk about her trip to Arizona in the spring. A group of aging conventioneers stood outside, eyeing a menu taped on the glass next to Al's seat. Suddenly Al began banging on the glass. Then he shook his head and gave the thumbs-down sign to those outside.

"Al," Jan said. "What in the world are you doing?"

Al laughed, undaunted by her unapproving look. It was a minor prank, really, but so unlike the pretense and control that formerly characterized their outings together. Al Canty was cutting loose, having fun, and not much giving a damn what anyone thought.

The Muirs had seen a lot of changes since early spring. Al was revealing things about himself, instead of remaining so tightly wrapped. He talked about his finances with John, seeking his advice as a stockbroker.

"Well, things are tight," Al said. "I can't seem to put any money away. My expenses are so great."

John was a little miffed. He thought, how is it I have savings and Al doesn't? I'm a junior stockbroker with kids and a wife who doesn't work. He's a psychologist who works day and night and has an income-producing wife. Jan sometimes complained that Al put all his money in his cars. But he'd been selling, rather than buying. Al even had sold the red Porsche, his beloved James Dean car.

One night two months ago he said he knew his mother "won't live forever," adding she had a lot of money.

"It's kind of a cold thing to think about, but it's a fact of life," he said. "And in a few months here I'm going to have everything paid off, Jan's car and my car. I'll be able to put some money away. I'll be able to start investing."

Already Al was investing more of himself in the time the four of them spent together. He gave Celia hugs and shook John's hand with conviction. He began talking about his youth, providing interesting anecdotes formerly kept concealed. He told stories about being a cook when he was in the National Guard in the fifties. He told them about his interest in theater. He named the plays in which he had roles in college: *Dark of the Moon, The Time of Your Life, The Beautiful People.* Celia and John were surprised. They never knew Al was a thespian.

Al also was giving away things that meant a lot to him. He showed up one night at their house with some props he'd used in his Project Indianwood skits. They included a noise-maker and a Viking's hat. He clowned around with the toys before giving them to their eight-year-old daughter. Even she was shocked. She knew Al rarely acted silly.

Al no longer appeared uncomfortable in their house, though they had adopted a third child, making it busier than ever. Al seemed to enjoy the activity. One night Celia and John sat in silent astonishment as he became very reflective and talked about an old friend he called Ray.

"He had a house like this where I'd go," he said. "I liked to spend the night there. They didn't have money and Ray didn't have a father. But it was comfortable. His mom didn't worry about the cleaning. She worried about wiping their noses, or hearing about their day at school."

Then he turned to Celia and touched the back of her neck.

"You're such a good mother," he said. "You have no idea how good you are by staying home with your children. You're a good mom, Celia. Stay that way."

And he wasn't looking for a cup of coffee. His eyes were warm, his smile genuine rather than cunning. Celia felt really good inside.

The four of them had been having a lot of fun together in recent months with the Muirs' new VCR. They popped popcorn and turned their living room into their private little theater. Al always wanted them to get mysteries, films about characters who were victims of thoughtful demise.

Al's favorite filmmaker was Alfred Hitchcock. He knew everything about the Master of Suspense. Often he asked that they rent a Hitchcock movie for the Saturday night get-togethers. Recently they'd watched *Rear Window,* the story of a man who witnessed a neighbor murder his wife through the window of a nearby apartment. The killer dismembered her body with a saw so he could shuttle her corpse out of the building unnoticed. Then he buried her head in the court-yard garden. Al thought it was great stuff.

But the most striking change in Al was the way he seemed

to be letting his feelings fly toward Jan. The Muirs always had guessed Al didn't like her competing with him for the center of attention. Before, when she was stealing the show, Al just remained silent. Now he was getting assertive. Celia suspected his little gag in the restaurant was engineered to put the brakes on Jan's monologue on Arizona.

When the four of them stopped by the Fisher Building the same night to see Jan's newly decorated office, he made a bolder move. As they ogled Jan's black lacquered furniture and rose-and-gray decor, Al stared out the window at the darkened city.

Finally, he turned and huffed, "Oh, come on now. Enough. Let's get the hell out of here."

He was jealous, but at least he was showing it. Gone was that old Alan Canty guard. Celia thought, who knows? Maybe soon they'll have a good old family argument instead of a *disagreement*.

As they got up to leave Floods after dinner, John Muir found himself trying to avoid one with Al. He couldn't believe what he was seeing. John had left a ten-dollar bill as a tip for the waitress. Out of the corner of his eye he could see Al had palmed it and put it in his pocket.

"Al, where you going with that?" he asked as Celia and Jan walked ahead. "That's for the waitress."

Al stopped suddenly and looked surprised, as though he'd picked up the cash absentmindedly.

"Oh, yeah. I guess it is."

John could see through the act, but he kept his shocked feelings to himself.

Why, he wondered, would a man of Al Canty's means and stature do some thing like that? And what in God's name made him think he could get away with it?

Chapter 74

A fifty-five-year-old divorcée named Dorothy Wilson cradled the telephone on her left shoulder and did what she did best any time John Fry called. She listened.

Ever since their mother died in 1967, John and his brother Jim had looked to her as close kin. Jim called her Ma, and John called her Aunt Dot, though they were in fact only second cousins. She never really sought the role, but she felt the two boys had turned to her to take Nell Ruth Fry's place.

"Gonna get married, Aunt Dot," John said. "I want you to come to the wedding."

As with most of John's plans, nothing was definite.

With Jim dead, Dot Wilson was hearing from John every couple of months. Before, she was the first person he called when he was in trouble. Over the years she'd taken many calls from police stations and probation officers in several states.

"John Fry will end up dying in a prison," one of his parole officers told her once.

Other times she figured the Fry boys just needed somebody older they could confide in. John took the privilege to extremes, bragging about his drug use, his girlfriend Dawn, and the doctor he said kept them well supplied with cash.

She'd ask him, "Johnnie, why do you tell me that stuff?"

Most of the time John kept her well confused. Dot later heard stories of John boasting he once owned several gas stations, though neither she nor anyone else in the family ever knew him to have even one. Outwardly, he didn't seem to be a troublemaker. In fact, he seemed like the kind of guy who got along with everybody. It didn't fit all the enemies he made.

Dot knew John didn't exclude the family, either. Once he

ran her phone bill so high with calls her service was cut off. Jim told her that John had stolen from him as well, including a stereo that he'd bought with the money left by his dead mother. But that was nothing compared to what happened to John's ex-wife, another girl named Dawn, ten years back.

Dot would never forget the day she dropped by. The girl looked as though she had been worked over by famished cannibals. She wept as she explained that she had just gotten out of the hospital. John and his motorcycle gang had paid her a visit, she said. Dawn said she was raped, beaten and bitten.

"Where was John as all this went on?" Dot asked her.

"He's the one who did it," she answered.

John's ex-wife gripped the hand of their four-year-old son, little Johnny, and vowed she was leaving for good. The last Dot heard, she was living somewhere in Australia.

Jim had his problems, Dot thought, but he would never hurt family like that. She still thought his death was tragic, and their dad Pete was convinced his death wasn't a suicide.

Jim knew his brother better than anyone, Dot figured, and she remembered the words he'd said for years: "John will be the death of me one day. If anything ever happens to me, have it looked into."

Jim also had some other advice, and Dot heeded it as she listened to John talk about some plan to move to Texas or California.

"Remember," Jim told her many times, "Never cross John, or he'll kill you."

Chapter 75

Actually, the wealthy kid is much more vulnerable to this kind of crime The inner-city kid is more sophisticated. He lives with violence; he has a much more rigid protective shell.

— W. ALAN CANTY,
Good Housekeeping, September 1977

A thirty-six-year-old unemployed cabdriver named John Oliver Bumstead was getting an earful from his neighbor John Fry. The two men were heading east in a U-Haul July 6, helping a neighbor move to New York. Fry had volunteered to share the driving during the twelve-hour trip. Talk always made a trip go faster, and Lucky Fry was a really good talker.

Bumstead had recognized Fry a few months back at Keith Bjerke's house as the same man who had processed him into Jackson Prison in 1977. Soon, Fry was dropping over to use his telephone, then to borrow money.

As the miles accumulated on the truck's odometer, a lot of subjects came up, including the man Bumstead knew as The Doc. From his house twelve doors from Fry's, he'd often seen the black Buick cruise down Casper. Often he was looking for it. Bumstead knew he had a chance to collect on one of Fry's loans after a visit from the man.

"Yeah, the money is funny," said John Fry. He looked pissed.

The Doc's support was waning, Fry explained. Fry said The Doc told him the problem was that his bank account was frozen and he couldn't get to all his funds.

"The doctor is fucking up," Fry said. "He's not paying me the money he should, and I'm gonna take him out if he don't get straight."

The comment held Bumstead's interest no more than the lane stripes on the freeway. Bumstead had wanted to "take out" a few people in his life as well. He doubted Lucky Fry meant it any more than he himself did when he made an idle threat. Posturing and talking tough. They were talents most everyone learned in Jackson Prison.

Keith Bjerke had been hearing the same tough talk from Lucky Fry for about a week. Fry told BJ several times that The Doc's money was getting "real thin" and that he and Dawn suspected he was getting ready to terminate his support.

"This shit has gotta change," Fry told him. "I'm gonna have to get him right."

Fry was preoccupied with the dwindling funds in two or three recent conversations. He looked angry and frustrated.

"I'm gonna kick his ass," Fry said.

But BJ had heard Fry complain about The Doc's cash flow before. A threat from the mouth of John Fry was like the air pollution on the south side. Some days you noticed it, but you never dwelled on it for long.

BJ had his own mounting troubles, including eviction from his place on Casper. Before Fry left for New York with Bumstead, he dropped by to talk on BJ's front porch. He mentioned that if BJ needed a place, his bungalow on Casper would probably be available in a week or so, probably the weekend of July 13. Fry said he wanted to leave Detroit. He was moving to California, he said, to "get my shit together." Fry said he'd asked The Doc for money to finance the trip.

BJ already knew about The Doc's $5,000 payoff a year ago. He suspected Fry was going to run the same scam. BJ assumed Dawn would be going west with him.

Since he was going to move, BJ asked him, could he have some of their things? BJ had his eye on the couple's new kitchen table and chairs. Fry nodded but was more concerned about what he might get from The Doc than what he planned to give away. He said the money issue was coming to

322

a head.

"I better get the money," Fry said. "Or the shit is going to hit the fan."

BJ put the plans for California in the same category as the threats about The Doc. After Fry walked home, BJ decided he'd better not plan on getting the dinette. He just never knew what to expect from Fry. Fry was a con man, he thought, and a real good one at that. Maybe he'd get the money from The Doc; maybe he wouldn't. The only mark Fry had for now, BJ figured, was BJ's next-door neighbor, John Bumstead.

Earlier, BJ told Bumstead so himself. He knew Fry owed Bumstead money. BJ was sitting on his porch when Bumstead walked by, heading for Fry's house. BJ mimed the cast of a fishing rod in the direction of his neighbor. He cranked the imaginary reel and yelled out:

"Right here, Bumstead. This is what Fry's doing to you."

BJ later explained, "If John Fry sees a way to get money from you or through you, you had better be on your guard."

A twenty-one-year-old southsider named Tamara Becker never understood why John Fry, the cousin of her old boyfriend, always called the doctor named Al "a pain in the ass." After living with Dawn and John earlier in the year, she was well aware of the steady supply of money he provided.

Tammy had liked Al ever since he took her to the hospital when she was sick. On Tuesday afternoon, July 9, she decided to return the favor after she saw his Buick parked in front of the couple's house. Inside, she found the doctor alone on the couch, and John and Dawn in the bedroom with their drugs.

"You should get out of this mess, because they treat you so rotten," she told him. He was still sitting on the couch when she left.

Two days later, on Thursday, Tammy saw John and Dawn walking down Pitt Street. She stopped to give them a ride. The couple began talking about their future.

"We're going to California to straighten out our lives," Dawn said.

John nodded his head, adding they were leaving on the

323

coming Monday. Tammy wondered out loud how they could do that with no money. John said he expected to make a lot of money over the weekend.

"It should be good for $10,000, $20,000," he said. "Maybe even $30,000 if things go right."

John ignored the question when she asked him how. Instead, he wanted to know if Tammy would be available to give him a ride somewhere Saturday if he called around 1 P.M. He offered to put gas in her car if she did. Tammy Becker told him she had plans that day.

Furniture merchant Robert Saleh sped back to the bungalow on Casper. This time he was taking the big warehouse man named Bosco, and a major league baseball bat.

Saleh cursed himself for putting up with the deadbeats. For weeks he had been begging Dawn Spens and John Fry for his payments for the color TV. Now there wasn't even one to repossess. Saleh tried calling this "Dr. Cantee." When his messages with the answering service went unreturned, he gave up.

Then he tried calling Dawn's father, Roy Spens.

"Look, I know you're not going to reimburse me for the money," Saleh told him. "But before something real bad happens, you better do something. I see her with marks on her arms. This guy Lucky Fry is no good. She's into heroin or something. I know she is."

"What the hell do you want me to do?" Saleh recalled Roy Spens saying. "You trying to make me feel bad? You make me feel ten times worse about this thing . . . You're just tearing me apart. Would you mind just leaving me alone? Leave us alone, and I'll take care of things myself."

Finally, Dawn Spens called on July 9 and told him she had a check from where she worked. She wanted to pay off her debt of $224. Saleh should have known there was a catch.

The check was drawn on an account held by Chuck's Equipment Rental for $410. Dawn said the doctor was a part-owner of the company. Saleh called the phone number on the check. There was no answer, but it was after 6 P.M. The paper was from a branch of Detroit Bank and Trust.

The furniture merchant gave her $186 change and took the

check. He was eager to rid himself of the woman and her boyfriend. But the next day he found the check was no good, the account closed.

"This company is no longer in existence," a bank manager said.

Back at his furniture store Saleh stared at the check and uttered a litany of expletives. He couldn't believe he'd been so foolish. It was drawn on the bank's Fort-Campbell office, which had been kitty-corner across Fort Street from his store. He looked out the window. The branch now was an abandoned building.

That's when he fetched Bosco and the bat. When Saleh got to the porch on the bungalow on Casper, he placed the bat next to the door. He was ready if Fry made one funny move.

"I want every penny right now," he barked when the couple answered. "This fucking check is no good."

John acted miffed.

"Well, she already used the money, to take care of some personal things. And how can you tell me it's no good?"

"The company is no longer in existence."

When Saleh said he was going to call the police, John turned overly friendly as Dawn handed him a $10 bill.

"Look, Bob," he said. "I'm really sorry about everything. The best I can do is give you $20 a day until I get it made up. You see, I need every dime I can get. We're getting married."

There's no end to the bullshit, Saleh thought. But he really didn't want the hassle of filing a criminal complaint. He would hold Fry to his word and be back, every day, right through the weekend.

That Thursday night, Lucky Fry picked up a razor and a pair of scissors and decided to return to the look he preferred during his biker days. When he was done, all that remained was a mustache.

Friends later commented he looked quite vicious. Fry gave different reasons for the new style. He told one friend he was trying out a new hair-growth tonic that required a shaved head. He told his neighbor Juanita Deckoff, "I just want the clean look."

A nationwide contest was announced that week for the

double of the Mr. Clean on the household product.

"You ought to enter it," Juanita suggested.

But John Fry and Dawn Spens had other plans. The concept had been around for a long time.

Back in April, John Fry had scribbled out a note to his girlfriend as his mind raced with cocaine one morning during the hours just before sunrise. He committed his thoughts to a blue notebook. They remained there among other pages of grocery lists and phone numbers.

It read:

Al: Arrange to spend more time with him "alone."

Go out to lunch at least once per week.

Maybe out to dinner or you fix him a special dinner. "After work" is best time.

This is all to prepare to get a nice chunk of money prior to goodbye.

Chapter 76

In recent weeks he'd driven her around the city so she could take photographs, the two of them looking for new images. She shot pictures of downtown buildings and tugboats on the Detroit River. She stalked for angles on pictures, and he sat in the car smiling. He looked patient, relaxed.

Jan Canty had reason to be optimistic. Al was sleeping better, eating better, and was increasingly enthusiastic about spending time with her instead of his patients, the courts, or the jailhouse. Finally, his priorities were changing. One Friday he scurried down from the bedroom dressed as though their outing was his top concern, though he had a couple of hours of forensic work also scheduled that day.

"Al," she said. "If you're going to the prosecutor's office, why don't you have a suit on? You've got your jeans and that junky shirt on."

He stopped, glanced down at his jeans, and did his best impression of the absentminded professor.

"Oh. Yeah. Maybe you're right."

On Friday, July 12, he woke up all fired up about driving to the Fisher Building.

"Let's go into the office," he said. "Let's get it finished up."

Al, she thought, doing housekeeping? Boy, he is changing. They had been in the new suite four months, but there were still minor touches left. After they arrived at the suite she watched in disbelief as he opened boxes and moved furniture. Then he pulled out a hammer and some nails. He said he was going to hang a few things on the walls. She couldn't remember the last time she'd seen her husband with a tool in his hand.

Later Jan took a break from putting away books in his

office and walked over to her counseling room. Al was hanging up her doctoral diploma and her state certifications in psychology and marriage counseling. He'd arranged them in a straight line.

"Why did you hang them like that?" Jan asked. "I thought you'd put them in a T formation like yours."

When Al turned to answer her she could see the change in him. He looked melancholy, as though he had resigned himself to something inevitable. He pointed to the empty section under the three frames.

"This," he said, "is for your future, Jan."

It wasn't the words, but the way he said them. The feeling she got at that moment was that Al was trying to say, "You're going to do much more than I ever did." He appeared to be mourning his own work, like a man coming to grips with the end of a long career. The moment was so poignant Jan didn't know what to say, but she would remember it vividly for many months.

Later in the day she heard other odd comments, Al becoming more melancholy with each one. He pulled a few Fisher Building office neighbors into the suite to show off her office. He repeatedly complimented her on how beautiful it was.

"I can't believe you pulled this together so quick," he said.

Later she found him standing silently, his arms folded as he surveyed the entire suite.

"I can't believe how well your practice has kicked off, Jan," he said. "You're where I was five years ago, and you've been only practicing five months."

How his mood has changed from this morning, Jan thought.

At noon, he refilled his thermos and headed for the door. He didn't appear too enthusiastic about another lunch hour crammed with forensic evaluations.

"I'll be back," he said. "I've got to go down to the damn courthouse again."

Juanita Deckoff was soaking up some sun in her backyard when she saw the familiar figure toddle past her on his way to her neighbor's bungalow.

"Golly," Al said. "You're going to get burned up if you don't stop that."

"You ought to get out here, Al," she said. "You look like you need some sun."

A few minutes later she dropped by the bungalow. Al was taking Dawn's blood pressure and lecturing her on her health.

"Dawn, you should be eating right because of your heart," he told her.

"I have, I have," Dawn said. "I've been trying to eat all I can."

"Yes, Dawn, but you've been eating junk food, not decent food."

Then he took her to score cocaine. When they returned, Dawn invited Juanita to get high. Dawn laid out a small line on the kitchen table for Juanita, then she went into the bedroom to mainline the rest.

Al was sitting in the living room. Dawn had dozens of snapshots from her years in Harper Woods spread all over the room. By the time Dawn came out of the bedroom, Juanita was feeling talkative from the coke.

"So, you're a shrink," she said, plopping down in a chair.

"Well, don't call me that," he said. "I don't appreciate that. I'm not a shrink, I'm a psychologist."

"Oh, fine," she chuckled.

"He even wrote a book on it," Dawn said.

Dawn's neighbor pulled out a paperback from the stuff scattered around the living room. She saw the author's name, Dr. W. Alan Canty. Al's picture on the back of the book caught her attention. He was wearing a turtleneck and black horn-rim glasses and looked twenty years younger.

"My goodness," Juanita said. "You're even good-looking."

"Yeah, that was me in my younger days," Al said. "Yeah, I wrote it. It's something I have accomplished that people will remember. They'll know I've been here."

Juanita told him the only trouble with his job was that he had to wear a suit.

"Yeah," he said, "but sometimes I get to wear jeans at the office on Fridays."

"Where's your office?"

"The Fisher Building."

"Well," she said. "You should go down to the Fisher Building and tell them they should wear bathing suits and shorts and get loose a little bit."

They talked about vacations. That afternoon, Juanita's mother was going to pick her up for a week near Traverse City.

"So you're going up north with your mom?" Al asked.

"Yeah, I'm gonna do a little horseback riding."

"I like horseback riding," Al said. "My wife and I are due for a vacation soon."

Later, after he left, she realized how much he had opened up during their conversation, as though he wanted her to know exactly who he was, where he worked, and what he did. She had found out in only a few minutes. Until then, Juanita had no idea he was married.

Lately Juanita had been hearing John and Dawn talk of matrimony as well, and a possible move to California. Juanita guessed they were right for one another. John told her once that Dawn was the only woman who ever really knew how to take care of him, the only one who didn't want him to be some thing other than what he was. Dawn said the same about John.

"John is the only man who ever really cared for me," she said.

Juanita never could figure out how Dr. W. Alan Canty figured into the scenario. Al had come up in a conversation with John that week while she was out hanging laundry. John mentioned Al had once paid him five thousand dollars to leave Dawn.

"You know," he said, "this guy still thinks me and Dawn are not having relations, that we're platonic."

"Yeah, so what, John?" she said. "We know better than that."

"Maybe," John continued. "Maybe I should try it again, but just get a little bit more money this time."

The conversation was only a couple of days after Dawn said John had broken her nose. She said there had been an argument over at their neighbor John Bumstead's house and John had hit her, by accident. Later Juanita heard otherwise. She always suspected John had a temper. It would be something Dawn would have to deal with if they got married, and Juanita knew the coke and late-night parties weren't helping matters either.

"John's mostly a nice, easygoing guy," Juanita later told a friend. "But you can tell. The man has got a tornado inside him."

Chapter 77

As for criminal psychopaths, these people have no conscience. They are usually dangerous people to deal with.

— W. ALAN CANTY,
Henry Ford Community College lectures

Jan couldn't believe her eyes. Al was wearing the new sport shirt. Impossible, she thought. She would have been shocked if he had taken it from the package after a week, let alone the day after she bought it.

"See the new shirt you bought me?" Al said.

He was beaming, standing tall.

"Gee, that's nice," she said.

More than nice. He also was wearing her favorite suit, the dark green one with the Western cut. Only his shoes looked unfit for the ensemble. He was wearing his black engineer boots with the steel-enforced toes. It was just another Saturday, but within Al's casual limits, he looked as though he was dressed for either a wedding or a funeral.

Jan gazed through her favorite set of leaded-glass windows as he brewed his coffee. The branches of the elms were overstuffed with leaves. For the first time in months, she was feeling better about their marriage. He was beginning to communicate again, beginning to open up.

"I was very scared in the hospital, Jan," he admitted recently as they lay in bed one night. "I'm going to work very hard to avoid that. I never want to ever go through it again."

After he filled his thermos, she walked with him to his car.

The temperature was in the low sixties; it was a classic Michigan summer morning, where the smells of flora and cool grass brought some comfort before the heat that always hit at midday.

Jan kissed Al goodbye and said, "I love you."

She waved as the black Buick backed up over the antique bricks, then glided away under the cathedral ceiling of big trees.

By July 13, W. Alan Canty had left the trail of a man who was planning to make a significant change in his life that weekend. He also left hints that he suspected it was not without risk.

Ray Danford had spoken to Al at his daughter April's graduation party just two weeks earlier. They planned to lunch again in mid-July.

"How's your little problem coming?" Ray asked.

"I'm almost out of this thing. I'll give you a progress report at lunch."

On the coming Monday, Al was scheduled to pick up a new pair of glasses from his ophthalmologist. They were tortoise-shells, but with larger frames — a more free-spirited look.

Gladys Canty had heard about the new glasses.

"Wait till you see them, Ma," he said. "They're really something. They're really different."

She received a card from her son in the mail July 13 — belated birthday wishes, sixteen days late. What struck her as uncharacteristic was the way he signed it: "love always, Bus." He'd never included the "always" in a greeting card before.

Buster was in high spirits when he called at noon, but overly concerned that she hang on to that card.

"Ma, you save your cards, don't you?" he said.

He knew she did, she said.

"Oh, that's nice, Ma."

He said he and Jan were busy preparing for a visit from her parents from Arizona, but that they would make time to visit her.

"Jan and I will be coming over on our bikes some Sunday soon," he said before hanging up. Gladys had never known her son to ride a bicycle to her house.

At 2518 Casper, there had been another jagged night of partying, even while a child slept innocently in Dawn and John's bedroom. The previous evening, the couple had stopped to see Fry's distant cousin Sue Stennett. Her seven-year-old daughter Tonya Sue begged to spend the night with her "Uncle John." Fry reluctantly relented. As the couple left with her daughter, John told Sue Stennett her daughter would have to come home early. He wanted the house clear of any guests.

"I'm trying to get some money out of Al," he said. "I'm expecting Al to arrive with a large amount of money."

Tonya Sue was dropped off back home around noon Saturday, the child reporting that Dawn and the man named Al had given her a ride. That lunch Al gave Dawn $40 in $10 bills, the prostitute would later say. He didn't linger at the kitchen table or take time to read the morning newspaper. In a half hour he was back at the Fisher Building.

John Fry spent the early afternoon out and about, visiting dope connections three times to buy cocaine and a handful of Tylenol 4s. Neither he nor Dawn had visited the methadone clinic in two weeks.

At 3 P.M., Al was wrapping up a session with a psychologist he supervised. The colleague found his supervisor pleasant and relaxed. At 3:30 P.M. Al phoned Jan. He told her he would come home right after his last session, which ended at 6 P.M.

"I think I'll stop at Kroger on the way home to pick up some coffee," he added. The grocery store was en route to his home.

At 5:15 P.M. Al began an appointment with his last patient of the day, a woman who received therapy three times a week and knew his habits and demeanor well. Sometime during that forty-five-minute session the phone rang. The patient later said she believed the caller was a female. As Al tried to end the phone call he became increasingly disturbed, so much so that the patient herself was jittery by the time he hung up. The psychologist apologized for the interruption.

"That was a very manipulative patient of mine," he said angrily.

334

At 6:30, the quick steps of a pair of engineer boots broke the silence in the empty hallway of the Fisher Building arcade. A few minutes later the black Buick sped down the ramp of the building garage. A garage attendant waved to the psychologist, but Al had no time for pleasantries. The attendant later said Al Canty looked "upset."

The car drove off into what had turned into a suffocating Saturday. The air swelled with humidity and the temperature was nearly ninety; it was the kind of night Detroiters pray for a rainstorm to take the fevered bloat from the soiled air.

It had been eighty-four weeks and three days since the psychologist saw the young prostitute standing on the corner of Peterboro and Second. Whether he was returning to the bungalow on Casper willingly or unwillingly, the fact remained that W. Alan Canty was broke. He had a $440 negative balance in his checkbook. But it was a paltry debit compared to what he owed a list of creditors that included his office landlord and the vigilant Internal Revenue Service.

Dawn Marie Spens's sugar daddy had no sweetness left. Somewhere between his last patient and his arrival on the south side, Al Canty decided to fortify himself with a couple of stiff drinks.

A nineteen-year-old southsider named Jimmie Carter was returning from a trip to the corner store when he saw the black Buick pull up to him on Clark Avenue well before sunset. The man he knew as John Fry rolled down the passenger's window.

"Hey, mon," he said. "You want to buy a watch?"

John was holding a gold Seiko. Carter peeked into the car. The girl he knew as Dawn Spens was in the backseat. Behind the wheel was a man in glasses. Carter later identified him as Al Canty.

"How much?"

"Twenty-five dollars."

Carter went into his sister's house nearby and returned with the cash. When he handed John the money, he noticed the two men had switched positions. Lucky Fry was in the driver's seat.

Sometime between seven and eight o'clock, John's imposing figure appeared in the small hallway of the bungalow. He and Al could see each other through the open doorway of the bedroom. Al was sitting in a chair next to Dawn, next to the dresser where they kept their works, a few feet from the mattress where they slept, just across from the doorjamb where a baseball bat rested against the wall.

An open pack of cocaine sat on the dresser. When Dawn finished with the syringe, she handed the works to her boyfriend. Al remained seated as John repeated the routine for himself.

As the drug took effect, Dawn ran into the bathroom, leaving the two men behind. As she retched into the toilet, she heard voices building in the bedroom. First there were postured comments, then insults. As the argument increased in pitch, Dawn stood up and walked around the corner, facing the open bedroom door.

Al was eye to eye with John Fry, yelling, "It's my money, I can give it or I can take it. I can do whatever I want to do. If you don't like it, fuck you. I don't have to justify *anything* I do to you."

Al stomped toward the bedroom doorway. John was partially blocking his way. Al shoved him with a one-handed push to his shoulder. John gave only slight ground, but a stool behind him clipped him at the calf and he fell backward. When he came to his feet, his chest was blown up and his face was bright red. He was gripping the Louisville Slugger with both his hands.

There were at least three blows, maybe four. Two hit home just above the right ear, another across the forehead as Al's tortoiseshell glasses flew across the room. The cracks of the bat sent ten intersecting fracture lines across Alan Canty's skull like the outstretched fingers of a lightning bolt.

Dawn Spens ran from the house after the first blow, hearing the smacks of the others behind her as she reached the front porch. Any of the three could have been fatal. The psychologist collapsed onto the floor. Blood spread across the surface of his brain and rushed into the vessels behind his eyes. He was convulsing, twitching, senseless. But he would take a few minutes to die.

Fry stood over the body, his hand still gripping the bat.

"Get up, motherfucker!" he thundered. "Get up!"

When Dawn returned inside, she kneeled over the body with Al's stethoscope, placing the sensor on his back. She heard the thumping of her own heart.

"I can't tell, John."

Fry ordered her to leave the house.

"Get the fuck out! Just get the fuck away from me."

"What am I supposed to do?"

"Fuck it. I don't care. Go make some money."

She went up to Vernor Highway and turned two tricks at thirty dollars each, peforming the sex acts in the tricks' cars.

John sat on the stool next to the body and smoked a cigarette, eyeing the body as he puffed. He decided to wrap Al's head in a blanket and drag him into the bathroom. He lifted the psychologist into the bathtub, propping his feet higher than his head. Then he slit his throat.

"I cut his throat to try and get some of the blood out of him," he later said. "I don't know why. It just seemed like a good idea at the time."

After John covered the body with the blanket he heard footsteps on the porch. At first he thought it was Dawn returning.

Outside, furniture merchant Robert Saleh rapped sharply on the screen door. He'd returned to the bungalow as promised, armed with a baseball bat and expecting another twenty dollars. When no one responded, Saleh pushed open the door and stepped a foot or two inside, clutching the bat in his hand.

As he scanned the living room his eye caught a cigarette resting in an ashtray. A stream of smoke wavered upward from its tip. He heard only a few birds chirping outside at the coming dusk. Something told Saleh to call it a night.

John could feel his own blood surging through his chest as he waited in the bathroom for the visitor to leave. Then he took the car keys to the black Buick, locked the house behind him, and went looking for Dawn. He found her sitting on a stool at a Coney Island on Vernor. They visited the dope house and bought cocaine, and also some heroin. By the time they returned to the house on Casper, John had come up with a plan.

"He's dead," he later recalled. "I would never have done it if he was alive. But I'm thinking, the guy has got to go. There's no doubt about that. He can't stay here. But there's an apartment house behind us. There's houses on the side. And there's people movin' in that neighborhood twenty-four hours a day."

Fry loaded up a syringe with a speedball. The coke provided the energy, the heroin the numb. He reached into the kitchen drawer and grabbed a knife, the long one with the serrated edge and the Ginsu trademark on the black handle.

In the bathroom he pulled off Al's boots, then the socks. He struggled with the green pants and the new sport shirt, finally tossing them in a growing pile on the bathroom floor.

Then John took off his own shoes, pulled his T-shirt from his muscular torso, and slipped off his jeans. He didn't want his own clothes stained with blood.

John stepped into the bathtub stark naked, placing one knee on each side of Al's body. His own skin met the corpse's flesh as he went about the task. Perspiration sparkled on his bald head beneath the harsh bathroom light and bright Formica walls.

Exactly where Dawn Spens was, what she did, and what she saw that night would be left to the courts and her own conscience. She later said she was away turning tricks. John later maintained she was sitting on the toilet seat, assisting him with the packaging during the grisly task.

It was about ten-thirty when he began.

First John took off the head, followed by the hands, cutting them just above the wrist. He cut off a foot, applying the Ginsu just above the ankle. The severance was so precise, a medical examiner later would fit the two pieces back together like a puzzle. The other foot followed. He was surprised by his fast progress

"It was easier than you might think," he later said.

The head, hands, and feet were wrapped in newspaper, which was then folded with the kind of sharp creases found in a butcher shop. These packages were placed separately in four green plastic garbage bags, the head and feet in separate bags, the hands put together in one. John wanted something to carry all the body parts that could potentially identify Al Canty's body.

"Where's that fucking brown bag?" he cursed.

The parachute satchel that Al once used to tote Dawn's gifts during her hospital stays became Al's own makeshift body bag. When it was full, the valise was placed in the refrigerator.

Fry broke for a cigarette. Then he finished the job. He cut the legs and arms from the torso, stacking them in one end of the tub like logs. He put each leg in a separate bag and the arms in one sack. He wrapped the trunk in the bedcover and triple-bagged the bundle. He carried bag after bag to the back landing of the bungalow. In another garbage bag he put the knife, the baseball bat, and Al's clothes. He wanted one more item.

"Where's that fucking thermos?" he asked out loud. "They find that thermos, they're going to expect to find him sitting here."

After it was bagged, he washed himself in a laundry tub in the basement.

By midnight Dawn was scurrying around the house, packing. She stuffed their clothing into plastic bags and gathered up her photographs, bill receipts, and other paperwork, heaping them by the handful into a cardboard box. The carpet was cut from the bathroom floor and the hallway, leaving only foam padding. Another portion was sliced and lifted from the bedroom.

"I've got to take care of something," John said. "You clean up. If you see any bloodstains, clean them up."

Dawn carried a bottle of bleach into the bathroom and washed out the bathtub. She could hear John's footsteps on the back stairs as he loaded the trash bags into the Buick parked in the back alley.

John stopped at garbage dumpsters in alleys throughout the south side. He muscled the torso into one off Buchanan near Thirty-fifth Street. He tossed limbs into another behind a gas station off Springwells near 1-75. He dropped the baseball bat, Ginsu, and other damning evidence behind a market at Lafayette near Livernois. When he returned, he toured the bungalow.

"I walked through the house," John said later. "It looked pretty much in order to me."

After the car was loaded with their belongings, Dawn

lifted the brown satchel out of the refrigerator and carried it to the trunk of Al's car. John paused in the kitchen before they left. He filled a syringe with what was left of the coke and pushed the needle into his arm just off the tip of the tattooed Harley-Davidson wing. A stream of blood squirted onto the kitchen floor.

"Come on, we're going up north," he said.

On their way they stopped to drop off the keys for the bungalow with a friend, telling him he could take whatever he wanted from inside. Thirty minutes north of Detroit, they stopped again. John parked the idling Buick on the berm of the Joslyn Avenue exit. He wanted a pillow from the trunk for Dawn, who had started to doze at his side.

As he rummaged, he noticed the shine of a green garbage bag in a far corner of the trunk. He grabbed the oblong bag with both hands and hurled it off into the weedy embankment of the freeway ramp. Dawn poked her head out the window.

"Whatya doin', babe?" she asked.

"Just throwin' away some garbage," he said.

Jan Canty had sat down in front of the TV at 7:30 P.M., right after she put out hamburgers and freshly sliced onion on the kitchen counter. From the start she was captivated by the three-hour concert special called "Live Aid." She watched Sting and Phil Collins sing "Long Long Way to Go" and "Driven to Tears." She listened as Led Zeppelin alumni Robert Plant and Jimmy Page reunited for "Stairway to Heaven."

Then it hit her. It was dark outside. She walked into the kitchen and looked at the clock Al bought her for Christmas. It was 10:30.

Al, she thought. Where is Al?

The clock must be wrong, she thought. She walked from room to room, checking other timepieces in the house. The shudder started somewhere in her upper body, then struck home deep in front of her lower spine. God, she thought, it's been *three hours*. How could I have failed to realize it was so late? Al never fails to call when he's held up, *never*.

Jan phoned his Fisher Building office. Then she phoned

the security desk. He'd signed out at 6:30.

She walked to the living room window, as though that would somehow make the black Buick come gliding down Berkshire. She found herself fighting off panic. She went into Al's home office and called the Muirs. Their eldest daughter answered. John and Ces were at a movie. She took a message.

As she sat in Al's overstuffed chair she thought of the cash Al carried in his pants pocket. She called the Grosse Pointe police, asking them to check the Kroger grocery store parking lot.

"He was supposed to stop there for coffee."

"Sure, ma'am," the officer said.

She phoned the Detroit police. They told her to wait twenty-four hours. Then the Grosse Pointe police phoned back.

"No," the officer said. "There's no sign of a Buick like that in the parking lot."

She began imagining things, none of them good. Maybe, she thought, he had a car accident on the way home. She called the Michigan State Police, which patrolled the Detroit freeways. She gave the dispatcher his plate number.

"No," the trooper said. "We've had no reports."

Jan wanted to go somewhere, go looking. No, she thought. He might call. I'd better stay home. She moved to a chair near the living room windows of the big Tudor and waited. She stirred with every pair of approaching headlights. She was sure some were even slowing to turn. It was as though the cars were deliberately taunting her.

By midnight, she could take the anxiety no more. She called a neighbor for help. Together they drove down to the Fisher Building but found everything was in order at the suite. It was almost too orderly. She could see Al had tidied up a few things before he left.

They drove back to Grosse Pointe Park. Jan tried to ignore the ever worsening scenarios that played in her head. She thanked her neighbor for the company, then let herself into the house.

The big Tudor never felt so empty. She waited this time on the leather couch in their living room, again keeping her eyes on the front windows.

341

Jan first noticed the lightning flashes from a distance, as though enormous camera bulbs were going off on the other side of town. Then the rain began falling. As the wind picked up it flailed the droplets against the glass. She'd heard that pelting before, against the window at University Hospital fifteen months ago.

The storm only reminded her all the more of Al. He always loved weather like this, she thought, but she'd always found it so frightening.

Soon the winds were whipping the big elms with fifty-mile-an-hour gusts. Through the leaded glass Jan watched the lightning bolts crack the sky in intersecting grids. With each flash she could see a sky that was a vivid green.

She hoped it wasn't a tornado and tried to shake the feeling that something had gone terribly wrong.

Chapter 78

Frank McMasters pulled on his robe and shuffled across his bedroom to investigate the gentle rapping on his window.

"Cheryl, you'll never guess who's here."

Cheryl Krizanovic looked up, then felt the muscles across her big tummy tighten. She was six months pregnant with Frank's child, but it wasn't the baby having its regular Sunday morning kick.

"Oh my God."

They hadn't seen John Fry in nine months. Cheryl wondered what kind of turmoil he was bringing this time into her life.

When the pair came inside, Frank could tell it wasn't just a surprise social visit. Dawn quietly took a seat on the couch, putting her hands between her knees. She looked as though she was kicking drugs. Fry wanted to talk to him outside.

"Frank, I've got to get cleaned up so I can get traveling."

Frank wondered what Al's Buick Regal was doing parked in his driveway. John said Al had loaned it to him for a couple of days because Dawn's car wasn't running.

Frank looked at John's shaven head. He began to chuckle.

"Hey, baldy."

John wasn't in a joking mood. He looked tired, strung out.

"Frank, I've got some incriminating evidence I have to get rid of, and I'm kinda on the run."

"What for?"

"Dawn passed a bunch of bad checks and shit. How about if we take this bag I got in the car and throw it in some of that quicksand?"

Frank laughed again. John hadn't been there five minutes and already the plotting had begun. Never a dull moment, he thought. But he was even more amused that John had actually bought that northern-woods tale a couple of years back about the sinkholes off his property. What did he think this was, Frank thought, the movies? He could see John's overactive imagination was still intact.

"Well, if you really want to bury it," Frank said, "we'll just take it out in the middle of the woods somewhere."

Frank suspected John had a bunch of checks and false IDs to dump. Maybe they could stop for coffee first.

"No, Frank, now."

John won't be satisfied until he plays out his little fantasy of cops and robbers, Frank decided. He put a shovel in the Buick. The two of them went inside to tell Cheryl and Dawn they were leaving.

"Cheryl, we're gonna be gone for a while," Frank said.

Dawn looked up at John and said, *"That?"*

"Yeah."

John began to talk as he drove north on U.S. 31 toward Pellston.

"Frank, I killed somebody back in Detroit last night."

"What, again?"

Frank was smiling. Lucky Fry and his continuing saga of murder and mayhem, he thought. When hadn't John killed somebody right before a visit to Alanson?

"No, no, no. I killed Al. I've got the identifiable parts."

"OK, baldy."

As the Buick sped north from Alanson ten miles, Frank wondered what John's plans were. He rambled on about having to get to Florida or Texas or somewhere. Frank had just the spot in mind for John's "incriminating evidence."

Just past the Pellston airport they turned east off U.S. 31 onto Douglas Lake Road. The area was designated a University of Michigan Biological Station, but the small signs posted on trees along the rural road were misleading. There wasn't a scientist or a station in sight. An old logging road, nothing more than a couple of ruts, led off of Douglas Lake Road into a good square mile of raw state forest. Hardly anybody ever went back there.

Local folk called the area the "animal boneyard." The Department of Natural Resources dumped dead deer and other animal carcasses found along the state highways in one clearing back off the trail. Frank had hunted that stretch of woods.

They took the car into the forest a good quarter mile or more before the center hump began scraping the Buick's underbelly. It was a hot, still morning. Mosquito and blackfly weather, and Frank suspected they would be waiting in swarms.

Frank waited for John as he pulled the brown valise out of the trunk. Frank could see the straps straining on the bag. He grabbed the shovel. John must have a hell of a load of stuff, he thought. What junkies do for money.

They marched through the underbrush, heading off the trail at an angle past stands of birch and oak toward the thicker woods ahead. Once under the big timber Frank looked for an open area among the ferns and pine needles. He found a spot under three pines.

Frank could dig a posthole the length of a shovel. For John's contraband he stopped at about three feet. John was complaining about the bugs. His bald head was covered with bites. The flies' handiwork showed up as little trickles of blood on his scalp.

Blackflies are such nasty little bastards, Frank thought. A lot of victims just wave the air, mistaking them for harmless fruit flies. By then they already were at work, taking flesh by the mouthful. By the time someone realizes he's been had, most of the damage is done.

Fry dropped the bag into the hole sideways, then sported a smirk Frank knew so well.

" 'Bye, Al," he said.

Frank thought, what in the hell is he talking about? Had he stolen some of Al's belongings too?

John covered the satchel with dirt. Frank scattered pine needles over the freshly turned earth. No one would ever find it. They fled the bugs, heading back to the car. Fry seemed to relax once they were back on the road to Alanson.

"Well," he said. "We got rid of the shit. Unless they find the ID and the checks Dawn can't go to jail for forgery."

They talked about plans for that day. Frank suggested they go grocery shopping. There wasn't enough food in the house for four. Then, maybe, they could do some sight-seeing.

"Lookit, man. Dawn and I have been up all night. Maybe

345

we'll sleep."

"Bullshit. You're not wasting the most beautiful part of the day. You're not going to waste it sleeping."

When they got back to the house, Frank was still thinking about what they might all do together. Dawn still was on the couch. Cheryl had just come out of the bedroom. John stopped, pointed his finger at Dawn, and said in a firm voice: "You know now, *this is for life*. One way or the other."

Dawn broke into sobs and ran into the bathroom. Cheryl was right behind her. Suddenly Frank McMasters felt as though someone had hit him in the diaphragm with the shovel he'd carried into the woods. "I killed Al." "Identifiable parts." " 'Bye, Al." He's got *Al's car.*

"John, what the fuck have you done?"

"Frank, I didn't want to kill the man. He was our life-support."

Cheryl came waddling out of the bathroom, saying, "John, it's true? This stuff?"

"Yeah, I didn't know what to do."

"Oh shit," said Frank.

John said Al had been drinking. They got into an argument. Al pushed him.

"I went out, man," John said

When he realized what he'd done he panicked, he said. He had to get the body out of the house. He cut him up in the bathtub. Al's head, hands, and feet were in the brown valise.

Frank was angry, scared, and curious all at once. My fingerprints are all over that Buick, he thought. Christ, I'm an accessory to murder.

Then he couldn't believe John's stupidity. He began firing questions at Fry as fast as they came to his mind, as though somehow that could change things, as though somehow that would keep him from being involved. But I already am, Frank thought. I'm fucking involved in something I have no business even being around.

"It was self-defense, Frank."

"Why didn't you just call the goddamn police?"

"With my record, who is gonna believe me?"

"John, you're taking a chance on a murder rap," as opposed to manslaughter or something simple."

"Frank, I don't want to go back to prison. It was self-defense. The guy pushed me first."

"Fucking pushing isn't killing. It's not a death situation. The law says if somebody hits you, you can hit him back . . . But if somebody pushes you with his hand, you can't pick up a goddamn club and beat him to death."

Manslaughter, maybe, Frank thought. Now, who knows? Cut him up! Christ. What would a jury think? Christ almighty!

Frank surveyed his living room. Dawn was crying. Fry was nursing his bites. And Cheryl. Jesus, Cheryl. She looked weak, nervous. The baby, he thought. She can't take this. The baby can't take this.

He had to do something. He had to get John and Dawn out of his house. How? What was he going to say? What would Fry do? I'm the only one that knows where those body parts are, he thought. Who else is Lucky Fry capable of killing?

Frank McMasters had to face it. I'm up to my ass, he thought. I'm right here in the middle of it with these goddamn junkies. How can I ever explain that trip out to the woods? How does anyone explain Lucky Fry to a cop, to a jury, to anyone?

The black Buick, he thought. It's sitting out there, right in my driveway. In his mind he could see fingerprints, his fingerprints, all over the Regal.

"The car," Frank said. "First thing we do. We've got to get rid of that fucking car."

Chapter 79

Celia Muir was going stir-crazy. Everyone looked paralyzed. Neither Jan nor Gladys Canty had moved since she'd arrived at the big Tudor in the heavy Sunday morning rain.

Jan was pressed into the corner of the couch, hugging a big pillow that had the same contours as the skin around her eyes. Celia would have thought Jan had been up for days, but only fifteen hours had passed. Al's new Hush Puppies were still tucked under the coffee table.

Gladys Canty's immobility was of a different sort. She'd arrived at dawn. Now it was late morning and Mrs. Canty had yet to stir from the formal wooden-backed chair in front of the window. Her view through lead-framed panes was distorted by the sheets of rain. She sat with her back rigid, her eyes never straying from the street.

Where's my son? Where *is* my son?"

Besides calling hospital emergency rooms, Celia had spent much of the morning shuttling back and forth between the two women — holding one's hand, patting the other's back. Not once had they sat together on the couch. The two women in Al's life are so divorced, she thought. They can't even connect in worry.

There must be something more they all could do, Celia decided. She had to get her friend out of that living room.

"Come on," Celia said. "We're going. We're not going to just sit here. We're going to look. Mrs. Canty's here. She can answer the phone."

Then Mrs Canty spoke up. No, she said, she did not in fact approve of the rule made by Detroit police of waiting twenty-four hours for a missing-persons report, not in Buster's case.

"I know people in high places," she said. She planned to call them while they were out looking.

Celia had feared the worst since she received Jan's message. Al must have had another nervous breakdown. Celia imagined him out there in his Buick somewhere, perhaps disoriented by the streets of Detroit. Then she remembered his monologue in University Hospital.

"Jan, remember he brought up the Cass Corridor, a girl?" she said as they got up. "Maybe we ought to look there."

"Oh no, Ces, no," Jan said. "That was all through a patient. He was mixed up, living a life of a patient."

Suddenly Mrs. Canty stood up, her eyes still riveted on the street.

"The Cass Corridor?" she said. There was disbelief in her voice.

"Well," Celia said, "he had mentioned in the hospital he'd gone down to the Cass Corridor."

"My son," Mrs. Canty said, "would have no reason to be in the Cass Corridor. We know what kind of people are down there."

There was much anger in her voice.

That was dumb, Celia thought. I should have never mentioned that in front of his mother.

Jan wanted no part of the Cass Corridor either during their several-hour search. Celia insisted Jan do the driving. The more active she was, the better, Celia thought. Jan put her Thunderbird on the track of her husband's predictable habits. They looked in the Kroger parking lot and checked a party store at the Detroit border where Al always bought his beer. They drove down the alley behind the store. Jan was reluctant to give anything a good look, especially when a black car appeared parked in the alley ahead.

"Check the license plate, Ces," she said, not looking herself. "Is it his?"

"No, Jan, it's not his."

The car wipers and freeway expansion joints beat out free-form rhythms as they headed for their next stop. From a distance on such a dull day, the Fisher Building looked as gray as an old cemetery monument. Its terra-cotta-tile roof, normally a smart green under bright sun, was the color of mud.

Celia didn't like the looks of anything when they stepped off the elevator onto the tenth floor. The corridor was very dark. Jan said they were working on the lights. Celia knew Jan had been there the night before. Yet her heart was slapping at her breastbone when they opened the door to the suite.

"Wait, Jan," she said, stopping her friend from sliding the key into the door. In her mind's eye she could see him inside, dead. Jan turned the tumbler on the lock, sending a metallic click reverberating down the polished marble corridor.

The smell hit Celia's nostrils only a few feet inside. Sweet, she thought. No, lemon. Lemon oil, or furniture polish. She walked around the waiting room, then followed the smell into Jan's office. The big oak desk once ruled by Al Sr. was dustless and bright.

"Oh, look, Ces," Jan said. "He's polished my desk."

Jan Canty fell into a chair and began to weep.

"He knew I wanted that done. No one had gotten around to doing it. Look, he's hung my picture frames. Celia, he's been trying *so hard*."

They discovered other housecleaning chores completed. Her books had been put in order on her shelves. The big Chinese cabinet was polished. Al must have done it all before he left the night before, Jan said. This is not Alan Canty, Celia thought.

Celia walked hesitatingly into Al's office. It was neat, clean. Gone were the little notes he usually left scattered everywhere for himself. Everything was so orderly.

Celia's worst fear crawled up inside her and curled up into a snake-tight spiral in her stomach. Al Canty has committed suicide. She knew it. Everything has been left so complete.

"The *bathrooms,* Jan," she said. "We've got to check the bathrooms."

"Why?"

"Why, you know, for Al. He might be in there. He might need help."

Jan stared at her quizzically. Celia grabbed her by the shoulders and looked into her eyes.

"Jan. We have to brace ourselves. Brace ourselves to the fact he might have harmed himself. You know, he's been having a lot of financial problems. Maybe he's been trying *too* hard. We've got to brace ourselves for the fact he might have killed himself."

One by one Celia checked the toilets on the floor. She tiptoed into the darkened rooms, checking the space under the

350

stall doors from a distance. She was ready to flee for help the minute she saw anything—a pant leg, a shoe, anything. She checked the women's as well as the men's.

They'd worked out a plan by the time they got to the Thirteenth Precinct. Technically, Celia and Jan figured, Al *had* been gone more than twenty-four hours After all, Jan hadn't seen him since the previous morning.

Celia watched Jan right herself into her best professional demeanor as they walked into the station. She had trouble getting her story out to the woman police officer behind the desk. The cop kept interrupting her to change her lunch-run order to a nearby Burger King.

The next officer they talked to was watching TV, a boxing match. He kept his eyes on the fights, turning only to ask questions

"Lady, did you have a fight?" he asked.

"No," Jan said. "Ces, you know that. You know I don't fight with him."

"That happens a lot, though," the cop said.

"I understand."

"Did you check his friends? Is he out with his friends?"

"Yes. No, he doesn't go out with friends. You don't seem to understand."

"Did you check the places he hangs out?"

"Yes. He doesn't hang out places. Officer, that's what I'm trying to tell you."

"Did you check the hospitals?"

"Yes, we checked all the hospitals. Celia, here, checked the hospitals."

There was a pause as the cop concentrated on the fight. The bell rung on the round, then he spun and said, "Lady, did you ever think to check the morgue?"

Celia watched Jan sit down suddenly in the chair behind her, as though she was about to collapse.

"Could you?" Celia asked.

"Well, you can call the morgue," the cop said.

The cop saw the shock on Jan's face and woke up. He admitted maybe this was out of character for the missing man. He apologized several times as he filled out the missing-persons report.

"Celia," she said as they walked out. "They don't see the seriousness of this. Al has been trying. You know things have been better than ever between us."

Gladys Canty still was at her post when they returned to the big Tudor. Jan pulled out Al's appointment book. It was getting late. They'd have to start calling his patients to cancel his Monday appointments.

"No," Gladys said. "You mustn't do that. You mustn't do that yet. Think of his practice. What will they think?"

"Look," Jan snapped. "We don't have to tell them what's happened."

They began leafing through the pages of a schedule that had become increasingly spotty. Some patients' names looked unfamiliar. They were odd-sounding names, as though they had been made up. The appointments for several weeks were printed out in block letters, each one in a different-colored felt pen — blue, yellow, orange, green. After Saturday, July 13, all the pages were blank.

When Mrs. Canty saw the empty pages, there were two women who suspected suicide.

Gladys Canty had picked up the telephone while her daughter-in-law was out searching with her friend. She dialed up an old friend from her tenure on the Detroit school board. The Reverend Nicholas Hood was a longtime member of the Detroit City Council, the city's legislative body.

"Nick," she told him, "this is not just another case of an errant husband. This is *my son*. I think he deserves something special. Whatever happened to him, it isn't run-of-the-mill."

He told her he would see what he could do.

She was still in her chair in front of the big window when Celia Muir left. Jan offered to fix her a bed in the guest room.

"No, I think I'll stay here at my post."

She was still there when the sun came up in the morning.

Chapter 80

Frank McMasters wanted to finish the half-built garage next to his house, park the Regal inside, cut it up, and scatter the pieces where nobody would find them.

But Lucky Fry saw dollar signs.

Dorothy Wilson, his surrogate mother back in Detroit, received one of the first calls he made from Alanson. She'd fallen asleep in front of the television when the phone stirred her from the couch.

"Hi," John said. "I think I've done it again. In fact, I know I have."

"Done what?" she asked.

"Killed a man. With a baseball bat."

"Why?"

"Because he didn't pay Dawn."

Before Dot could question him further, John offered her the car. Did she want an '84 Buick Regal for only a hundred dollars? Johnnie Carl, she thought, you ought to know better than to offer me what has to be a stolen automobile.

He told her he loved her, then hung up.

"John, you gotta get that goddamn car out of here," Frank said.

John remained convinced he could fence the Buick in the Motor City, where it would be dismantled in a chop shop. He and Dawn, John decided, were driving back to Detroit. Then after Frank got off work, he and Cheryl could drive to pick them up.

Before leaving, John wanted to destroy Al's identification, which he'd found in a wallet in the glove compartment. Everyone in Frank's house already had seen the name.

"Frank, until I went through the guy's wallet he had me

fooled too," John said.

After Frank left for work, John told Dawn to go to the bedroom and bring in Al's papers. Cheryl fed them into their wood-burning stove in the living room. Dawn lit a roll of newspaper.

"Add more paper," John said. "Make sure it's all burned."

He held back Al's Mobil credit card. He'd already used it to gas the car up in Flint.

After another sleepless night, Jan Canty decided she would enlist the help of the media. Early Monday morning she phoned the influential news department of WJR-AM, the station located in the Golden Tower of the Fisher Building. Maybe reporters would be receptive to helping a fellow tenant.

Jan heard the first news report in her Thunderbird on her way to the Fisher Building. She'd decided work was the only thing that might take her mind off Al.

Few residents of the Morrell Apartments listened to WJR, but John Fry and Dawn Spens were well known by many of the tenants in the three-story building on Morrell and Toledo streets. So was the black Buick and the man they knew as The Doc.

John Bumstead was one of the first people to spot the couple as they pulled up to the building shortly after noon. Bumstead had gone to the Morrell Apartments to see Keith Bjerke, who had moved into an apartment there.

Fry hit the brakes when he saw Bumstead on the sidewalk. He spit several obscenities at his former neighbor. Fry demanded to know why Bumstead hadn't told him when he called from northern Michigan the day before that police cars were spotted on Casper on Sunday.

Tammy Becker was looking out the window of her friend Cecelia Ramirez's apartment when she spotted the Buick parked across from the building. A few minutes later she went out the front door. Dawn was sitting on the concrete steps in front. Then Fry approached her from the direction of the car. He wanted Tammy to follow him in her car so he could drop the Buick off somewhere.

"Where's Al?" she asked.

"Things have backfired," John said.

Tammy told him she didn't want to get involved.

"Tammy, it's very important that I get rid of this car."

John was looking for a neighborhood car thief. He offered to fill up her tank with gas. John pulled a gasoline card from his pocket. She saw the name Alan Canty.

"John, I don't want to know any more," she said.

She turned to go back into the apartment building, but John grabbed her arm, repeating again that he had to dump the Buick. Then he explained why.

"Al didn't bring what he was supposed to," he said. "He finally stuck up for his rights."

The Doc stuck out his arm, John said, and he "went to town" on him with a baseball bat.

"Al's history," John said. "The body will never be found. It's scattered in five different states."

Tammy refused to help again, but before she scurried into the building, John told her she was the only person he'd told about the killing.

"If it gets back," he said, "I'll know it was you."

Later, Cecelia Ramirez also talked with John and Dawn outside.

"Where's The Doc?" she asked.

Fry smirked. Dawn was still sitting on the steps, her limbs shaking.

"Would you believe that The Doc started drinking and got brave and stood up to John?" Dawn said. "He even pushed John."

A short while later John and Dawn showed up at the apartment door of a thirty-three-year-old ex-convict named Gary Neil, asking to use his phone. Neil had many dealings with Fry over the summer. He'd also heard several days before the killing about John's plans to score a large amount of money from The Doc.

"What happened to your move?" Neil asked.

"It backfired."

"What happened to The Doc?"

"He pushed me over the edge."

John said that Al had shown up "with only sixty-six dollars." He said Al told them he was through with them and he was "going to straighten his life out." Then Al threw up his fists, Fry said.

"The body is in five different states," he added. "I just got back from Ohio."

John wanted to know if Neil could help him sell the black Buick. He'd split the money. Neil asked him if he had a title. John said he didn't.

"John, I can't sell a car without the fucking title."

Dawn, meanwhile, was on the telephone. Neil noticed she was crying as she talked.

"You'd better watch Dawn," Neil told John. "She's going to crack."

"After all she's been through I don't have to worry about her," Fry said. "She won't crack, man. I'd put my life in her hands."

Gary Neil's girlfriend, Consuelo Flores, overheard Dawn's conversation. Dawn called her mother in Windsor and told her she'd almost been raped and had to leave Detroit — for California or Florida, perhaps. She warned her mother not to tell anyone she'd called. She needed as much money as possible.

A few minutes later, outside the apartment building, Tammy Becker's boyfriend, Steve Kovach, was just leaving in his girlfriend's car when John Fry ran up and asked for a ride. Kovach knew John had been hassling Tammy that afternoon. He decided to give John a lift to get him away from his girlfriend. Dawn got in his car and John told him to follow the Buick.

John parked the Buick two miles away on a main street near I-75. Kovach was nearly out of gas. Fry offered to fill his tank, pulling out a Mobil credit card. Kovach saw the name on the plastic and told him to forget it. He'd take his chances on the fumes.

As they drove back to the Morrell Apartments, he heard

John tell Dawn, "If we can't sell the car, we're going to have to burn it."

By late afternoon, the word about The Doc's fate had spread through the entire apartment building. But two days earlier Keith Bjerke already had hints Al was in trouble. On Saturday, before the killing, he was on his way to the showers located in the basement of the building when Gary Neil yelled from his second-floor apartment, "Hey, watch the papers. The Doc is in big shit."

By early evening, the Buick was parked in front of the Morrell Apartments again. When BJ saw the car, he approached his old neighbor, who was sitting with Dawn on the front steps.

"Well, where's The Doc?" he asked sarcastically.

"On an extended vacation," John said. Then Lucky laughed.

Gladys Canty's influence was already being felt by the time the afternoon shift reported at the Thirteenth Precinct. Sergeant Carl Robinson was already up to his neck in other work as he took a seat next to the broken air conditioner. He was pulling off his tie when he saw a familiar six-footer with a linebacker's build walk into the detective bureau. Greg Osowski was wearing his trademark shit-eating grin.

"Goddamn, look at this missing," Robinson told the seventeen-year veteran. "I'm gettin' bugged by cases. I'm gettin' bugged by the phone. Now I'm getting bugged by the commander."

Osowski waited for the punch line.

"Greg, if I get calls, will you help out and take them."

He'd take more than that. Osowski snatched the missing report from Robinson's desk. Fifteen years in the Thirteenth Precinct, two years in Morality, and he still was a sucker for a case. He hadn't worn a uniform in thirteen years, but he remained the only cop in the investigations section with the bottom rank of police officer. He'd broken in half the guys in the detective bureau.

The thirty-nine-year-old once asked a superior why he was

357

never promoted. He responded, "Somebody's got to take the blame when things go wrong. Shit always rolls downhill."

Osowski phoned Jan Canty. She detailed her husband's predictable nature.

"Sounds like the perfect husband," he later told another investigator.

By 8 P.M., Osowski decided he'd better start at the beginning. Twenty minutes later he was shooting the breeze with a couple of security guards at the Fisher Building.

"He's a strange one," said one "The man worked twelve to fourteen hours a day, every day."

After an elevator ride, Osowski found himself standing in the middle of Al Canty's office in the Detroit Guidance Center. He saw the red Mustang on the wall and the wood cube with the brass ball. He looked up at the African sculptures, their distorted faces peering at him from the bookshelf. It was only a vibe, but he had learned to trust his instincts.

"What did you mean by a strange one?" he asked the security guard when he returned to the Fisher arcade.

"He's a sexicle."

"What the fuck is that?"

"He had a second office in here years ago and a lot of gorgeous young girls coming and going."

A few minutes later, Osowski stood looking out on the open vista from the tenth floor of the Fisher parking structure where Al Canty kept his car. Overworked. Young girls. Where, he thought, does a guy like that go to party after a long day?

From his high post on a hot night, he eyed Second Avenue stretching south, directly into the heart of the Cass Corridor.

Frank McMasters didn't know how much longer he could stand the waiting. It was well past 8 P.M., and John Fry and Dawn Spens were late. Frank and Cheryl Krizanovic were sitting in his Dodge Aspen at the predetermined corner on the south side. Frank was surprised when the black Buick pulled up next to him.

"Hey," he said to John. "I thought you were gonna get rid of that damn thing."

"I've got to talk to a couple of people first and then we'll get rid of it, then get the hell out of here."

Frank struggled to keep up as John steered the Buick recklessly through the streets of Detroit. He sped, blew stop signs, and cut corners through gas stations at lights. He stopped at a house, went inside, then came out saying the fence didn't want the car.

Then they drove to the Morrell Apartments, where John met Gary Neil. Dawn got into Frank's Aspen. Neil and a friend were in another car. Now there were two cars chasing the Buick to another location where another unsuccessful attempt was made to unload the Buick.

By 11 P.M. Frank was fed up. Cheryl had spent the entire evening swaying back and forth in the passenger's seat. John came up with another plan as the three cars sat idling on the street.

"Frank, we're gonna strip it, then burn it. Go get a gallon of gasoline."

Frank drove to a nearby twenty-four-hour gas station. The two other cars were right behind him. While Dawn paid for the can of gasoline, Fry, Neil, and the third man began fumbling with the Buick, their hands shaking as they tried to unlock the wire wheel covers. The spare tire and jack were put in Frank's trunk.

Next, they wanted to take the Buick to a remote location to pull all four tires and the radio. Lucky Fry was going to get every dollar he could out of Al Canty's car. That's when Frank drew the line.

"Fuck this, John, I'm leaving. I can't take this pressure. I don't want these junkies around me. I'm leaving."

"No, we're just going to get these tires —"

"No, we're not going to get the goddamn tires. We're gonna get rid of this goddamn car."

Neil and the other junkie disappeared into the night with the wheel covers. Frank followed John, who was driving the Buick, to a remote section of Federal Street across from a warehouse. John parked the car in a vacant field near a stretch of railroad tracks. John fumbled with the license plate, trying to turn the fasteners without a screwdriver. Frank grabbed it with two hands and ripped it off.

Then John doused the car with gas. He started limping. He complained of an old abscess that was acting up on his leg, then asked Frank to torch the car. Frank lit the rag, threw it on the Regal, and ran. About five seconds passed before the flames met the fumes.

They sped off as the flames lit up the desolate area. Frank was relieved. He no longer had to worry about fingerprints.

No one had any money for gas or food for the five-hour trip back to Alanson. John and Dawn had spent their money on a bottle of Somas—muscle relaxants to soothe their nerves. They stopped at a local restaurant and waited while Dawn turned a trick on Vernor Highway.

By the time they reached Pontiac, thirty minutes north of Detroit, Frank had a headache that pounded every time the car hit an expansion joint. He asked John to take the wheel and took him up on his offer for one of the Somas. John and Dawn already had swallowed a handful.

Frank began questioning Fry again about the murder. Frank knew he was totally involved now, and he demanded that John tell him everything. Earlier, John had told him that the fatal argument with Al was over the psychologist supplying her drugs.

The Aspen rolled north on 1-75, while John unfolded a different story as Frank pressured him. John said the plan was to get Al to pay him ten thousand to twenty thousand dollars to leave Dawn alone—the same move they had pulled over a year ago. This time, however, John was to leave Detroit entirely and relocate in California. John also had added a twist to the deal, the kind Frank considered characteristic of his scheming personality.

It went like this: Dawn put in the request for the money. John, meanwhile, pretended to take Al into his confidence. John then told Al privately that he had Dawn believing that once they got the money, they would both flee to California, leaving Al with nothing. But that was a smoke screen, he told the psychologist. John told Al that what he really planned was to take the money for himself and leave Dawn behind for him. That way the money could be transferred through Dawn without alerting her to John's departure.

God only knows, Frank thought later, what Lucky Fry actually would have done if he had received that money.

Al Canty, however, failed to show with the cash on Saturday night. As Dawn ran into the bathroom to throw up, he and John began arguing about it. Words were exchanged and Fry demanded to know why the deal no longer stood.

"Fuck you," Al said. "I don't have to justify anything I do to you."

Then Al pushed him. Frank McMasters already knew what happened when someone touched Lucky Fry. He'd seen the man before with a baseball bat in his hands.

No, it probably wasn't premeditated murder, Frank thought. But he doubted there was a lawyer in Detroit who could explain Lucky Fry to a jury. He just hoped John had kept his mouth shut.

"The guy can't be traced to me," John had already assured him. "And Frank, I haven't said a thing to anybody."

Around midnight, Greg Osowski pulled up to the three hookers standing on Temple just east of Cass. The old cop rule still applied: Treat a whore like a lady and a lady like a whore.

"Yeah," said one. "There's a girl named Dawn who has a good trick with a Buick. She used to live on Second and Charlotte."

Back at the precinct Osowski took a call from Ray Danford. Ray had been worried since he had heard from Jan. He had to tell somebody, but it wasn't going to be Al's wife. Osowski listened as Ray told him about their lunches.

"I think the name is Spens," he said.

"Dawn Spens?"

"Yeah, that's it."

At 1:30 A.M. the precinct computer produced a rap sheet and an address — 645 Charlotte. A few minutes later Osowski sat in an idling unmarked car, looking at a vacant lot. Across the street he saw the Homewood Manor. He recognized the girl sitting out on the steps.

For years Osowski had nurtured a select group of snitches, many of them whores. They were always looking for breaks the next time they found themselves in the Thirteenth lockup. Sometimes the cop wondered whether it was worth all the favors he handed out. He decided he'd walk across to the Homewood and find out from the girl *Suzy Q.*

"Yeah, Dawn," she said. "She hangs with a guy named Lucky."

"I need more than that, come on."

She blinked her eyes. Thirty minutes later she called him at the station.

"Greg, its Fry," she said. "I think the name is Lucky Fry."

The Dodge Aspen blew by the state police car as it lurked in the median near Bay City. When John Fry saw the flasher in his rear-view mirror he remembered what Frank had said about the faulty speedometer.

"Frank, Frank," he shouted. "Drive! Take the wheel, man! I don't have a driver's license and I just killed a motherfucker."

"No, man." Frank was drowsy from the Soma.

"Fuck this, you will!"

The car swerved as John kept his foot on the pedal, and the two of them switched places. Fifteen minutes later the trooper handed Frank the speeding ticket. The cop was cordial and unsuspicious

"I figured I had at least a seventy-two-hour grace period," John said.

Frank learned later why John Fry was so adamant about turning over the wheel. He had four arrest warrants on statewide police computers—for shoplifting in Petoskey, contempt of court in Allen Park, assault and battery in Detroit, and a traffic violation in Saginaw, one of the towns they'd just passed.

Frank McMasters still could see John's reckless drive through Detroit and their brush with the trooper. Shit, he thought. Maybe that's why everyone called him Lucky.

Chapter 81

Tuesday morning W. Alan Canty's picture hit the streets. On its second front page, the Detroit *Free Press* carried a story along with a photograph copied from the back of Al's book *Therapeutic Peers*. It was a portrait from his thirties. He wore a turtleneck and a pair of black horn-rim glasses. The headline: PSYCHOLOGIST DISAPPEARS AFTER LEAVING OFFICE.

Afternoon police-beat reporter Betsey Hansell picked up the Canty story the night before while chatting with a friendly sergeant in Police Headquarters. There, the city's twelve precincts reported dozens of cases day and night to an information control center. But the name Alan Canty stood out.

"You ought to check into this Dr. Canty," the sergeant told the reporter. "He used to teach at the police academy. He was quite a flamboyant character."

The mix-up between father and son was further muddled as Hansell sat in the police department newsroom listening to a *Free Press* librarian read clips to her over the telephone. Dr. Canty's background, the librarian said, included expertise on criminal sexual psychopaths and LSD experimentation for the CIA.

Another clip she read in the Alan Canty file did in fact quote Al Jr. The 1975 story was about hypnosis, keying on the news angle that a *psychiatrist* was hypnotizing witnesses on the case of missing labor leader Jimmy Hoffa. One expert quoted liberally in the story on the effectiveness of hypnosis was *psychologist* W. Alan Canty. Somehow, as reporter and librarian raced to meet deadline, that clip prompted another mix-up.

The lead paragraph on Tuesday's story: "A Detroit psychologist who hypnotized witnesses in the search for missing Teamsters leader Jimmy Hoffa and who tested LSD for the CIA has been missing since Saturday."

Even as a missing man, Al Canty seemed to be fashioning illusions as his identity remained clouded by his father. The basic information, though much of it inaccurate, generated a flurry of television reports. Jan Canty provided TV stations with the picture of her and Al standing on the brink of the Grand Canyon.

"He likes to go to the same restaurants," she told one Minicam. "He likes to go to the same grocery stores . . ."

One TV report led off with footage of Jimmy Hoffa. "It was ten years ago to the month since Hoffa was last seen getting into a car outside a suburban Detroit restaurant." Soon the Canty case would command the kind of widespread curiosity associated with the former Teamsters leader. Al Canty would join Jimmy Hoffa in the ranks of Detroit's most baffling crime stories, but for entirely different reasons.

The media attention relieved some of the frustration that had pursued Jan since that night filled with lightning and green sky. At least people are looking for him now, she thought. Her parents flew in from Arizona, pushing up their scheduled visit a couple of weeks. It wasn't until they had arrived on Monday night that she realized how out of touch she had become with her own needs.

"Jan, what's this?" her mother asked, arriving in her kitchen.

The Saturday night hamburgers were still on the kitchen counter. Onions and lettuce she cut were brown and wilted. She suddenly realized she hadn't eaten in two days.

With her father in tow, Jan went to the Fisher Building Tuesday afternoon. She saw a couple of her patients and fielded calls from Al's.

One of the callers was Ray Danford. He wanted to see her, so she told him to come to the office. He arrived just ten minutes before a patient's appointment.

* * *

Ray Danford wished he had a stiff drink as Jan closed the door in the consultation room, leaving her father outside in the waiting room. His lip was shaking. He felt like the stammering boy of his youth.

"Did — did Al tell you about these dopers he was hanging out with?" he stuttered.

Ray tried to tell her about the drugs and Dawn and John and the south side and Al's visits every day. But he found himself speaking in fragments. Jan just kept looking at him in disbelief as he tried to get it out.

As he left he was nearly in tears. He wanted to tell Jan what he figured had already happened. He wanted to tell her that he was convinced his old friend was dead. But he couldn't bring himself to say it.

Jan Canty's mind wandered as Ray mumbled about some drug addict Al was treating. She found it hard to concentrate with a patient scheduled only a few minutes away. Drug addicts. The south side.

Who, she thought, is this man talking about? Not Al. She thanked him for coming. He's as traumatized as I am, she thought.

After the patient left, she decided to tackle the money. A lot of Al's bills were due. She thought of his evaluations at the Wayne County prosecutor's office; she thought of a private attorney Al had said owed him money for forensic work.

Her father offered to call both to see about payment. He was pale when he reported back. The prosecutor's staff said they had never seen W. Alan Canty, let alone given him any cases. As for the private attorney, he reported no dealings with Al.

He must not have talked to the right people, she thought. Then she began thinking about other things Al had said recently. Jan didn't like the pattern she saw falling into place.

Chapter 82

Greg Osowski dismissed any hope of more than six hours' sleep as he reached for the ringing telephone late Tuesday morning.

"Hi, Greg, this is Suzy Q," she said. "Woke your ass, didn't I?"

Single, the cop gave his home phone number to his best snitches.

"Buy me lunch. Might have somethin' for ya."

They agreed to meet at 1 P.M. on the south side.

Osowski already was taking the missing case personally. He liked to look at his two dozen informants as growing infants he was teaching to walk. But for months they all had been falling on their butts. He felt like a proud father—one of them was now taking some giant steps.

The way it was shaping up, Lucky Fry and Dawn Spens were running in turf he knew well. Besides his connections in the Corridor, his own house was only a half mile from the Michigan Avenue strip where Dawn turned tricks. His next tip from Suzy Q put the couple right in the neighborhood where he grew up.

The hooker was waiting for him in the Cruise Inn Bar on Vernor Highway near Springwells. He bought her a bag of chips and a screwdriver.

"They call the trick The Doc," she said. "And, The Doc is a good john, Greg."

"Yeah."

"They live right near here, on Casper, I think it is."

"Can you do better than that?"

"Let me call you this afternoon."

Osowski left a twenty-dollar bill on the bar rail in front

366

of her.

"Hey, Greg," she said, grabbing the twenty. "Watch yourself. Lucky is a crazy motherfucker."

"Why? Does he carry a gun?"

"He doesn't have to carry a gun," she said.

Dan Hall, Al Canty's fellow car buff, was watching a 6:00 news report on the missing psychologist as his family sat around the kitchen table in his Bloomfield Hills home. Hall wondered now if Al would ever make their lunch date. The newscast mentioned police were looking for Al's 1984 black Buick Regal. Hall turned to Jim Campbell, his son-in-law.

"I've ridden in that Regal they're looking for," he said.

Campbell flashed on what he saw earlier that day on Detroit's south side as he supervised a crew laying a fiber-optic line near the Grand Trunk Railway. He saw a black Buick parked among some debris near the tracks.

"I saw a car like that today—all burned up," he said.

Hall suggested Campbell call the police.

"Naw, I'm sure they've checked it out."

"Jim, you better call anyway."

Hardly a half hour had passed since Greg Osowski had taken the call from Suzy Q. Dawn Spens and John Fry lived "one or two doors down" from Pitt, she told him, then she went one better than that.

"They were trying to unload The Doc's car on Monday," she said. "Supposedly it's fucked up over on Federal somewhere."

Before he could find a partner for the outing, the precinct phone rang again. Osowski listened to the caller from Bloomfield Hills. Jim Campbell wasn't quite sure of the name of the street where he saw the burned car.

"It begins with an F," he said. "Near the railroad tracks and Livernois."

"Federal?"

"Yeah. In a field, across from the warehouse there."

Osowski pulled a fifteen-year veteran named Robert Carroll from his desk and headed toward the location.

"Greg," he said. "I don't know what the fuck you're doing, but you run with the ball."

When Osowski saw the blistered car near the tracks he sensed they were about to score.

Nothing was left inside the Regal but bare seat springs and charred metal framing. They copied the vehicle ID number from under the hood. Minutes later they fed the vehicle number into the Fourth Precinct computer and waited. It was nearly 9 P.M. when the printer chattered out the response.

After notifying Homicide and Armed Robbery, the two cops returned to secure the burned Buick. They were met there by five scout cars and a canine unit poised to search the area. Just after 10:30, Osowski and Carroll were back in their car, heading in the direction of Casper and Pitt.

"Call the station," the dispatcher said.

Osowski pulled into a police Mini Station on Vernor, one of many small, volunteer-staffed units scattered in neighborhoods throughout the city. They were only a long block and a half from the bungalow on Casper.

Inside, Carroll cradled a telephone, while Osowski found himself eavesdropping. A volunteer was shooting the breeze with a burly guy who had just dropped into the storefront operation. Osowski heard the visitor say "The Doc."

His name was John Oliver Bumstead.

"Yeah, I know Lucky Fry," he said.

"Bob, let's not blow this," Osowski told his partner. "Let's call the boys at the big store."

Later, Osowski would write it all off as Polish luck.

Celia Muir escorted her best friend out of the big Tudor for a long walk as evening fell on the Pointes. They strolled down Berkshire, then along Windmill Pointe Drive. They found themselves glancing in the driveways and looking at cars as they passed. Celia even had found herself looking up the aisles of a grocery store earlier in the day.

In time, they were able to nurture a few lighthearted moments. Celia even prompted a laugh out of Jan. Then her friend stopped suddenly. She heard Jan's breath rush out.

"Look!"

Celia's eyes focused on the figure a hundred yards away on the sidewalk ahead. Through the summer haze she could see him, his shoulders seesawing with each step. He's walking our way, toddling our way, Celia thought. His head was topped with red.

They stood there frozen for a few seconds, watching the figure approach. Then they began breathing again. Somebody else owned that distinctive Al Canty walk. Jan wanted to go back to the big Tudor.

"I thought that was Al," Jan said. "I thought that was Al, coming home."

Chapter 83

The child who is sometimes licked, and on other occasions barked at by the family dog, really never knows where he stands with the animal: just as the child who is sometimes praised and at other times punished for what he views as similar behavior will have difficulty determining what is expected of him.
— W. ALAN CANTY,
Principles of Counseling and Psychotherapy

A soft-spoken public relations consultant named Doris De Deckere was telling a friend over lunch about the name in the newspapers. She met W. Alan Canty when he was in high school. The teen showed up one day outside his father's office in the Recorder's Court clinic, where she worked as a secretary at the time.

"I was alone in the office. Young Alan Canty came in, though I didn't know who he was at the time. He asked for Dr. Canty. And he was so nervous — so obviously nervous — that I perceived him to be disturbed. I said that Dr. Canty would be right back, that he was with one of the judges.

"Well, he was really agitated and pacing back and forth, saying, 'When do you think he's coming?'

"So I went back to his office and called the judge's chambers and said that there was a disturbed young man downstairs who was asking for him, and I thought it important he come and see him.

"When Canty did, and spotted his son, he said, 'Jesus Christ. What are *you* doing down here? What do *you* want?'

"It had something to do with the dentist. Then he took him into the office and yelled and yelled and *yelled*. I mean it was just really horrible. It's not the sort of temper you expect to see between father and son, especially in a business place. You might expect some controlled anger. But he knew I was there, and there were no holds barred. I mean, he really and truly blasted this kid and called him lots of names, including 'stupid' . . .

"I haven't forgotten it because it was so shocking to me. And I felt an incredible sense of stupidity that I didn't know it was his son. I thought how stupid to call him 'disturbed.' And maybe I was to blame for the railing he got. It was one of those incidents where when you think of it, your blood runs cold.

"But the man always spoke very disparagingly of his son. He never spoke of him with any great love; he never spoke of him with any pride. The only references I ever heard was that he wished his son was doing something else; he wished he was smarter; he wished he was . . . you know, *'that damn son of mine.'* If he got that kind of thing at the office, I can imagine what he got at home.

"So, I'm reading about all this in the newspapers that the young Canty was missing and I said to my husband, 'Look at this. I haven't seen this man in years. Isn't this funny? It brings it all back to me again.'

"And I wasn't surprised. When you diminish somebody, and they feel they have no self-worth, you lay them open to seeking the level of self-worth they have. If it's nothing, that's the level they seek.

"I turned to my husband and said, 'You know, they're gonna find him in some garbage dumpster somewhere.' "

Chapter 84

*The successful interrogator must be a convincing actor.
He must learn how to play several roles.*

— ALAN CANTY, Sr.
"The Psychological Training of Police Officers," 1953

The week Homicide took over the Alan Canty case, its top cop, Gilbert Hill, was getting his teeth capped. Seven months earlier the inspector had made his acting debut as Eddie Murphy's boss in the film *Beverly Hills Cop*.

Gil Hill, a lean black man with penetrating eyes and a penchant for three-piece suits, snagged the role when Hollywood producers showed up in his office one day, looking for inspiration for the film sets. They found plenty in the dark-oak-and-cork-trimmed confines of the homicide section.

For fifty years the face of child killer and sex deviate Merton W. Goodrich and the tall headline CATCH GOODRICH greeted visitors at the door. It was part of a framed display of news clips on the 1932 case. Nobody in Homicide knew who first put them up, and nobody knew why they still remained. But the charge and photo set the tone of the section's fifth-floor offices in Police Headquarters. Goodrich's odd mug was anyone's stereotype of a twisted killer.

Hill's dental work was in anticipation of more film work. He'd already lost his favorite role when he became supervisor of the section's fifty detectives, who probed more than six hundred killings a year. The promotion took him out of the daily case-cracking routine, where his skills once earned him a spot on a task force imported by Atlanta to solve its rash of child killings. Hill still couldn't resist getting involved when a hot case came down the pike.

The first paperwork on the Canty case showed up next to a pack of Kools and a cup of black coffee on Hill's desk Wednesday morning. The inspector already had one of his best investigators involved, a thirty-eight-year-old detective named Bernard Brantley.

Sergeant Brantley was Hill's successor as the head of the section's special assignment squad, a group of a half-dozen detectives who probed police shootings and high-visibility cases. With his paunchy frame and balding head, Brantley looked more suited for a desk in City Hall than for one of the toughest jobs in Homicide. It was a deceptive demeanor.

"Outright brilliant is what he is," Hill once said of him. "He ain't scared of nothin'—not even me."

Brantley watched his boss slide his preliminary report back to him across that kind of well-greased track of compliments late Wednesday morning.

"We're going to call it a homicide, even though we don't have a body. It's all yours, Bernard."

Brantley should have suspected as much. It was his first day back on the noon-to-eight shift following an all-night rotation that had introduced him to the Canty case in the first place

When Brantley arrived at the sweltering Vernor Mini Station the night before, he found John Bumstead surrounded by more than a dozen question-shooting cops who had packed the storefront, anxious to get a piece of the action. Bumstead said that he heard Fry and Spens were at the Morrell Apartments, trying to raise money to get out of town.

"Well," Brantley said. "If Fry is at the apartment building, and this guy is saying he probably killed him, let's go get him."

Cops covering the back exit heard a chorus of flushing toilets when Brantley and eight officers made the location. Some tenants obviously mistook their arrival as a drug raid.

There were a half-dozen people who said they knew the couple. Brantley suspected they all had information, especially when one woman pulled him aside in a hallway.

"Lookit," she said. "They said they did it. You oughta get 'em. They're probably going to be here again."

As he returned to the squad room from Inspector Hill's office late Wednesday morning, Brantley knew right where his outfit would begin. They were going back to get the talkative girl from the Morrell Apartments, but he planned to offer a half dozen the trip downtown. That would take the heat off the snitch.

"Well, everybody," he said, "let's go take some hostages."

The squad concept of concentrating a half-dozen detectives on one case had served the homicide section well. Brantley liked to fit a cop's personality to the task at hand. The spectrum was well covered.

On one end was Gerald Tibaldi, a grinless sergeant with more pepper than salt in his hair. Eight years of facing reams of cases as a precinct detective had blessed the twenty-year veteran with no tolerance for hand-holding.

On the other was a detective Brantley called The Social Worker — Marlyss Landeros, a soft-featured cop who had taken a lot of crap as the first black woman in the section. But even her critics had to admit she could "work the religion angle" better than most anybody. The thirty-seven-year-old cop called her aim for the heart "The Gift." She'd learned from Gil Hill, who, one cop once said, "had the uncanny talent of making you think you were his best friend as he put you away for life."

The Canty case officially was assigned to Landeros, meaning she'd cover the formal paperwork and see that prosecution witnesses made it to court. The latter was another forte. Landeros already fielded fifty phone calls a week from her "friends" made on past murder cases. Some called collect from Jackson Prison.

A new slew of friends arrived in the homicide section late that afternoon when Brantley and a cruiser returned from the Morrell Apartments. Tammy Becker, Consuelo Flores, and Gary Neil were in the first group. Later Keith Bjerke, Steve Kovach, and Cecelia Ramirez followed. Not all were talkative, but Landeros found a common thread among those who were.

"I couldn't help but get the feeling," she later said, "that many of them really liked this guy called The Doc. He was a symbol of prestige to a lot of them, and some felt John and Dawn had abused his generosity."

The stakeout at 2518 Casper produced only one temporary captive — furniture merchant Robert Saleh, when he returned to collect another twenty dollars. By Wednesday evening Homicide had a search warrant.

The squad dismissed John Fry's boast of scattering the body as high street drama until detectives and evidence technicians entered the bungalow just after sunset.

Right off, Brantley noticed the missing carpeting. Then he began spotting the blood: A smudge at the base of the toilet. Splatters on the white wall above the tub. Dried droplets on the doorframe of the back bedroom.

He saw blotches of darkened blood on two towels left in the living room and front bedroom. Another small stain marred the kitchen floor. Squad members followed a trail down the stairs from the kitchen; they discovered a pool dried on a rubber step mat at the back landing. Underneath the basement stairs was a piece of bloodstained formica. Next to the stairs was a small storage area, and more blood.

Brantley walked over to an old concrete laundry tub and looked in. It was dry except for a recessed groove in the basin. A channel of water had yet to evaporate. It was bright red with blood. An evidence tech pointed to a box under the last basement step. It was an empty trash-bag box, and it was smeared with blood.

"Jesus," Brantley said. "We need samples of all this."

Marlyss Landeros found herself studying the junk left behind in the back bedroom. Items on a dresser reinforced what people had been telling her all day. A spoon for cooking dope. Empty prescription bottles. A couple of dozen used paper seals for cocaine. There was a stethoscope, a Comerica Bank envelope, an eviction notice, and a book, *Psychology of Industrial Conflict*.

Landeros looked at a copy of the Yellow Pages at the foot of the dresser. Scrawled across a page was "Dawn Marie Spens Fry." On the floor she found a sheet of paper ripped out of a notebook: "Canty, W. Alan, Ph.D. 906 Fisher Building." The psychologist's home and office phone numbers were also there. A clump of red hair stood tall atop the fibers of the bedroom carpet.

As camera strobes sent bursts of light into the yard from the bungalow's windows, Brantley talked to neighbor Mike Oliver outside. His girlfriend Juanita Deckoff was still vacationing in the north. Oliver told Brantley what the squad already knew, about Al Canty's daily visits and the money for Dawn Spens. Then he said that last week he had eavesdropped on John Fry as the pimp sat at a picnic table beneath his kitchen window.

"One day I'm going to kill that fuckin' doctor," Oliver said he heard Fry tell a companion.

When Oliver mentioned garbage bags, Brantley began tapping his pencil on his thumb. The neighbor said he saw a pickup truck and two people carrying bags out of the bungalow in the back alley late Saturday night.

"How many bags did you see?" Brantley asked.

"At least five, but not more than six bags."

"Have you seen those kind of bags before?"

"Yeah. They look like big leaf bags."

"Have you seen John or Dawn use garbage bags before?"

"No. They never used plastic bags for garbage. They would throw garbage out the window, or put it in paper bags and throw it out the window."

Back at Homicide, the squad checked the garbage pickup schedules after they found the alley dumpster empty. The trucks had hauled away the entire south side early in the week. Brantley was convinced the body had left with the empty soup cans and milk cartons.

"We've just run out of luck, everybody," he said.

As far as the squad leader knew, no one had ever been convicted of murder in Michigan without a body, and the detective figured an ex-con such as Lucky Fry knew that as well. Brantley called the Wayne County prosecutor's office anyway. He wanted a murder warrant for John Fry and Dawn Spens.

"Lookit," he told an assistant prosecutor. "We've got blood. We've got great witnesses. We've got a witness seeing the plastic bags."

The assistant prosecutor wanted a body.

"Damn it, how much more circumstantial evidence do you

need?" Brantley said. "We'll never find the body."

"Bernard, we're reluctant to issue a warrant without a body."

The squad bitched about the wording of the teletype. John Fry and Dawn Spens were wanted for "questioning" in the disappearance of W. Alan Canty.

Gil Hill wasn't surprised that Jan Canty was a class act. He knew the name Canty well. Alan Canty, Sr., was one of his favorite lecturers at the police academy. But the inspector pondered how the old man would have handled the task he faced as she waited outside his office Thursday morning.

Hill was convinced Jan Canty was a widow. Duty dictated he tell her about the picture that was emerging of her husband on the south side.

She was wearing a smart blue suit as she took a seat across from his desk. He began with the torched car. He said they had executed a search warrant and were seeking two suspects.

"I believe that your husband is dead because of these circumstances. There's always room for hope, of course. But based on my experience, I like to tell people what I believe to be the truth."

Jan's lip began to shake. She asked if her parents could join her. The family held hands as he continued. Hill couldn't decide which was more difficult, revealing the possible homicide or the next installment.

"We've been getting a lot of rumors as to what was going on with your husband," he began again.

He told her about the prostitute named Dawn, her husband's clockwork visits, and the money he reportedly had been bringing every day.

"That's what people were saying," he said. "And these people also have told us he's been killed and his body cut up."

During the silence, Hill remembered the last time he broke the news to a family about a dead john. An entire squad was detoured two weeks because a wife wouldn't be candid. He could hear her shouts echoing: "Why you want to do that to him! The man is dead now. There ain't been no money missing. He ain't been fuckin' around with no whores."

Hill pressed on anyway with questions. He needed to find out if all he had was a bunch of junkies with big imaginations. He had a hard time believing their story himself.

They talked for a good hour. They talked about money, sex, and work schedules. She cried. Her mother and her dad cried.

"I knew something was wrong," she stammered. "The finances are not what they should be. But we both work. It didn't make sense. But this makes sense. In fact, this is the only thing that has made any sense for months."

"And now, Mrs. Canty," Hill said, "it all makes sense to us."

The circuit of circumstances over the past nineteen months lit up all at once for Jan. Then came the overload. Only one light was left blinking as her parents drove her back to the big Tudor.

This, she thought, explains why we never had lunch. Now Al might be dead. What am I supposed to do? Hope? Mourn? Or be furious?

She was too shocked to feel any one of the three.

Gladys Canty got the call from Jan's mother just before noon Thursday.

"Gladys, can you get someone over there to be with you?" she said. "We're on our way."

She knew they were bringing terrible news. She summoned her eighty-seven-year-old friend named Edna, a doctor's widow she'd known for years. Her friend arrived shortly before Jan's parents. Jan's mother's face was florid. Her father sat with his hands folded and his head down.

Out with it, Mrs. Canty thought.

"Alan has been murdered," Jan's mother said. Gladys closed her eyes.

"And it's worse than that. He was involved with a prostitute. Her pimp killed him. He's been dismembered."

"I'm just glad his father isn't here."

She didn't think Al Sr. could have handled this kind of strain.

"How was he killed?" she asked.

"We don't know how."

They didn't stay long.

This is all some kind of mistake, Gladys thought after they left. The truth will eventually come out. It has to come out.

Then she felt a stillness in her home she'd never known before. She and Edna sat together on the couch, as her old friend gently patted her hand.

Over the next several days, the tips kept the squad phones ringing. Many callers reported Fry's handiwork with a baseball bat and his attempts to sell the Buick. One caller said he'd overheard a clerk in an auto-parts outlet saying Lucky Fry had been shopping in his store for a saw.

One anonymous informant tried to connect Fry with another death. Fry, the frightened caller said, had killed his own brother on Christmas in Tennessee. Street talk was that Jim Fry had witnessed his brother kill a south-side couple and was planning to talk before Lucky staged a suicide.

When Marlyss Landeros pressed for details, the caller hung up. The squad already had all they could handle with Fry on one case.

"Maybe Fry got cocky," Landeros said near the end of one of the squad's eighteen-hour days. "Maybe he thinks 'cause he got away with murder before he's gotten an extra sense of self-confidence."

But nobody knew where John Fry and Dawn Spens had gone. By late in the week the Canty story was all over the papers and the television.

Then, late Friday afternoon, somebody else balanced an old delinquent account with Lucky Fry.

"It's a place he goes to hide out and dry out," said the informant. "It's in Alanson, not far from Petoskey. They're up there right now."

Chapter 85

By midweek Frank McMasters was sleeping very lightly with an old handgun tucked between his sheets.

John Fry already had tried to move the body parts while Frank was at work. The only set of wheels available was Frank's old motorcycle. The plan never got farther than the kick starter and John working up a heavy sweat.

John spent most of his time hanging around the house, pontificating about his next move as Dawn sulked. When someone mentioned the murder, she burst into tears. Frank's first concern was Cheryl. She was growing more jittery by the day. Frank was worried about the baby.

When he got an unexpected day off, Frank decided he had to do something about everyone's nerves. They bought a couple of six-packs and spent a day sight-seeing to the north. They drove across the Mackinac Bridge and strolled down the strip of little gift shops in the Upper Peninsula town of St. Ignace. On the way back, they stopped in Indian River at a pay phone. Dawn called a relative in Texas who she said was a former addict. He might help them out, she said. She asked him to send two bus tickets. He turned her down.

On Thursday a money order arrived from Dawn's mother for fifty dollars. It was made out to Frank. He cashed it and split it with his houseguests. They bought some more beer and went driving again. That night their outing took them down Douglas Lake Road, past the state land where Al's remains were buried. John was smirking when he recognized the area.

"There's where Al's buried," he said. "He has his own personal cemetery."

He looked out the window, chuckled, and waved his hand.

"Bye-bye, you motherfucker," he said.

Dawn started sobbing again.

Frank figured the problem at hand had nothing to do with laughter or tears. Somebody had better make a move, he thought. The Detroit daily newspapers they bought earlier that day reported the burned Buick and a police search of 2518 Casper. One story reported a couple as being sought for questioning.

Early Friday morning Frank went to work. Shortly after the rest of the household woke up, the Detroit *News* and *Free Press* were spread out on the kitchen table. John's and Dawn's names and descriptions were in front-page stories.

"His goodness may have got him," Gil Hill was quoted as saying about Al. "Some people are telling us he was trying to get her off drugs."

"Shit," Fry said. "Maybe they'd like to know about all those prescription pills he was bringing her."

Cheryl Krizanovic thought John was missing the point.

"John," she said, "your pictures are going to be in the paper tomorrow. Count on it."

In fact, back in Detroit, Homicide was releasing the mug shots that morning. They showed John in a full beard and Dawn with long, straight hair pulled back from her forehead. When Frank returned from work, the couple was already packed, waiting for a ride to Detroit.

"We gotta go," John said, handing Frank the newspaper.

"I guess you do," he said.

Frank McMasters didn't need any convincing.

As freeway signs charted their progress south, John and Dawn discussed where they might go after they connected with a friend in Detroit. Texas, Florida, California, anywhere.

Then they began working on a story. The pair had been seen by too many people in Alanson, the four of them decided. It only would be a matter of time before they were traced to the village. They decided Frank and Cheryl, if questioned by police, were to say the two of them had visited, then left.

Fry then began telling Dawn what to do in case they were

arrested. There was no body, he said. There was no way he or she could be charged for murder if everyone kept silent. But he added an amendment to the plan in case something did go wrong.

"If it comes down to it, put it on me," John said. "Put all the weight on me."

"Babe, what do you mean?" Dawn said.

"Make a deal to testify against me for immunity, damn it. You make a deal because it's gonna come out anyway."

"But John, I don't want to do that. I don't want to lose you."

"Goddamn it. It's not gonna do any good if we're both in the goddamn penitentiary. We're still not going to be together. You may as well take your way out."

Then Frank and Cheryl listened as Fry instructed them about their role in a worst possible scenario.

"You guys do everything you can to help her out and let me go to the dogs," he said. "Because if it gets down to murder, that's where I'm gonna go anyway."

It wasn't Dawn who took batting practice with Al's head, Frank thought, but he knew she could face a number of charges.

Earlier that week, when Frank grilled John about the killing, John emphasized Dawn wasn't in the house during the mutilation. Later they talked about that alone, during a trip to the beer store.

"John, that's all bullshit and I don't want to hear it," Frank said.

"Well, what the fuck do you want me to tell you, that she was packaging it up when I was cutting it up?"

"That sounds more like you. That sounds more feasible."

"OK. So it happened that way, man. But don't tell Dawn I told you. She don't want anybody to know that she was there."

Dorothy Wilson had already entertained a visit to her modest west-side home from Marlyss Landeros, telling the detective about John Fry's Sunday phone call. She fell asleep on the couch after the Canty reports on Friday's eleven o'clock news, absolutely convinced now that Johnnie Carl was a killer.

Dot's feet skated on the carpet as she struggled to clear her head and reach the ringing kitchen telephone. It was half past midnight.

The voice was deep and low.

"This is John. I'm around the corner on Kentfield and I'm coming to your house."

He hung up before she could speak.

Dot Wilson's mouth went so dry so fast she couldn't swallow. Oh Lord, she thought, he told me about the murder. *John Fry is coming to kill anyone who knows about the murder!*

She dialed as fast as she could. She called her brother down the street. His phone had been cut off. She called her son across the street. There was no answer. She called her mother, who answered.

"John's comin' for me. Get help. Get the police."

Dear God, I can't even think, she thought. *Police.* Her panic was so great she dialed everything but the emergency 911 number. She called her next-door neighbor, Ray Brewer. He was a detective in the Fourth Precinct. There was no answer. That's right, her mind raced. He works afternoons. She dialed up a local Mini Station. The number was right there next to the phone.

An officer later logged the call from "a hysterical female."

"Listen to me," she stammered. "I can't talk long. The guy who killed the doctor just called me. He's coming to get me! He's just a few houses down."

"Who?"

"Johnnie Fry! Please send a car. Please send one! But be careful, he's right nearby."

An unmarked car three miles away was alerted, the dispatcher suggesting the two plainclothesmen investigate a hysterical female near the foot of Heyden Street.

Then Dot called Bernard Brantley in Homicide. They spoke only briefly. What good is he? she thought. He's all the way downtown. Then she tried neighbor Ray Brewer again, getting his wife out of bed.

"Well, Ray ought to be home any minute," she said.

She dialed again, this time her sister who lived down the street. The answering machine came on. Later her sister would listen to the message on the tape:

"Oh Lord, please let her get on. Oh God, please let her answer. Oh God . . ."

Then Dot dropped the phone. She had to get out of the house. She ran in her slippers several houses down to her sister's house. Her sister had been woken by the pleading through the answering machine intercom and was waiting for Dot at the door.

Ray Brewer, a thirty-year veteran police sergeant, was anticipating his easy chair and some late-night TV when he was met by his wife inside the door of his home. As she explained the call from their neighbor, he noticed a van pull up on the street out front. He saw the big guy with the baseball cap heading for Dot Wilson's door, and the young girl trailing behind.

"Call for a backup," he told his wife, then he walked outside.

Brewer put his hand on his gun and identified himself. Then, as he walked from his porch, he felt flanked. He had a man he suspected was John Fry on his right, and the van idling on his left, just across his front lawn. He was relieved when the guy in the cap motioned to the van and it sped off. Now he just wanted to stall.

"What are you doing?"

"Well, my aunt lives here."

"I don't believe it," Brewer said. "You look like you're up to trouble. Show me some ID."

Brewer didn't want him to get into that house. He assumed Dot Wilson was still there and figured if the man was Fry, he might try to take a hostage. Brewer was handed the license of a Julienne Scott. The girl just sat on the porch, resting her head in both her hands.

Where, Brewer cursed to himself, is that damn squad car? The guy in the cap remained cordial.

"My cousin lives across the street," he said. "I'll show you."

"As long you remain in my sight," Brewer said.

Brewer stood next to the girl but kept his eyes on the guy, who walked across the street and banged on the door. He expected one of them to bolt anytime.

"I've got an uncle next door, let me go check there," he said, moving further down the street.

The girl remained on the porch. He was beginning to think she was too tired to run.

At 12:45 A.M., a fourteen-year veteran named William Johnson and his partner, William Deck, reached the last block of Heyden just as John Fry was about to try another relative's house.

"It's him, right there," Brewer whispered into the unmarked car.

"Who?" one officer said.

"Fry. John Fry."

Deck jumped out, running in his sneakers like a crouched cat as the figure walked to another house. Fry was reaching for another door when Deck announced himself with the cold touch of a .38 Smith & Wesson on the back of John Fry's slick head.

"Don't move or I'll blow your brains out."

Fry tried the Julienne Scott ID again, but both cops saw the bald dome shining under a streetlight when they ordered him to take off the baseball cap.

As the unmarked car headed downtown to Police Headquarters, John leaned over in the backseat and whispered to the only living witness to his murder of W. Alan Canty.

"Honey, they're gonna put the best they got on you, 'cause they know you're the weak link. Now, you gonna be the weak link, or you gonna be the woman I think you are?"

"Don't worry, babe," Dawn said. "I'll never say a word."

"All you gotta do is sit cool for three days, man. They're gonna bring everything they got to bear on you."

"They gonna beat me up?"

John laughed.

"No, they ain't gonna beat you up. You may wish they beat you up after they get through with you, wish they kicked the dogshit out of you to make you feel better 'bout yourself. That's how good the motherfuckers are at twisting you all around."

Chapter 86

*Sometimes [the interrogator] will confront the sub-
ject with evidence of his guilt, while in another case
he will keep him guessing. He may repeatedly remind
one subject as to the symptoms of the subject's ner-
vousness, while with the next suspect he will be overcome with emotion and will join the suspect in
shedding tears over the disgrace he has brought on his
family.*

— ALAN CANTY, Sr.,
"The Psychological Training of Police Officers"

Bernard Brantley decided to give Dawn Spens a few
thoughts to sleep on before she was shown her cell in the
eighth-floor lockup. He'd already targeted her as the weak
link in the case.

It was nearly 2 A.M., and Brantley was putting the final
touches on a search warrant for Frank McMasters's house.
A police plane would be waiting for squad detectives Saturday afternoon. Brantley never looked up as she was es-
corted- into the squad room not even two hours after her
arrest.

"Do you know what type of people you're dealing with?"
he asked her. "You *know* the people that Dr. Canty went to
college with just aren't going to stand by and let something
like this happen."

She said nothing. Then he looked up.

"You know, I really don't want to talk to you," he said.
"I'm tired and I want to go home and sleep. But I want you

to think about some things. We've got John for murder one. That's a given. We're sure you helped him. We're not sure how much. Maybe you didn't help him at all. Maybe you just consoled him. But you know all about this case."

Brantley's tired monotone sounded like that of a weary bureaucrat instructing his next applicant to fill out a government form.

"Now," he continued, "the bottom line is, do you want to go to prison for the rest of your life, or do you want to help the police? Think about it. We've got everybody you can think of that knows anything about this case. We've got Tammy. We got Gary. Dawn, we really don't need you.

"So if you want to take the chance on going across the street and being charged with murder one, do it. I'm too tired. Even if you wanted to talk, I don't want to talk to you. I don't even want to sit here right now and type a statement."

The twisting had begun. Dawn Marie Spens hardly slept.

When Marlyss Landeros reported to the squad room early Saturday morning, she thought the girl in the shaggy perm sitting across from her desk was just one more incidental witness. She offered her a donut.

"Hi," the cop said. "You want some coffee?"

The cop flashed a warm smile, trying to meet her eyes. The girl in blue jeans and a halter top looked up coldly. The cop felt the girl look right through her. Later someone told her that was Dawn Spens. She didn't look at all like her picture.

"That girl has got the personality of a straight razor," she said.

Frank McMasters and Cheryl Krizanovic heard about John and Dawn's arrest on the radio as they drove around in the hours before sunrise, trying to find Cheryl's brother's house.

"We better go in to Homicide," Frank said.

He wanted to run their fabricated story and get the worst of it over with. But the worst was just beginning.

By early afternoon, he had no idea what had happened to Cheryl or what she was telling police. He was sitting in the squad room with Marlyss Landeros and a detective named Madelyn Williams.

Williams, a ten-year veteran detective, possessed the kind of gutty guffaw that enlivened laugh tracks. Frank still couldn't believe her greeting when he introduced himself as Dale McMasters that morning.

"Hello, Dale, I mean Frank," she chuckled. "You do like to be called Frank, don't you?"

"How did you know that?"

"We know all about you, Frank. We have the whole book. Two years' probation for receiving and concealing stolen goods. Still on probation, aren't you?"

She was smiling. Christ, he thought. Five more months. He'd been convicted in Emmet County. He'd unknowingly bought stolen construction materials and would eventually win the case on appeal.

But that couldn't do him a damn bit of good now as he sat with both Williams and Marlyss Landeros. He'd already gone into as much as he wanted to about John and Dawn's visit. Then, Williams stood up. She was laughing.

"I've seen some awfully good liars in my life, but you are one of the worst," she said. "You can't even sit still for two seconds in that chair."

"What?"

"You know you're telling a bullshit lie. We know you're telling a bullshit lie. And it shows on your face. Face it. You're a lousy liar, Frank."

Landeros wasn't laughing. She touched his hand, searched his eyes, and said softly:

"Frank, it's the arm. You've got a vein in your arm that twitches when you lie."

He looked down at his forearm.

Williams left, then Landeros began laying evidence out on her desk: Photos of blood on Casper. Blood-type reports from the lab. Statements about John Fry's boasting.

Jesus Christ, Frank thought, he shot his mouth off to everybody in the neighborhood. Frank knew he was in big trouble.

"Want something to drink?" Landeros asked.

"What the hell is this?" Frank stammered. "Good cop, bad cop?"

"You know, Frank," she continued, "I've got police officers sitting up there right now at your house."

"No."

Frank watched as she dialed. He knew the number of the Petoskey state police post by heart. He heard her ask for Sergeant Gerry Tibaldi.

"Yes, Sergeant," she said into the phone. "I think the inspector would OK a bulldozer. I can't see a problem with that."

My house, Frank thought. It's all I own.

"Sergeant, would you talk to this young man?"

Frank grasped for the receiver.

"Lookit, McMasters, this is Sergeant Gerald Tibaldi of the homicide section," he said. "I've got a goddamn search warrant and it's signed by a judge. I'm gonna execute this search warrant on your house. If I don't find anything in the house, I'm comin' back with a bulldozer for your property."

"No," Frank said. "The keys. The neighbor has the keys. You can get anything you want. Just leave my house alone."

"Frank, I'm comin' with dogs. I'm comin' with bulldozers and cranes. But I'm gonna find that body."

Frank was ready to deal. He wanted immunity from prosecution. He watched Landeros call the prosecutor's office. Then he gave Marlyss Landeros a six-page statement. He told her about the satchel and the car burning, but he danced around John's utterances as to the reasons for the killing. Besides, he thought, which version am I supposed to tell?

"Did anyone help John cut the body up?" Landeros asked last.

"I don't know," he said.

Later, before he signed the statement, he wanted to amend that response.

"Also," he said, "the last answer about 'Did I know if anyone helped John cut the body up' I answered, 'I don't know.' But as I recall now, John told me he sent Dawn out of the house and nobody was in the house until it was all over with."

Later Landeros took Frank into another room to see Cheryl. She had stuck by her story. Her loyalty to John Fry still ran deep. She had never been able to shake it, despite what he'd done to her life.

"Cheryl," Frank said. "I've told them the truth. You should too."

"Why?"

"Lookit, Cheryl. John Fry has already caused you to lose one child. What do you wanna do, lose another one because of him?"

Cheryl was all twisted up inside. Only a week ago she'd felt secure in a new life. Every time she tried to free herself, her old boyfriend found a new grip. Somehow she had to cut herself loose. She looked at Frank, then the detective.

"No, Frank," she said. "He ain't worth that much."

Later Cheryl found herself in Frank's car, heading to her brother's house. She had forty dollars Frank gave her before the homicide detectives took him away in the police airplane. She hadn't slept in three days and her nerves were spent.

"You know," she said to her brother, "if there was ever a time in my life when I needed drugs, it would be now."

She knew more tests were coming. There would be a trial. She knew she'd have to take the stand.

"But you know what?" she continued. "I don't want it. I don't want any drugs at all."

She'd feel that way for a long, long time.

Gilbert Hill had come in on Saturday to introduce himself to Lucky Fry. He made little progress. Rumor had it that Fry had returned to Detroit to kill someone who had talked to police. Hill couldn't resist one more question.

"Tell me," he asked him, "why did you bother to stop in Detroit, anyway?"

"I had some business to take care of, mon."

"I see," Hill said. "I'm glad we found you before you got to your business."

Fry laughed.

Dawn Spens had been shuttled from one room to another throughout the day. Three times she'd declined to make a statement. Sometime during the day a squad member told her, "You know John is likely going to make a statement against you."

In the late afternoon, Hill decided to invite her into his office for a chat. The inspector's popularity was high anytime he was near his desk. Phone calls from the media and his daughters came with regularity. The telephone could be unnerving for any visitor. One minute he could be serious, the next laughing with some unknown entity on the other end of the line.

Between the calls, he asked Dawn Spens if she wanted to make a statement. She declined. Then he brought in Roy Spens. Her sister Patty was waiting in the hallway outside.

"If you're going to make a statement, Dawn, you better hurry up and do it," Hill said after her father left.

A few minutes later he brought Sergeant Brantley, Sergeant Williams, and Marlyss Landeros into the little office and closed the door.

"Marlyss, Dawn is going to make a statement," Hill said.

Dawn hesitated. Then Bernard Brantley stood up. He muttered angrily, then stormed out of the office and slammed the door.

"Don't piss Bernard off now," Hill said. "Dawn, you do not want to piss him off. He's the only one in your corner."

By 6 P.M., Marlyss Landeros was nearly finished typing the eleven-page statement from Dawn Spens.

Dawn had given a thumbnail sketch of her relationship with Al Canty. She said she only knew him as Dr. Alan Miller. She said she found out his real name in the newspaper after the murder. She said she never knew he was married. She said she thought he worked at Harper-Grace Hospitals.

She said that the day of the murder she was expecting him to bring some "extra" money, but no more than four hundred dollars. She admitted she'd told other people that there had once been a five-thousand-dollar payoff, but she said she had lied. She skirted a question about plans for California. She said she was throwing up when John and

Al argued. She said she saw one swing of the bat and heard another hit home. While she was out turning tricks, she said, Al's body disappeared from the house.

At one point Dawn's voice started to crack. Landeros kept her fingers on the typewriter. The cop had put The Gift away for the night. She'd already made her mind up about Dawn Spens after she offered her the donut.

"She swept a lot away from her," Landeros said later. "She's Little Miss Innocent Two Shoes. And she sure can bat those big eyes of hers when she has to."

But Dawn also broomed John Fry right into a murder charge, if only the squad had a body.

Detective Tony Brantley cursed the thought. A cold beer. He'd left a cold beer, his easy chair, and a deadlocked Detroit Tigers ball game in the seventh inning for this. And the mosquitoes. The last time he'd seen them this big was twenty years ago. Vietnam. These northern woods might as well be Nam, he thought. It was hot and humid enough.

Bernard Brantley had never mentioned that Tony would be flying 250 miles in a twin-engine Beechcraft and ending up in the goddamn woods. He felt like a banker at a lumberjack ball. He'd shown up for duty in a suit, a tie, and a brand-new pair of street shoes.

The bugs found his style impressive. They seemed attracted to all the sweat. The forty-year-old stocky detective envied the three state troopers from the Petoskey post, who'd dressed more appropriately for the search.

"You know this land is owned by the University of Michigan," said one state evidence technician. "They raise mosquitoes out here for tests."

Brantley could hear the little bloodsuckers buzzing.

"This guy McMasters better not be blowing smoke up our asses," he complained. "Maybe we ought to just forget about his goddamn immunity and lock his ass up."

Brantley, Sergeant Tibaldi, a Detroit evidence technician, and the state troopers had been following Frank for nearly two hours as he zigzagged the area off the logging trail. Frank was in a short-sleeve shirt and his big arms were covered with red welts from the bites.

"Lookit," he said. "It's here, I'm telling you. Give me a polygraph. Hypnotize me. But it's here."

They decided to try a new tactic. They went back to where the trail met Douglas Lake Road and put Frank in a car. They chauffeured him in on the logging road about a quarter mile.

Suddenly he yelled, "Stop. Right here."

Frank made a beeline about 80 yards in, past the stands of birch and oak into the deeper woods ahead. Then he saw the three big pines.

"I found it," Frank yelled.

A police dog had already tracked right over the spot.

The only hint that the ground had been disturbed earlier was the ease with which the evidence technician's trowel slid into the black earth. A foot and a half deeper it struck the satchel. Brantley watched the straps stretch as the valise was carried from the hole.

They laid it all out on a sheet of plastic amid the swarming mosquitoes. The team stood in a circle as the garbage bags were opened. Frank noticed how neatly the contents were wrapped. The hair and skin were heavily matted with blood. But Brantley, Tibaldi, and McMasters all recognized the facial features. They had been well preserved by the cool ground.

It was 7:40 P.M. — one week since Jan Canty had placed the hamburgers on the kitchen counter for her husband in the big Tudor in Grosse Pointe Park.

The squad had its case. They had the hands and the feet. They had the head of psychologist W. Alan Canty.

Chapter 87

Jan Canty wondered what more could be waiting for her as she walked again past the face of Merton W. Goodrich early Sunday morning. Marlyss Landeros had called and wanted her at Police Headquarters immediately.

Jan had found much comfort in the way the detectives treated her. They made her feel as though they'd dropped everything to find Al. Earlier in the week Bernard Brantley had visited her at the Fisher Building. He seemed so big standing over her desk.

"Does it ever happen where these kind of cases don't get solved?" she'd asked him.

"Rarely," Brantley said.

Later she would write an open letter to local newspapers praising the section's professionalism and sensitivity. But no one there could have eliminated the shock of what had to be done on this Sabbath.

First she identified Al's gold Seiko watch. Then Gerald Tibaldi handed her a burned remnant he'd fished out of the stove during a search of the house in Alanson.

Jan recognized the corner of a newspaper cartoon Al had laminated in plastic and carried many years in his wallet. It was one of those special things couples savor. It was an Ashleigh Brilliant cartoon from his syndicated feature "Pot-Shots."

The caption read: "One of my favorite places in the world is anywhere with you."

Jan listened as Landeros gently told her about the mutilation and the body parts at the morgue.

"We have something for identification," she said. "We need you to come over to the medical examiner's office and identify your husband."

I'm not hearing what she's telling me, Jan thought. Identify *what? What will I see?* The proposition terrified her. How much more of all of this, she thought, can I be expected to take?

Her thinking began to take on a dark, whimsical quality. Maybe, she thought, this was all a bad dream, a bad joke, a Hitchcock movie scripted by Al on a stormy walk to the lake.

Al Canty, my husband, she thought. I don't even know my husband anymore. Who is he? What has he been doing? *And why is he doing this to me?*

"Jan," Landeros said, patting her shoulder. "It's important for the case. It's important for you."

Landeros continued preparing her as they drove to the morgue. The identification was a legal requirement, she said. They conducted it now with a video on a black-and-white television. She would see only his head.

"It's going to be him," she said. "We know it's him. There's no doubt in our minds. All you have to say is 'yes' and you can close your eyes."

The fluorescent lights and tile walls reminded her of an insane asylum. Jan's father wanted to tackle the task for her, but now she felt she had to do it.

"No, Dad, nobody should have to do this," she said.

"OK, then, I'll do it with you," he said.

They held her under her arms as she approached the TV screen, Landeros on one side and her father on the other as she waited for the image.

The second or so she saw him would fashion nightmares for many months to come. The white sheet was wrapped around his neck like a collar. He looked as though he'd been beaten badly. The right eye was heavily bruised. His mouth was open, his tongue swabbing the lower lip, just like that night in University Hospital.

She hung her head. She couldn't speak. The three-letter word would not come.

They had to repeat the entire procedure again. The image flashed again on the screen.

"Yes," she said.

"You look so gray," her mom said when she walked out.

She just wanted to go home. She began to walk to the front door of the morgue. Then she saw the people outside through the glass doors. Her first thought was *machine-gun turrets,* the spindly-leg kind from old World War I documentaries. No, she thought, those are the legs of camera tripods. What are those cameras for? Then Jan realized they were aimed at her. Reporters were waiting outside.

My God, she thought, there's just no end to this. She felt as though she was about to be raped.

Landeros spun Jan around and whisked her down a corridor and out the back door of the morgue. A police car was waiting. They laid her down in the backseat and sped away.

Jan felt as though her entire life had been turned upside down. This has to be it, she thought. There can't be anything more left to learn.

Her mother told her to rest in the backseat as they drove back to the big Tudor. The next day her mom told her that was when she'd fallen asleep.

Landeros wasn't exaggerating when she told Jan she was sure of Al Canty's identity. The medical examiner had already made the ID from fingerprints. One set came from his stay in jail as a repeat traffic offender.

A newer set was lifted on February 28, 1983. That night Alan Canty had solicited a female Detroit police officer acting as a decoy in the Cass Corridor. He'd offered her twenty-five dollars for sexual favors. The misdemeanor cost him a seventy-five-dollar fine.

Mark Bando wanted a piece of the Canty case from the time he'd seen the teletype. Earlier in the week he rounded up a Corridor regular who had spent the evening partying with Fry before the murder.

The whore car was no longer his to command. He'd burned out on the detail and requested transfer. One of the reasons was a nineteen-year-old hooker named Sheila Blanton. Bando had high hopes for the attractive girl with the long chestnut hair. But she overdosed on prescription drugs and booze a month before her twentieth birthday in February 1983.

He talked to Sheila in the whore car the night she died. She told him about a doctor she'd found for a sugar daddy. His name was Al, and he wanted to set her up in an apartment so she could straighten out her life. One day she'd gone into his glove compartment and seen his name. It was Dr. Alan Canty. When Sheila asked him about it he said, "Please keep this confidential. It would be very, very devastating if anyone found out."

Bando had always wondered what happened to the guy.

The TV cameras didn't get footage of Alan Canty's widow, but one station shot something far more compelling for its Sunday evening audience.

Late in the afternoon Gerald Tibaldi and Madelyn Williams drove out I-75 to the exit ramp at Joslyn Avenue. When the police plane had returned from Alanson, John Fry had told Gilbert Hill the location of the "garbage" he'd thrown out a week ago.

The squad tried to keep the search secret. Hill wanted a news blackout until he could get Fry and Spens arraigned on Monday. Tibaldi told headquarters he would radio "we have arrived at our destination" if they found what they suspected.

Tibaldi saw the green garbage bag about fifteen feet from the pavement, three quarters of the way up the ramp. A section of newspaper was sticking out of the end. The maggots were already at work.

The TV crew arrived with the coroner's van. They shot footage as an evidence technician used both hands to lift the green bag into the body wagon. Inside was Al's left leg.

The next day the morning newspaper would erroneously report that his torso had been found. Back at headquarters, Marlyss Landeros already was upset.

"My God, his wife," she told another cop. "How many more pieces are we going to find? How many times does she have to be slapped in the face with this?"

By early Sunday evening the squad was talking to the prosecutor's office about charges Homicide could expect

Monday morning. John Carl Fry: murder in the first degree and mutilation of a dead body. Dawn Marie Spens: accessory to murder after the fact and mutilation.

Several squad members, including Landeros, wanted first-degree murder charges against the prostitute.

"That statement of hers is packaged," she said. "She's as involved as he is. He's taking all the weight."

But an assistant prosecutor said even the mutilation charge was pushing it. Dawn Spens hadn't confessed to cutting up Canty, or helping in the packaging. In fact, she had distanced herself from the act, saying she was turning tricks.

Nevertheless, she fell under the mutilation statute because of the wording of the statute. The law, passed in 1846 to deter grave robbers, declared it a felony to "carry away a portion of the dead body of a person . . ."

Dawn had admitted to carrying the brown valise from the refrigerator.

Squad detectives had doubled their forty-hour work week in five days on the case, but Gerry Tibaldi wasn't finished. Threatened with criminal charges on the black Buick, Gary Neil had been locked up for three days. The squad wanted to refresh his memory about his dealings with John Fry. Tibaldi had yet to take Neil's fourth and final statement.

By late Sunday the twenty-year veteran was running on fumes when he got word from the lockup that Lucky Fry wanted to talk to him.

"I want to make a statement," Fry said.

Tibaldi took the offer back to the squad room. Nobody was interested. "It's such a good case, why screw it up?" Tibaldi said.

On Monday morning John Fry and Dawn Spens were led to the Frank Murphy Hall of Justice for arraignment in Thirty-sixth District Court. Marlyss Landeros and Gerald Tibaldi strolled the pair through a mob of reporters and cameramen waiting in the one-block walk from headquarters to the courthouse.

Everyone got their first look at the pair they'd already

heard so much about. Dawn still was wearing the tight jeans and halter top, and she hid behind a pair of sunglasses. With his bald head and massive chest poking from an open Western shirt, Fry looked like a character from a slasher film. TV reporters kept yelling the same questions at them:

"Why did you do this? John Fry, why did you do this?"

"Dawn, did you love Dr. Canty? Dawn, why did you do this?"

They were mute. They remained that way during their arraignment. Fry was ordered held without bond. As tears glistened in Dawn Spens's eyes, she was ordered jailed on $100,000 cash bond. The arraigning magistrate looked at the couple and said:

"The conscience of the court is shocked."

Chapter 88

In the days following the arraignment, headlines thickened from POLICE FEAR PSYCHOLOGIST WAS KILLED GIVING AID to PSYCHOLOGIST'S DOUBLE LIFE TRACED.

At first news editors treated the sordid details of Canty's exploits as delicately as they would have for a priest. Once the story was out, the pendulum swung, sometimes with little basis in fact. One TV report featured a talkative prostitute. Her identity obscured by the shadows, she knew what the TV reporter wanted. She claimed she introduced Dawn Spens to Canty.

Canty, she said, was "into fantasies . . . bondage—chain me to a wall with my arms spread in chains and my legs spread apart."

The popular David Newman radio talk show from the Fisher's Golden Tower buzzed several nights with callers and their theories. Detroiters' imaginations ran wild. One caller claimed firsthand knowledge that Dawn Spens "was the only one who could dress up like a little girl for him."

Some of Canty's patients came to his aid, calling reporters and saying Al sometimes talked of helping a Cass Corridor prostitute. He was a skilled, helpful professional, they said. But they had no desire to give their names for the record.

The coverage unleashed a flood of memories for a social worker named Carla McGuire. She first met Alan Canty sixteen years ago as a student in his psychology class at Henry Ford Community College. He gave her academic and career guidance at first. That blossomed into having drinks together once a week, always at the same time, the same place.

In 1969, she was a twenty-three-year-old single mother with big baby-sitting bills and the tastes of a marginal flower child. He seemed to do a lot of vicarious living through her. He was fascinated that she smoked pot, went to rock concerts, and attended antiwar rallies. Then he began giving her about fifty dollars a week.

"Take this and buy something for yourself," he'd say.

They talked a lot about psychology. He delighted in revealing details about prominent Detroiters who were his patients. She later learned that was unethical, but she thought psychology the perfect profession for him. He seemed to find excitement in picking up the shades on other people's lives.

Carla's father thought Al was a prize catch. But she became more uncomfortable with him as the relationship heated up. His awkward advances and tight-lipped kisses reminded her of an adolescent. She couldn't believe he'd once been married. He said he and his wife Maggie were separated, and that she was a full-blown schizophrenic. She later learned he was lying.

When Al gave Carla a used car, she realized she had to break it off. She felt uncomfortable about his fifty-dollar handouts. She never went to bed with him in their six months' relationship. But she was feeling like a whore. She wasn't surprised by the stories in the paper.

A forty-eight-year-old Mount Clemens attorney named Bruce Karash saw the news stories and felt cosmic justice had been served. He'd always thought Al Canty unethical. Now everybody knows it, he thought.

Karash met Canty through the young woman who would later become his first wife. In the mid-1960s Jane was an extremely attractive twenty-year-old with long dark hair. She worked for an advertising agency in the Fisher Building and met Canty one day in a Fisher coffee shop. Jane had a peripheral interest in psychology and was fascinated by the program for autistic children Canty told her about.

Then Canty offered her a job. He would pay her five dollars an hour, more than double the minimum wage, to read stories he said were for children in the project. For six months she worked early evening hours in his office one or two times a week.

Karash suspected Canty had something other than autism on his mind. All she did was read fairy tales while he sat in his big chair and listened. Some stories he wrote. Others were traditional. Canty said the stories were "being developed" for presentation to the kids. But Jane never saw an autistic child, or any child for that matter. Later he hired several of her friends. They never saw children either.

"Broom him, Jane," Karash said. "The guy is a fraud."

"Oh, you attorneys are all alike," she told him. "Always skeptical."

Later she saw his point. Canty told her his wife Maggie was critically ill with cancer, ready to die at any time. Then they ran into Canty and his wife in a restaurant.

"Bruce, she's as healthy as a horse," she admitted.

Jane became more watchful of his behavior. Canty unsuccessfully tried to hypnotize her a couple of times. Then she noticed that as she read the psychologist fairy tales, he often had an erection.

She quit soon after that.

Dr. Lorraine Awes heard about her patient's murder and the arrest of the two suspects when her former secretary telephoned her in Anchorage. The psychiatrist recognized the descriptions of Dawn and John. She was deeply disturbed by the news.

But the psychiatrist was glad she was in Alaska. She knew she could be subpoenaed and forced to testify in a criminal case. She had no desire to detail her patient's psychological profile in an open courtroom. And from the news reports, it sounded as though the prosecutor had everything he needed.

Gladys Canty couldn't read enough about her son. She was quite pleased the homicide section had been so proficient. If Al Sr. was here, she thought, he would commend the detectives on their fine work.

She was stately, often helpful, when reporters called. She wanted to lift Buster's name out of this scandal.

402

"He's still my son," she told one. "And I love him very much."

Mrs. Canty also had a conference with Gilbert Hill. The inspector speculated that Al was being blackmailed. He told her he doubted sex alone could have motivated him to spend that much money. Then he complimented her late husband, Al Sr.

"We used to ask him," Hill said, " 'How are we supposed to stand the gore that goes with this job?' He would say, 'Leave your job here. Never take it home.' I remembered that."

"I thought that was ironic," Mrs. Canty later said, "considering the way Al Sr. regaled Buster and me with his cases."

The news media that had provided so much comfort only a week ago now became Jan Canty's tormentor. She perceived reporters as persistent window peepers. The phone calls and people at her door were continuous. On Berkshire, where local residents never parked their cars on the street, the television trucks stood out like high-tech invaders among the old homes and tall trees.

Jan knew what the media wanted. But how, she thought, can I ever explain the last two years? Who would believe me? And what business is it of theirs anyway?

She saw the scenario as another segment in her husband's Hitchcock script: Everyday psychologist goes from relative obscurity to the nightmare of the public eye. God, she thought, everyone must think I'm stupid, *naive*. She wanted to rip that word out of the dictionary.

Jan's parents acted as buffers. They met people at the door, answered the phone, and gave her verbal synopses of what was being reported. She'd caught a glimpse of just one TV account, the footage inside the house on Casper. Blood appeared to be everywhere. She feared Al had been chased down, beaten, and tortured throughout the house.

Several times reporters greeted her in her waiting room at the Fisher Building. One waited with one of her patients. When he didn't identify himself, she thought he was one of Al's patients. Then he began asking questions. She asked Fisher security to keep reporters off her floor.

Jan resolved that she wasn't going to close up shop and

403

hide. She'd yet to miss a day of work. She was worried about her patients and her practice. She thought, a psychologist and marriage counselor whose husband had been off whoring around for nearly two years. What will they think of the profession? What will they think of *me?*

No one taught her how to handle something like this in graduate school. Jan knew she had to wing it. She decided not to let the subject of Al dominate therapy, but she wouldn't make it taboo either. She tried to be sincere. Her patients came in with white knuckles and dry mouths. She tried a straightforward approach with all. She started each session along these lines:

"I'm sure you weren't sure whether you should have come in today or not, but I'm glad you did. I don't want you out there wondering how I'm doing. Or, I'm sure you have questions that need answering. You're entitled to know. It's been forced on you by the media, and now my problems, in some respects, are your problems. If I was in your shoes, I'd have unanswered questions myself. Don't worry about me. I'm not delicate. Feel free to ask. If I don't feel the question is appropriate or I don't feel ready to answer it, I'll tell you so."

She lost only one patient. The most frequent question was "Are you leaving Detroit?"

Reporters had a plethora of angles to pursue. They went to Harper Woods, where school officials and old schoolmates portrayed Dawn Spens as an honor student who mysteriously went bad. One reporter found Roy Spens in his Harper Woods bungalow. They chatted.

"She didn't do heroin; she did cocaine," he said. "I visited her in jail . . . She's not going through withdrawal. She's doing great. She feels good. She's a very strong girl. She was in love [with Fry]. At eighteen you fall in love pretty easy.

"She's an intelligent girl. She was going to school, then two and a half years ago she crushed me. I said she wasn't a prostitute, then the police showed me her arrest reports. This is obviously the worst thing that ever happened to me."

Dawn's old soul mate Dee Cusmano was having a few pops

404

in the East Warren Lanes bar when a story on the Canty case came on the TV. She scrambled to turn up the set. A number of Dawn's old friends were there. The bar became still.

"It was very hard to accept," she said later. "It was very upsetting."

Then Dee Cusmano got a collect call at home from Dawn Spens from the Wayne County Jail. Dawn began calling every night. She wanted Dee to visit.

One night she drove down to the jail. Dee couldn't believe what she was seeing and hearing through the little glass window.

Dee asked her old friend what happened. Dawn told her that John had demanded $5,000 from Canty, but he'd arrived with only $100. In recent weeks, she said, his payments had been cut down to $10 or $20. She relayed the story about the argument and the baseball bat. Then John had ordered her out of the house to turn tricks, she said. When she got back the body was already cut up and packaged, she said.

Dawn was scrawny, full of needle tracks, and laughing. Dee was stunned. How, she thought, can Dawn be so flippant, especially after a story like that? Doesn't she realize where she is?

After Dawn was taken back to her cell, Dee couldn't find her visitor's pass. As deputies checked with the front desk, she remained jailed inside the small visiting cell for a half hour. One of the turnkeys began teasing her, saying they were going to keep her there for the night. The place must have been a hundred degrees. She slid into a dizzy panic.

"Let me out, damn it!" she screamed. "I'm not a criminal."

When she finally hit the fresh air at the door, she vowed never to go back. But Dawn called her every night for a week. When Dee missed a couple of calls, her old friend stopped phoning.

Dee didn't know whether to feel sad or relieved.

Chapter 89

It was so hot the day of the W. Alan Canty's memorial service, the pavement shined by noon. Inside the big parlor of the Verheyden Funeral Home, air conditioners dropped the temperature to an uncomfortable chill.

Jan Canty arrived at the Grosse Pointe Park mortuary clutching two of her husband's precious paving bricks. As she set them down outside, a man approached her.

"What are those for?" he said.

"I'm going to have them buried with Al's ashes," she said. "Al was so attached to these crazy bricks I thought it would be a nice gesture."

"I wouldn't go to that kind of trouble for him," he said. "In fact, considering what he has done, I don't even know why you're bothering to give him a decent burial."

She was speechless. All week Jan had been trying to postpone her anger. She'd reasoned I was a good wife to him and I'm going to finish that role with this memorial service. I'm not going to stop before the last act of the play—then I'm going to get good and pissed off.

Celia and John Muir were at her side. Celia sensed the tension building between two of the most important women in Al Canty's life. She was relieved that the third was in the Wayne County Jail. Celia knew Jan and Gladys Canty were at odds over some of the funeral arrangements. She suspected Jan's smoldering anger toward Al was finding a target in Gladys Canty.

And anger was everywhere in the funeral home. At first it looked like hardly anyone was going to show up. Jan, her parents, her sister, and the Muirs sat on one couch to the right of the aisle. Gladys Canty was sitting alone on the left.

Mrs. Canty's nephew and sister-in-law were expected from Cleveland, but had not arrived yet.

"I'm going to go sit with Mrs. Canty," John Muir said. "I see a woman who has lost her son."

Then the parlor quickly filled. Al Junior's turnout would equal Al Senior's nine years earlier in the same room. Some of the nearly 300 in attendance found out about the arrangements at the end of a long story delivered by their local paper boy this Sunday morning.

In its July 28 editions, the Detroit *News* laid out everything three reporters could find in the week following the discovery of the leg off I-75. The story "Police Look for the Hook" proposed a half dozen theories about the psychologist. They ranged from extramarital thrills to a research project that had "gotten out of hand."

Print journalists assigned to cover the service sensed the hostility from mourners. They sat in back chairs and kept their notebooks obscured at their hips.

"You bastards," one mourner muttered to a nervous writer. "You'd think you had your fill."

Another tapped the same reporter for some information.

"Hey," he said, pointing to a tall black man. "Tell me, is that Gilbert Hill, the movie cop?"

One after another the people came from the hot parking lot into the rose-perfumed chill. Celia noticed one couple who looked like street people. A southsider had been quoted in the *News* story that she was coming. There were patients, colleagues, antique car collectors, the curious, and many old friends of Gladys Foster Canty. There weren't enough seats.

Gladys Canty was shocked by what the man in his midthirties was telling her.

"Mrs. Canty, I'm the one who bought Al's coin collection," he said, shaking her hand. "I thought it would be a good investment for my kids."

Ever since Gilbert Hill told her about the kind of money involved, Mrs. Canty had been worried about the coins. Earlier that week, she asked Jan to check the attic of the big Tudor where Buster said he kept the collection hidden. Grandpa Canty started amassing the coins for his grandson.

Al Senior continued it, buying the pieces of gold and silver. He spent substantial amounts of his pension on the shiny inheritance for young Alan.

Jan reported back after a visit to the attic. She'd found only empty envelopes scattered about.

"He must have been really desperate to sell that," she said later. "He'd always told me, 'Oh, I'll guard it with my life Ma.' "

Mrs. Canty estimated its value exceeded well over $10,000. Ray Danford signed the guest registry and led his family into the room. He spent a lot of time looking at the carpet, but it had nothing to with his second job. He found facing Jan difficult. He felt bad that he hadn't taken Al's situation more seriously.

Also among the mourners was the budding child psychologist Bob Willing and Al's long-time patient, John Mosey, the recovering alcoholic.

Willing felt cheated. He figured his 2,000 hours of supervision might turn into another wasted chapter in his long, rambling career. Just a month earlier Al Canty had signed his recommendation forms for his state licence. One section attested to Willing's "good moral character." The board is going to laugh me out of the state capital, he thought.

John Mosey hadn't seen his therapist in a year. Al cut him lose a year ago, agreeing his self-destructive thinking problems were over. Then two close friends of Mosey died. One was another recovering alcoholic who relapsed and drank himself to death at 29. Mosey recently called Al, wanting a refresher to cope with the anger over the deaths. The psychologist told him he was booked, but would have some openings in the fall. Just knowing Al would be available had subdued much of his anguish.

All week Mosey had been reading the papers. Earlier in the week he took some ribbing. "Hey, isn't that the sonovabitch you wanted me to see," said one acquaintance. "You asshole, his body is strewn halfway up and down I-75."

He thought of compulsion and two dead friends. The last thing he wanted was a drink.

Jan Canty felt as if she was caught between two echoes. She could hear her mother on the end of the parlor sofa.

"That sonovabitch. That sonovabitch. How could he do

this to you?"

Then she heard her sister.

"Oh Jan, I'm going to miss him. He was so good to me, so supportive."

She just wanted it all to end. Why, she thought, hasn't the service started? She had asked Dr. Thomas Mooney, a Port Huron psychologist Al was supervising, to deliver a eulogy. She wanted no religious symbols. Al would have never gone for that.

"It's been all over the newspapers," she told Mooney. "We need something appropriate." He was one of the last people to see Al alive that Saturday.

"Leave it to me," he said.

The service opened with the Twenty-third Psalm. Gladys Canty had asked John Muir to read it. Then Dr. Mooney tackled what might well have been the toughest speaking assignment in Detroit that day.

"When Jan called me a week ago today to ask if I would give this eulogy . . . My response was instant: 'Yes, I would be honored and privileged.' Had it not been for Al and his incredible skills, I would not be the person I am today. The only reservation I had was that I may fall apart emotionally while giving the eulogy for my friend, my mentor, my therapist. Jan assured me that would be all right."

Mooney struggled through the thirty-minute delivery, but it did not diminish a message culled from the philosophies of leading psychologists of the century. He cited Al's professional competency, then went right after the emotions in the room.

"I want to remember, too, the many lessons that Al helped people with. One important lesson that is so timely now is that we not vilify and judge as this leads only to our own anger and blame. Let us seek comfort in the thought that wherever there is intense sun, there is a shadow. Let us not dwell on the shadows cast by Al Canty but rather focus on the sunlight he shed."

He evoked the writing of Elizabeth Kuebler, citing the stages of grief: denial and isolation, anger, bargaining, depression, and finally acceptance.

"As the news of this tragedy and of Al's death unfolded, I am sure that all of us experienced in some degree the first

409

four stages . . . As the news stories progressed, my thoughts became: *How could he? How could they?* They only led to my own anger . . ."

He spoke of Albert Ellis's rational thinking, urging his listeners to let go by changing the way they thought. Then he quoted Leo Buscaglia from *Loving Each Other:*

"Forgive. There is a wonderful aura surrounding the verb forgive, great warmth and strength. It is a word suggesting a letting go, a releasing, an action which has the power to soothe, to heal, to reunite, to recreate . . ."

Later he added, "With Al's death, we are all faced with a unique opportunity for growth. His death has left all who knew him and loved him feeling vast emptiness — perhaps anger, resentment, betrayal, fear, or perhaps questions that seem to haunt security and peace . . . The emptiness will lessen, the anger will subside, forgiveness will unfold, and we will all start to heal and accept.

". . . Some people come into our lives and quickly go. Some stay for a while and leave footprints on our hearts and we are never, ever the same."

The bright light from the TV camera flooded the parlor after Mooney's last words. Jan Canty collapsed weeping into Celia Muir's lap. John Muir covered the lens and ordered the cameraman from the funeral home.

John came up with a plan to switch cars. He wanted Jan's as a decoy so they wouldn't be followed by the TV crew back to the big Tudor.

"I felt absolutely violated," Jan later said.

Gladys Canty returned to her retirement bungalow with her forty-year-old nephew and seventy-eight-year-old sister-in-law. She wondered what she would do with the chickens. She'd cooked up a bunch hoping that Jan and her parents would stop by after the service.

Mrs. Canty had been informed that her son's widow planned something home alone with friends. "I'm sure she won't mind if you come," one of her relatives said. She didn't consider that an invitation.

She and the few surviving members of her family loaded the roses from the funeral home in her nephew's van. They drove to Elmwood Cemetery where her son's ashes were to be buried. Because of the criminal case, his remains would not be released by the medical examiner for many weeks.

Like his life, the date of W. Alan Canty's death was split in two. The death certificate fixed it at July 21. That was the date Jan identified the remains of the man she married. The man John Fry killed died on July 13. Mrs. Canty was having the latter chiseled on Buster's headstone.

The grave was at the top of a hill in Detroit's most historic cemetery, the burial place of Territorial Governor Lewis Cass. Elmwood's many mausoleums and towering monuments carried the names of some of Detroit's oldest and wealthiest families. Many of the city's street names were represented in family stones.

The Canty plot was marked by a family memorial of brightly polished red granite. It was a stark newcomer among the gray-weathered stones. Gladys Foster Canty was having a marker made for herself with Buster's. She knew now that nobody else would be around to see to that task.

Oh, Mrs. Canty thought, how Al Senior and Junior loved this old place. She remembered the many times their tightly knit trio visited Elmwood just to study the historic grounds. Then Al Senior picked out their spot, overlooking a stretch of water called Bloody Run.

"I've always wanted to live on the water," Al Senior said. "Ma, I'll be able to come out at night and see the ducks."

The Canty name now was two full generations old in Detroit. It's the end of it, Gladys thought. Maybe now father and son could walk together at night.

In just a couple of weeks an erroneous rumor worked its way from the Grosse Pointes twenty miles west to Detroit's struggling Brightmore district and the open ear of Dot Wilson, John Fry's surrogate mom. Dot listened as a friend told the story. It supposedly came from somebody who worked at the Verheyden Funeral Home.

"The widow was so mad at the doctor, she gave the undertaker a couple of bricks," the friend said. "She wanted them put in a bag with the remains and wanted it thrown in the Detroit River. That's right, bricks. That's how bad his wife wanted to be rid of him."

Chapter 90

No one doubted that Thirty-sixth District Court Judge Isidore B. Torres would find enough evidence to bind Fry and Spens over for a full trial. But in the wake of the news blackout at Homicide, the state had to lay out its case for public consumption at their preliminary examination July 31.

Reporters, patients, former students, colleagues, and the plain curious were looking for clues that would explain Al Canty's involvement with the suspects. Everyone wanted a good look at the man who could cut up a body. Everyone wanted to see the superhooker who could milk a man for $140,000.

All the seats in the two-hundred-person courtroom were taken a half hour before the start.

Marlyss Landeros had been preparing Jan Canty for her testimony all morning. At first Jan was reluctant, but then she realized the detective was right. It was time she took back some of the control of her life. This was her chance to stand up and have her say.

Under the mutilation statute, Jan only had to testify that she'd not given anyone permission to carry away or dissect her husband's body. She wore her most professional blue suit and put her hair in a twist. Just as she finally was psyched up for the task, the prosecutor offered to cut her from the witness list. The defense would stipulate what she was going to say.

"No, please," she said. "I want to do it. I need to do it."

Jan was the first witness. Landeros let go of her hand at

the courtroom door and she walked up the aisle between the jammed benches of spectators. At the end, just to her left, sat Fry and Spens. She looked only at their hands as she passed. She thought of what they had done with them.

She was not frightened anymore. She was angrier than hell.

Her testimony lasted less than two minutes. As Assistant County Prosecutor Robert Agacinski began the first of twenty terse questions, she heard the abrasive strokes of chalk from the TV artist in the jury box to her left.

Then she forced herself. Look up, she thought. Jan Lucille Canty, look up at Fry and Spens.

There.

He is so big, she thought. His chest is so big. Fry was wearing a gray plaid Western shirt and gray corduroys. But he looks like Mr. Clean, she thought. But no, I could never be alone in a room with that man.

"How long have you been married to Dr. Canty?" the prosecutor asked.

"In September it would have been eleven years."

Then she saw Dawn. Her eyes were sleepy, her hair wildly unkempt. She had a ruffled blue blouse and blue jeans. But her clothes were worn and dirty. Jan saw her ankles. They were swollen above her cheap black high heels. She was almost yellow. God, Jan thought, she's got liver disease.

"And did you come down to the morgue?" the prosecutor asked.

"Yes, I did."

As the attorney continued she wanted to ask the questions. She had a thousand of them for Dawn. What did you think of him? Did you know about me? Did he treat you kindly? How did you treat him? Did you love him? Did he love you? Why did you do this to him? Did he suffer? Do you know how I suffer now?

"Did you give medical authorities or anybody permission to perform an autopsy or dismember the body in any way?" the prosecutor asked.

"No."

Then she saw past the frizzy hair and careless posture at the defense table. Dawn Spens looked so young. My God, she thought. What has happened to you to end up here?

414

Jan found the prostitute bewildering.

"You may step down, Doctor," said the court clerk.

One after another, Robert Agacinski called his witnesses. A half-dozen southsiders were summoned to tell their stories about Lucky Fry, Dawn Spens, and the man they called The Doc. Cheryl Krizanovic. Frank McMasters. John Bumstead. Mike Oliver. Tammy Becker.

Through many of their brief testimonies Dawn Spens looked bored and indifferent. She fiddled with a dead, half-burned cigarette next to a legal pad. Halfway through the three-hour exam the hooker looked as though she was going to nod out in open court. She laid her head on her arm, her upper body draped over the edge of the defense table.

John Fry looked every witness in the eyes, sometimes slightly nodding his head.

Then Gary Neil took the stand. He was wearing a new sweatshirt with a hood, its long sleeves pulled down past his wrists this hot summer day. Dawn Spens sat up. John Fry's eyes followed him to his seat. Neil looked straight ahead, ignoring him. Then everyone discovered why Fry was charged with premeditated murder.

"Did there come a time in July of '85 when you had a conversation with John Fry about Al?" Agacinski asked after establishing Neil and Fry's relationship.

Neil said he did, on a Saturday afternoon in the basement of Fry's house on Casper.

"And who all was present, at the time?"

"Just me and John."

"And the conversation was about Al?"

"Yes."

"What did he say?"

"Said he had a big score that was coming at him, between twenty and thirty thousand dollars, supposedly . . . Doc was supposed to bring the money over for him and Dawn . . . He was going to kill The Doc, chop him up, and wanted to know if I wanted—if I wanted to be in on it. I said no, and he said not to tell anybody else about it or else I'd be out, and that's about it."

415

It was the information Sergeant Gerald Tibaldi and other interrogators had pumped from Neil after priming him with a three-day stay in the headquarters' lockup.

"Did he indicate why he was going to do that to Al?" Agacinski continued.

"Yes, to get rid of the body."

"Did he indicate why he was going to kill Al to begin with?"

"Yes, for the money."

"Did he indicate to you when he expected to do that, when he wanted you to help him?"

"He said about a week."

On cross-examination, Jay Nolan, Fry's court-appointed attorney, extracted Neil's lengthy prison record. Then Nolan introduced John Fry's worst enemy — his own bragging mouth. He asked Neil:

"Out of the clear blue, did he initiate this conversation down in the basement? Had there been anything that led up to it?"

"No. He was more or less bragging, 'I'm going to have a lot of money. If you want to help me, I could use some help. I'll let you in on the money. If not, don't grab on my shirttail when I get this money.' "

"Was he the kind of guy that did a lot of bragging?"

"Yes."

Al Canty's relationship with Dawn Spens also became public record that day. The prosecution introduced her eleven-page confession. Soon a copy was warm on a nearby copying machine.

Now there was no doubt. The psychologist was the prostitute's trick. But many who saw her during the exam were as perplexed as Jan Canty. She didn't seem to fit anyone's concept of a siren who could cost a prominent psychologist his fortune, his life, and, finally now, his reputation. And Dawn's statement left more questions than answers.

Judge Torres ordered John Fry and Dawn Spens to stand trial in early December as charged.

Chapter 91

The missing sex life that had troubled Jan Canty through three years of marriage now seemed a godsend. The reports linking AIDS, intravenous drug use, and prostitution were just emerging. She went for a full workup from her physician anyway.

She was relieved with the test results. She'd nurture any good news she could find.

Several days later, she dropped by Gladys Canty's house to pick up the registry from the memorial service. Gladys hinted that Al hadn't been entirely honest with Jan about his finances, that he'd been borrowing large sums of money.

"Jan, do you think he didn't want us to be close?" she asked.

For a brief moment they connected. They'd both been manipulated by Al.

"Don't worry," Jan said. "You'll always have a daughter in me."

But Jan made little time for visits to Al's mother. Her parents planned to stay with her for two months, and the first order of business was a garage sale. Jan wanted to weed any hint of Al out of the big Tudor, out of her life. Celia Muir helped with the task. They began with the clothes—pulling them off the racks, out of the dressers, stuffing them into plastic garbage bags for charity. Jan slammed the drawers shut when they were empty.

All day Celia had tried to mask her sadness. Then she picked up one of Al's shirts and put it to her nostrils. It smelled like him.

"Ces, what are you doing?" Jan demanded.

"Well, it—it's Al. It smells like Al. I'm going to miss him."

"Well, *I'm not*"

Jan continued stuffing the plastic bags. She found the Al Miller mechanic's smock from the Halloween party. She wanted to burn it. Then Jan's twin sister made a discovery in an obscure corner of one of the big closets.

"Look at this," the twin said. "Jan, I want it."

Jan was perplexed by the shiny blue jacket with the monogram "Cadieux Bar" across the back. She wondered where and why her husband bought such a thing.

"This just isn't his style," she said.

Soon they were packing the knickknacks, boxes of them. Jan found herself grabbing anything associated with Al. Then she came upon the white coffee cup—the one fired in a kiln with the rim depressed, as though someone had tried to smash it. Inside was the ceramic figure of a little man trying to push the cup back into shape. Al brought it home to her the day she almost quit college.

"That's a struggle cup," he said.

When Al was hospitalized she took it to him to cheer him up. She asked herself, do I really want to get rid of this?

Yes, she did.

Old books, paintings, records, tools from the garage, Al's home office furniture. Later the antique cars and parts would be sold. The antique-brick driveway was covered with odds and ends by the time they were done.

Later, Jan was thankful Celia and her parents were around. Without them she would have made some bad decisions. She tried to haul a $1,000 Oriental rug to the driveway just because Al had picked it out. Her mother put on the brakes.

"Jan, you're going to be angry with me and I'm not getting into your business, but you *are not* going to sell that."

"Don't tell me what I can sell and not sell," she barked. "I'll sell what I want."

Anything she couldn't sell she dragged into a big pile below the tall elms, where it waited for the Grosse Pointe Park garbage trucks. Next to the heap she put Al's Jeep Junior, the little car he'd held on to for years.

Al's office was another two weeks' work. Two discoveries

418

in particular disturbed her. She was bewildered by copies of two money orders for $250 she found in his desk. Al had forged her signature at the bottom. Later, she realized the negatives of her photos that had documented their home and its belongings were missing. Al must have taken them to make copies. But why? she thought.

What a sloppy record keeper Al was, she thought, as she worked her way through piles of paperwork. She found grocery lists mixed in with health records. She found car magazines piled with psychology journals.

As she rummaged, she found a file labeled "Project Indianwood." There were only a few sheets of paper. Where, she wondered, are the records of the ten hospitals that have his videotapes?

When she was finished, she closed the door to his office in the Fisher Building suite. She wouldn't open it again.

Al followed her everywhere nonetheless. One day she bagged a half-dozen telephones Al had lying around and took them back to the telephone company for credit. She handed the clerk their phone bill with the bag. The clerk looked at the phone bill, looked at the phones, looked at the bill, and then looked back at her.

"Oh," she said, turning to a coworker. "It's him. It's her. That's the guy . . . You're his wife."

"It's wonderful being a celebrity," she snapped. "Now, just take the phones."

Jan felt people staring at her in the Ram's Horn, a Grosse Pointe restaurant where she often grabbed a quick meal.

A month after his death, she returned to the University Health Center to supervise other psychologists. A nurse greeted her with "Good morning, Dr. Canty." A half-dozen people stopped in their tracks and looked.

Everybody already knew her professionally at the center, but everybody now was so quiet. They looked at her as though they wanted to ask questions but couldn't get up the nerve. Jan felt like a walking item of curiosity.

When the questions did start, they didn't stop.

"Tell me, Jan, did you know?"

What a dilemma, she thought. How do I explain it? Do I want to explain it? It just would put me more center stage.

419

She wanted to find the shadows.

After a while she stopped answering questions. She suspected nobody believed her anyway. She formulated a standard response.

"Lookit, you're going to believe what you want anyway, so I'd just rather not talk about it."

And Al, *always Al,* she thought.

"What's going to happen to his patients?"

She hated that question the most. She thought, what about me? Am I invisible?

Al's patients were brutally frank. They seemed to perceive her as just another therapist who could handle anything they said.

"How is this going to affect *your* patients?"

"Are you going to have a nervous breakdown?"

Al's patients haunted her. She called many of them, offering referrals.

"No thanks," many said. "I was near termination anyway."

One kept calling nearly every day for weeks. She wanted her records; Jan couldn't find them. She called repeatedly at home.

"Look," Jan finally said. "He kept sloppy records. All he probably kept was insurance forms, anyway. I just don't have time to deal with it right now."

She contacted the Michigan Psychological Association for advice. Yes, a staffer said, his records could be destroyed. After she secured permission from probate court, she burned them.

Jan wished she could have torched all the bills as well. They never stopped coming. Al had let the Fisher Building rent slide for nearly a year. He was nearly fourteen thousand dollars behind. He owed more than seven thousand dollars in back income taxes. She feared the IRS would be at her door any day. Hospital bills, the answering service, accountants—he'd left her with a tab exceeding twenty-five thousand dollars.

And Al's mother, Jan thought. She seemed oblivious to Jan's pain. How could this have happened to poor Bus? Bus. Buster. Al Jr. Alan Canty. W. Alan Canty.

Damn it, she thought, doesn't she realize the destruction

he's left in his wake? Me. His patients. Jan wanted to shout at her: "Wake up, damn it!"

By late August, she'd lost twenty-five pounds. She still couldn't get a good night's sleep. She had nightmares. She woke up mornings wondering how she'd gotten the bruises on her arms and legs.

"Jan, you've been bumping into doorjambs and things," her mother told her.

One of many trips to the doctor revealed she'd developed an irregular heartbeat and gone into early menopause.

There was comfort, of course: Letters from people she hadn't heard from in years. People who knew Al, offering to help. A neighbor who put out a standing invitation for a guest room if she got lonely or frightened. Author and psychologist Albert Ellis sent her two letters. He wrote:

"He has been one of the pioneer rational-emotive therapists in the country . . . And I have always heard excellent things about him from several of his clients. His loss to these clients and of course to RET will be a severe one. I hope you are bearing up well under this enormous strain and if there is anything I can do to help, please let me know."

Rational thinking, she thought. Where was Al's rationality?

Jan's feelings took on the nature of Al's life and death. He'd left her heart mutilated like his body. When she was out among people she found herself angry.

"Did you know about this, Jan?" a neighbor asked in her backyard.

"If I did I would have killed him myself." She couldn't believe she'd said it.

Alone, she looked at old photos and found herself missing the man she married. She felt sorry for him. He seemed so pathetic. She wanted to talk to him.

Then, she thought, how dare he leave me with these questions? But I can't punish him. He's already paid the ultimate price. What would I have done if he had lived and I had found out?

"Ces, do you think he loved me?" she found herself asking her friend many times.

Just before Labor Day, her parents returned to Arizona.

Alone her first day in the big Tudor, she couldn't connect with herself. When she sat down, she decided she had to stand. When she decided to do paperwork, she wanted to go outside.

It was a gorgeous Saturday. She mounted her bike and rode down to Windmill Pointe Drive, stopping by the city park. As she looked at Lake St. Clair she noticed the couples. How dare you be together? she thought. Don't you know what a miserable day this is? Everybody in the world seemed to have a partner.

She pedaled home and called Celia Muir, who urged her to visit.

"I'm on my way right now," she told her.

Three hours later she found herself sitting alone in the Ram's Horn restaurant, thinking she ought to be heading to the Muirs' house. When she arrived there, Ces was worried sick.

Jan spent the night. The next morning she rose just before dawn and tiptoed out of the Muirs' house. She saw one of the most pictorial sunrises of her life over a set of railroad tracks aimed toward the horizon.

She found herself again with two questions that had been unrelenting: How could you do this to me, Al? Why didn't you come to me for help? Forget the fact I was your wife. *Damn you, I was your friend.*

Jan didn't reach for her camera. She just wanted it to rain.

Chapter 92

Gladys Canty had hoped it wouldn't get worse, but it had. She couldn't understand why her daughter-in-law was being so cold.

Her first hint was the way Jan had dropped off Buster's high chair that day before the garage sale. Mrs. Canty already was hurt she hadn't been asked to help out. Jan drove up in her red Thunderbird and wrestled it out of the trunk.

"How come you've brought this back?" Mrs. Canty asked.

"My mother told me you *particularly* wanted this back," Jan snapped. Then she sped off, leaving the chair on the porch.

Mrs. Canty probed her own memory. She couldn't remember ever saying that to Jan's mother. She even checked with her friend Edna, who was there that day Jan's mother visited. No, Edna didn't remember her saying anything about the chair either.

Some weeks later there had been another problem.

"Jannie, I just can't shake the feeling that we've let Alan down," she told her one night on the phone.

Several nights later they talked again.

"You hurt me a great deal with that comment," Jan told her. "I've been a good wife."

"I didn't mean to hurt you. I meant 'we' in general. Society and such."

Now, Mrs. Canty thought, I've done this foolish thing. Why didn't I realize? In September, she sent Jan a card and a check for twenty-five dollars, marking what would have been their eleventh anniversary. The letter that came back was blistering. The word "whoremonger" stood out.

423

"Why would you want to celebrate a mockery of a marriage?" Jan wrote, adding she didn't want to see her again. On matters of the estate, they would deal through attorneys from now on.

In the weeks ahead, Gladys was thankful she had her friends. They took her on outings to historic sites and club functions around the city. Sometimes they gathered for an afternoon of tea. But the company couldn't ease her wonderment whether he had suffered during his death.

One night she had a dream. At least it seemed a dream as she was falling asleep. It couldn't have been Buster, she thought, sitting there at the typewriter he'd bought her one year for Christmas.

"Oh, Ma," he said. "It wasn't that bad."

She wanted to believe the apparition.

Chapter 93

Dawn Spens passed her days writing love letters to John Fry and sending them through the inmate mail as the couple waited in the county jail for trial. She scribbled away like a young teen with her first box of stationery. She dotted every letter "i" with big circles. She printed "I LOVE YOU" as though she was carving a sturdy oak. She enclosed "Dawn + John" in a heart of hearts.

Right after the preliminary examination she wrote that she was trying to "be strong" and missed John after seeing him in court. She continued:

"My love for you grows stronger with each passing day. I reminisce about days and nights passed. Right now it is about 6 A.M. I haven't been sleeping very well. Isn't that strange? My mind won't slow down to let me sleep anymore.

"Please don't ever question my love for you. It's as deep as the ocean, as wide as the sea, and as high as the mountains. I do know you love me and thank God for that every night."

A couple of days later she added:

". . . I can't tell you how much I miss having your strong arms around me, supporting me. I can't help but think about the days when all I'd have to do is ask and you would put your arms around me and hold me as long as I needed. You probably don't know this, but when you would do that you were the only reason for me to continue living . . . You're my whole life and you will continue to be my whole life, for as long as you wish. I hope that's forever!!"

There were at least thirty letters in all across the four-month wait. Fry was not nearly so prolific in his answers, often causing his girlfriend to dash off a flurry of writings in an attempt to get an answer. When he did, he often probed her sentiments on the pending murder case. He wrote her about her shortcomings in the interrogation by Gilbert Hill. He added that greater tests were ahead. Near mid-August, she wrote back:

". . . Babe, you know me better than anyone else could ever hope to. How did you know I felt that way about the deal with Hill? You never stop amazing me. I love you so deeply. My head was so fucked up that night, I honestly don't remember what they told me to say or what I said. That isn't any bullshit. I hate myself for it. Please believe I've never meant to hurt you, because I love you. Ya know you're one hell of a good man!!!"

Dawn hoped to get out of the county jail before the murder trial. Her attorney petitioned the court to have her bond reduced. She wrote Fry again, indicating she'd been in contact with her father, Roy:

"My dad got into my ass on the phone. He said, 'You think it was hard here before, it's going to be five times harder this time. If you fuck up one time, I'm going to kick your ass out.' Ain't that a bitch!"

". . . If by another miracle I get out on bond, I'll have to stay with him until this shit is over. I think that may be the best thing because I definitely plan on staying away from drugs. Dig. All drugs do is ruin people's lives, and we definitely don't need that. Right?"

Dawn's father, as well as her court appointed lawyer, Robert Slameka, repeatedly urged her to stop corresponding with her boyfriend. She sent him cigarettes as well as letters. Her bond was reduced to fifty thousand dollars, but her family decided not to bail her out. By September, Roy Spens no longer was sending for her inmate account.

Dawn continued writing anyway, adding candy as well as cigarettes in her letters. She wrote that she regretted they had not married sooner, adding "as soon as possible I want us to get married and have a baby."

Not all their communication would be on jail stationery. Dawn and John were housed in an outdated lockup built in the Purple Gang era. For years the old county jail has served inmates with what they affectionately call "the phone," a system of heating vents that ran through the walls. Prisoners have used the air ducts to talk from floor to floor. John was in ward 511, while Dawn was in 612, almost directly above. The couple sent messages through other inmates and sometimes talked directly.

On September 9, John made an attempt to avoid his trial altogether. Working through a female contact he'd made on the vent, he reportedly bribed an unscrupulous guard to smuggle a pistol and a couple of hacksaw blades into his cell. That Monday, John and two other inmates forced two jail guards into a cell and stripped them of their uniforms.

John waited on a fifth-floor catwalk as his cohorts put on the uniforms and tried to find a way out. One inmate got as far as a stairwell between the first and second floors, where he held sheriff's deputies and Detroit police at bay for nearly four hours before surrendering. All three were charged with escape.

On the first day of October, Dawn Spens went to court in an effort to get her homicide confession back. Her attorney wanted the statement declared inadmissible in the upcoming trial. Dawn took the stand and claimed she'd requested a lawyer after her arrest but was denied. She also maintained she'd been promised she could go home if she made a statement.

Recorder's Court Judge Michael F. Sapala, who would also hear her full trial, denied the motion, saying he found Dawn Spens "totally lacking in credibility." Later, Dawn asked Sapala to assign her a new attorney, saying she and Slameka couldn't get along.

The hearing also initiated a lover's spat. John wondered if she had incriminated him. He wrote Dawn to say her charges were insignificant, "a bullshit meatball case," compared to the life sentence he faced.

Four days after the hearing she wrote back:

"I'll tell you what 'the fuck' my problem is: The real truth is that I'm pissed at you for getting me into this. No I shouldn't be in your shoes, because it was your decision, or don't you remember? Don't get me wrong, I'm not blaming you, I just don't feel you have the right to put me down. I'm trying to be strong, but it is hard for me right now, even though I'm *only* facing fifteen years."

Later in the letter she added: "I don't want this fucking place to break us up. Do you feel the same way, or do you even care?"

And, "I do love you, honey. Don't let this situation make you forget that."

The two began arguing over other matters, in their letters and over the vent. Dawn was upset over jailhouse rumors that her boyfriend had fallen for another girl, one of his "rap partners" on the phone. John criticized her for talking with other male inmates through the heating system. Dawn's letters began dropping off. In late October she wrote one of the last letters he would receive before the trial:

"This place is really getting to me. I don't know what I'm going to do in prison. I guess I'll live. I have to. I don't know why, but I've been thinking a lot about that lately . . .

"I can see your feelings for me are changing already. You don't trust me anymore (if you ever did) and every time I talk to you, we argue. We never used to argue before. I don't know why all this shit is running through my head. I really don't know much of anything anymore.

"I do love you. I know I always will, even if we're forced to be separated for a long time. Please don't play with my feelings or me. I miss you so much it hurts. I hurt every night when I lay down to go to sleep, and I know you won't be there to hold me. You wouldn't believe how much I miss you holding me. I need you so badly. I hope some day we'll be able to embrace again. I know one day we will, but it just seems so far off right now . . ."

Chapter 94

They portrayed me to the jury as this Cass Corridor street pimp junkie that's doin' these evil things and using young girls—and now he's done fucked up and killed somebody.

— JOHN CARL FRY,
March 1987

The trial of John Carl Fry began in December under the threat of another killing. Sheriff's deputies sent word over to Judge Michael F. Sapala that the vents at the county jail were blowing with rumors that Fry would be executed in open court.

Fry reportedly had information about other murders, the deputies said. Jail talk had it that if testimony didn't go his way, he would plea-bargain to a lighter charge in exchange for incriminating information. Sapala had the capacity courtroom audience searched one by one with hand-held metal detectors.

That meant at least two searches for the capacity audience. Visitors already had to negotiate an airport metal detector at the front door of the Frank Murphy Hall of Justice. People had pulled guns before in Recorder's Court, including one pistol-packing judge, who later was disbarred for other judicial indiscretions.

The twenty-three judges on the Recorder's bench disposed of more felonies in one day than most Michigan counties handled in a year. Despite the caseload, Recorder's showed few signs of wear. Its courtrooms were smartly appointed with soft lighting and polished wood. Sapala's was in the shape of a trapezium, like a half theater-in-the-round.

One of the bench's most respected jurists, Sapala would oversee legal talent that was quite familiar with the kind of trench warfare fought in one of the most active criminal courts in the country.

Robert Agacinski was in his tenth year as a trial prosecutor, the Canty case his third highly publicized murder of the year. The wiry, bespectacled prosecutor looked less like the stalwart of the people and more like a family dentist. He often tried cases like one as well. Agacinski possessed the disarming talent of comforting witnesses with an almost sighing delivery. Just about the time a tough customer dismissed his experience in the chair as uneventful, Agacinski began drilling through a nerve.

Jay Nolan, Fry's attorney, had emerged over two decades as one of Recorder's most colorful practitioners. A former assistant prosecutor, Nolan possessed a wit matched only by his fondness for suspenders and dapper boaters. He bore a striking resemblance to Clarence Darrow, but his humor was entirely his own. Probably his most famous one-liner came when he showed up very late for a well-reported trial some years back. Nolan strolled into the packed courtroom, tossed his straw hat onto a hall tree, turned to the annoyed defense team, and said:

"Well, ladies and gentlemen, let the perjury begin."

Nolan, however, found nothing funny about John Fry's unshakable request to be tried by a jury. Nolan feared that with a panel of twelve the details of the mutilation would overshadow his argument for manslaughter. He planned on arguing that Fry had killed Alan Canty in a rage rather than cold blood. Nolan had urged his client to put his life in the hands of Sapala, as Dawn Spens would by requesting a bench trial. Not that the forty-three-year-old judge wasn't streetwise after seven years on the bench. But Nolan knew that Sapala, like most Recorder's judges, was reluctant to dispense a first-degree murder verdict and its mandatory life sentence unless the element of premeditation was rock solid.

But Lucky Fry wanted a jury, and he got one on December 3—a panel of twelve women, with two female alternates. Nolan preferred it that way. He was hoping for some sympathy for Fry because the murder victim had been playing around on his wife.

The first full day of testimony was December 4. Sapala announced the jury would hear all testimony concerning Fry, then be excused when witnesses were questioned about the role of Dawn Spens. Her trial would run concurrently with her old boyfriend's. Her defense would not begin until after Fry's verdict.

In the courtroom Fry might have passed for an assistant professor, as long as he didn't roll up his sleeves. He wore a brown tweed suit and a green tie, loaners from an acquaintance of Nolan's. His grayish blond hair had grown to the bottom of his collar. His beard was neatly trimmed, and he was decked with a walrus's mustache that concealed his lip. Two attorneys sat between Fry and his girlfriend at the defense table. The defendant's eyes rarely met during the entire trial.

It took two days for sixteen of Fry's friends, relatives, and street associates to tell what they saw and heard. Agacinski avoided exact dates or days of the week. Many time-frame discrepancies existed between police statements, preliminary exam testimony, and other accounts.

But the central story remained consistent. Frank McMasters and Cheryl Krizanovic told what they knew of Al, about Cheryl's repeated trips from Detroit to the north, and about John and Dawn's arrival with the body parts in mid-July. Dot Wilson told of Fry's late-night calls. The people of the Morrell Apartments repeated Fry's one-liners the day he burned the car. Neighbor Michael Oliver told what he heard Fry say at the picnic table. John Bumstead testified about the conversation on the trip to New York.

As they testified, many avoided the discerning eyes of the defendant. Fry hardly moved from an upright, but relaxed, posture. Occasionally testimony would prompt a slight smirk at the corner of the mustache. Then his eyes rolled deep into his head.

Many aspects of the full story never made the court record. The trial revealed little about Alan Canty. Jan Canty not only wasn't a witness, she didn't attend the trial. She was at an international symposium of psychotherapists in Arizona.

431

Attorneys agreed to stipulate her testimony from the preliminary exam.

One bemused member of the audience was neighbor Juanita Deckoff, who also wasn't called as a witness. She'd returned from her vacation after the investigation was completed. The early testimony confused her.

"I couldn't figure out who this Dr. Miller was everybody was talking about," she said later. "Then I realized they were talking about Al Canty. I only knew him by that name."

The continuing contention by Fry and Spens that they knew the psychologist only as Dr. Al Miller would go unchallenged through the entire trial. Evidence from the Casper bungalow—the sheet of paper with Al's real name—never reached the prosecutor's office. Neither did the note suggesting Dawn set Al up for "goodbye."

Agacinski called a nervous Tammy Becker, who testified about the conversation in her car and the couple's plans to move to California "to straighten out their lives." She told how the couple expected "ten to thirty thousand dollars" on the weekend of the murder. She relayed Fry's statement that his deal had "backfired."

But a hole widened in the narrative as attorneys battled over the more bloody aspects of the case. The prosecution argued that Fry had planned to extort a large sum of money from Dr. Al Miller. That assumption left a big question that begged to be asked: How does someone blackmail a man whose identity is a fabrication?

The question never was posed.

As Agacinski presented his case, Jay Nolan found himself in a unique position for a defense attorney. He had to convince a jury that his client was a liar, and for that reason he should be exonerated from murder one. Fry's bragging that he was going to "kill The Doc," Nolan argued, was nothing more than puffing.

But Gary Neil had the smoking gun. He was the last witness on a Thursday afternoon, the third day of the trial. Neil took the stand in another one of his long-sleeve sweatshirts. His voice was low and slow. His testimony was more graphic than in the preliminary exam. Neil described his relationship

432

with Fry:

"Well, I met him in the penitentiary. I didn't know him that well there . . . On the street I ran into him again about a year ago and became more or less drug-related buddies. We both like coke."

Neil testified how John and Dawn had a plethora of names for Al Canty—"a chump," "the sugar daddy," "a lame." Then he testified about the basement conversation in the days before the killing.

"Then he asked me if I knew how to get rid of a body after it happened, how to get rid of the bones and everything completely. I said, 'I don't know, John.' That was about it."

"How long did the conversation last?" Agacinski asked.

"It lasted about twenty minutes. He was showing me the layout of the basement and the plastic and 'put the body on here' and take it apart and so forth."

Jay Nolan sprung out of his chair for the cross-examination. He carried in his hand four printed statements Neil gave to police on four separate occasions. The first two contained no reference to the basement conversation. Nolan boomed his first question.

"It was after this that they had locked you up and told you that you would stay until you told the truth that you gave this version about the basement conversation, is that right?"

"That and after the visit from my sister, who told me I better tell the truth, no use holding back information on this guy."

"This visit from your sister was when you were in the jail-house locked up?"

"Yeah."

"So the time you decided to implicate him with this story you were in the jailhouse?"

"Right."

"Now, you are in the jailhouse and you now remember things, right?"

Agacinski objected. Sustained.

Nolan extracted Neil's criminal record, then went back to the four statements. He tried to impeach him with a discussion of the exact date of the basement conversation with Fry, using the varying reports he gave homicide detectives.

"Now, in this statement you are fixing this conversation as

five days before the homicide?"

"I said about a week before, eight days before that he would kill the doctor. That's what I told them."

"Here it says five days before," said Nolan, pointing to one of the statements.

"I said a week or eight days before."

"I am asking, your statement was five days before?"

"One says five and one says eight."

"This one says five days before?" Nolan asked, pointing again.

"Yes."

"There was another time you said eight days before?"

"Right. I didn't keep up on the days."

Neil soon had most everyone in the courtroom as confused as his own confused memory. Nolan was losing his witness, and nothing would rattle Neil's relaxed demeanor. Several friends later said Neil was stoned, but he stuck to the mutilation story.

By then it was late afternoon. Judge Sapala recessed the trial until the following Monday. Nolan's cross-examination was scheduled to begin with Neil on Monday morning, but Neil didn't show up. Sapala ordered more witnesses brought forth.

When Neil finally arrived that afternoon, Nolan tried to fight his way out of a hole with the ex-con in the sweatshirt. Now Neil remembered not one, but three conversations about the extortion and killing.

Assistant Medical Examiner Marilee Frazer was an odd contrast to the imposing homicide cops she followed on the witness stand. The young examiner stood hardly five feet, wore pop-bottle glasses, and spoke in a high-pitched voice. Courthouse regulars had nicknamed her The Giggling Pathologist because of the way her enthusiasm for her grisly work sometimes appeared as delight in open court.

Monday afternoon, Dr. Frazer described in rich detail the effect of the blows to Canty's head. The ten intersecting fracture lines, she said, were "like the shell of an egg cracking."

With a look of bewilderment, she discussed in detail what instrument might have been used in the mutilation. It cut

434

cleanly like a knife, she said, but had also severed the bone. "There are very few basic knives that will cut through this entire tissue," she said. "It would have to be more like a saw."

The jury was motionless, except for the repeated blinking of several sets of eyes.

After further discussion of the bruises and blows to Al Canty's face, Jay Nolan tried to lessen the impact on cross-examination.

"He was dead at the time of the amputation?" he asked.

"Yes," Dr. Frazer said.

Jay Nolan had been impressed that Fry's story had never varied from their first meeting, and he personally remained convinced Fry had not killed Canty in cold blood. He thought Gary Neil had lied to save himself from charges related to Canty's Buick and a check-kiting scheme. Nolan had been publicly critical of the homicide section's ability to extract statements from a witness by detention, while a murder *suspect* was protected by *Miranda* warnings and rights.

Over the past week the jury had heard an unfolding narrative filled with profanity, street slang, prostitution, and drug addiction, not to mention the more gruesome aspects of the case. The panel had been shuffled in and out of the courtroom more than a dozen times as testimony on Dawn's charges was heard from the same witnesses who had implicated Fry.

Now it was Nolan's turn. On Tuesday, seven days after the trial began, John Carl Fry took the stand as the only witness for his defense.

Many of the twelve women readjusted themselves in their seats, straightening their postures as the central character was sworn at the stand.

"What is your name, please?" Nolan began.

"John Fry."

"You are the defendant in this case?"

"Yes, I am."

"You killed Dr. Canty?"

"Yes, I did."

"You dismembered his body?"

"Yes."

Fry was frank about his past criminal record, telling the jury that he lived "off the proceeds of a prostitute." He said he was, essentially, everything everyone said he was — a pimp, a junkie, a thief — but he was not a cold-blooded killer.

Then the defendant and his attorney put W. Alan Canty on trial before the twelve women.

Fry told of Dawn meeting Canty and their growing dependence on Al for money for drugs. He told of Al's own purchases of heroin and his visits to Dawn in the hospital. He told of his own attempt to get clean in Alanson, and of Canty sabotaging Dawn's effort to stay straight. He explained the five-thousand-dollar payoff and the stickup that brought him back in the picture. Fry said he himself was dependent on the doctor for his habit. Fry was emotionless, but articulate in his description of drug withdrawal while waiting for Canty's money. Often he mixed street jive with the precise words of an English major.

"Were you in pain?" Nolan asked.

"Yes, I was."

"Was Dawn in pain?"

"Yes, she was."

"When you said something like 'I'm going to kick his ass, I'm going to kill him,' were you laying plans to kill the goose that laid the golden egg, were you going to kill him?"

"No."

"What did you mean by those words?"

"I was pissed. It was a street *vernacular,* you know. Over a period of years I probably said I would do something to four, five people, you know, maybe twenty people, but I never did."

"A figure of speech?"

"Right."

Later the story moved to the period when Canty was giving them rides to the methadone clinic.

"Did he have any comments as you were going to the methadone clinic?"

"He thought we were wasting our time. Once a dope fiend, always a dope fiend."

"Dr. Miller told you that?"

"Yes."

Then Fry said Dr. Al Miller introduced them to cocaine to

436

combat the sleepy effects of the methadone. He claimed Al one day brought them a gram of pharmaceutical cocaine. By July, Fry said, he and Dawn had quit the methadone clinic but were addicted to coke. They made plans to move to California, where Fry said he had a job waiting for him in a bar. The "big score" that weekend of the murder was not an extortion attempt, but a stolen-truck scam.

Then Nolan introduced his client's version of the fatal argument. Fry said he and Dawn had made an agreement not to do any more coke that Saturday of the murder. When he returned and found Al had bought her drugs during his evening visit, he was angry.

"He proceeded to tell me point-blank, 'Fuck you, I don't have to justify anything I do to you.' He shoved me like he was walking out."

"What did you do at that moment?"

"I really went out . . ."

Fry said he told Dawn to leave the house while he cut and packaged the body. Nolan asked him why he dismembered Alan Canty. He said he saw no other way to get him out, and he feared returning to prison. He feared police would never believe him about the argument.

"I am an ex-con," Fry explained. "I recognized I am a dope fiend, you know . . . He is established; he is a doctor."

"Is that what seemed like a good idea at the time?" Nolan asked concerning the dissection.

"Yeah, it seemed."

"Does it now?"

"No, sir."

Prosecutor Agacinski went for the enamel with his first question on cross-examination.

"Mr. Fry, why did you call Dr. Canty a pinhead when he wasn't around?" he asked.

"It was a nickname that was given to him."

"Who gave him the nickname?"

"Dawn."

"Why did you adopt the nickname?"

"I don't know. No specific reason."

Now Agacinski had the witness in a combative mood,

right where he wanted him.

". . .Why did you tell Tammy Becker that Dr. Canty was a pain in the ass?"

"Evidently, Mr. Agacinski, you never dealt with tricks. Most tricks are pains in the ass. They interrupt your life."

"How was he a pain to you?"

"Just by being around at times when it would be inconvenient."

Agacinski moved in on Fry's conversations with Canty about California. Fry stuttered, the only time he would during his entire testimony. He admitted Al was supposed to give him money for the trip, but he said Al didn't want him to go.

Agacinski posed his questions in a bemused tone, gesturing with his expressive hands, looking as though he was trying to understand. He took Fry through everyone else's testimony.

"Tamara Becker is mistaken about the amount involved?" he asked.

"Yes."

". . . You told Dorothy Wilson you killed a man because he didn't pay Dawn, is that correct?"

"Yes, I did."

"That's why you killed Dr. Canty—he didn't pay Dawn?"

"No."

"So you lied to your cousin?"

"Yes."

Then, later:

"Let me ask you specifically then . . . did you tell John Bumstead that the money was funny and you wanted to take him out . . ."

"The statement was made."

"By whom?"

"There was no 'I wanted to take him out.' That statement wasn't made."

"The money was funny, and if [you] didn't get it straightened out, you had to take him out; that's what you said to John Bumstead?"

"Possibly."

"And you told Dorothy Wilson that he didn't pay Dawn the money?"

"Right."

438

". . . And do you remember telling Keith Bjerke at other times that if the money didn't come in, that the shit was going to hit the fan?"

"The shit was always hitting the fan."

"Tell me what you mean by that."

"When you live in that environment, there is always some shit hitting the fan. That can mean a million different things."

"It could mean killing somebody, couldn't it?"

"I never consider it that way. I suppose it could."

"But did you say that to Keith Bjerke?"

"I possibly did."

"Before Dr. Canty died, do you remember sitting at a picnic table outside of Mike Oliver's kitchen table and telling somebody you were going to kill the fucking doctor?"

"No."

"John Bumstead was wrong when he heard you say that?"

"Yes."

"And Michael Oliver is wrong?"

"Yes."

"He is wrong too, Michael Oliver is wrong?"

"I didn't say that. If that makes him wrong, he is wrong."

"Who else did you complain to that the doctor didn't provide enough money?"

"Half of the dope fiends in the Vernor-Clark area."

Then, Agacinski asked about Gary Neil and lowered the cap on his handiwork.

"He was probably wrong when he heard you say that you were going to kill the doctor and cut the body up?"

"He is definitely wrong."

"The way Oliver . . . is wrong?"

"No."

"The way Tammy Becker is wrong?"

"No."

"They are wrong in different ways?"

"Yes. There are degrees of wrongness," John Fry said.

"There certainly is . . ." Agacinski said.

When Fry was done, everyone broke for lunch.

When everyone returned, Agacinski pled to the jury in his

closing argument that Fry's admission of the killing and mutilation was a ploy to get them to believe his other statements. Agacinski apologized for the foul language that had been evoked in the testimony. He talked of Alan Canty.

"Dr. Canty is not a sympathetic figure," Agacinski said. "He did not do right. He shouldn't be in this world, but we could shed tears. He didn't deserve to die."

Jay Nolan had crafted an eloquent final argument, and his heart literally was pumping. Every morning of the trial the sixty-one-year-old former distance runner scurried up the twelve flights of the Frank Murphy Hall of Justice "to get the blood flowing." On a wall at the top of the courthouse stairwell were dozens of Nolan's pencil marks noting his times for the many previous trips during many previous trials.

Nolan had already run up the stairs Tuesday morning. He took a second trip up during a 3 P.M. recess, right before his closing argument.

The defense attorney began with a backhand at the prosecutor for his remarks about the victim.

"There is not a person in this courtroom who is not in sympathy with Dr. Canty and what happened to him. He certainly did not deserve to die and did not deserve the ignominy of his burial, and we grieve for his family, we all do."

Then Nolan himself portrayed the psychologist as a modern-day Dr. Jekyll and Mr. Hyde.

"He wrote a book on therapeutic peers, which means your equals," he said at one point. "He comes in from Grosse Pointe, and he descends to these wretched people and becomes a part of their lives . . . I suggest he was playing with them as guinea pigs. He is a trained psychologist, and he has control."

Building resentments caused John Fry's hot blood that led to the killing, Nolan argued.

"I don't think John Fry realized, when he was on the witness stand today, what was being done to him by this skillful doctor of psychology. I don't think John Fry realizes he was being manipulated . . . Dr. Jekyll knew what he was doing. He was manipulating these people."

Nolan hammered at the book *Therapeutic Peers,* turning it into an indictment of W. Alan Canty.

"John Fry is not his peer. Dawn Spens is not his peer. Frank

McMasters is not his peer. Cheryl Krizanovic is not his peer."
He went on for a minute, naming every south-side witness with the same phrase.

It was a rousing argument with a rousing climax.

"[Canty] raises to full height and says, 'I don't have to justify anything.' He pushed him aside and dismissed him as if he is not human.

"Finally here is the end. He has treated these people as toys and twisted and twisted and twisted that spring, and the twisted spring broke. It broke Fry . . .

"This is the type of situation which is manslaughter, and I ask you to return a verdict of manslaughter and guilty of dissecting a human body."

The next day, after less than three hours of deliberation, the jury found John Carl Fry guilty of first-degree murder. Fry never blinked as the verdict was read.

Chapter 95

None of the jurors lingered for a courthouse lunch. One sprinted on the toes of her high heels out the front doors of the Frank Murphy Hall of Justice, trying to escape reporters. Some feared recrimination from the man in the tweed suit,

One year later, a juror would write a letter, sending it to a journalist who wrote a magazine article on the case. It read in part:

"You probably would never have heard from me if it wasn't for your article yesterday . . . I didn't read it, but I began shaking again. I didn't sleep well again last night. After the trial was over I pushed it away. I found out yesterday that isn't the solution. I do not want you to interview me . . . but I want you to hear my story.

"I am a person who tends to trust people too much. That's probably why God kept me on that jury. When [we] were chosen we were surprised to see no men among us.

"As each person testified I could hardly believe my ears. As a group we, the jury, became more scared. Waiting for the elevators, going into the bathrooms, in the cafeteria, etc. The only place we felt secure was in the jury room.

"Let me tell you about after Frank McMasters testified. We went to lunch in the cafeteria. We were talking about our families, jobs, the weather—anything but the trial—when Frank McMasters walked in with some other witnesses. It was as if we rehearsed it . . . All the jurors who were there stood up, leaving our lunches, and headed toward the elevators. My heart was pounding . . . All through the trial we had the hope of being the two [alternates] who would be excused at the end.

"I guess you'd like to know what happened while we were

in deliberation . . . I know the whole courtroom thought we were going to rely on what Gary Neil said, but no—there was more . . . We had a short open forum and took a vote. It came up ten guilty murder one, two murder two . . . We pieced together the evidence a little slower. *The money is getting funny. I'm going to take The Doc out. The bat was always in the living room. Now it was in the bedroom. Several blows to the head. Use this credit card for gas. The Doc's on an extended vacation.* And then the plan in the basement. There was kind of an eerie silence as we took our second vote . . . The room was silent except for: 'Murder one.' 'Murder one.' 'Murder one.' . . .

"We looked around at each other. Some women lit cigarettes, some used the rest room, others just sat quietly . . . I came to the reality that I'd been sitting not fifteen feet from a man who actually planned the death of another person. We didn't even let the judge know we were ready for another fifteen or twenty minutes.

"Later a television reporter tried to talk to several of us. When he approached us I began to cry again. He asked if it was because I was scared. I said no . . . I lied. You see, the whole thing occurred in a place very familiar to me. As each witness testified, more streets were named and as I went home each night, I passed through that area . . . The house where he was murdered I pass each time I visit my grandmother. My parents shop at the [grocery store] behind that house . . .

"I guess I'm getting better . . . This hit too close to home, I think.

"All I can conclude for you is that John Fry had the most fair jury as possible. Thanks for listening—and now, I can begin again."

Chapter 96

Do you know what the first thing is I want to do when we can be together again? Give up? Well I'll tell you I want to have your baby.
— *Letter from Dawn Spens to John Fry,*
August 27, 1985

Sheriff's deputies put away their metal detectors as the defense of Dawn Spens began the day after John Fry's verdict. There were a lot of empty seats, and one TV crew instead of three trying to snag witnesses in the courtroom lobby.

It was as though Dawn Spens was left to tidy up the drama with a few short lines, even though the hooker was the catalyst that brought killer and victim together on that bloody night.

Ray Danford remained for the final act. He sat quietly on a back bench through most of the trial. Another onlooker was Roy Spens, who now stood out among a sparse courtroom audience. He'd avoided reporters and friends of his daughter. Frank McMasters approached him earlier in the trial, asking if he could bring clothes and paperwork Dawn had left at his house while she was on the run.

"I don't give a shit what you do with it," Spens said. "You can burn it for all I care. I don't want anything to do with this."

In appointing a new defender for Dawn Spens, Sapala wanted a lawyer he considered a worthy opponent for a tough prosecutor like Robert Agacinski. The judge wanted a fair fight over the charges in the Canty case that would be his alone to decide.

Twenty years ago, defense attorney Robert Ziolkowski was an offensive tackle for the University of Iowa and a Green Bay Packers draft choice. Like a good lineman, "Z" still went about his job without drawing much attention. A lesson often learned by new young prosecutors was the faultiness of the assumption that Ziolkowski's size and slow movements related in any way to his mental agility. He'd learned his trade well in the trenches of Recorder's Court.

Sapala himself was a tougher judge than when he first took the Recorder's bench seven years ago. The unrelenting parade of repeat offenders had changed many of his early beliefs about criminal rehabilitation. But Sapala, the only lawyer in a family of physicians, still was capable of mercy when he saw a lawbreaker he felt needed healing.

From the first day of the trial there was no sign of the stoned hooker who had shown up at the preliminary exam four and a half months ago. Dawn Spens had gained twenty pounds in the county jail. She was escorted into court wearing a clinging purple knit dress that accented her lumps and rolls. Her calves were swollen by the starchy jail food. Her permanent had grown out, replaced by strings of hair that was now ash brown and pulled back from her head. She wore a little black bow on top, as though she was trying to reclaim youthful innocence. But with the dress, the jail-white skin, and the circular scars showing through her nylons, the total effect was one of pathos.

The role Dawn would play out in the courtroom was one the prostitute knew well, one she had played with her high school chums, her johns, the doctors at Receiving Hospital, and psychologist Alan Canty.

Ziolkowski had already laid out his defense in an opening statement the week before.

"I think the facts in this case will show that prior to coming in contact with Mr. Fry, Dawn Spens led a rather ordinary life," he told the court.

His defense was twofold. First he sought to prove that Dawn Spens was not subject to the mutilation statute. True, he argued, she had "carried away" the valise with Al Canty's body parts from the refrigerator, but she'd had no idea what was inside.

Second, Ziolkowski would argue that Dawn was not an accessory after the fact to murder because she had acted under duress. She destroyed evidence, raised money for their flight, and sought to cover up the crime under orders from her pimp.

Dawn Spens followed those orders, he would argue, because she was terrified of Lucky Fry.

As Fry's jury filed in and out on previous days, Agacinski had little difficulty establishing Dawn's role as an accessory. The concealment of body parts. The cleanup of blood. Driving to northern Michigan. Destruction of Canty's documents. Buying gas for the car-burning. Raising money for their flight. All these elements easily were established by Frank McMasters, Cheryl Krizanovic, and Dawn's own statement to police. Other witnesses told of her sobbing outside the Morrell Apartments.

With little fanfare, Ziolkowski rose from his seat, lumbered a few feet into midcourt, and cross-examined some southsiders, opening holes he'd later fill with his defense.

"Did you ever see John beat Dawn?" he asked Tammy Becker.

"Not literally beat her, no . . . I seen him slap her a few times," Tammy said.

"You don't consider that beating somebody?"

"No, I don't."

". . . And do you recall having told the police that Dawn would be afraid to leave?"

"I felt she was afraid to leave."

"What gave you that impression?"

"The way she acted."

"What about her actions that led you to believe she was afraid to leave Mr. Fry?"

"Because he was so demanding with her."

Ziolkowski cross-examined Cheryl Krizanovic, probing her violent relationship with her old boyfriend. Cheryl told the court how John introduced her to drugs and prostitution, about the many beatings and the time he shattered her spleen. She explained his threats to kill her if she ever left.

"Did you ever discuss that with Dawn Spens?"

"Yes."

"Did you discuss the fact that Mr. Fry had struck you on numerous occasions?"

"Yes."

"Had Dawn Spens—did she ever tell you about being struck by Mr. Fry?"

"On one occasion."

"Did you ever see her being struck by Mr. Fry?"

"No."

Ziolkowski questioned John Bumstead early in the trial on the argument at his house when Dawn's nose was broken.

Bumstead said the argument was among the four of them—himself, his wife, and John and Dawn. Under redirect examination Agacinski tried to put the group's lifestyle in context.

"He was hollering at Dawn Spens the way you holler at your wife?" Agacinski asked.

"I don't know. I holler at my wife very hard. I don't know how to compare him with me."

". . . After blood is coming from Dawn Spens's nose, what happened?"

"She got up and she said, 'My nose is bleeding.' "

"Then what happened?"

"They left."

". . . Do you hit your wife?"

"I used to, and I am not proud of it, but it happens."

"Did blood come from her nose too?"

"I don't know. You have to ask her that."

As for Dawn's knowledge of the contents of the valise and the plastic bag hurled out off I-75, neither Cheryl, Frank, nor any other witness testified that they had heard Dawn say she knew what was inside.

On Thursday morning, the day after Fry's verdict, Agacinski added the final installment of the people's case by calling Marlyss Landeros to testify about Dawn's confession. She read the entire document into the record.

In her statement Dawn reported: "John told me to go to the kitchen and take the overnight suitcase with the body parts of Al in it out of the freezer."

And as for the garbage bag Fry dumped on I-75: "Nobody told me but I knew he was throwing away body parts of Al."

John Fry was locked up in the county jail cell when Dawn took the stand later that morning. Wearing the same dress she'd worn for six days of the trial, she raised her hand, was sworn, then sat, crossing her legs. Her scars were visible from the last row of the courtroom.

Dawn's audience was a dozen onlookers, the court staff, the attorneys, and, most importantly, Judge Michael F. Sapala. Roy Spens sat on a bench near a wall, his eyes focused on the floor, his head in his hands.

"Miss Spens, tell us your full name, please," Ziolkowski began.

"Dawn Marie Spens."

Ziolkowski moved to the center of the courtroom. The big attorney walked slowly back and forth as he continued with his questions.

"And how old are you, ma'am?"

"Twenty."

Her voice was soft, her brown eyes attentive.

It was a moving narrative of human bondage but quite unlike the one that would be told outside the courtroom later by Dolores Cusmano, Donald Scott Carlton, Juanita Deckoff, Sue Stennett, Mark Bando, Cheryl Krizanovic, Frank McMasters, Dr. Lorraine Awes, John Carl Fry, and thirty of Dawn's own jailhouse letters written before and after the trial.

According to her testimony she'd left high school and Harper Woods to move in with Donald Carlton in the Cass Corridor. There she took a job working in a party store. Don beat her often. One day, John Fry showed up on the scene. He threatened Carlton, delivering Dawn from his beatings. She moved in with John. But then Fry introduced her to intravenous drugs. Before that she had only smoked some marijuana and drank. Fry introduced her to prostitution, she said. Yes, she'd heard about Cheryl's ruptured spleen, and she was afraid to leave John. She told of the time he broke her nose and other times he slapped her. She said she feared he would kill her or her family if she left him. She said she had no place to go if she left.

"Did you love John Fry?" Ziolkowski asked, pushing his

glasses higher on his nose and looking into her eyes.

"At one time I cared about him. I thought I owed him something at the beginning because he had gotten that one guy away from me."

"And did there come a time when your feelings changed?"

"Yes."

"And how did it change, what were your feelings then about John Fry?"

"I resented him."

"But you stayed with him?"

"Yes.

"Why?"

"I didn't feel I had any other choice."

Then Ziolkowski moved into the circumstances surrounding the murder. John and Al began arguing while she was vomiting, she said. She really didn't know what they were arguing about. After the killing Fry ordered her to listen for a heartbeat. Then he ordered her to turn tricks. The body disappeared while she was gone.

"Why didn't you go to the police at that time?"

"I was afraid of John, and I knew that — Well, he had told me before that he had escaped from jail. I knew if I went to the police he would get me."

Dawn testified she didn't know what happened to the body until she made her statement to Marlyss Landeros in Homicide. She only "suspected" Al's body part was being thrown out on I-75. She did not know what was in the valise. She offered an explanation for her statement to Landeros about the brown bag.

"Did you tell Officer Landeros that you took the bag with the body parts in it from the refrigerator?"

"I explained it to them what the bag looked like, and they told me that was the bag with the body parts in it. So then, from that point on, whenever I referred to it, she put 'the bag with the body parts' rather than going into the explanation that [it was] just the bag I had seen."

"She characterized the bag you described as 'the bag with the body parts in it'?"

"Yes."

". . . Was that your language?"

"No."

A taped confession would have settled the dispute. But there had never been time for tape recorders and transcripts in a homicide section handling six hundred murders a year.

Ziolkowski concluded her testimony with Dawn saying she'd received threatening letters from Fry in jail.

"He told me that if I didn't — In the letters he wrote, he said if I didn't let him know something by December 3, he would assume that I was on the other side and act accordingly when he saw me; that there was either time to 'be right or be gone.' "

At Agacinski's request, the court ordered he be allowed to see the letters, but neither side entered them into the record.

After lunch, Agacinski got out his drill. He led Dawn Spens again through her account of her early days with John Fry.

"So after a month or two of being with Mr. Fry your feelings of love or affection *went away?*"

The prosecutor stood in the middle of the courtroom, seemingly bewildered.

"Yes," Dawn said calmly.

". . . But because [of] what he would do on the streets, did you feel some affection or some respect or some debt that you owed John Fry as well?"

"It wasn't really — I can't explain it very well. In some respects I guess I did feel indebted to him."

The prosecutor ground at the defendant's story for an hour. Then Agacinski cited Tammy Becker's testimony about their plans to go to California.

Dawn denied there were any such firm plans at all. She portrayed the day of the killing as another routine visit by Dr. Al Miller.

He tried to impeach her testimony about being ordered to clean the bathtub.

"Did John come in and criticize your clean-up job at the time?"

"No."

"You were afraid he was going to come in and criticize your clean-up job?"

"I just did what he told me to do."

"You were just being thorough."

450

Agacinski paused and smiled, then quickly switched to her story about the brown valise.

"Then after you cleaned up the bathroom, you got this overnight case. How did it feel? Tell us how it felt in your hand."

"I grabbed it by the handle."

"How heavy was it?"

"Fairly heavy."

". . . How long had that overnight case been in your house?"

"Ever since we moved there."

"How long had it been in the freezer?"

"I don't know."

"Did it look out of place to you?"

"Yeah."

"Had you ever seen that in the freezer before?"

"No."

"But you didn't want to think what was in it?"

"No."

Agacinski pled, gestured, and paced, but Dawn responded in short, soft answers. Sometimes she knitted her brow slightly, looking as perplexed as her interrogator. He prompted her to admit she was never physically threatened when she aided Fry after the crime. But he never found a nerve.

On redirect, Robert Ziolkowski asked one more question.

"Miss Spens, I noticed some marks on the back of your legs. Can you tell me what those are?"

"Scars from using drugs," she said.

Dawn Spens's trial was adjourned until the following Monday. The Sunday night before what would be the last day of testimony, Dawn penned another letter to John:

"I truly hope this letter finds you doing as well as can be expected. You wouldn't believe how shocked I was when I heard the verdict. Tomorrow is supposed to be my last day of trial . . . My nerves are shattered. It really pisses me off that it is taking so long to finish this trial . . .

"Everyone up here was bummed out when they heard the verdict on you. My mom and my sister cried. There are a couple of girls up here who wanted me to tell you that they admire your style."

When the trial resumed after the lunch hour Monday, Ziolkowski introduced Michael Abramsky, a clinical psychologist versed in drug and spouse abuse. Abramsky had conducted a clinical workup on Dawn Spens, based on a two-hour interview with her in the jail in early November.

Abramsky remarked that during their interview Spens's "emotions were flat."

"She did not show a normal range of emotions," he said. "There was little spontaneity. There were very little emotions of any kind."

Abramsky said it could be a product of longtime drug abuse or her "lifelong habitual behavior," but he couldn't tell which one. He characterized Dawn as a person who was dependent on others, who made no decisions of her own.

"Is that thought process or lack of a thought process consistent with one who is drug dependent?" Ziolkowski asked.

"It is also consistent with someone who has certain historical factors that Miss Spens shares. She comes from a broken home. There was a lot of substance abuse in the family. There was very little guidance. . . ."

He compared her with an abused spouse, saying she suffered from the kind of passive behavior associated with the syndrome. Given her makeup, Abramsky said she was acting under duress after the murder.

Attorneys made their closing arguments after a short afternoon recess. Agacinski tried to evoke what might have prompted Al Canty to visit the bungalow on Casper on July 13.

"Two things concern me about her relation—her talking about the facts in this case," he told the court. "The first is her contradicting Tammy Becker [on] going to California. Miss Becker was clear in testifying that the week before the death of Dr. Canty, Miss Spens herself mentioned that the coming weekend was [when they were] to go to California . . .

"It is my argument that Miss Spens was much more involved in the perpetration of some financial fraud from Dr. Canty, that she was an active participant in getting a large sum of money to finance [her flight] to flee with John Fry to California. She had no care for the consequences of Dr. Canty, whether he would survive or not . . ."

He also pointed out her 3.8 grade point average in high school but questioned her "candor" in her testimony. After taking the court again through the testimony, Agacinski, a prosecutor not normally prone to metaphor, closed by creating one for Judge Michael F. Sapala:

"I believe Miss Spens is accountable as to both counts, and I ask the court not to be seduced by Miss Spens as Dr. Canty was, and to find her guilty on both counts."

Ziolkowski opened by saying he found the prosecutor's comment about seduction "interesting." There was some spring in his step as he added, "From all the evidence and testimony I heard, Dr. Canty seemed to be the one that initiated this whole process."

The big attorney then stood motionless in front of Judge Sapala and matter-of-factly painted Dawn Spens as helpless.

"I believe," he said in closing, "what we have heard from Dawn Spens from the witness stand is the case, and that is that she is the true victim of this case. We feel some compassion for Dr. Canty but no compassion for Mr. Fry, but I think the true victim, the person both these individuals were feeding off of, if you will excuse the expression, was Dawn Spens . . ."

Twenty-four hours later on December 17, the parties gathered again for Judge Sapala's verdict. But first, he expressed the frustrations that awaited anyone who was prone to investigate the case of W. Alan Canty.

"We," Sapala said, "are left to determine the fact of this shameful and disgusting episode via an odd and bizarre parade of dope addicts, prostitutes, thieves, and admitted lawbreakers. Such never makes the job of a fact finder easy . . .

"The core of this strange universe is narcotics. We have been exposed to a hedonistic and cruel world where the pursuit of powdery substances shapes and molds every relationship of thought, every desire, and ultimately compels an end of pain and misery and death.

"Whether it was Dawn Spens or John Fry or Gary Neil or McMasters or Krizanovic or Becker or Bumstead or . . . W. Alan Canty, Ph.D., we see only self-gratification of individual appetites.

"The people I have seen live in a community where there is absolutely no love. They are only users of dope and users of each other."

Judge Sapala found Dawn Marie Spens guilty of being an accessory to murder after the fact, but not guilty on the charge of mutilation of a dead body.

Then he referred her to the Recorder's Court Psychiatric Clinic for evaluation.

"Miss Spens, I know you talked to Dr. Abramsky, but it won't hurt that you talk to one of the psychologists or psychiatrists here at the clinic. It may help in terms of the -ultimate sentence in this case."

"OK. Thank you," Dawn Spens said as she stood, trying to smooth the wrinkles on her clinging purple dress.

Chapter 97

Clearly our stories must contain aggression. The common denominator amongst most inhibited patients was aggressive and destructive fantasies toward adults whom they imparted with evil and villainous characteristics early in the story and subsequently destroyed . . .

— W. ALAN CANTY
Therapeutic Peers

Two weeks after Judge Sapala's verdict, the same Recorder's Court Psychiatric Clinic that Alan Canty, Sr., had headed for many years diagnosed John Carl Fry as a "textbook" psychopath.

"He can mimic emotions, feelings, and even guilt, but has no capacity for real empathy or compassion," its report stated. "Guilt is an emotion that is foreign to him. We can only recommend the maximum period of incarceration by sentence."

It was a moot point. Lucky Fry faced a life term, with no allowance for parole, under the state law covering first-degree murder. Judge Michael Sapala, however, had ordered the report done to aid prison officials.

On a Monday morning, December 23, Fry returned before the judge for the formalities. Jay Nolan had a few words for the record.

"My client stands before the statutory gallows of this state now . . . I mean no disrespect of Dr. Canty's family, and I take note that John Fry's life has been disaster and tragedy. He has been a man of great capacity and still has

455

those capacities. He at one time owned three gas stations in Pontiac and was a successful businessman. We are now faced with devastation."

"Mr. Fry," Judge Sapala said. "Is there anything that you would like to say before the court passes sentence?"

John Fry, his hands clasped in front of him, looked up at Sapala and said:

"Throughout this whole trial I have been betrayed as a cold individual. I have a lot of regrets about the way things happened. I regret for Dr. Canty and his family. Anytime an individual's memory is sold, it's a shame to humanity.

"My main regret is to Dawn Spens. She was subjected to jail and possible prison. Anyway, I ask the court for mercy, not for myself but for Miss Spens."

Ten days later, on January 2, Dawn Spens needed a little charity. The probation department and the psychiatric clinic recommended a prison term. Sapala had before him a psychiatric clinic report that suggested she wasn't really "regretful" about the incident, indicating "her remorse most likely is situation-specific, namely, it probably would disappear as soon as she is released from custody."

Her attorney Robert Zilkowski objected strongly to both the probation and psychiatric reports. And Jan Canty, in an interview with the probation department, said she saw Dawn as a "victim" and didn't object to probation, as long as she went into a rehabilitation program.

There were hardly any burial expenses Dawn should have to pay, Jan also indicated in the report. There was hardly a body to bury.

Judge Sapala asked the prostitute if she had anything to say before sentencing. Dawn, dressed as she was during the trial, looked up at the judge.

"I would like to say I am sorry to Dr. Canty's family and my family for all the pain they have suffered."

Dawn was speaking in a low, barely audible voice. The chatter in the courtroom was high. It was just another Thursday morning in Recorder's Court, with attorneys coming in and out with paperwork for the clerk. Gone was the fanfare of the Canty trial. By the time Sapala ordered the courtroom silent, the court reporter had missed what Dawn said next for the record. But it was heard by a journalist covering the sentencing.

"But," said Dawn Marie Spens, "I feel like I'm a victim too. I would greatly appreciate another chance to prove myself, that I can live in society without getting into trouble."

Judge Sapala decided to spare Dawn Spens the penitentiary. He gave two reasons for not imposing the five-year sentence. One was the overcrowding in state prisons, a condition that often caused the early release of felons. The other was that he wanted to see her get help.

"Even if the maximum sentence were imposed, I am satisfied given their policies, she would probably be released fairly quickly . . . Frankly, I don't have much confidence in their programs that might exist to help people with drugs and alcohol and emotional problems."

Sapala said he thought Dawn Spens was a "retrievable human being."

"I have been here long enough to have most of my optimism stripped from me, given what I see every day," Sapala said. "But I still think there is a chance."

Prosecutor Robert Agacinski objected, saying incarceration was in her best interest as well as society's. But Sapala had tailored a sentence especially for the prostitute.

She would be on probation for three years, the first ten months to be spent in the Wayne County Jail. With time served before and after the trial, Dawn Spens already was more than halfway home. After her release from the jail, Sapala ordered, she was to enter a drug rehabilitation program and undergo periodic urinalysis. If it was an outpatient facility, she would have to do one hundred hours of community service. If she went to an inpatient drug program, she would have to remain there until medically discharged.

"Thank you, your honor," Dawn said.

"Good luck," said Judge Sapala. He said it twice.

Dawn Spens was ecstatic with the sentence. As she waited for her out date, she wrote John Fry more love letters, thanking him "for helping me out."

Fry was headed for Jackson Prison, but he still had some bargaining power left. The county sheriff's department wanted information about its own security problems during Fry's attempted jailbreak. Soon Fry's escape charges were dismissed. Lucky also secured a face-to-face meeting with Dawn in mid-January, the day he left for Jackson.

They were left alone together in the jail's old lineup room. Fry was in irons. Dawn sat on his lap, kissing him and rubbing his balding head. He was nearly forty years old. He'd already spent a quarter of his life in prison. Already he had plans not to spend the rest of it there as well.

A day later Dawn wrote:

"John, when it comes down to it, you are one hell of a man, and after being with you, I know that even if I were to look—which I'm not—I would never be able to find a man who could show me the love and affection you have."

But her recent letters no longer bore hearts and adolescent drawings. They were on legal stationery and were often printed in boldface. She promised she would visit him and "do things" for him on the outside when she got out. If her probation officer wouldn't let her visit him, she would correspond with him, she promised. Then she repeated one more promise:

"I just want you to know how I feel, so maybe you can understand me a little more. Remember that promise I made you yesterday? If my feelings ever do change, I will tell you face-to-face. I owe you at least that."

Fry went to Jackson, marked a year in Huron Valley Men's Correctional Facility, and finally ended up in the drafty cells of Marquette, a maximum security prison at the northern tip of Michigan's Upper Peninsula. He worked on his appeal and boasted how he had "taken the weight" for his girlfriend, claiming she had helped package the body parts.

Two years after his last letter from Dawn he'd yet to hear a word from his old girlfriend.

"It's spelled s-u-c-k-e-r," Lucky said. "I guess that's how much I loved the bitch."

On March 19, Dawn Spens was released from the Wayne County Jail and transferred to a small holding cell behind Judge Sapala's courtroom.

She waited there for the director of Dawn Farm, an inpatient drug treatment facility forty-five minutes west of Detroit. Earlier she'd tried to get into a program in Windsor to be close to her mother. The plan was abandoned because of restrictions against convicted felons crossing the Canadian border.

The director of Dawn Farm arrived with a couple of former addicts. The young women were Dawn's age and had eyes bright with recovery. They would be her company for the ride back to the treatment center, set on a farm in a rural section of Washtenaw County. It was a nine-month residency program.

Dawn immediately began chatting with her companions as she walked from the Frank Murphy Hall of Justice. She was twenty-one years old when she sucked in her first breath of free air in eight months. It was a rainy, blustery day outside.

Dawn Marie Spens didn't have a coat. She wore her purple dress and the traces of her last three years etched in circles on her legs.

The rest of her belongings she carried in a brown paper bag.

Chapter 98

Gladys Canty was troubled by the sentence given Dawn Spens, but even more so by the unanswered questions surrounding her son's death. Did he try to stand up to a threat of blackmail, or did he simply pick a fight with John Fry?

She couldn't fathom her son willingly turning over large sums of cash to the pair. She wondered if the sale of his coin collection might have precipitated his breakdown and hospitalization. She faced other mysteries, one in particular that troubled her for months.

By tax time in the year following his death, she still hadn't received an interest earnings statement from one of her certificate of deposit accounts. The ten-thousand-dollar CD had been gathering interest for two 3-year terms in a bank in Grosse Pointe. Buster had helped her invest it there; his name was on the certificate as well.

Finally, when she inquired by telephone, an assistant banker told her the account had been closed some time ago, but he couldn't provide a date. She would have to come in so the staff could pull the records.

Gladys couldn't remember cashing that CD. Then she thought of her son, his loans, and the whole sordid story. Later, a friend proposed they both go to the bank, pull the records, and see who cleared the account. The CD would have matured to more than fifteen thousand dollars. She agreed, then changed her mind the day before the planned trip to the bank.

"No," she said. "I don't believe I want to go through with this. Buster's name has suffered enough. I can't help but think I did withdraw it and invest it somewhere."

One day in spring, Gladys Canty heard a gentle rapping at the side of her bungalow. She opened the door to find a girl in her thirties standing there in her driveway alone, the sun casting highlights on her raven-black hair.

When the woman introduced herself, Gladys realized it was a former patient of her Alan's, a Greek girl who had been calling her periodically on the phone. She invited her in for tea. They sat and chatted for a couple of hours. The former patient was very emotional, telling how much she admired her son, how much he had helped her through ten years of therapy. She'd first met Alan when he taught her psychology class at Henry Ford Community College. She missed him dearly, she said.

The girl was one of two sisters who lived with their mother, a widow. Soon not only the patient was calling, but her mother as well.

"How are your nephews, how is your sister?" she would ask.

Gladys could see they were trying to befriend her or maybe were looking for her to fill a void. The entire family had been in therapy with her son at one time.

One Sunday, the entire family proposed that they come out and visit her. Maybe they could have dinner together that night.

"I don't cook dinners anymore," Mrs. Canty said.

As a compromise, Gladys agreed to meet them later in the week. On a Thursday evening they picked her up at her bungalow and drove her back to their house on the west side. They prepared a beautiful meal for her, a main dish of chicken and rice. There was a lovely salad and a beautiful dessert of strawberries made by the patient with the raven-black hair.

"A fine man, Dr. Canty was," the girl kept saying. "Such a tragedy. Such a tragedy."

The whole family was quite animated. The mother kept saying in a mourning voice, "Your son, he was a *good* man. He was such a very good man."

"Such a tragedy," said the girl.

The mother sat next to Gladys at the table, patting her and gesturing as she spoke. Gladys felt very uncomfortable, and

461

she was such a long way from home.

I have so very little in common with them, she thought.

Later she wrote them a letter. She told them she really didn't know them until after Buster died. Now, the memories were too painful. She believed it was in both their best interests that they didn't see one another again.

Gladys Foster Canty wasn't 100 percent certain about the decision. She wondered for a long time if it was the Christian thing to do.

Chapter 99

I am equally grateful to my wife Jan-Jan, whom I first met through her work on the project . . . The greatest debt of all is owed to the many dedicated young women who have served as Indianwood guides from 1962 to the present. Many . . . spent long tiring sessions rehearsing and performing — often with no feedback from children. Some left the program after great dedication with little awareness of their impact on autism These tireless efforts have touched me more deeply than they can ever know . . .

— W. ALAN CANTY,
Therapeutic Peers

Jan Canty was a widow, but she was only thirty-five. Al had counseled her that in this situation she should remarry, but what Al had told her really didn't matter much now.

The questions and answers came in waves.

One day she found herself reaching for the telephone, ready to call Al's first wife. "Tell me," she wanted to say, "just who is this man I married? Can you tell me that, please?"

On another, she tried reaching Dr. Lorraine Awes but found she had moved to Alaska. Jan knew she could probably find Al's therapist, but what's the point? she thought. What could it possibly change?

She spent more time talking to Ray Danford, who filled her in on what he knew. Later another friend came into her life. He wanted to dig out everything he could find and put the entire fragmented story together. At first she was reluctant, but then she became more comfortable as she began to

463

understand. As she heard stories from Al's exploits, she found herself still disbelieving.

"That just doesn't sound like Al," she'd say. "It's totally out of character."

Then her own words would hit her. "Character" had become a relative term.

How, she thought, could he have compartmentalized his life so thoroughly? For more than ten years she only knew part of him. An Eve, a Sybil, a true split personality would be easier to accept. What energy it must have taken to keep everything so separate, she thought, to run concurrent narratives of so many, many lies.

"In retrospect, I hardly knew him at all," she told a friend.

Then came the implications concerning her own judgment. What, she asked herself, does this say about me? I am not *naive,* damn it. I do not suffer from delusions. It was not me that did this. I only was in love with him. She didn't know whether she could love and trust a man again that much.

Then, over time, the question began to arise about the very project that had brought them together—the little book about the troubled children and the skits.

She kept waiting for mail, for something, from the hospitals where Al had said he sent his tapes from Project Indianwood. She knew the videos had been made. She had a dozen of the originals on three-quarter-inch tape.

She searched for sales records of *Therapeutic Peers,* the paperback book she had typed. She knew Al had distributed them to some bookstores, but certainly there were no royalties on the seven printings he claimed had funded her education. Then her friend pointed out Al published the work himself on a vanity press. Anyone could do that with any work, as long as they had the money.

She thought, maybe that's what Al meant during his psychotic break: "They'll find out Indianwood is a fraud." Did he mean the tapes and the book sales? Or was there more?

The revelations darkened as her friend searched for answers. Leading experts and longtime counselors in the field of autism had never heard of W. Alan Canty; some reported they were puzzled by newspaper reports that he was an expert on the childhood disorder. Al's claims of a high success rate with his Indianwood techniques drew scorn.

"Believe me, word travels like wildfire in this field, parents are so desperate for help," said Dr. Joseph Fischhoff, director of psychiatry at Detroit Children's Hospital and a longtime leader in the field. "It's just not true. If somebody had a 70 percent success rate with autism, he would have the Nobel Prize."

That explained why Al refused to go to professional conferences, Jan thought, why he often criticized such gatherings. He couldn't talk about his work there.

Indianwood guides who worked for Al in the 1960s were located. All reported skits and readings of violent fairy tales. All were told their work would be presented to autistic children. All performed for the same audience of one — W. Alan Canty, his theater seat his chair in the Fisher Building suite.

One former boyfriend of a girl involved in the project from 1964 to 1967 explained what he knew and saw. At the time, Al's first marriage was floundering.

"It got to be a joke around a clique of mine," he said. "He always had the cutest girls. They did a lot of dying for him. We knew something wasn't right, even at sixteen. But the girls really didn't care. Nobody was paying that kind of money, five dollars an hour. And he never once made an advance at them.

"The funny thing was, I was in therapy with him at the time because of personal problems and a bad trip with LSD. He really did help me. I'd have to say he was a very good psychologist, despite his strange behavior concerning the girls."

Jan began to wonder if there ever were *any* children, then about her true role as a young applicant for the project. She thought, Did our entire relationship evolve from an initial deception, grow into a quirk in some kind of ongoing psychodrama?

Therapeutic Peers mentioned only one other professional who knew about Al's research — James Clark Maloney — but he'd died before the work was published. The rest of the participants were children. There were only first names, and the story of an Indianwood guide called only Connie.

Connie, according to the book, made the first breakthrough — to a group of seven autistic children in the basement of the Birmingham Psychiatric Clinic in 1962. Her chapter described the children sitting in a half circle, watching her "spellbinding performance" of a story about black swans. Then one of the autistic kids outside the circle made a noise—first a cackle, then a laugh.

"Within minutes primitive laughter was percolating through the circle," Al wrote. It was the birth of the therapeutic peers.

Then Jan remembered. The guide had gone on to become a professional actress. Al had pointed her out in a movie he insisted on seeing called *W.W. and the Dixie Dancekings.* She had a part with Burt Reynolds in the film.

"That's her," Al said during the film. "See, the one who touched the children. Isn't she a fine actress?"

Al talked that night as though he and Connie were old friends separated only by time and profession. If there was at least one group of autistic children, at least one particle of truth to the book he had dictated off the top of his head, the actress could confirm it, Jan thought.

Her stage name was Conny Van Dyke.

Jan's friend found her in Naples, Florida, retired from the screen. She was forty-one and working as a turnkey in the Collier County Jail on the midnight shift. At fourteen she was chosen the prettiest teenager in America by *Teen* magazine. She'd made five hundred TV appearances and several films.

She spoke in a soft voice. Unlike most of Al Canty's other guides, she had long blond hair.

"Have you ever heard of Alan Canty?" Jan asked.

"No, but that doesn't mean a thing. Who is he?"

"A psychologist in Detroit. Did you know him from the early sixties?"

There was a long pause.

"Him," she said. "Yes, I know him."

Then she began to cry.

"People like to think that somewhere along the line they made a difference," she began. "I'm still trying to do that.

"I was a senior in high school. I met him while modeling at an auto show. I only did it three or four times, put on the plays for him. I was modeling, singing, and recording at that time. I volunteered for the job.

"I don't remember the room, but I remember the kids. There *were* children, five or six of them. One skit had to do

466

with a machine gun or something, the girl being threatened with the machine gun. I couldn't do it mean, he said. It had to be done Punch and Judy. Not as sinister and macabre.

"He gave me the script. And told me the story, and what he was aiming for—to trigger something in the mind of the child. I was alone. I didn't work with anybody else. I remember the group of children, sitting in a circle. Except one child—she was off by herself. Sitting with her arms wrapped around herself, cuddling herself like an orphan.

"I remember doing it, then I remember the laughter. Yes, laughter, the speaking."

The former actress began crying again. She said she was moved because the memory was linked with a recent event.

"The funny thing is, a couple of years ago I worked at an old persons' home in Naples," she said. "Two days a week. I'd sing and dance, make up songs at the piano. They'd give me words and I'd make up songs—and the very same thing happened.

"There was an old man who hadn't spoken for a year . . . and people thought he was totally nuts. I went over and started scatting with him. And he scatted too. Then I started saying words and he started saying words. And the staff was amazed. It's the first time he'd spoken in a year.

"When that happened it triggered that memory from long ago, you know, how sometimes something like that will get people to speak.

"The funny thing was that the old man later said he could speak all the time. He just didn't like the way they were treating him. The staff at the home were saying, 'Come on now, it's time for us to have our dinner, time for us to go beddie-bye.'

"But he was putting them all on. He said he was just sick of always being treated like a child."

Chapter 100

By late winter, the big Tudor had been up for sale for six months with no takers. Jan wrote a list for the realtor stating the recent improvements: the new hot-water heater, the new roof, the brick driveway, and anything else that would help sell the house.

She could also pen her own list covering why she wanted out: high taxes, high heating bills, high mortgage bills, living alone with the six bedrooms and six bathrooms—not to mention the memories.

The realtor also insisted they inform any potential buyers of a so-called "hidden defect": "The former owner was murdered and dismembered." If they didn't, a troubled or superstitious buyer might sue down the road, he said.

She didn't need that sort of grief. One by one, she was paying off Al's debts. Her own practice was growing. She left Al's old suite for a new office more suited to her tastes. When the movers picked up Al Sr.'s big old walnut desk, it fell into pieces. She sent it away to be fixed, asking repairmen to also cut it down to size.

Mainly, she just wanted to get on with her life. But interest rates were high and the real estate market slow. She'd never expected to have to go through the entire winter in the house alone.

When the frigid weather came, she shut most of the rooms to save energy and money. She heated only a couple—the kitchen and the guest room, where she moved after Al's death. Even then, she kept the living space at sixty degrees.

A warm electric blanket waited for her on the bed when she returned home every night from work. She ate her dinners on the bed, watched television from the bed, and fought her way out of nightmares on the bed.

One was particularly terrifying. She dreamt she was back in the morgue, looking at the TV screen. His severed head turned, looking at her. She woke in the pitch dark, sweating heavily, wondering where she was. Finally, she focused on the thick strips of lead that intersected the windows in the room.

The people kept coming to see the house month after month. It got plenty of traffic. There were many compliments.

"Oh, look at the leaded glass," they'd say. "The whole house is so beautiful. Look at the lead on those windows."

Yes, she thought, it's beautiful. But it's my ball and chain. It's my prison.

That's it, she thought. *My beautiful prison.* She began calling Al's big Tudor that.

Then one day just before the break of spring, the realtor delivered a buyer—a couple who wanted the home, hidden defect and all. She was glad there were young children who would fill up all the space with toys, tiny fingerprints, and noise.

Jan found a condominium in the Pointes—something nice, but quite scaled down. She liked the lines of the new place. Later she discovered it was designed by Albert Kahn, the architect of the Fisher and the home on Berkshire. Some things, she thought, will always be with me.

The seasons were balancing somewhere between winter and spring when she made her last trip to the house. She drove down Jefferson Avenue, then aimed her red Thunderbird under the elms of Berkshire. Then she noticed another car coming in the distance as she approached the house.

It was a Buick—a black Buick Regal. She felt a surge of blood through her chest. The driver looked so much like him, but the resemblance was only a cruel coincidence.

The house seemed as immense as ever when she walked inside for the last time. She paused in the living room, looking at the expanse of carpet stretching to an empty fireplace and bare mantel. How, she thought, did we ever fill all this?

She decided to check all the rooms to make sure she hadn't left anything behind. She looked everywhere—the closets, the basement, the linen cabinets. She searched last in the kitchen. She opened all the drawers and cupboards in her favorite room.

Finally, she ran her hand across the shelving of the last of the upper cabinets, the one where Al used to keep his precious coffee. As her hand swept above her, she felt her fingers hit something small.

It was a toy, one she remembered Al saying his parents had bought for him at an antique show when he was just a young boy. It had been missing for years.

The toy was a little monkey, but unlike any she'd ever seen. He was made of several types of hardwood. The limbs and extremities — the head, the arms, the legs, the feet — were separate, held together only by frail wires at the joints. He could flip and flop in any direction, take on most any posture or form.

She could see how Al's monkey had remained hidden there for so long. He stood only two inches tall.

Jan found herself squeezing him in her palm as she walked out the door.

Acknowledgments

The most valued discoveries in researching and writing this book have been the counsel, support, and experiences offered by many good people along the way.

I would especially like to thank Russell Galen, Scott Meredith, Jack Olsen, and Ruth Coughlin for their key roles right from the start. I'm also indebted to Tom Murphy, my research assistant, for his fleet-footed legwork; my editor, Nick Bakalar, for his ways with writers as well as with words; Michael Novak and Pat Freydl for their valued legal expertise; and Debbie, Jessica, and John for their love and tolerance.

Special appreciation goes to Jan Canty, who cooperated without remuneration, as did every source in this work. Also, I wish to acknowledge Dr. Lorraine Awes for agreeing to detail her patient's case history at the request of his wife.

For their help when I was at the Detroit *News,* I would like to thank Lisa Velders, Ben Burns, Jim Vesley, Lionel Linder, and Bob Giles. Also much thanks to Anne E. Sweeney, Robert Ficano, Nancy Mouradian, Chris Kucharski, Anita Mack, Gladys Canty, and Jeanne McAllister.

Finally, there's no greater gratitude than the kind I've discovered in the company of Bill's many friends: Al, Richard, Pete, the late Don Ball, and all the rest.

About The Author

Lowell Cauffiel, who has won journalism awards from UPI, AP, and the Columbia Graduate School of Journalism, covered the Canty case for the Detroit *News*. He has done freelance work for many magazines, and presently is on the staff of *Detroit Monthly* Magazine. This is his first book.